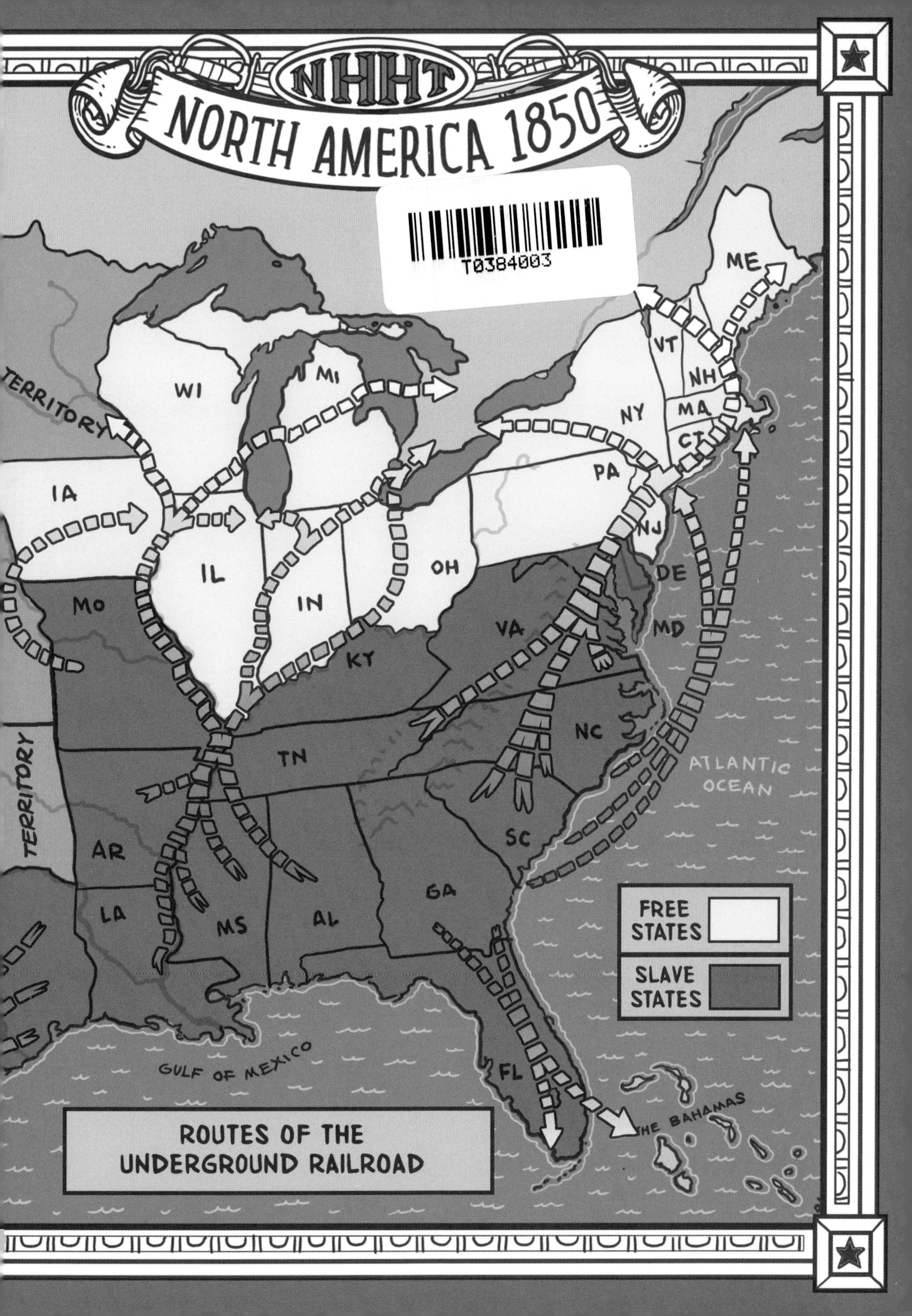
NHHT
NORTH AMERICA 1850
T0384003
TERRITORY
WI
MI
IA
IL
IN
OH
PA
NY
VT
NH
ME
MA
CT
NJ
DE
MD
VA
KY
MO
TERRITORY
TN
NC
SC
AR
LA
MS
AL
GA
FL
ATLANTIC OCEAN
GULF OF MEXICO
THE BAHAMAS
FREE STATES
SLAVE STATES
ROUTES OF THE UNDERGROUND RAILROAD

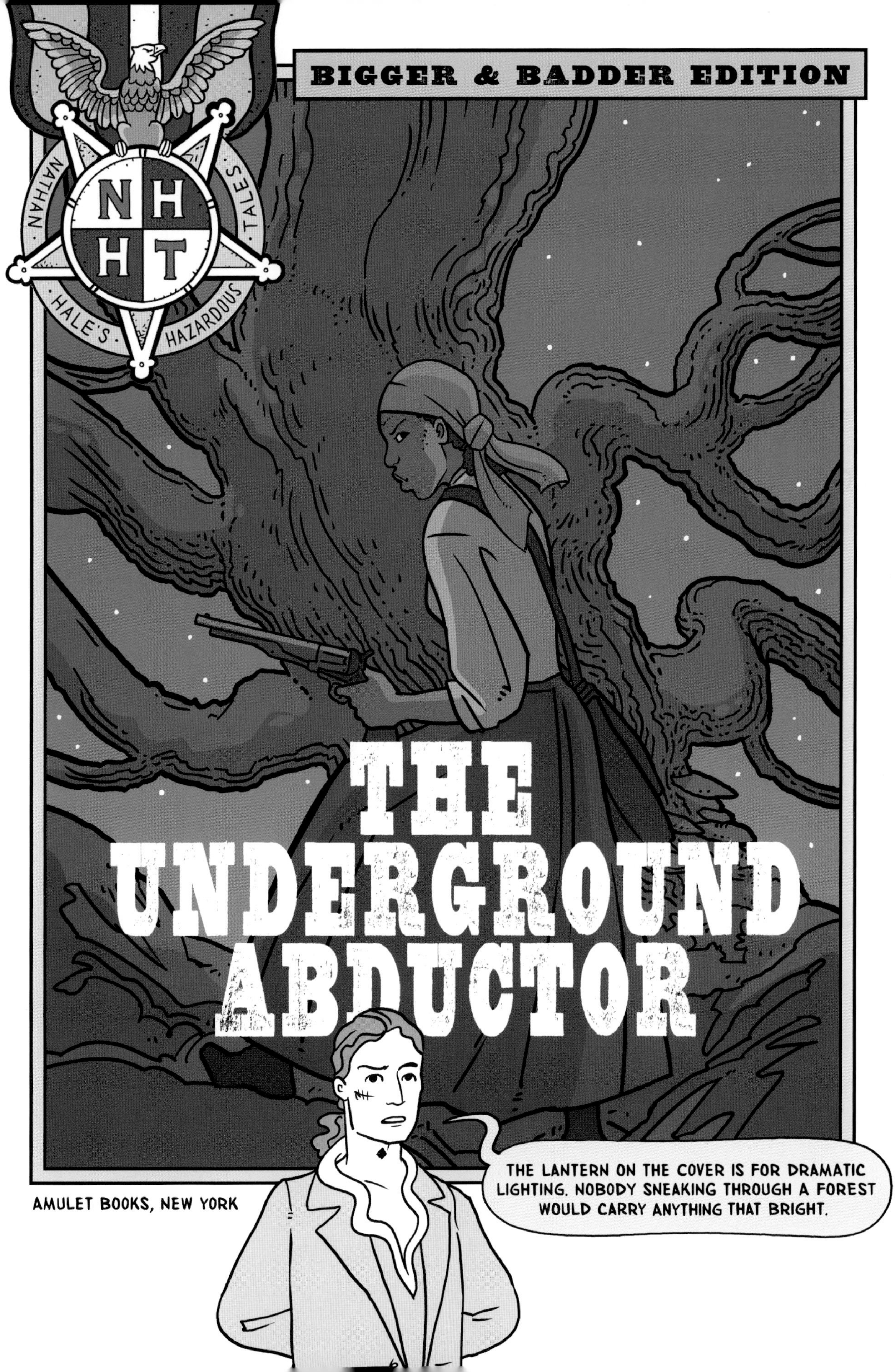
NATHAN HALE'S HAZARDOUS TALES
NH HT
BIGGER & BADDER EDITION
THE UNDERGROUND ABDUCTOR
THE LANTERN ON THE COVER IS FOR DRAMATIC LIGHTING. NOBODY SNEAKING THROUGH A FOREST WOULD CARRY ANYTHING THAT BRIGHT.

AMULET BOOKS, NEW YORK

LIBRARY OF CONGRESS CONTROL NUMBER FOR THE 2015 HARDCOVER:
2016297698
ISBN FOR THE 2015 HARDCOVER: 978-1-4197-1536-5
ISBN FOR THE 2022 BIGGER & BADDER EDITION: 978-1-4197-6217-8

TEXT AND ILLUSTRATIONS © NATHAN HALE
BOOK DESIGN BY NATHAN HALE AND CHAD W. BECKERMAN

PRINTED AND BOUND IN CHINA
10 9 8 7 6 5 4 3

AMULET BOOKS ARE AVAILABLE AT SPECIAL DISCOUNTS WHEN PURCHASED
IN QUANTITY FOR PREMIUMS AND PROMOTIONS AS WELL AS FUNDRAISING
OR EDUCATIONAL USE. SPECIAL EDITIONS CAN ALSO BE CREATED TO
SPECIFICATION. FOR DETAILS, CONTACT SPECIALSALES@ABRAMSBOOKS.COM
OR THE ADDRESS BELOW.

AMULET BOOKS® IS A REGISTERED TRADEMARK OF HARRY N. ABRAMS, INC.

ABRAMS The Art of Books
195 Broadway, New York, NY 10007
abramsbooks.com

TO MY MOM

NHHT

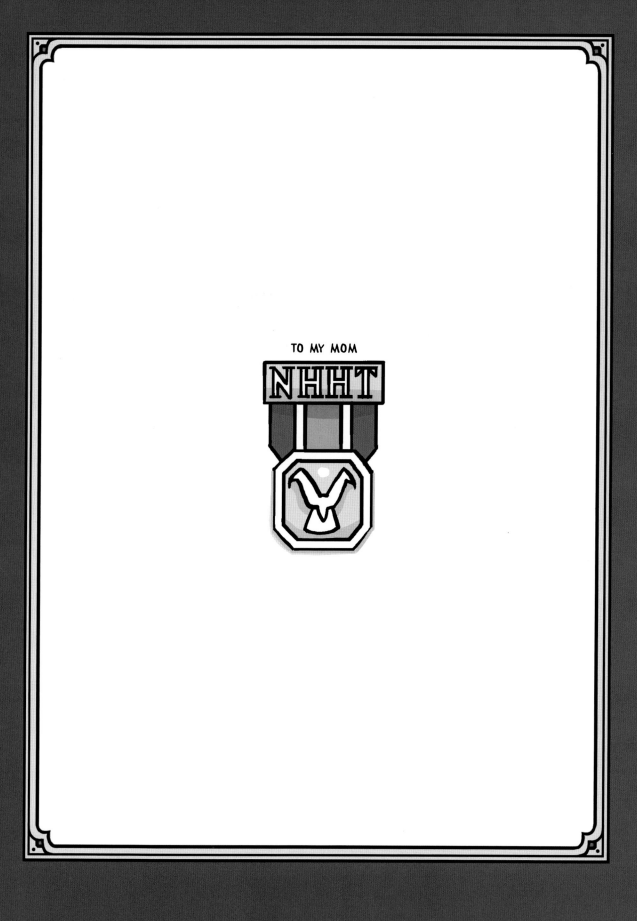

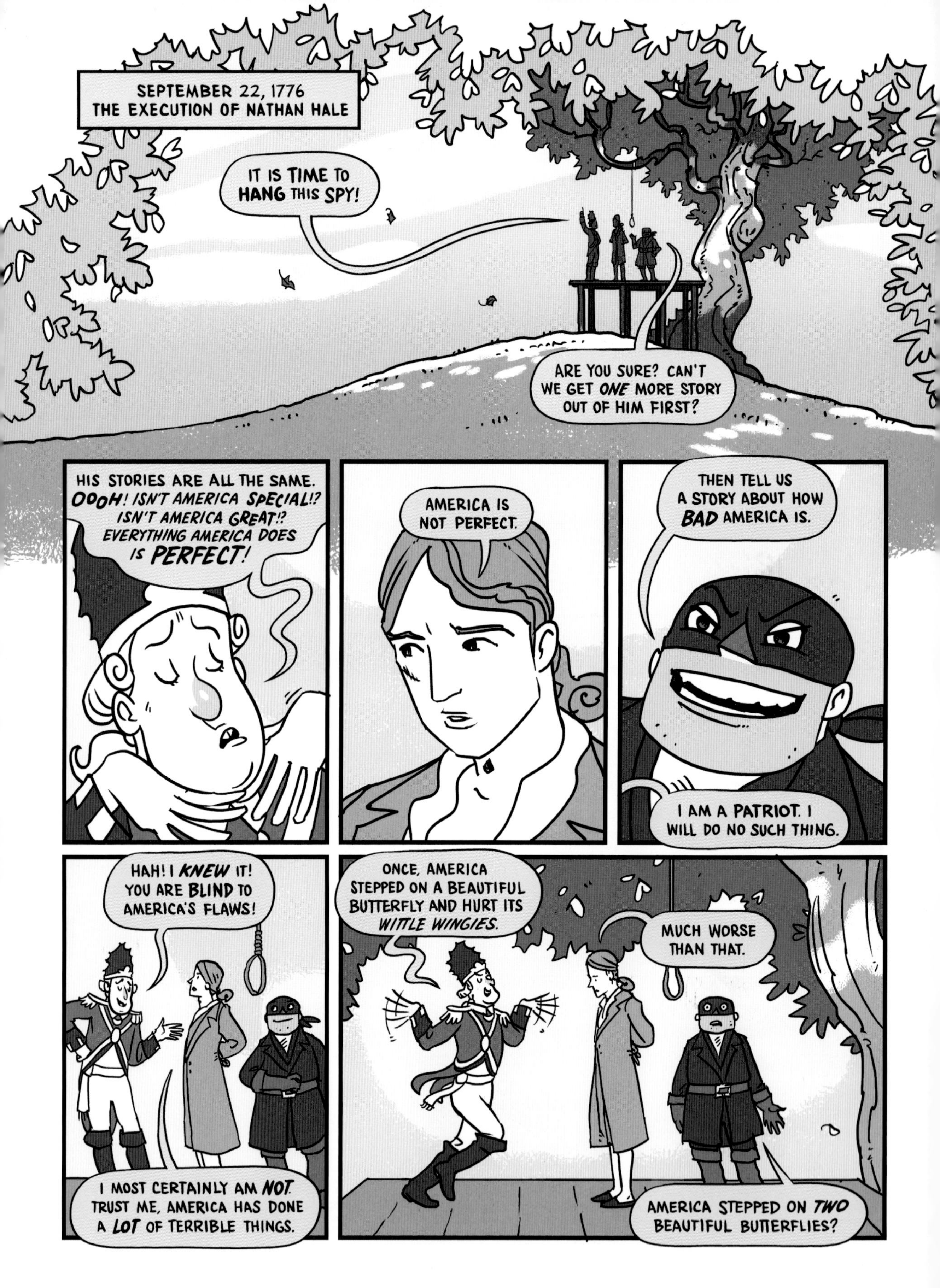
SEPTEMBER 22, 1776
THE EXECUTION OF NATHAN HALE
IT IS TIME TO HANG THIS SPY!
ARE YOU SURE? CAN'T WE GET ONE MORE STORY OUT OF HIM FIRST?
HIS STORIES ARE ALL THE SAME. OOOH! ISN'T AMERICA SPECIAL!? ISN'T AMERICA GREAT!? EVERYTHING AMERICA DOES IS PERFECT!
AMERICA IS NOT PERFECT.
THEN TELL US A STORY ABOUT HOW BAD AMERICA IS.
I AM A PATRIOT. I WILL DO NO SUCH THING.
HAH! I KNEW IT! YOU ARE BLIND TO AMERICA'S FLAWS!
I MOST CERTAINLY AM NOT. TRUST ME, AMERICA HAS DONE A LOT OF TERRIBLE THINGS.
ONCE, AMERICA STEPPED ON A BEAUTIFUL BUTTERFLY AND HURT ITS WITTLE WINGIES.
MUCH WORSE THAN THAT.
AMERICA STEPPED ON TWO BEAUTIFUL BUTTERFLIES?

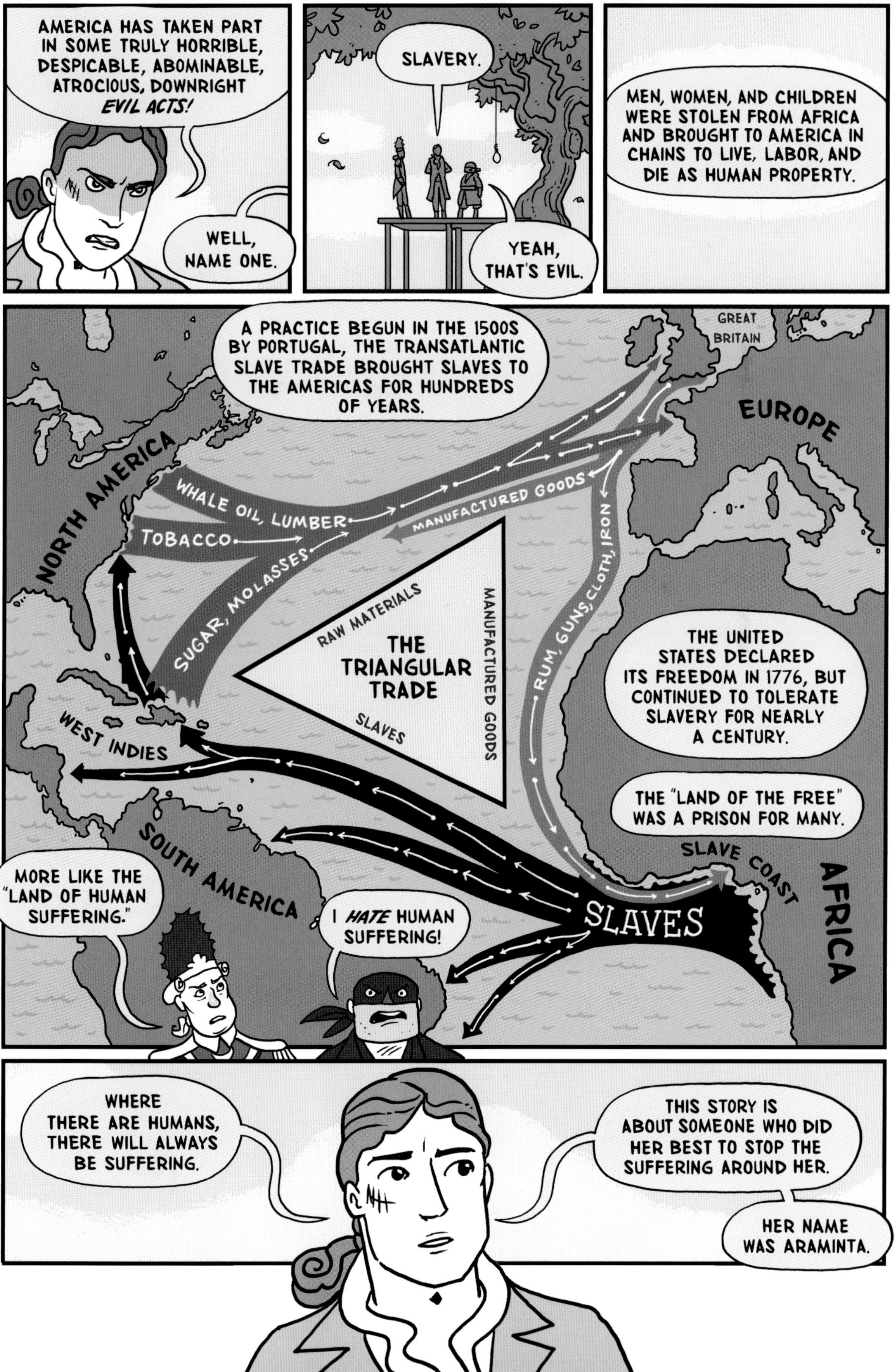
AMERICA HAS TAKEN PART IN SOME TRULY HORRIBLE, DESPICABLE, ABOMINABLE, ATROCIOUS, DOWNRIGHT *EVIL ACTS!*
WELL, NAME ONE.
SLAVERY.
YEAH, THAT'S EVIL.
MEN, WOMEN, AND CHILDREN WERE STOLEN FROM AFRICA AND BROUGHT TO AMERICA IN CHAINS TO LIVE, LABOR, AND DIE AS HUMAN PROPERTY.
A PRACTICE BEGUN IN THE 1500S BY PORTUGAL, THE TRANSATLANTIC SLAVE TRADE BROUGHT SLAVES TO THE AMERICAS FOR HUNDREDS OF YEARS.
GREAT BRITAIN
EUROPE
NORTH AMERICA
WHALE OIL, LUMBER
TOBACCO
SUGAR, MOLASSES
MANUFACTURED GOODS
RUM, GUNS, CLOTH, IRON
RAW MATERIALS
THE TRIANGULAR TRADE
MANUFACTURED GOODS
SLAVES
WEST INDIES
SOUTH AMERICA
SLAVE COAST
AFRICA
SLAVES
THE UNITED STATES DECLARED ITS FREEDOM IN 1776, BUT CONTINUED TO TOLERATE SLAVERY FOR NEARLY A CENTURY.
THE "LAND OF THE FREE" WAS A PRISON FOR MANY.
MORE LIKE THE "LAND OF HUMAN SUFFERING."
I *HATE* HUMAN SUFFERING!
WHERE THERE ARE HUMANS, THERE WILL ALWAYS BE SUFFERING.
THIS STORY IS ABOUT SOMEONE WHO DID HER BEST TO STOP THE SUFFERING AROUND HER.
HER NAME WAS ARAMINTA.

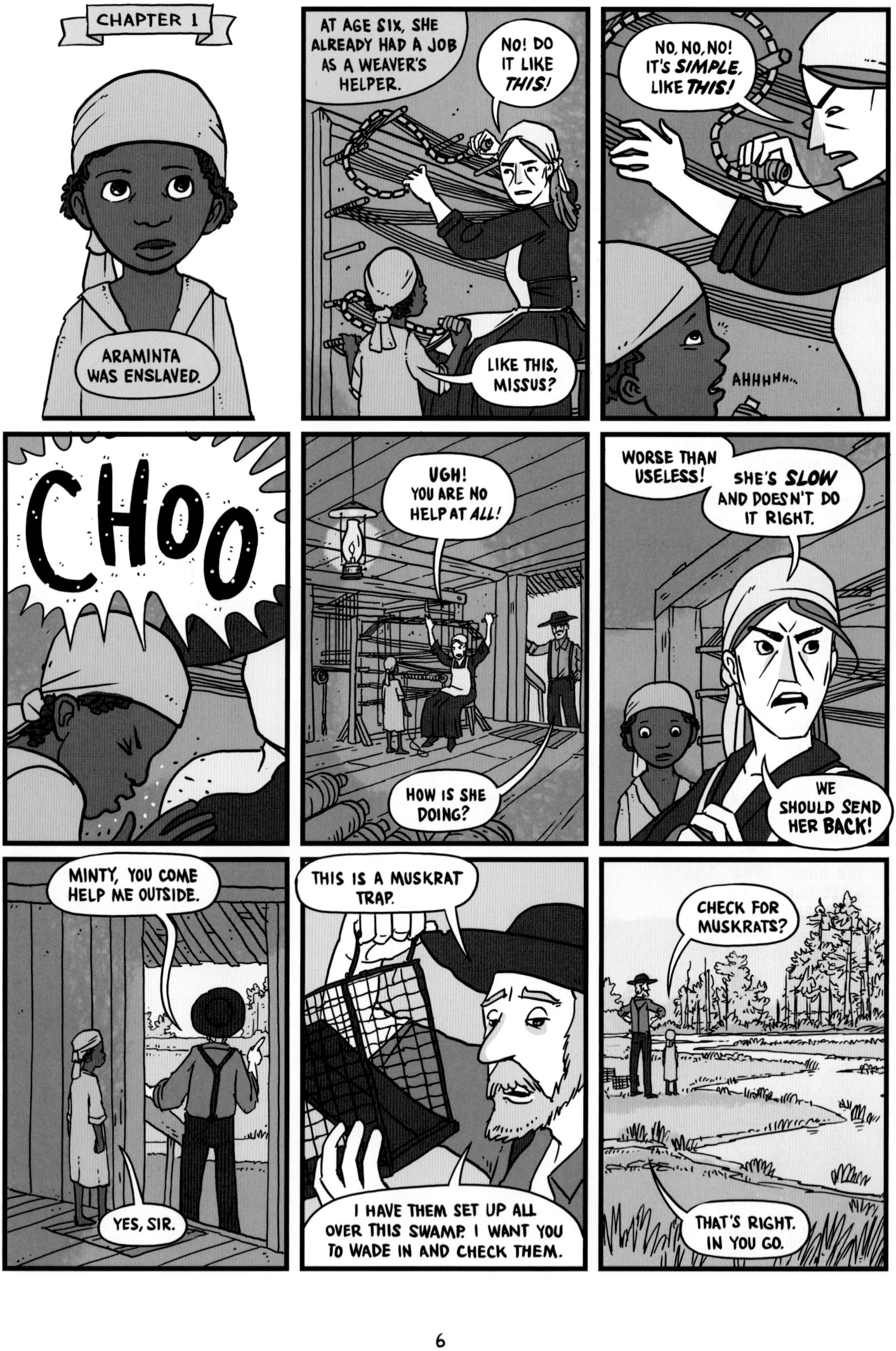
CHAPTER 1
ARAMINTA WAS ENSLAVED.
AT AGE SIX, SHE ALREADY HAD A JOB AS A WEAVER'S HELPER.
NO! DO IT LIKE THIS!
LIKE THIS, MISSUS?
NO, NO, NO! IT'S SIMPLE, LIKE THIS!
AHHHHH...
CHOO
UGH! YOU ARE NO HELP AT ALL!
HOW IS SHE DOING?
WORSE THAN USELESS!
SHE'S SLOW AND DOESN'T DO IT RIGHT.
WE SHOULD SEND HER BACK!
MINTY, YOU COME HELP ME OUTSIDE.
YES, SIR.
THIS IS A MUSKRAT TRAP.
I HAVE THEM SET UP ALL OVER THIS SWAMP. I WANT YOU TO WADE IN AND CHECK THEM.
CHECK FOR MUSKRATS?
THAT'S RIGHT. IN YOU GO.

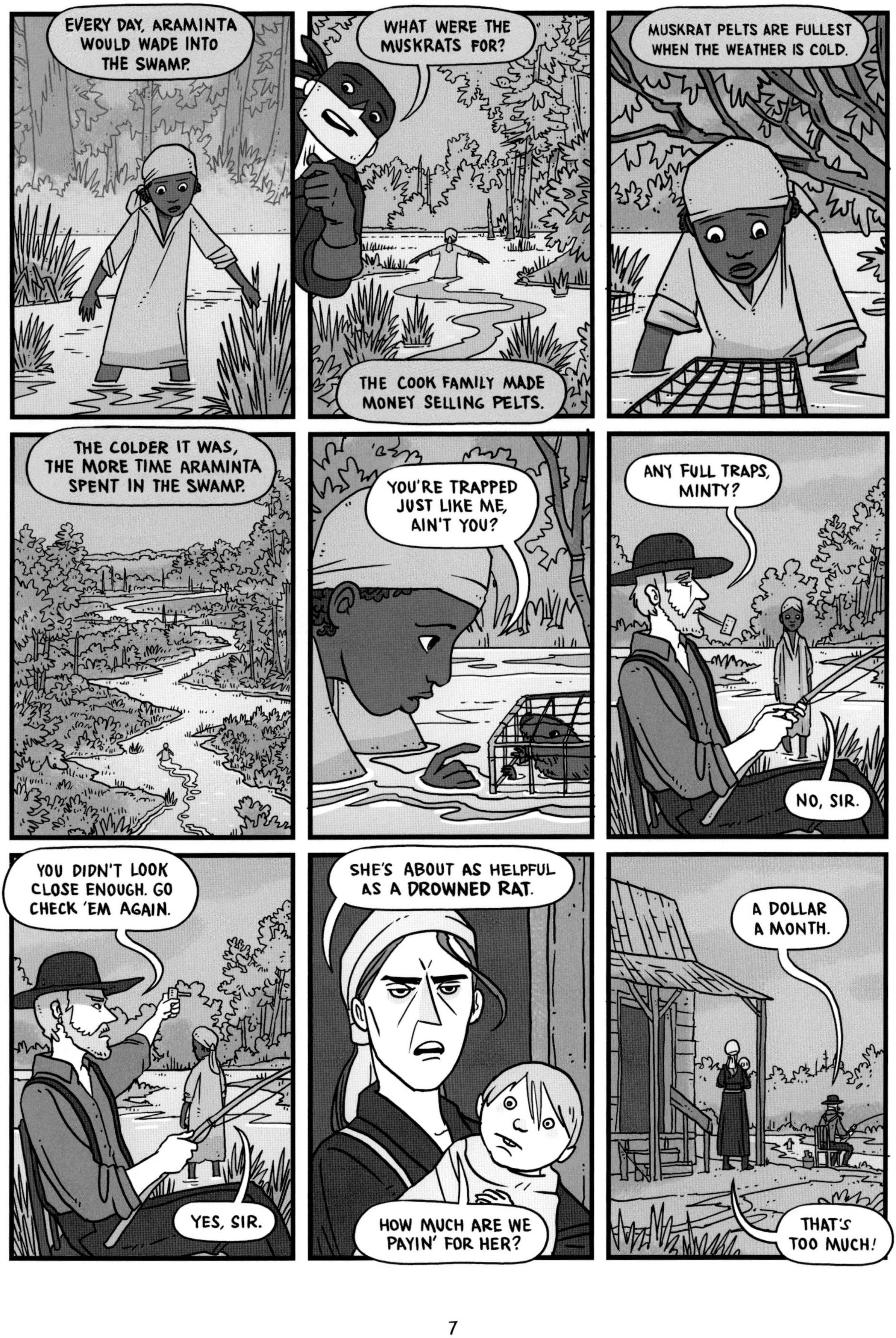
EVERY DAY, ARAMINTA WOULD WADE INTO THE SWAMP.
WHAT WERE THE MUSKRATS FOR?
THE COOK FAMILY MADE MONEY SELLING PELTS.
MUSKRAT PELTS ARE FULLEST WHEN THE WEATHER IS COLD.
THE COLDER IT WAS, THE MORE TIME ARAMINTA SPENT IN THE SWAMP.
YOU'RE TRAPPED JUST LIKE ME, AIN'T YOU?
ANY FULL TRAPS, MINTY?
NO, SIR.
YOU DIDN'T LOOK CLOSE ENOUGH. GO CHECK 'EM AGAIN.
YES, SIR.
SHE'S ABOUT AS HELPFUL AS A DROWNED RAT.
HOW MUCH ARE WE PAYIN' FOR HER?
A DOLLAR A MONTH.
THAT'S TOO MUCH!

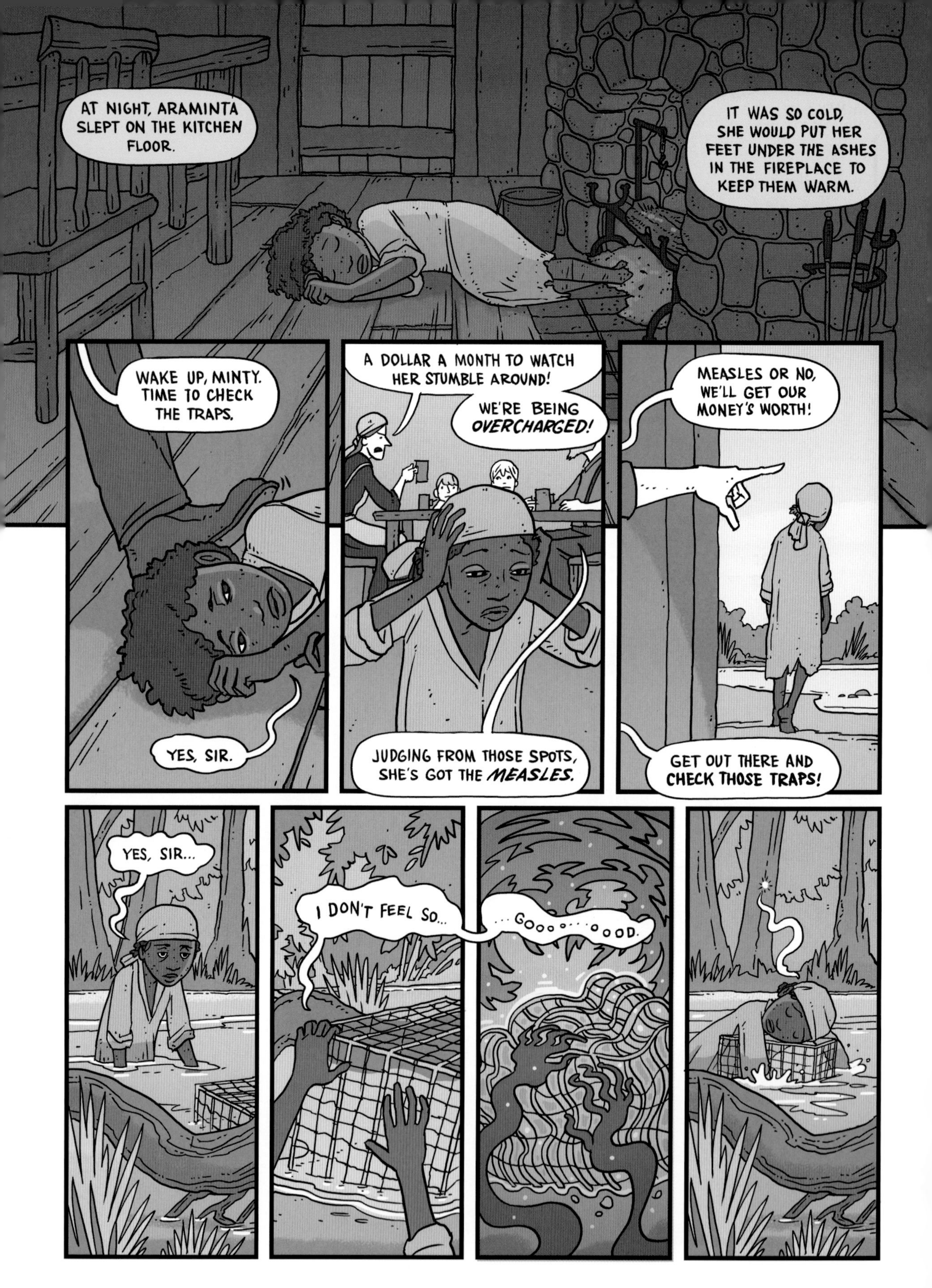

AT NIGHT, ARAMINTA SLEPT ON THE KITCHEN FLOOR.
IT WAS SO COLD, SHE WOULD PUT HER FEET UNDER THE ASHES IN THE FIREPLACE TO KEEP THEM WARM.
WAKE UP, MINTY. TIME TO CHECK THE TRAPS.
YES, SIR.
A DOLLAR A MONTH TO WATCH HER STUMBLE AROUND!
WE'RE BEING OVERCHARGED!
JUDGING FROM THOSE SPOTS, SHE'S GOT THE MEASLES.
MEASLES OR NO, WE'LL GET OUR MONEY'S WORTH!
GET OUT THERE AND CHECK THOSE TRAPS!
YES, SIR...
I DON'T FEEL SO...
...GOOO...OOOD.

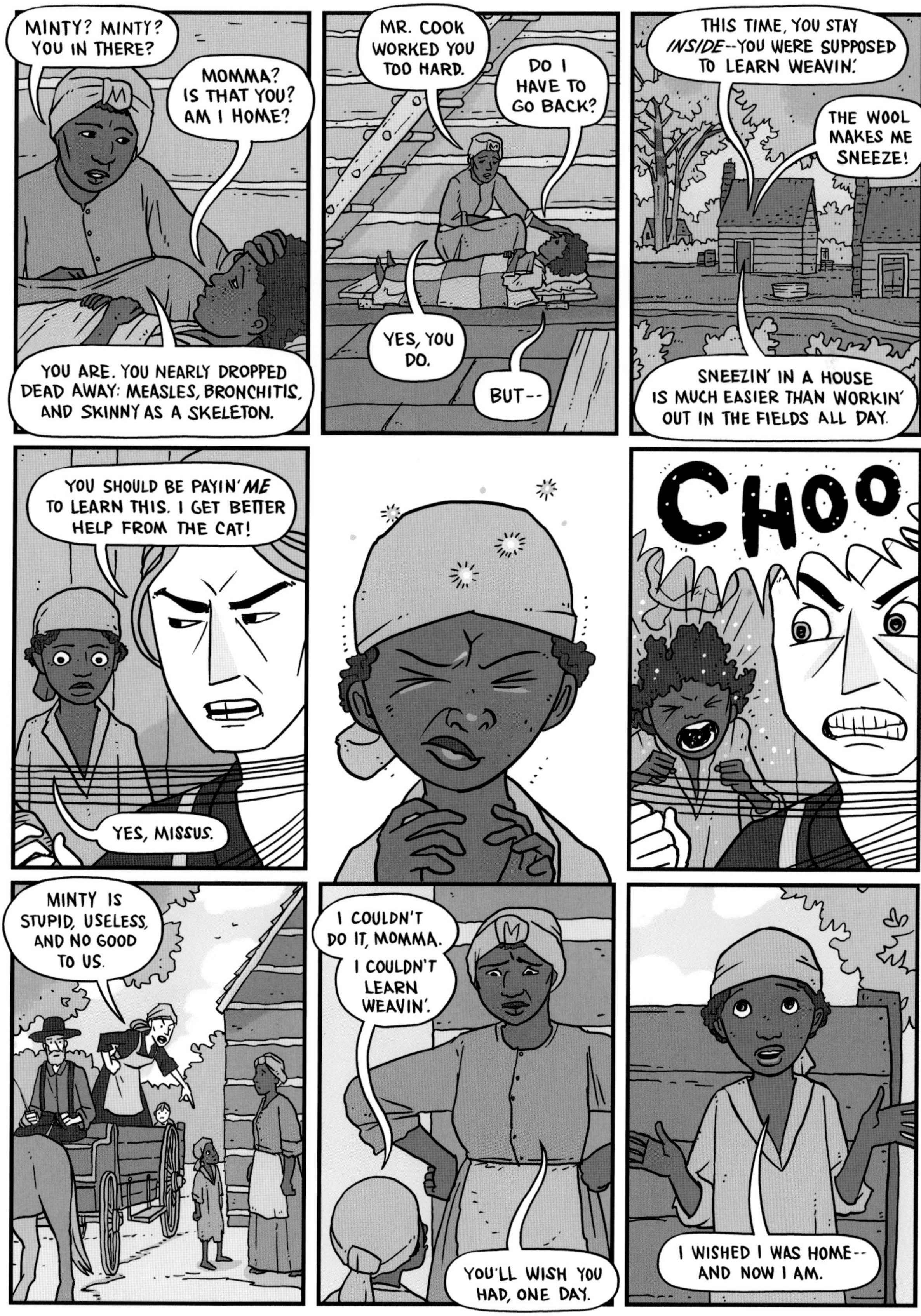
MINTY? MINTY? YOU IN THERE?
MOMMA? IS THAT YOU? AM I HOME?
YOU ARE. YOU NEARLY DROPPED DEAD AWAY: MEASLES, BRONCHITIS, AND SKINNY AS A SKELETON.
MR. COOK WORKED YOU TOO HARD.
DO I HAVE TO GO BACK?
YES, YOU DO.
BUT--
THIS TIME, YOU STAY *INSIDE*--YOU WERE SUPPOSED TO LEARN WEAVIN'.
THE WOOL MAKES ME SNEEZE!
SNEEZIN' IN A HOUSE IS MUCH EASIER THAN WORKIN' OUT IN THE FIELDS ALL DAY.
YOU SHOULD BE PAYIN' *ME* TO LEARN THIS. I GET BETTER HELP FROM THE CAT!
YES, MISSUS.
CHOO
MINTY IS STUPID, USELESS, AND NO GOOD TO US.
I COULDN'T DO IT, MOMMA.
I COULDN'T LEARN WEAVIN'.
YOU'LL WISH YOU HAD, ONE DAY.
I WISHED I WAS HOME-- AND NOW I AM.

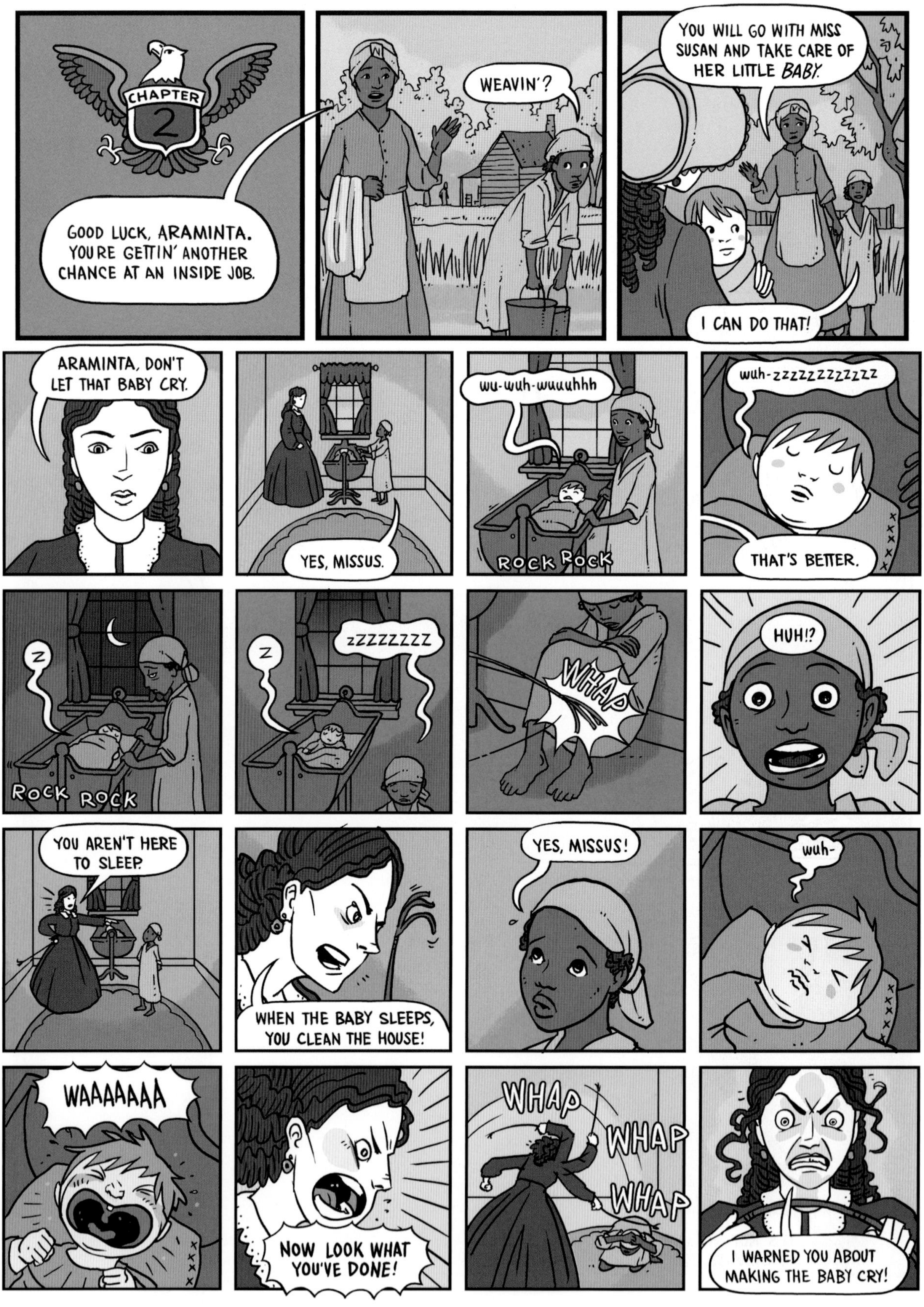
CHAPTER 2
GOOD LUCK, ARAMINTA. YOU'RE GETTIN' ANOTHER CHANCE AT AN INSIDE JOB.
WEAVIN'?
YOU WILL GO WITH MISS SUSAN AND TAKE CARE OF HER LITTLE BABY.
I CAN DO THAT!
ARAMINTA, DON'T LET THAT BABY CRY.
YES, MISSUS.
wu-wuh-wuuuhhh
ROCK ROCK
wuh-zzzzzzzzzzz
THAT'S BETTER.
Z
ROCK ROCK
Z
zzzzzzz
WHAP
HUH!?
YOU AREN'T HERE TO SLEEP.
WHEN THE BABY SLEEPS, YOU CLEAN THE HOUSE!
YES, MISSUS!
wuh-
WAAAAAAA
NOW LOOK WHAT YOU'VE DONE!
WHAP
WHAP
WHAP
I WARNED YOU ABOUT MAKING THE BABY CRY!

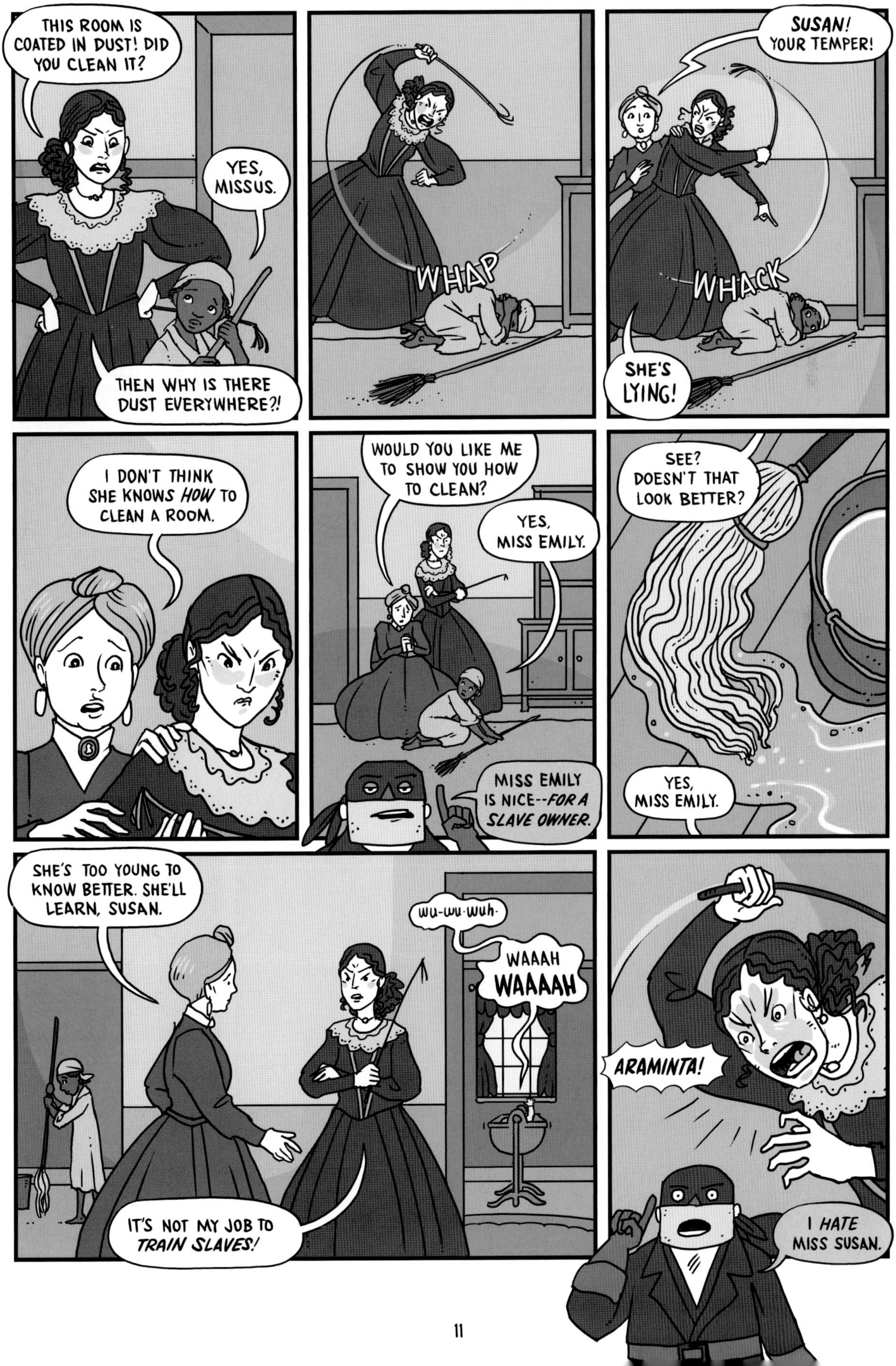
THIS ROOM IS COATED IN DUST! DID YOU CLEAN IT?
YES, MISSUS.
THEN WHY IS THERE DUST EVERYWHERE?!
WHAP
SUSAN! YOUR TEMPER!
WHACK
SHE'S LYING!
I DON'T THINK SHE KNOWS *HOW* TO CLEAN A ROOM.
WOULD YOU LIKE ME TO SHOW YOU HOW TO CLEAN?
YES, MISS EMILY.
MISS EMILY IS NICE--*FOR A SLAVE OWNER.*
SEE? DOESN'T THAT LOOK BETTER?
YES, MISS EMILY.
SHE'S TOO YOUNG TO KNOW BETTER. SHE'LL LEARN, SUSAN.
wu-wu-wuh
WAAAH
WAAAAH
IT'S NOT MY JOB TO *TRAIN SLAVES!*
ARAMINTA!
I *HATE* MISS SUSAN.

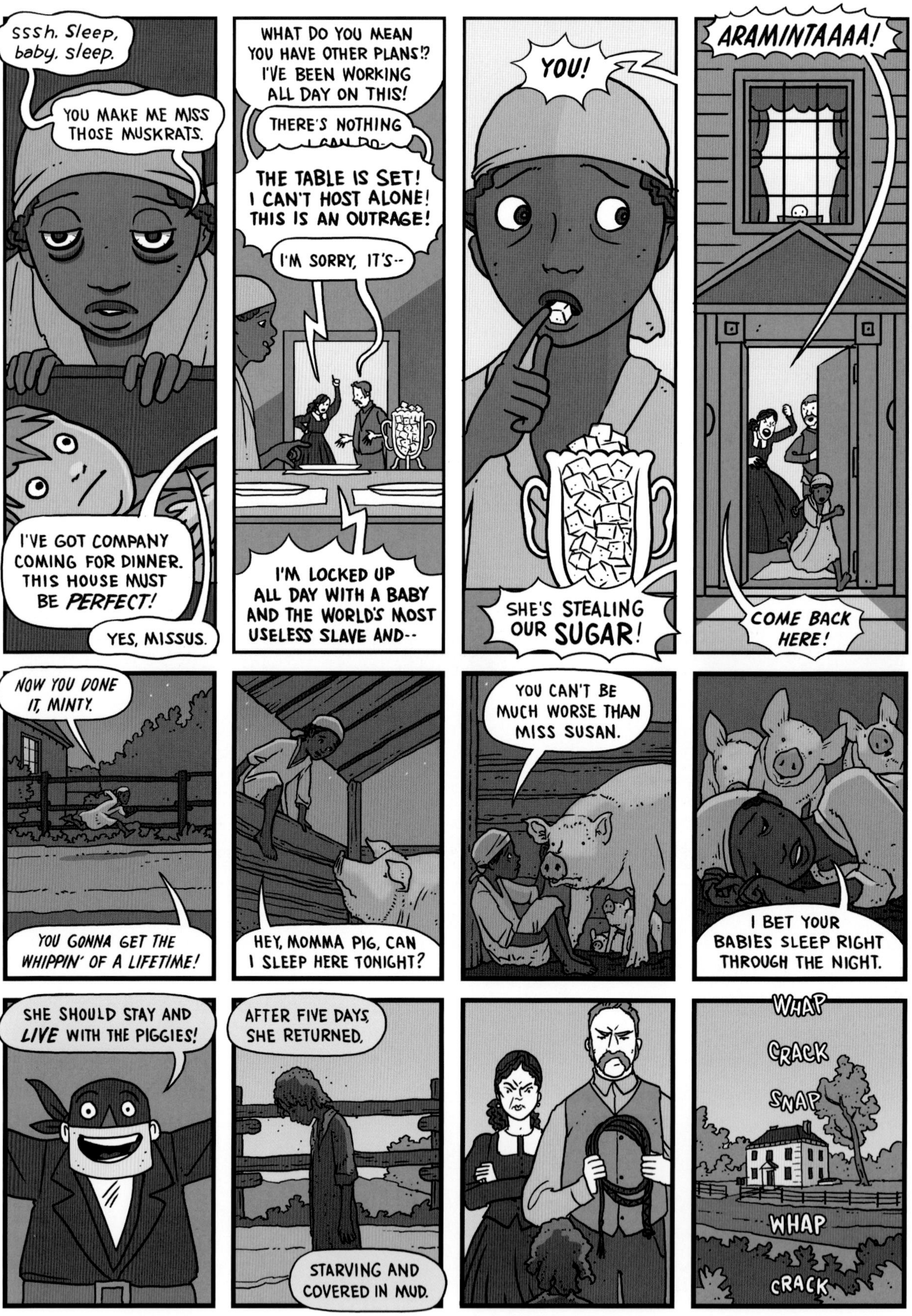
sssh. Sleep, baby, sleep.
YOU MAKE ME MISS THOSE MUSKRATS.
I'VE GOT COMPANY COMING FOR DINNER. THIS HOUSE MUST BE *PERFECT*!
YES, MISSUS.
WHAT DO YOU MEAN YOU HAVE OTHER PLANS!? I'VE BEEN WORKING ALL DAY ON THIS!
THERE'S NOTHING
THE TABLE IS SET! I CAN'T HOST ALONE! THIS IS AN OUTRAGE!
I'M SORRY, IT'S--
I'M LOCKED UP ALL DAY WITH A BABY AND THE WORLD'S MOST USELESS SLAVE AND--
YOU!
SHE'S STEALING OUR SUGAR!
ARAMINTAAAA!
COME BACK HERE!
NOW YOU DONE IT, MINTY.
YOU GONNA GET THE WHIPPIN' OF A LIFETIME!
HEY, MOMMA PIG, CAN I SLEEP HERE TONIGHT?
YOU CAN'T BE MUCH WORSE THAN MISS SUSAN.
I BET YOUR BABIES SLEEP RIGHT THROUGH THE NIGHT.
SHE SHOULD STAY AND *LIVE* WITH THE PIGGIES!
AFTER FIVE DAYS, SHE RETURNED,
STARVING AND COVERED IN MUD.
WHAP
CRACK
SNAP
WHAP
CRACK

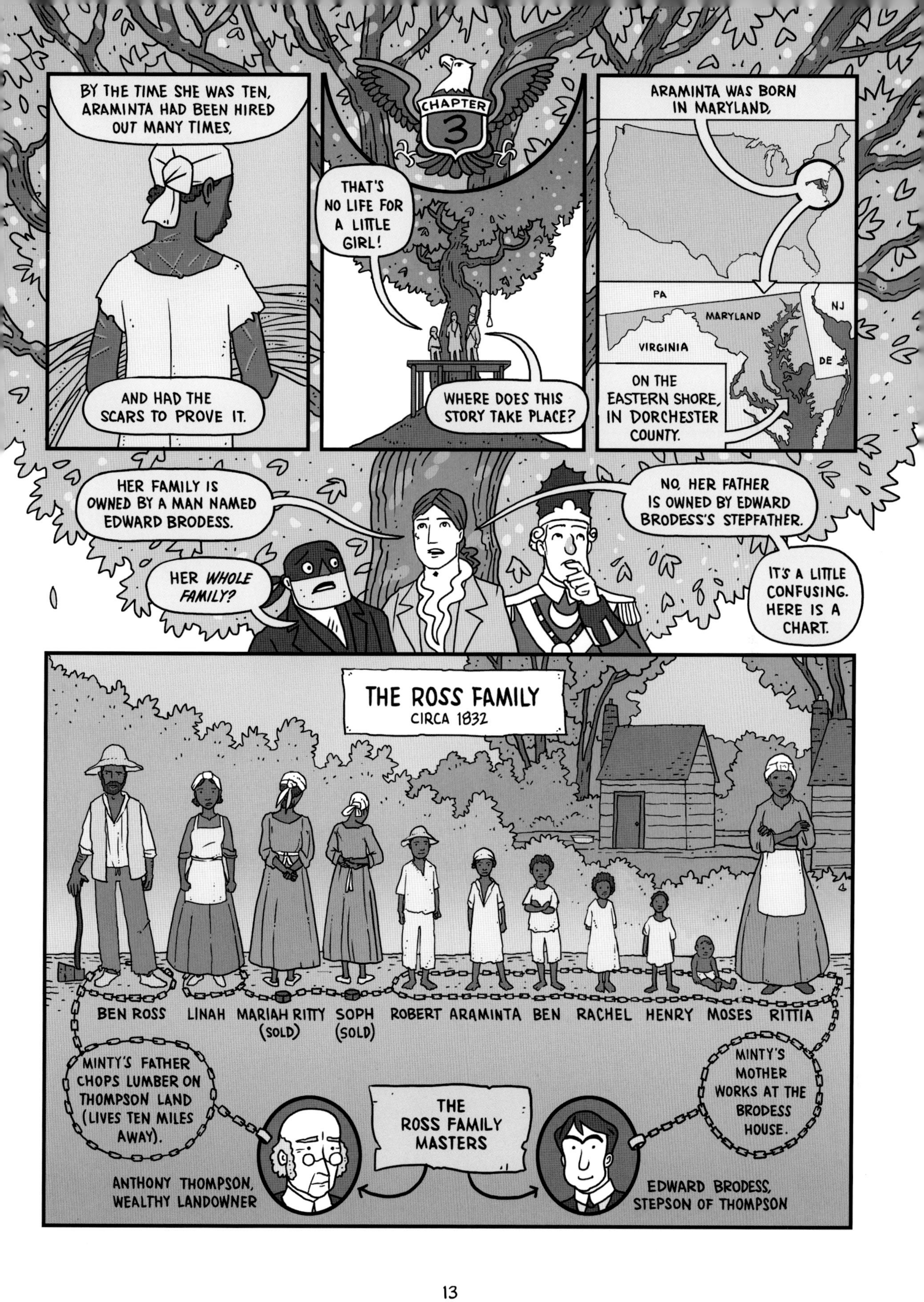
BY THE TIME SHE WAS TEN, ARAMINTA HAD BEEN HIRED OUT MANY TIMES,
AND HAD THE SCARS TO PROVE IT.
CHAPTER 3
THAT'S NO LIFE FOR A LITTLE GIRL!
WHERE DOES THIS STORY TAKE PLACE?
ARAMINTA WAS BORN IN MARYLAND,
PA
NJ
MARYLAND
VIRGINIA
DE
ON THE EASTERN SHORE, IN DORCHESTER COUNTY.
HER FAMILY IS OWNED BY A MAN NAMED EDWARD BRODESS.
HER WHOLE FAMILY?
NO, HER FATHER IS OWNED BY EDWARD BRODESS'S STEPFATHER.
IT'S A LITTLE CONFUSING. HERE IS A CHART.
THE ROSS FAMILY
CIRCA 1832
BEN ROSS
LINAH
MARIAH RITTY (SOLD)
SOPH (SOLD)
ROBERT
ARAMINTA
BEN
RACHEL
HENRY
MOSES
RITTIA
MINTY'S FATHER CHOPS LUMBER ON THOMPSON LAND (LIVES TEN MILES AWAY).
THE ROSS FAMILY MASTERS
MINTY'S MOTHER WORKS AT THE BRODESS HOUSE.
ANTHONY THOMPSON, WEALTHY LANDOWNER
EDWARD BRODESS, STEPSON OF THOMPSON

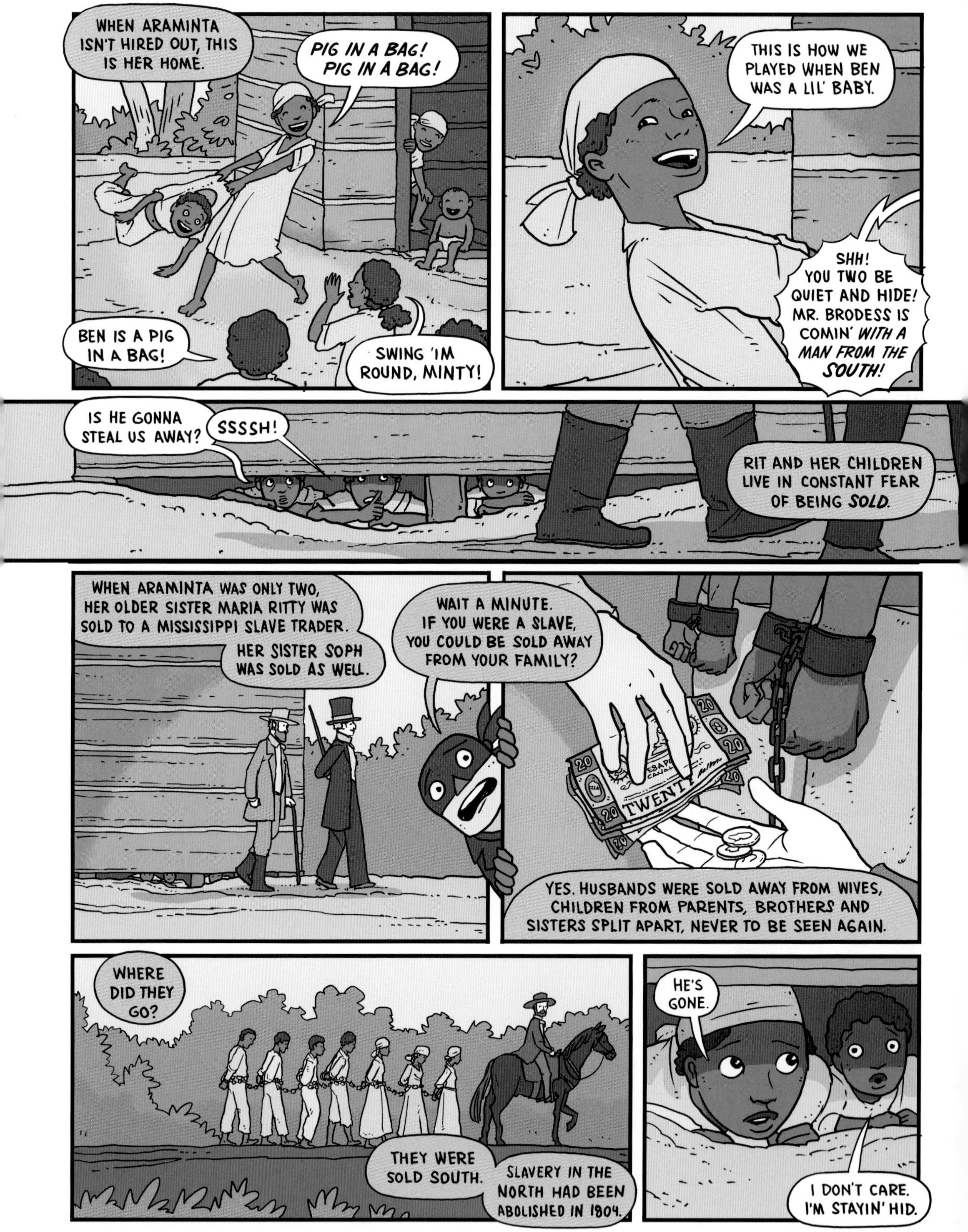

WHEN ARAMINTA ISN'T HIRED OUT, THIS IS HER HOME.
PIG IN A BAG! PIG IN A BAG!
BEN IS A PIG IN A BAG!
SWING 'IM ROUND, MINTY!
THIS IS HOW WE PLAYED WHEN BEN WAS A LIL' BABY.
SHH! YOU TWO BE QUIET AND HIDE! MR. BRODESS IS COMIN' WITH A MAN FROM THE SOUTH!
IS HE GONNA STEAL US AWAY?
SSSSH!
RIT AND HER CHILDREN LIVE IN CONSTANT FEAR OF BEING SOLD.
WHEN ARAMINTA WAS ONLY TWO, HER OLDER SISTER MARIA RITTY WAS SOLD TO A MISSISSIPPI SLAVE TRADER.
HER SISTER SOPH WAS SOLD AS WELL.
WAIT A MINUTE. IF YOU WERE A SLAVE, YOU COULD BE SOLD AWAY FROM YOUR FAMILY?
TWENTY
YES. HUSBANDS WERE SOLD AWAY FROM WIVES, CHILDREN FROM PARENTS, BROTHERS AND SISTERS SPLIT APART, NEVER TO BE SEEN AGAIN.
WHERE DID THEY GO?
THEY WERE SOLD SOUTH.
SLAVERY IN THE NORTH HAD BEEN ABOLISHED IN 1804.
HE'S GONE.
I DON'T CARE. I'M STAYIN' HID.

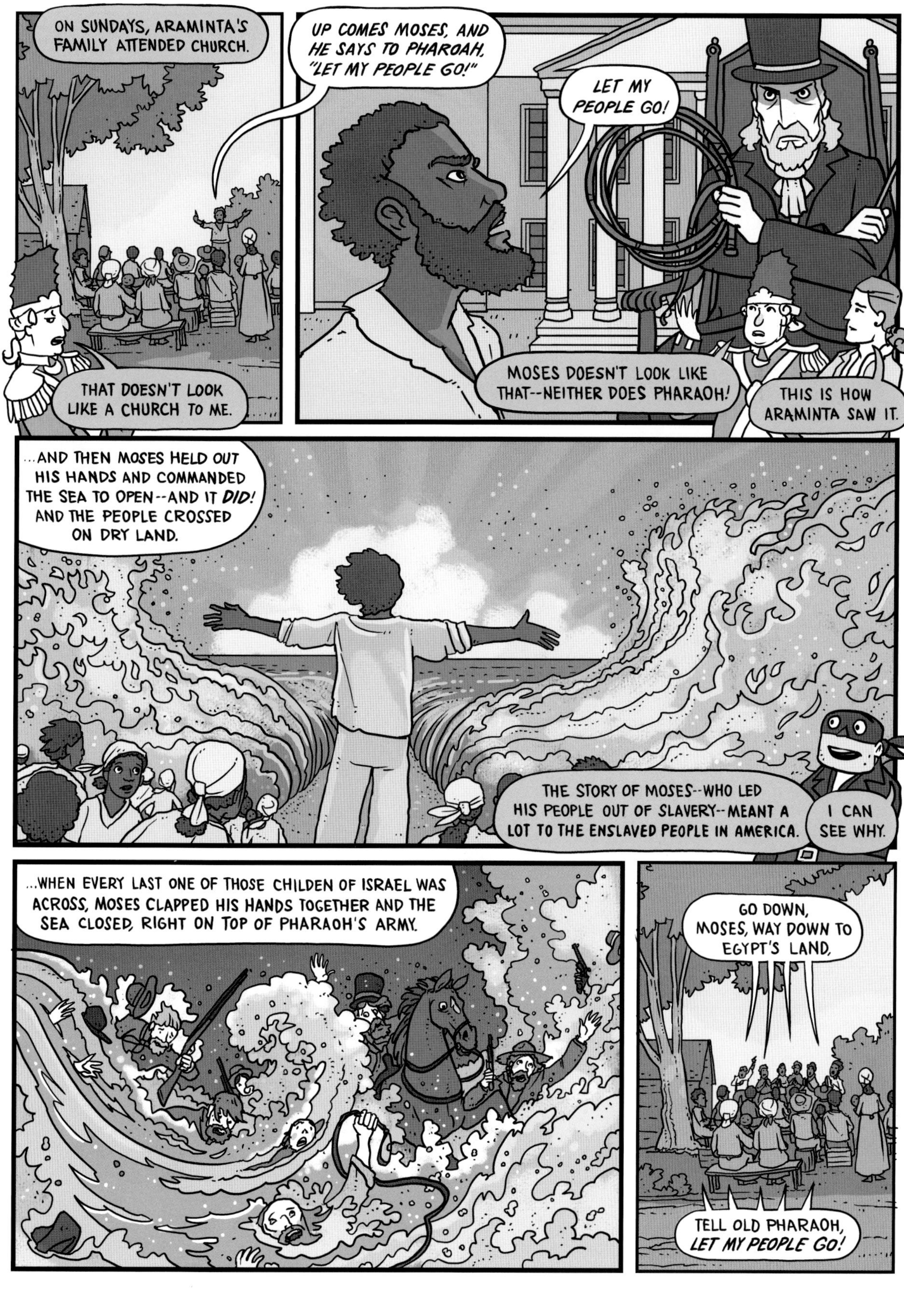

ON SUNDAYS, ARAMINTA'S FAMILY ATTENDED CHURCH.
THAT DOESN'T LOOK LIKE A CHURCH TO ME.
UP COMES MOSES, AND HE SAYS TO PHARAOH, "LET MY PEOPLE GO!"
LET MY PEOPLE GO!
MOSES DOESN'T LOOK LIKE THAT--NEITHER DOES PHARAOH!
THIS IS HOW ARAMINTA SAW IT.
...AND THEN MOSES HELD OUT HIS HANDS AND COMMANDED THE SEA TO OPEN--AND IT *DID*! AND THE PEOPLE CROSSED ON DRY LAND.
THE STORY OF MOSES--WHO LED HIS PEOPLE OUT OF SLAVERY--MEANT A LOT TO THE ENSLAVED PEOPLE IN AMERICA.
I CAN SEE WHY.
...WHEN EVERY LAST ONE OF THOSE CHILDEN OF ISRAEL WAS ACROSS, MOSES CLAPPED HIS HANDS TOGETHER AND THE SEA CLOSED, RIGHT ON TOP OF PHARAOH'S ARMY.
GO DOWN, MOSES, WAY DOWN TO EGYPT'S LAND,
TELL OLD PHARAOH, *LET MY PEOPLE GO!*

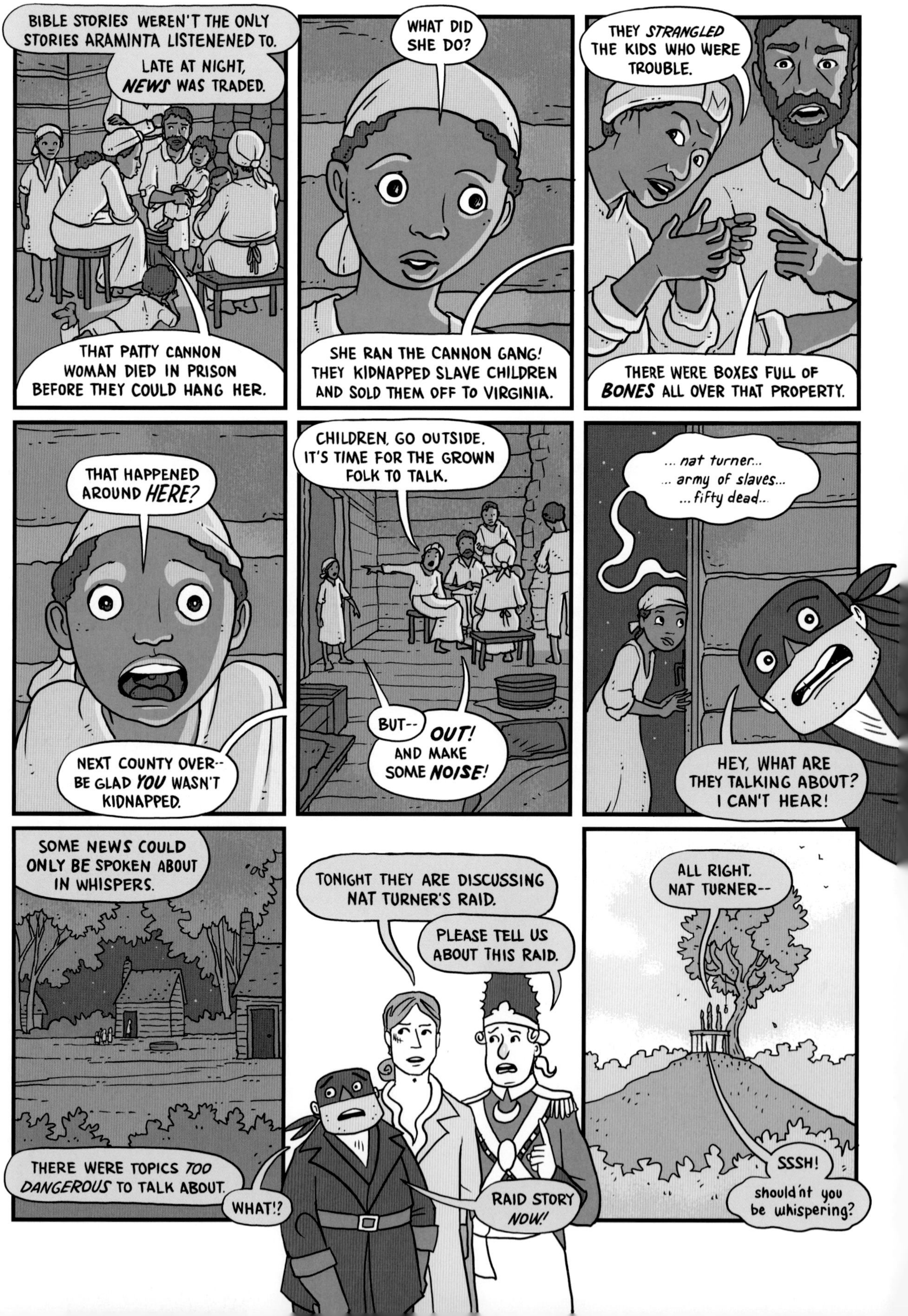
BIBLE STORIES WEREN'T THE ONLY STORIES ARAMINTA LISTENENED TO.
LATE AT NIGHT, NEWS WAS TRADED.
THAT PATTY CANNON WOMAN DIED IN PRISON BEFORE THEY COULD HANG HER.
WHAT DID SHE DO?
SHE RAN THE CANNON GANG! THEY KIDNAPPED SLAVE CHILDREN AND SOLD THEM OFF TO VIRGINIA.
THEY STRANGLED THE KIDS WHO WERE TROUBLE.
THERE WERE BOXES FULL OF BONES ALL OVER THAT PROPERTY.
THAT HAPPENED AROUND HERE?
NEXT COUNTY OVER-- BE GLAD YOU WASN'T KIDNAPPED.
CHILDREN, GO OUTSIDE. IT'S TIME FOR THE GROWN FOLK TO TALK.
BUT--
OUT! AND MAKE SOME NOISE!
... nat turner... ... army of slaves... ... fifty dead...
HEY, WHAT ARE THEY TALKING ABOUT? I CAN'T HEAR!
SOME NEWS COULD ONLY BE SPOKEN ABOUT IN WHISPERS.
THERE WERE TOPICS TOO DANGEROUS TO TALK ABOUT.
TONIGHT THEY ARE DISCUSSING NAT TURNER'S RAID.
PLEASE TELL US ABOUT THIS RAID.
WHAT!?
RAID STORY NOW!
ALL RIGHT. NAT TURNER--
SSSH!
should'nt you be whispering?

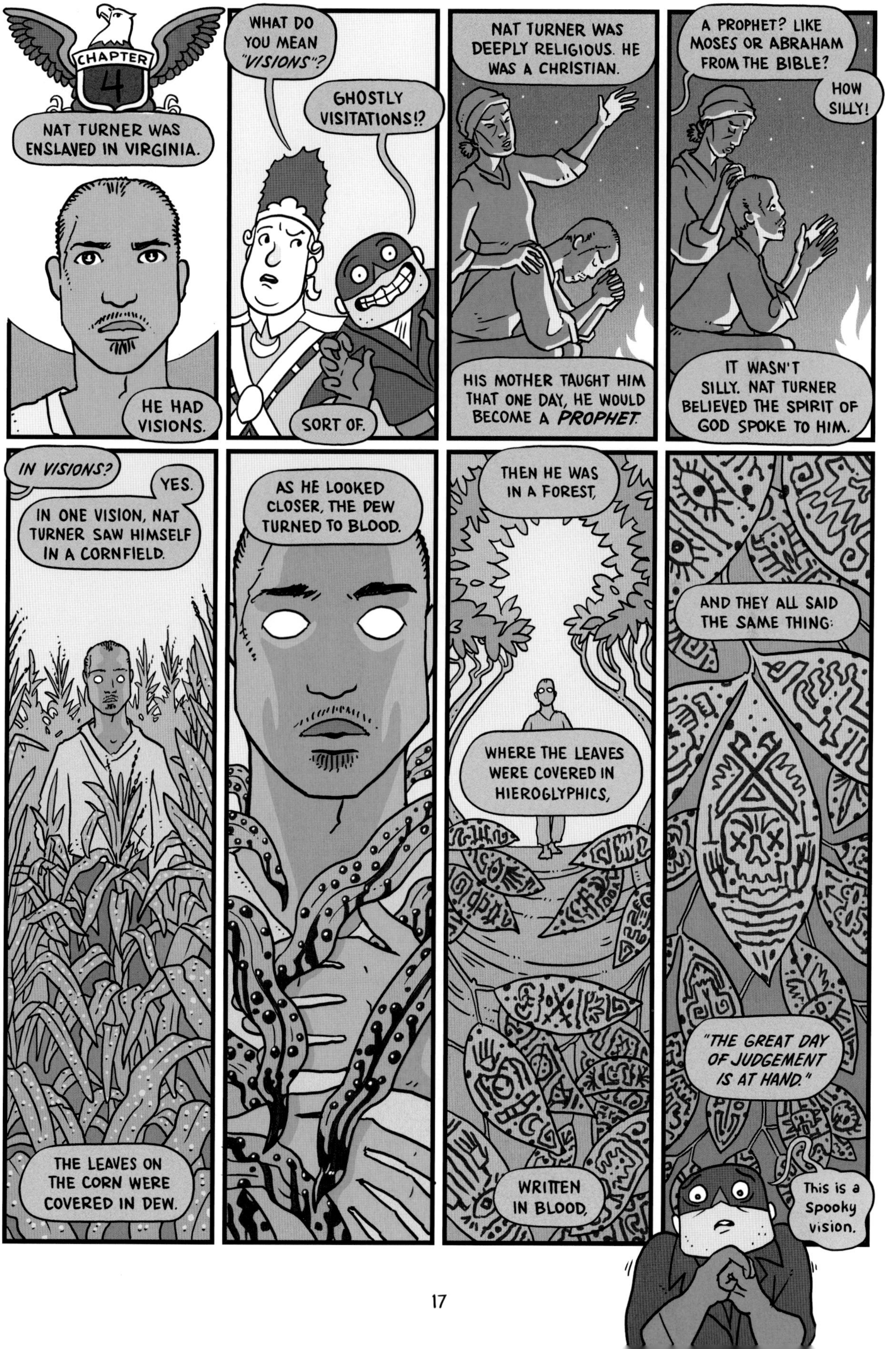
CHAPTER
4
NAT TURNER WAS ENSLAVED IN VIRGINIA.
HE HAD VISIONS.
WHAT DO YOU MEAN "VISIONS"?
GHOSTLY VISITATIONS!?
SORT OF.
NAT TURNER WAS DEEPLY RELIGIOUS. HE WAS A CHRISTIAN.
HIS MOTHER TAUGHT HIM THAT ONE DAY, HE WOULD BECOME A PROPHET.
A PROPHET? LIKE MOSES OR ABRAHAM FROM THE BIBLE?
HOW SILLY!
IT WASN'T SILLY. NAT TURNER BELIEVED THE SPIRIT OF GOD SPOKE TO HIM.
IN VISIONS?
YES.
IN ONE VISION, NAT TURNER SAW HIMSELF IN A CORNFIELD.
THE LEAVES ON THE CORN WERE COVERED IN DEW.
AS HE LOOKED CLOSER, THE DEW TURNED TO BLOOD.
THEN HE WAS IN A FOREST,
WHERE THE LEAVES WERE COVERED IN HIEROGLYPHICS,
WRITTEN IN BLOOD,
AND THEY ALL SAID THE SAME THING:
"THE GREAT DAY OF JUDGEMENT IS AT HAND."
This is a Spooky vision.

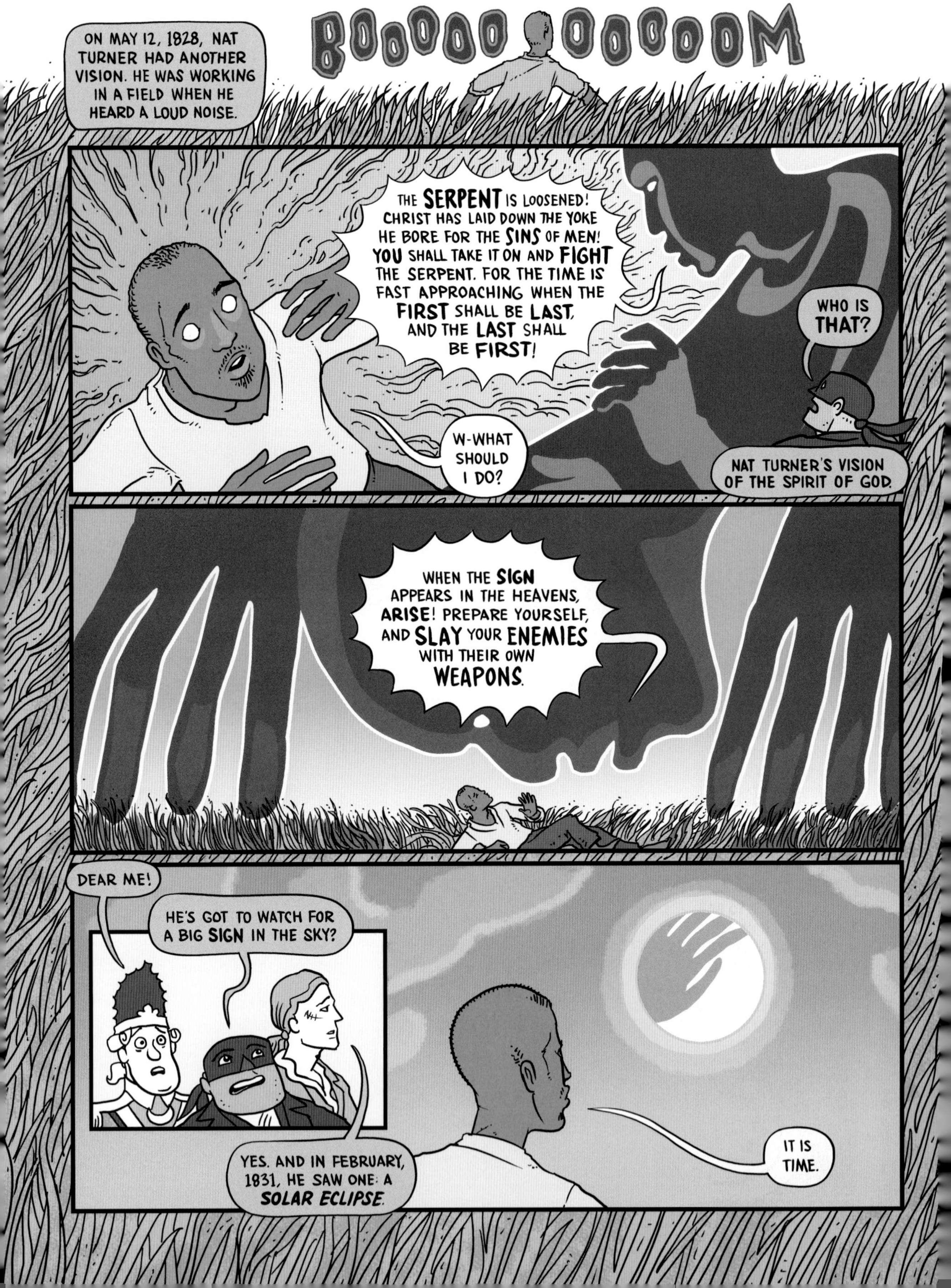
ON MAY 12, 1828, NAT TURNER HAD ANOTHER VISION. HE WAS WORKING IN A FIELD WHEN HE HEARD A LOUD NOISE.
BOOOOOOOOOOOOM
THE SERPENT IS LOOSENED! CHRIST HAS LAID DOWN THE YOKE HE BORE FOR THE SINS OF MEN! YOU SHALL TAKE IT ON AND FIGHT THE SERPENT. FOR THE TIME IS FAST APPROACHING WHEN THE FIRST SHALL BE LAST, AND THE LAST SHALL BE FIRST!
WHO IS THAT?
W-WHAT SHOULD I DO?
NAT TURNER'S VISION OF THE SPIRIT OF GOD.
WHEN THE SIGN APPEARS IN THE HEAVENS, ARISE! PREPARE YOURSELF, AND SLAY YOUR ENEMIES WITH THEIR OWN WEAPONS.
DEAR ME!
HE'S GOT TO WATCH FOR A BIG SIGN IN THE SKY?
YES. AND IN FEBRUARY, 1831, HE SAW ONE: A SOLAR ECLIPSE.
IT IS TIME.

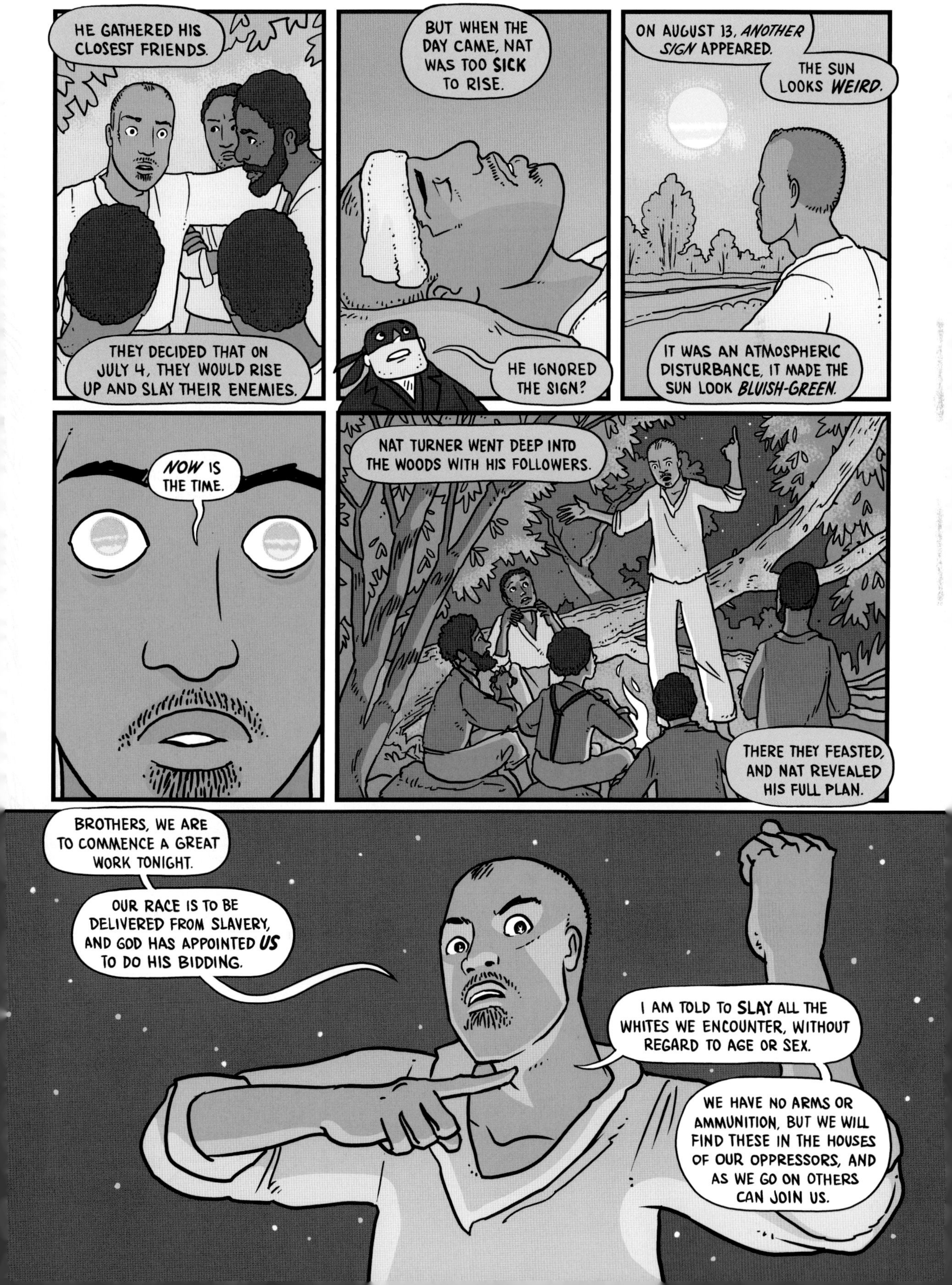
HE GATHERED HIS CLOSEST FRIENDS.
THEY DECIDED THAT ON JULY 4, THEY WOULD RISE UP AND SLAY THEIR ENEMIES.
BUT WHEN THE DAY CAME, NAT WAS TOO **SICK** TO RISE.
HE IGNORED THE SIGN?
ON AUGUST 13, *ANOTHER SIGN* APPEARED.
THE SUN LOOKS ***WEIRD***.
IT WAS AN ATMOSPHERIC DISTURBANCE, IT MADE THE SUN LOOK ***BLUISH-GREEN***.
NOW IS THE TIME.
NAT TURNER WENT DEEP INTO THE WOODS WITH HIS FOLLOWERS.
THERE THEY FEASTED, AND NAT REVEALED HIS FULL PLAN.
BROTHERS, WE ARE TO COMMENCE A GREAT WORK TONIGHT.
OUR RACE IS TO BE DELIVERED FROM SLAVERY, AND GOD HAS APPOINTED ***US*** TO DO HIS BIDDING.
I AM TOLD TO **SLAY** ALL THE WHITES WE ENCOUNTER, WITHOUT REGARD TO AGE OR SEX.
WE HAVE NO ARMS OR AMMUNITION, BUT WE WILL FIND THESE IN THE HOUSES OF OUR OPPRESSORS, AND AS WE GO ON OTHERS CAN JOIN US.

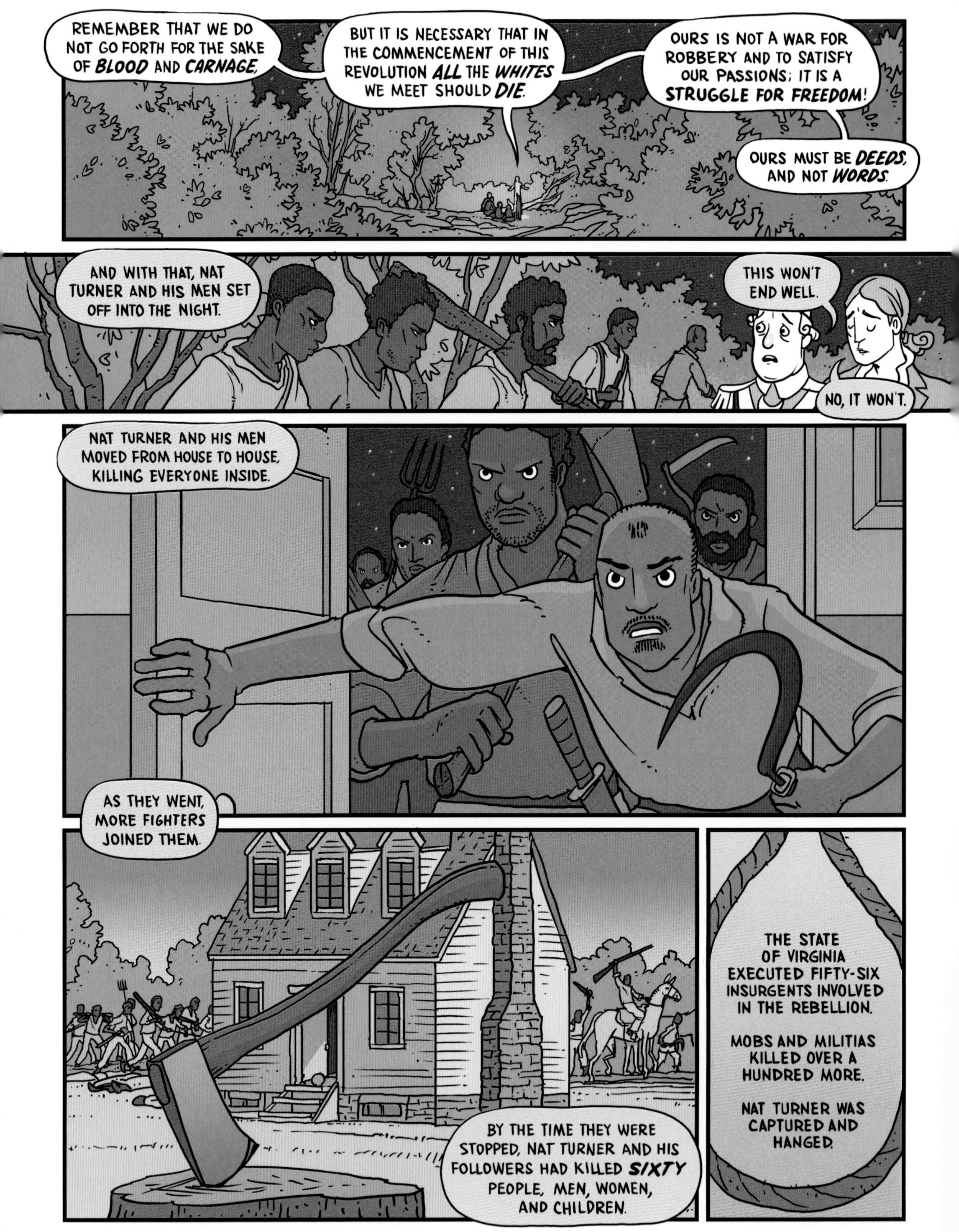

REMEMBER THAT WE DO NOT GO FORTH FOR THE SAKE OF BLOOD AND CARNAGE,
BUT IT IS NECESSARY THAT IN THE COMMENCEMENT OF THIS REVOLUTION ALL THE WHITES WE MEET SHOULD DIE.
OURS IS NOT A WAR FOR ROBBERY AND TO SATISFY OUR PASSIONS; IT IS A STRUGGLE FOR FREEDOM!
OURS MUST BE DEEDS, AND NOT WORDS.
AND WITH THAT, NAT TURNER AND HIS MEN SET OFF INTO THE NIGHT.
THIS WON'T END WELL.
NO, IT WON'T.
NAT TURNER AND HIS MEN MOVED FROM HOUSE TO HOUSE, KILLING EVERYONE INSIDE.
AS THEY WENT, MORE FIGHTERS JOINED THEM.
BY THE TIME THEY WERE STOPPED, NAT TURNER AND HIS FOLLOWERS HAD KILLED SIXTY PEOPLE, MEN, WOMEN, AND CHILDREN.
THE STATE OF VIRGINIA EXECUTED FIFTY-SIX INSURGENTS INVOLVED IN THE REBELLION.
MOBS AND MILITIAS KILLED OVER A HUNDRED MORE.
NAT TURNER WAS CAPTURED AND HANGED.

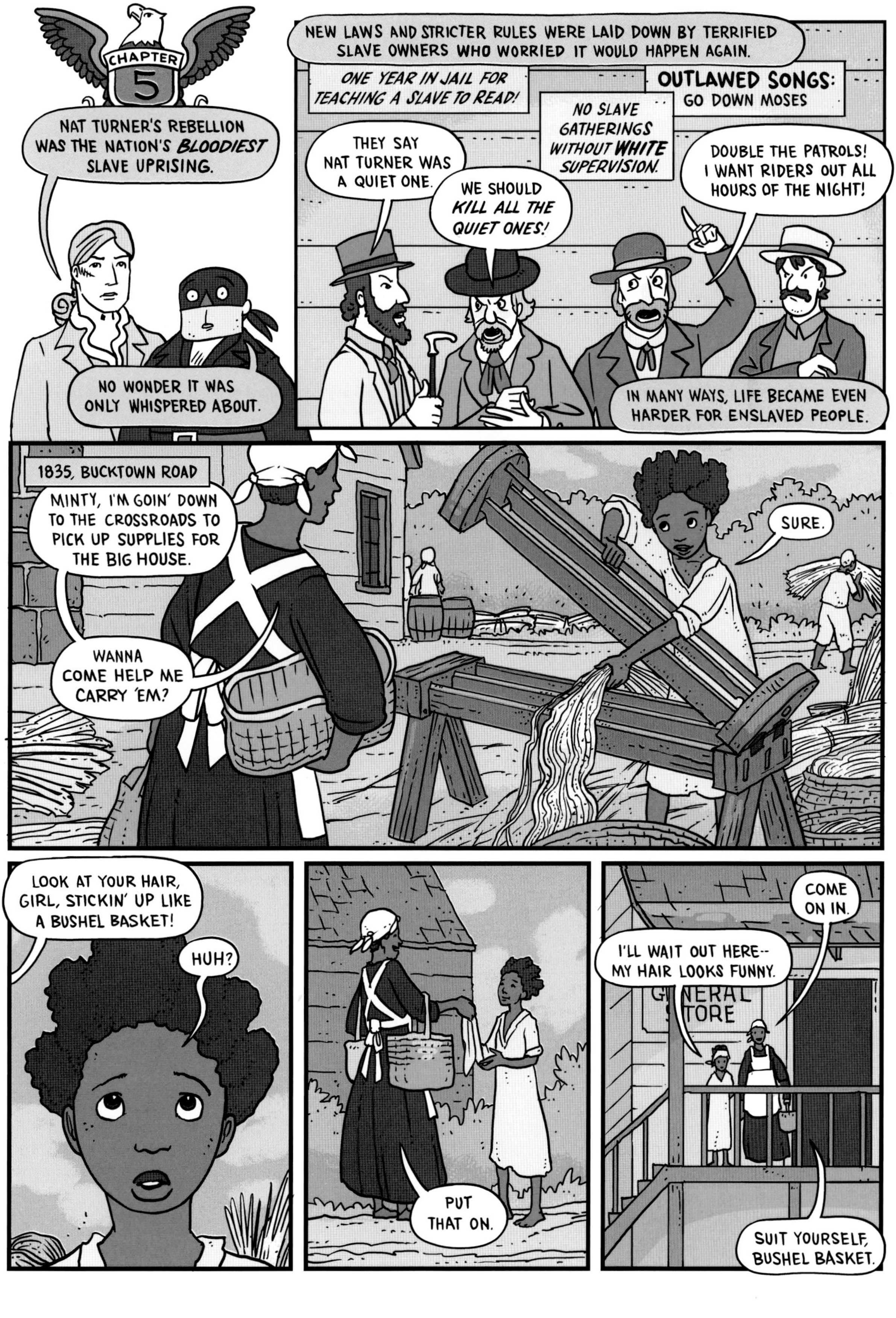

CHAPTER 5
NAT TURNER'S REBELLION WAS THE NATION'S *BLOODIEST* SLAVE UPRISING.
NO WONDER IT WAS ONLY WHISPERED ABOUT.
NEW LAWS AND STRICTER RULES WERE LAID DOWN BY TERRIFIED SLAVE OWNERS WHO WORRIED IT WOULD HAPPEN AGAIN.
ONE YEAR IN JAIL FOR TEACHING A SLAVE TO READ!
NO SLAVE GATHERINGS WITHOUT WHITE SUPERVISION.
OUTLAWED SONGS: GO DOWN MOSES
THEY SAY NAT TURNER WAS A QUIET ONE.
WE SHOULD *KILL ALL THE QUIET ONES!*
DOUBLE THE PATROLS! I WANT RIDERS OUT ALL HOURS OF THE NIGHT!
IN MANY WAYS, LIFE BECAME EVEN HARDER FOR ENSLAVED PEOPLE.
1835, BUCKTOWN ROAD
MINTY, I'M GOIN' DOWN TO THE CROSSROADS TO PICK UP SUPPLIES FOR THE BIG HOUSE.
WANNA COME HELP ME CARRY 'EM?
SURE.
LOOK AT YOUR HAIR, GIRL, STICKIN' UP LIKE A BUSHEL BASKET!
HUH?
PUT THAT ON.
COME ON IN.
I'LL WAIT OUT HERE-- MY HAIR LOOKS FUNNY.
GENERAL STORE
SUIT YOURSELF, BUSHEL BASKET.

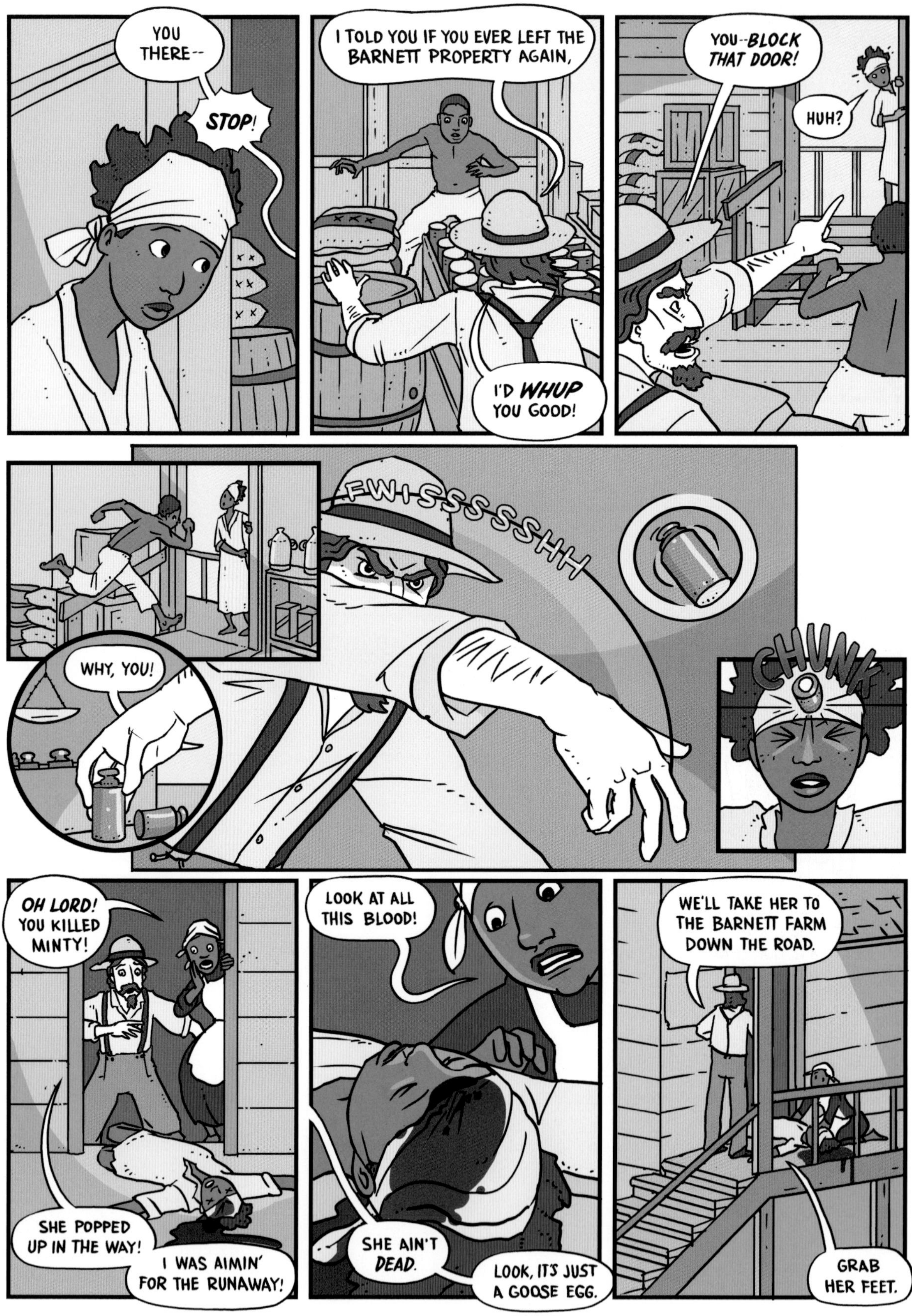
YOU THERE--
STOP!
I TOLD YOU IF YOU EVER LEFT THE BARNETT PROPERTY AGAIN,
I'D WHUP YOU GOOD!
YOU--BLOCK THAT DOOR!
HUH?
FWISSSSSSHH
WHY, YOU!
CHUNK
OH LORD! YOU KILLED MINTY!
SHE POPPED UP IN THE WAY!
I WAS AIMIN' FOR THE RUNAWAY!
LOOK AT ALL THIS BLOOD!
SHE AIN'T DEAD.
LOOK, IT'S JUST A GOOSE EGG.
WE'LL TAKE HER TO THE BARNETT FARM DOWN THE ROAD.
GRAB HER FEET.

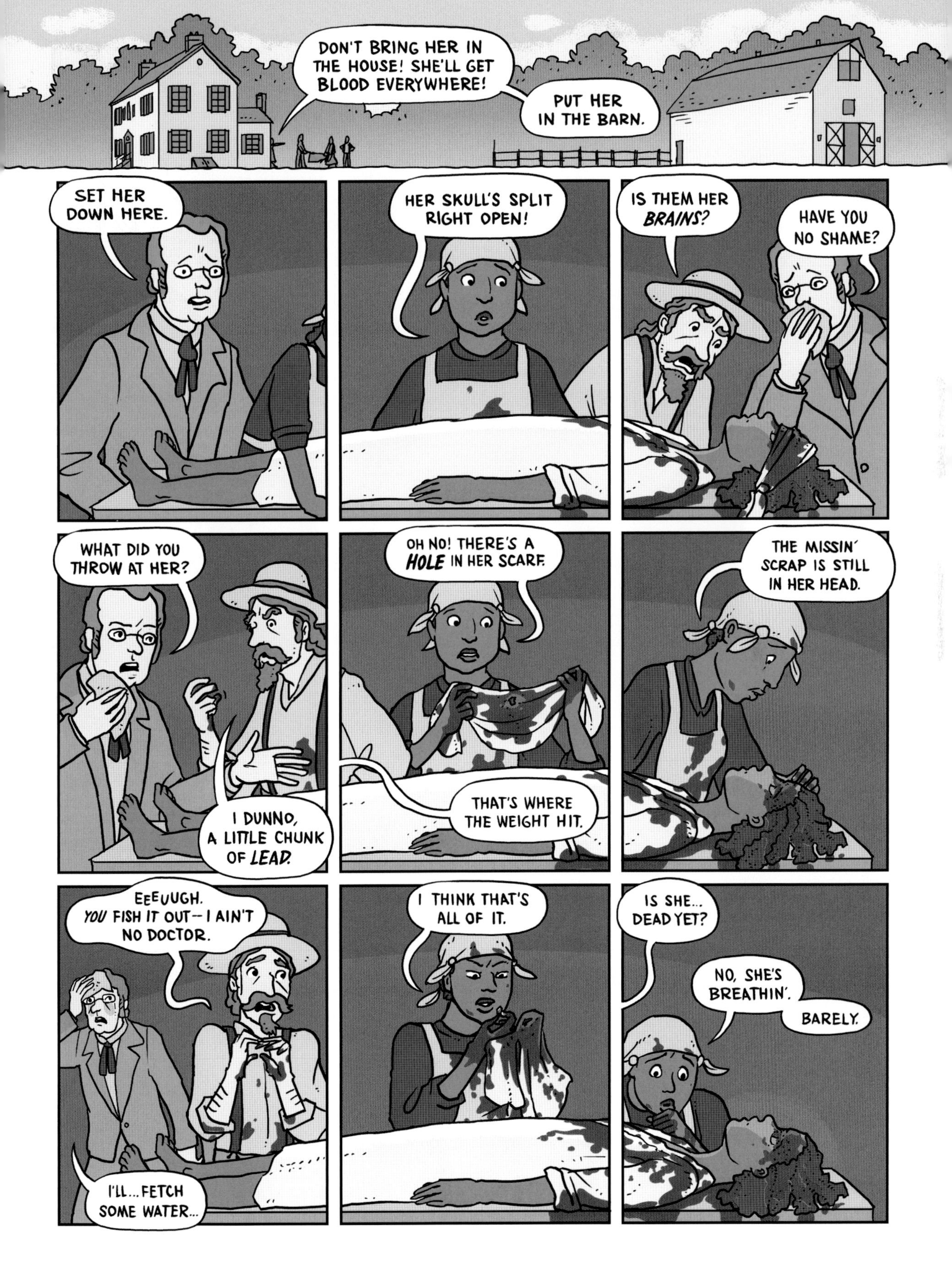
DON'T BRING HER IN THE HOUSE! SHE'LL GET BLOOD EVERYWHERE!
PUT HER IN THE BARN.
SET HER DOWN HERE.
HER SKULL'S SPLIT RIGHT OPEN!
IS THEM HER *BRAINS*?
HAVE YOU NO SHAME?
WHAT DID YOU THROW AT HER?
I DUNNO, A LITTLE CHUNK OF *LEAD*.
OH NO! THERE'S A *HOLE* IN HER SCARF.
THAT'S WHERE THE WEIGHT HIT.
THE MISSIN' SCRAP IS STILL IN HER HEAD.
EEEUUGH. *YOU* FISH IT OUT-- I AIN'T NO DOCTOR.
I'LL... FETCH SOME WATER...
I THINK THAT'S ALL OF IT.
IS SHE... DEAD YET?
NO, SHE'S BREATHIN'.
BARELY.

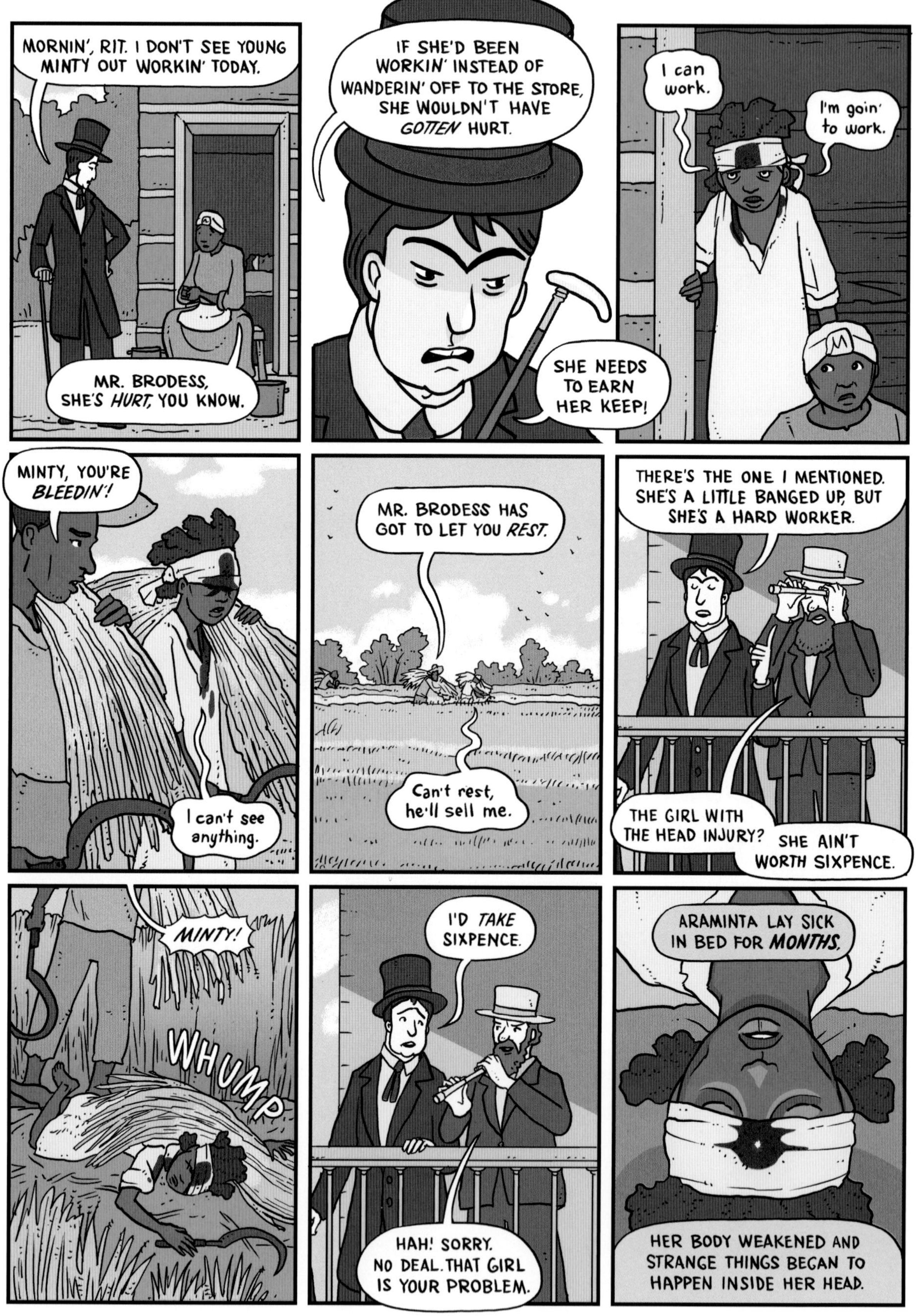
MORNIN', RIT. I DON'T SEE YOUNG MINTY OUT WORKIN' TODAY.
MR. BRODESS, SHE'S HURT, YOU KNOW.
IF SHE'D BEEN WORKIN' INSTEAD OF WANDERIN' OFF TO THE STORE, SHE WOULDN'T HAVE GOTTEN HURT.
SHE NEEDS TO EARN HER KEEP!
I can work.
I'm goin' to work.
MINTY, YOU'RE BLEEDIN'!
I can't see anything.
MR. BRODESS HAS GOT TO LET YOU REST.
Can't rest, he'll sell me.
THERE'S THE ONE I MENTIONED. SHE'S A LITTLE BANGED UP, BUT SHE'S A HARD WORKER.
THE GIRL WITH THE HEAD INJURY?
SHE AIN'T WORTH SIXPENCE.
MINTY!
WHUMP
I'D TAKE SIXPENCE.
HAH! SORRY. NO DEAL. THAT GIRL IS YOUR PROBLEM.
ARAMINTA LAY SICK IN BED FOR MONTHS.
HER BODY WEAKENED AND STRANGE THINGS BEGAN TO HAPPEN INSIDE HER HEAD.

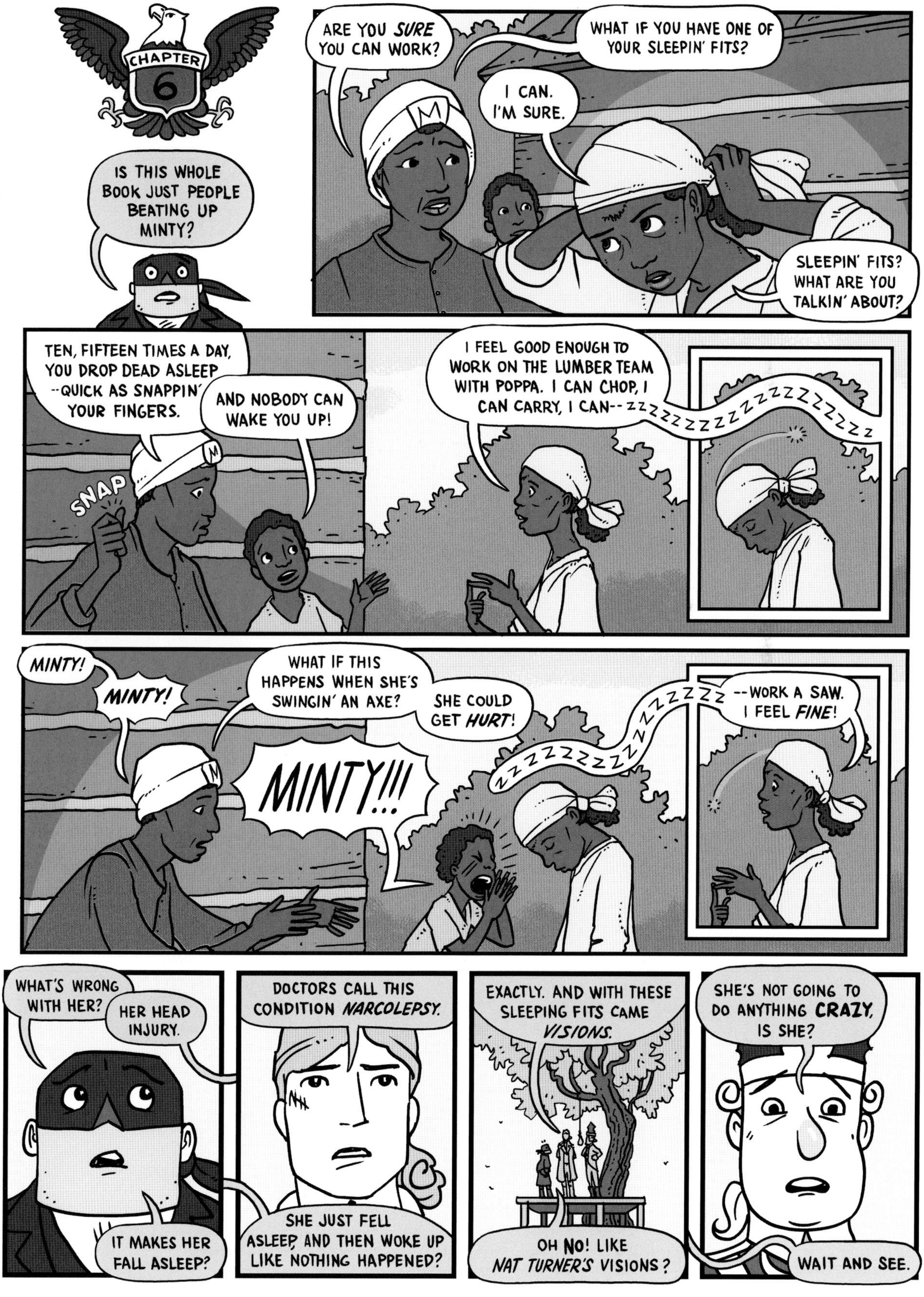
CHAPTER 6
IS THIS WHOLE BOOK JUST PEOPLE BEATING UP MINTY?
ARE YOU *SURE* YOU CAN WORK?
WHAT IF YOU HAVE ONE OF YOUR SLEEPIN' FITS?
I CAN. I'M SURE.
SLEEPIN' FITS? WHAT ARE YOU TALKIN' ABOUT?
TEN, FIFTEEN TIMES A DAY, YOU DROP DEAD ASLEEP --QUICK AS SNAPPIN' YOUR FINGERS.
SNAP
AND NOBODY CAN WAKE YOU UP!
I FEEL GOOD ENOUGH TO WORK ON THE LUMBER TEAM WITH POPPA. I CAN CHOP, I CAN CARRY, I CAN-- ZZZZZZZZZZZZZZZZZZZZZZ
MINTY!
MINTY!
WHAT IF THIS HAPPENS WHEN SHE'S SWINGIN' AN AXE?
SHE COULD GET *HURT*!
MINTY!!!
ZZZZZZZZZZZZZZZZZZZZZ --WORK A SAW. I FEEL *FINE*!
WHAT'S WRONG WITH HER?
HER HEAD INJURY.
IT MAKES HER FALL ASLEEP?
DOCTORS CALL THIS CONDITION *NARCOLEPSY*.
SHE JUST FELL ASLEEP, AND THEN WOKE UP LIKE NOTHING HAPPENED?
EXACTLY. AND WITH THESE SLEEPING FITS CAME *VISIONS*.
OH **NO**! LIKE *NAT TURNER'S* VISIONS?
SHE'S NOT GOING TO DO ANYTHING **CRAZY**, IS SHE?
WAIT AND SEE.

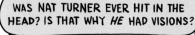

WAS NAT TURNER EVER HIT IN THE HEAD? IS THAT WHY *HE* HAD VISIONS?

NO. IN FACT, THERE MAY BE NO LINK BETWEEN MINTY'S INJURY AND HER VISIONS.

THE VISIONS STARTED SOON AFTER SHE RECOVERED.

WHAT DID SHE *SEE* IN HER VISIONS?

WAIT AND SEE.

QUIT BEING SO MYSTERIOUS! WHAT DID SHE *SEE?*

ARAMINTA SPOKE OF BOTH GOOD AND BAD VISIONS.

HEAVENLY MUSIC OR TERRIBLE RIDERS WITH CHAINS -- BUT WE'LL GET TO THAT SOON ENOUGH.

AS LONG AS SHE DOESN'T HAVE VISIONS OF *BLOODY CORN.*

ARAMINTA WORKED WITH HER BROTHERS ON HER FATHER'S LUMBER CREW.

SHE GREW STRONG HAULING AND CUTTING WOOD.

LOOK AT THIS!

I'VE ALREADY CHOPPED HALF A CORD OF WOOD!

BEAT THAT!

THAT'S A FINE STACK, MINTY. MY BEST CUTTERS CAN BARELY KEEP UP.

IT'S 'CAUSE SHE'S ALWAYS STEALIN' NAPS.

WELL, WHATEVER SHE'S DOIN' IT *WORKS.*

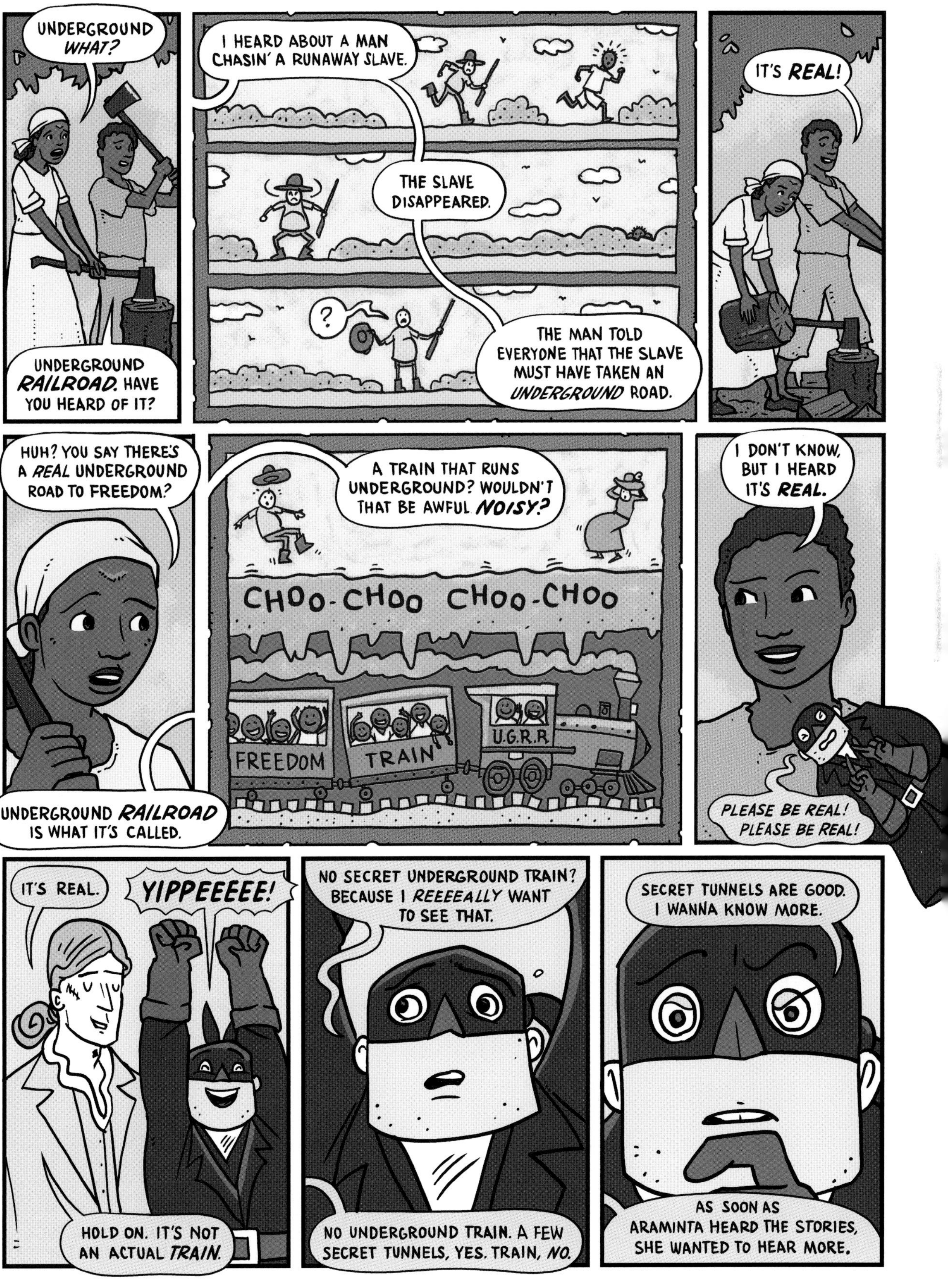
UNDERGROUND WHAT?
UNDERGROUND RAILROAD. HAVE YOU HEARD OF IT?
I HEARD ABOUT A MAN CHASIN' A RUNAWAY SLAVE.
THE SLAVE DISAPPEARED.
?
THE MAN TOLD EVERYONE THAT THE SLAVE MUST HAVE TAKEN AN UNDERGROUND ROAD.
IT'S REAL!
HUH? YOU SAY THERE'S A REAL UNDERGROUND ROAD TO FREEDOM?
UNDERGROUND RAILROAD IS WHAT IT'S CALLED.
A TRAIN THAT RUNS UNDERGROUND? WOULDN'T THAT BE AWFUL NOISY?
CHOO-CHOO CHOO-CHOO
FREEDOM TRAIN
U.G.R.R
I DON'T KNOW, BUT I HEARD IT'S REAL.
PLEASE BE REAL! PLEASE BE REAL!
IT'S REAL.
YIPPEEEEE!
HOLD ON. IT'S NOT AN ACTUAL TRAIN.
NO SECRET UNDERGROUND TRAIN? BECAUSE I REEEEALLY WANT TO SEE THAT.
NO UNDERGROUND TRAIN. A FEW SECRET TUNNELS, YES. TRAIN, NO.
SECRET TUNNELS ARE GOOD. I WANNA KNOW MORE.
AS SOON AS ARAMINTA HEARD THE STORIES, SHE WANTED TO HEAR MORE.

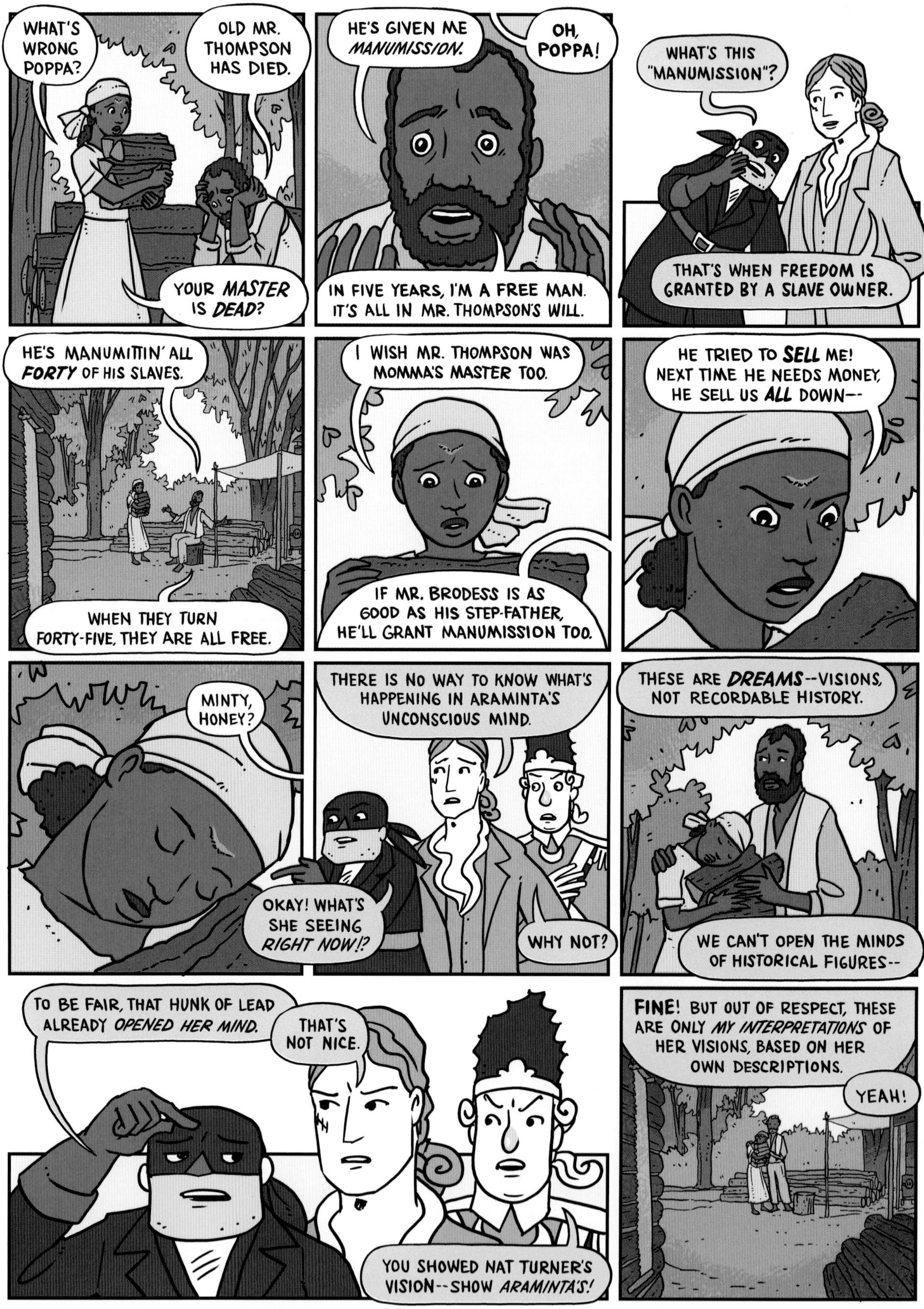
WHAT'S WRONG POPPA?
OLD MR. THOMPSON HAS DIED.
YOUR MASTER IS DEAD?
HE'S GIVEN ME MANUMISSION.
OH, POPPA!
IN FIVE YEARS, I'M A FREE MAN. IT'S ALL IN MR. THOMPSON'S WILL.
WHAT'S THIS "MANUMISSION"?
THAT'S WHEN FREEDOM IS GRANTED BY A SLAVE OWNER.
HE'S MANUMITTIN' ALL FORTY OF HIS SLAVES.
WHEN THEY TURN FORTY-FIVE, THEY ARE ALL FREE.
I WISH MR. THOMPSON WAS MOMMA'S MASTER TOO.
IF MR. BRODESS IS AS GOOD AS HIS STEP-FATHER, HE'LL GRANT MANUMISSION TOO.
HE TRIED TO SELL ME! NEXT TIME HE NEEDS MONEY, HE SELL US ALL DOWN--
MINTY, HONEY?
THERE IS NO WAY TO KNOW WHAT'S HAPPENING IN ARAMINTA'S UNCONSCIOUS MIND.
OKAY! WHAT'S SHE SEEING RIGHT NOW!?
WHY NOT?
THESE ARE DREAMS--VISIONS, NOT RECORDABLE HISTORY.
WE CAN'T OPEN THE MINDS OF HISTORICAL FIGURES--
TO BE FAIR, THAT HUNK OF LEAD ALREADY OPENED HER MIND.
THAT'S NOT NICE.
YOU SHOWED NAT TURNER'S VISION--SHOW ARAMINTA'S!
FINE! BUT OUT OF RESPECT, THESE ARE ONLY MY INTERPRETATIONS OF HER VISIONS, BASED ON HER OWN DESCRIPTIONS.
YEAH!

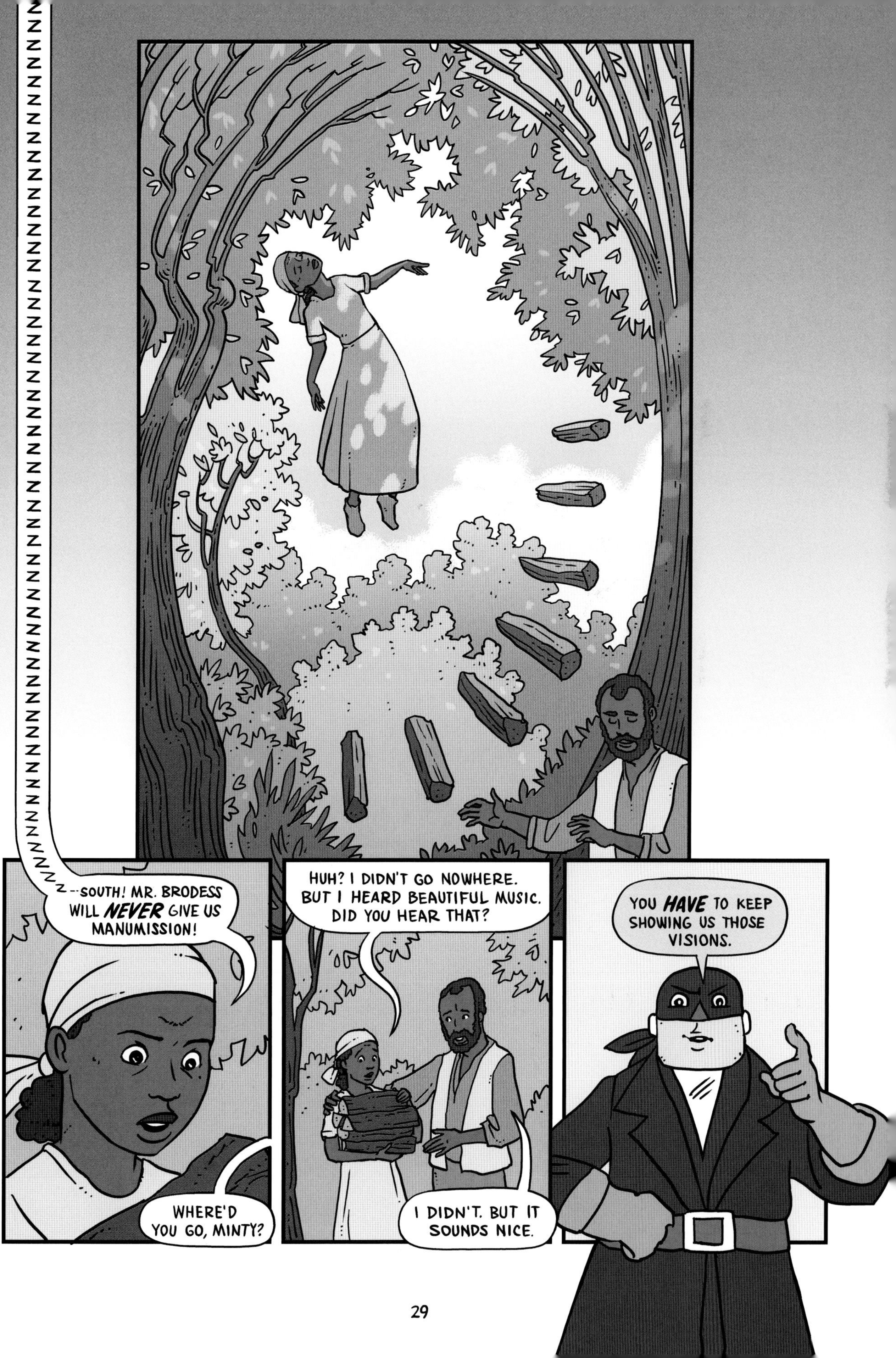
ZZZZZZZZZZZZZZZZZZZZZZZZZZZZZZZZZZZZZZZZZZZZZZZZZZZZZZZZZZZZZZZZZZZZZZZZ--SOUTH! MR. BRODESS WILL NEVER GIVE US MANUMISSION!
WHERE'D YOU GO, MINTY?
HUH? I DIDN'T GO NOWHERE. BUT I HEARD BEAUTIFUL MUSIC. DID YOU HEAR THAT?
I DIDN'T. BUT IT SOUNDS NICE.
YOU HAVE TO KEEP SHOWING US THOSE VISIONS.

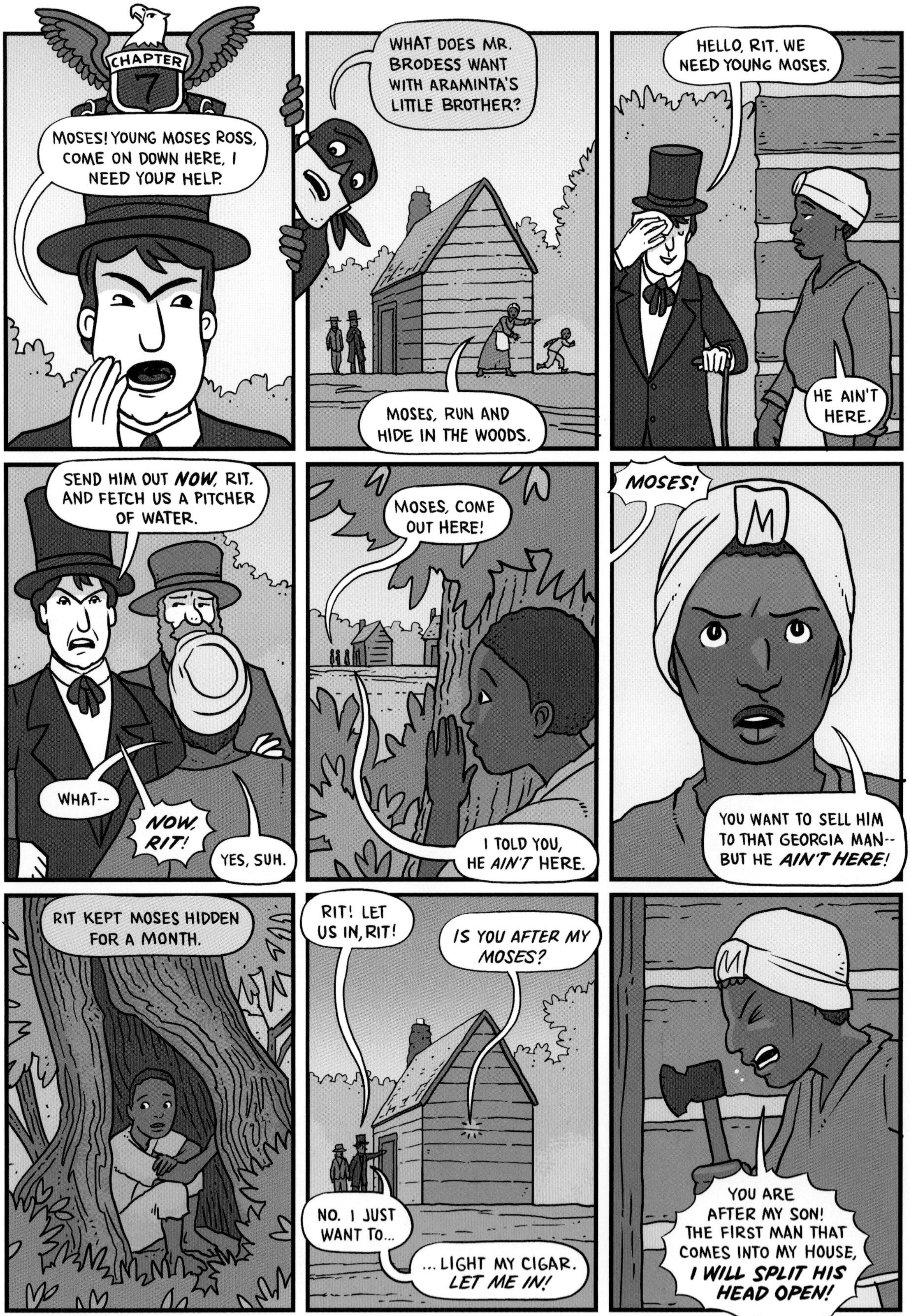
CHAPTER
7
MOSES! YOUNG MOSES ROSS, COME ON DOWN HERE, I NEED YOUR HELP.
WHAT DOES MR. BRODESS WANT WITH ARAMINTA'S LITTLE BROTHER?
MOSES, RUN AND HIDE IN THE WOODS.
HELLO, RIT. WE NEED YOUNG MOSES.
HE AIN'T HERE.
SEND HIM OUT ***NOW***, RIT. AND FETCH US A PITCHER OF WATER.
WHAT--
NOW, RIT!
YES, SUH.
MOSES, COME OUT HERE!
I TOLD YOU, HE *AIN'T* HERE.
MOSES!
M
YOU WANT TO SELL HIM TO THAT GEORGIA MAN-- BUT HE ***AIN'T HERE!***
RIT KEPT MOSES HIDDEN FOR A MONTH.
RIT! LET US IN, RIT!
IS YOU AFTER MY MOSES?
NO. I JUST WANT TO...
... LIGHT MY CIGAR. *LET ME IN!*
M
YOU ARE AFTER MY SON! THE FIRST MAN THAT COMES INTO MY HOUSE, ***I WILL SPLIT HIS HEAD OPEN!***

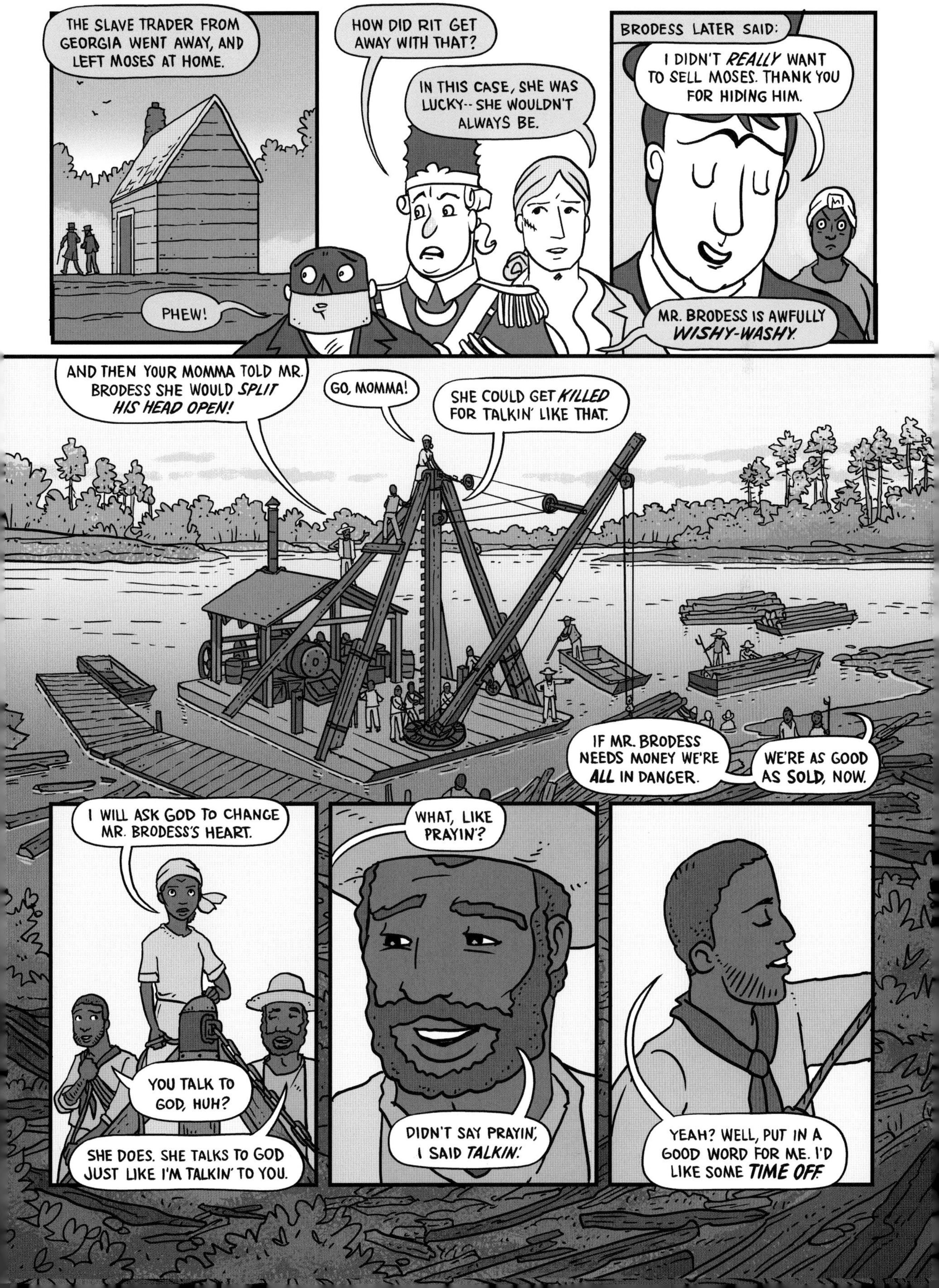
THE SLAVE TRADER FROM GEORGIA WENT AWAY, AND LEFT MOSES AT HOME.
PHEW!
HOW DID RIT GET AWAY WITH THAT?
IN THIS CASE, SHE WAS LUCKY-- SHE WOULDN'T ALWAYS BE.
BRODESS LATER SAID:
I DIDN'T REALLY WANT TO SELL MOSES. THANK YOU FOR HIDING HIM.
MR. BRODESS IS AWFULLY WISHY-WASHY.
AND THEN YOUR MOMMA TOLD MR. BRODESS SHE WOULD SPLIT HIS HEAD OPEN!
GO, MOMMA!
SHE COULD GET KILLED FOR TALKIN' LIKE THAT.
IF MR. BRODESS NEEDS MONEY WE'RE ALL IN DANGER.
WE'RE AS GOOD AS SOLD, NOW.
I WILL ASK GOD TO CHANGE MR. BRODESS'S HEART.
YOU TALK TO GOD, HUH?
SHE DOES. SHE TALKS TO GOD JUST LIKE I'M TALKIN' TO YOU.
WHAT, LIKE PRAYIN'?
DIDN'T SAY PRAYIN', I SAID TALKIN'.
YEAH? WELL, PUT IN A GOOD WORD FOR ME. I'D LIKE SOME TIME OFF.

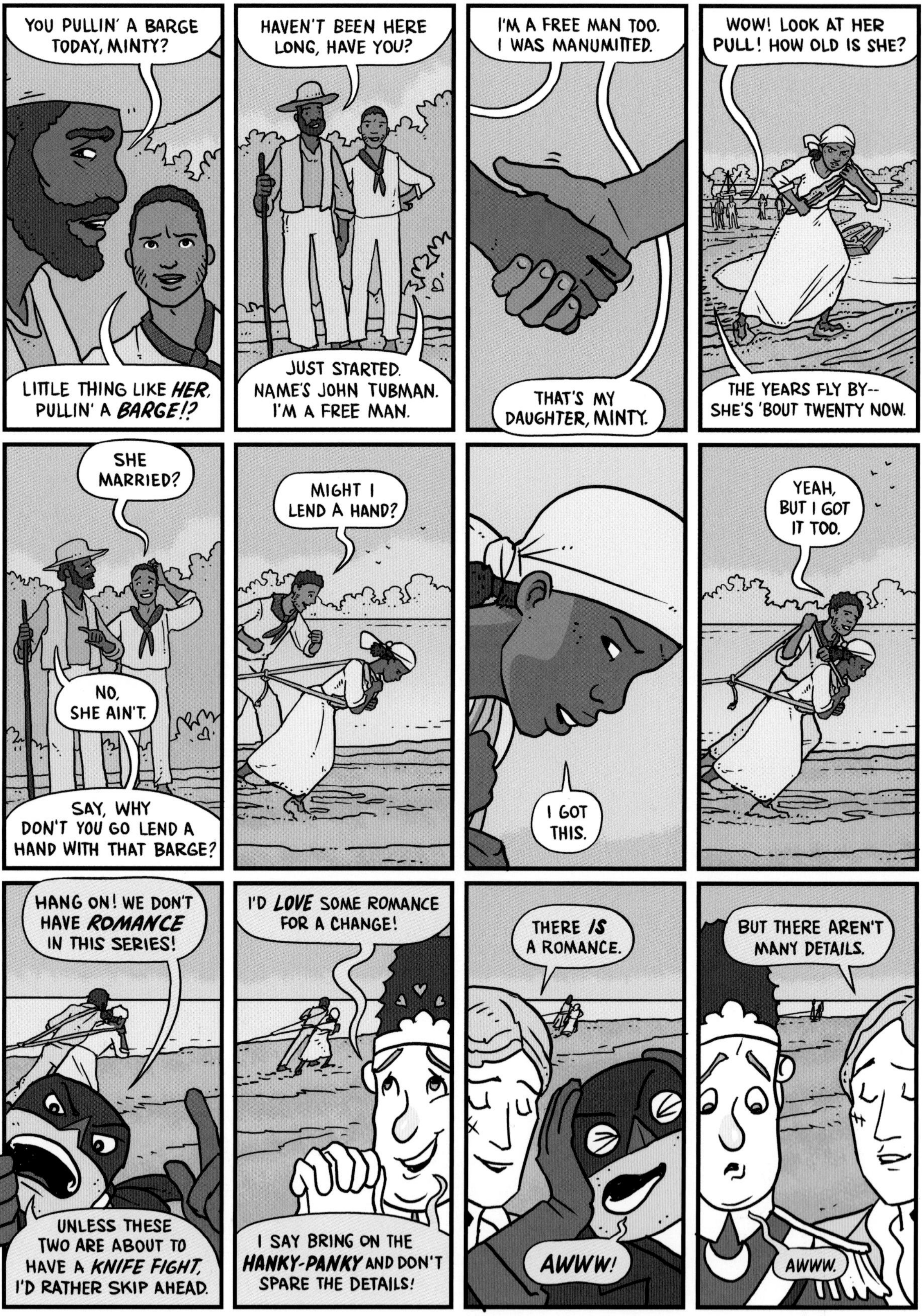
YOU PULLIN' A BARGE TODAY, MINTY?
LITTLE THING LIKE *HER*, PULLIN' A *BARGE*!?
HAVEN'T BEEN HERE LONG, HAVE YOU?
JUST STARTED. NAME'S JOHN TUBMAN. I'M A FREE MAN.
I'M A FREE MAN TOO. I WAS MANUMITTED.
THAT'S MY DAUGHTER, MINTY.
WOW! LOOK AT HER PULL! HOW OLD IS SHE?
THE YEARS FLY BY-- SHE'S 'BOUT TWENTY NOW.
SHE MARRIED?
NO, SHE AIN'T.
SAY, WHY DON'T YOU GO LEND A HAND WITH THAT BARGE?
MIGHT I LEND A HAND?
I GOT THIS.
YEAH, BUT I GOT IT TOO.
HANG ON! WE DON'T HAVE *ROMANCE* IN THIS SERIES!
UNLESS THESE TWO ARE ABOUT TO HAVE A *KNIFE FIGHT*, I'D RATHER SKIP AHEAD.
I'D *LOVE* SOME ROMANCE FOR A CHANGE!
I SAY BRING ON THE *HANKY-PANKY* AND DON'T SPARE THE DETAILS!
THERE *IS* A ROMANCE.
AWWW!
BUT THERE AREN'T MANY DETAILS.
AWWW.

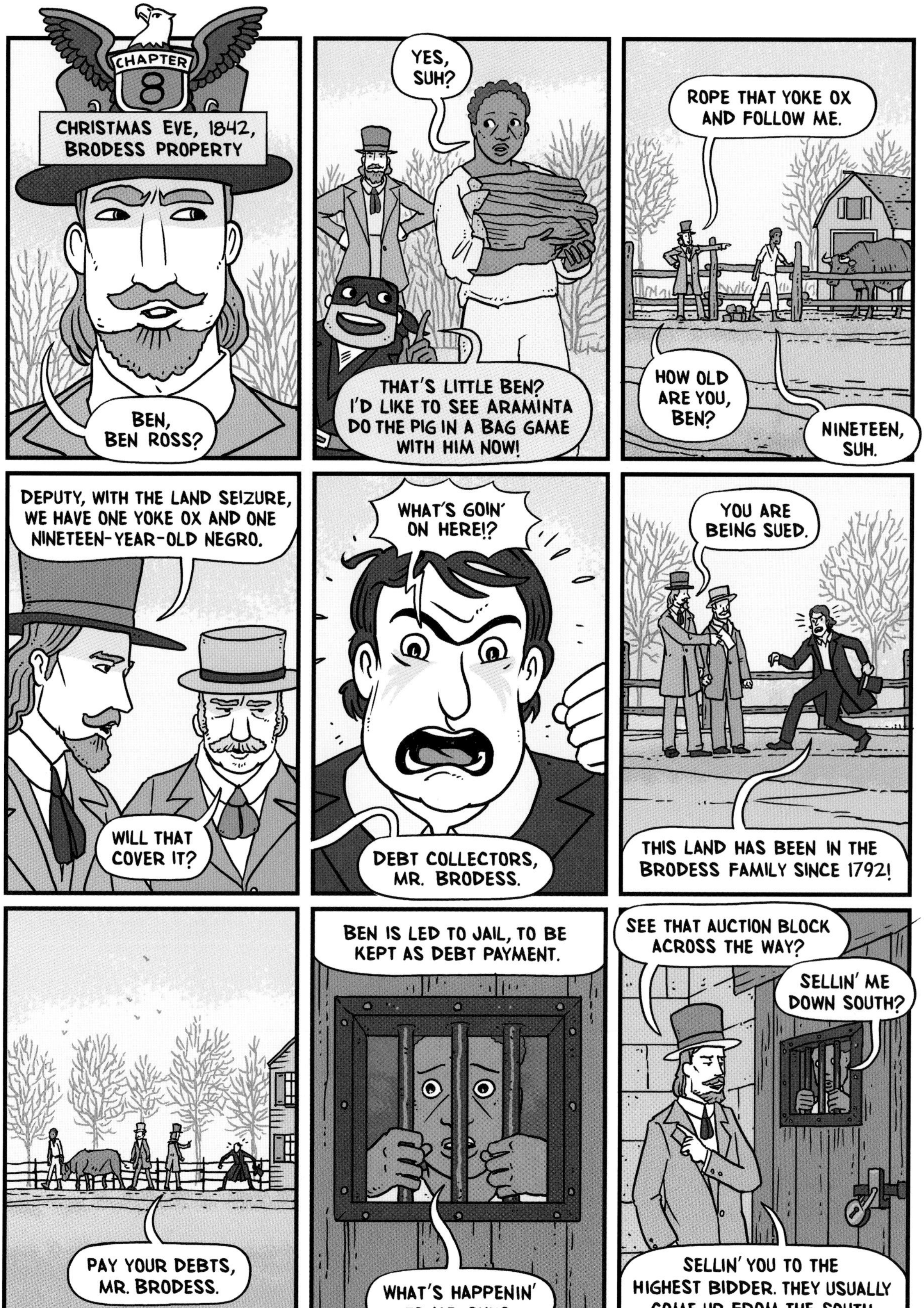
CHAPTER 8
CHRISTMAS EVE, 1842, BRODESS PROPERTY
BEN, BEN ROSS?
YES, SUH?
THAT'S LITTLE BEN? I'D LIKE TO SEE ARAMINTA DO THE PIG IN A BAG GAME WITH HIM NOW!
ROPE THAT YOKE OX AND FOLLOW ME.
HOW OLD ARE YOU, BEN?
NINETEEN, SUH.
DEPUTY, WITH THE LAND SEIZURE, WE HAVE ONE YOKE OX AND ONE NINETEEN-YEAR-OLD NEGRO.
WILL THAT COVER IT?
WHAT'S GOIN' ON HERE!?
DEBT COLLECTORS, MR. BRODESS.
YOU ARE BEING SUED.
THIS LAND HAS BEEN IN THE BRODESS FAMILY SINCE 1792!
PAY YOUR DEBTS, MR. BRODESS.
BEN IS LED TO JAIL, TO BE KEPT AS DEBT PAYMENT.
WHAT'S HAPPENIN' TO ME, SUH?
SEE THAT AUCTION BLOCK ACROSS THE WAY?
SELLIN' ME DOWN SOUTH?
SELLIN' YOU TO THE HIGHEST BIDDER. THEY USUALLY COME UP FROM THE SOUTH.

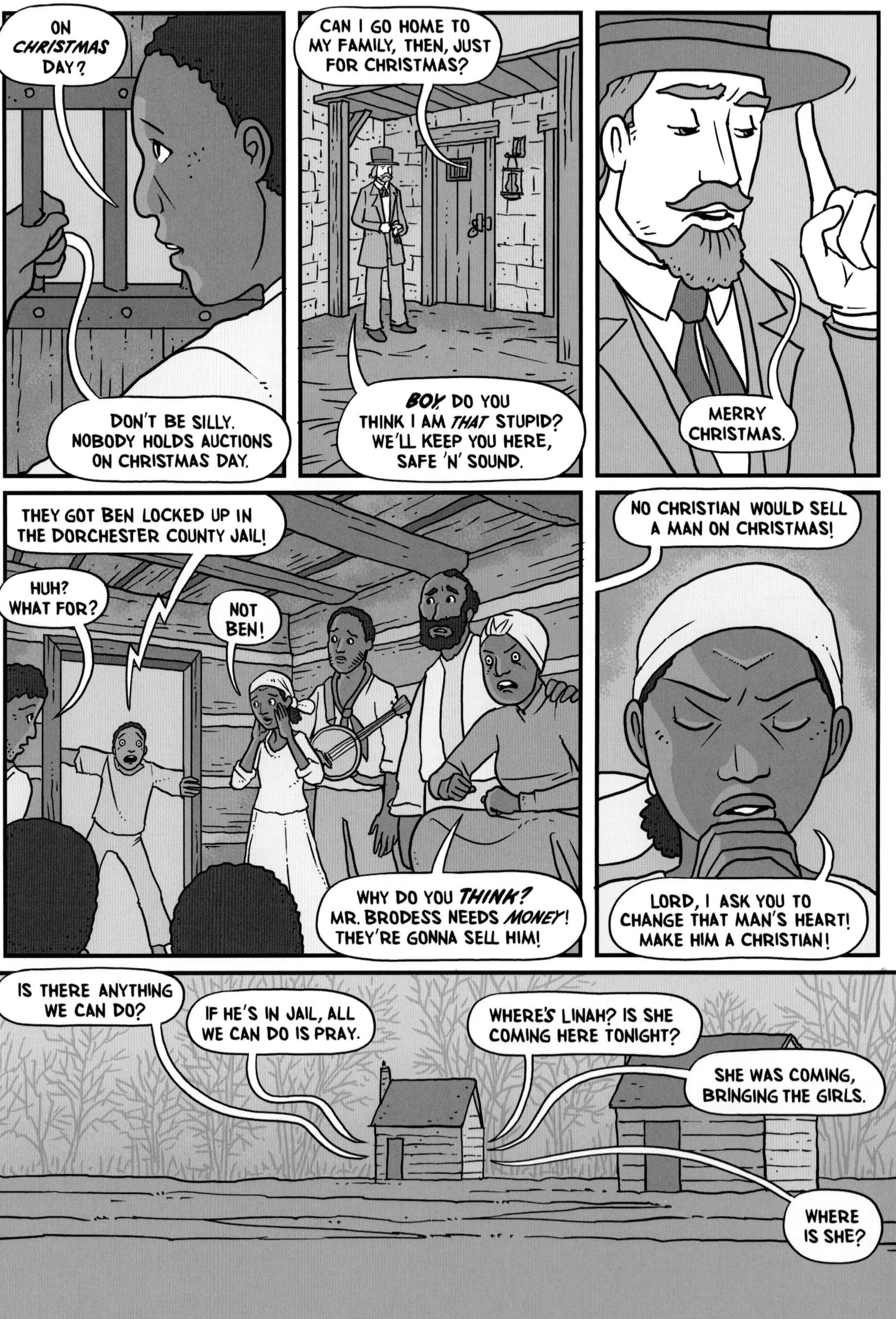
ON CHRISTMAS DAY?
DON'T BE SILLY. NOBODY HOLDS AUCTIONS ON CHRISTMAS DAY.
CAN I GO HOME TO MY FAMILY, THEN, JUST FOR CHRISTMAS?
BOY, DO YOU THINK I AM THAT STUPID? WE'LL KEEP YOU HERE, SAFE 'N' SOUND.
MERRY CHRISTMAS.
THEY GOT BEN LOCKED UP IN THE DORCHESTER COUNTY JAIL!
HUH? WHAT FOR?
NOT BEN!
WHY DO YOU THINK? MR. BRODESS NEEDS MONEY! THEY'RE GONNA SELL HIM!
NO CHRISTIAN WOULD SELL A MAN ON CHRISTMAS!
LORD, I ASK YOU TO CHANGE THAT MAN'S HEART! MAKE HIM A CHRISTIAN!
IS THERE ANYTHING WE CAN DO?
IF HE'S IN JAIL, ALL WE CAN DO IS PRAY.
WHERE'S LINAH? IS SHE COMING HERE TONIGHT?
SHE WAS COMING, BRINGING THE GIRLS.
WHERE IS SHE?

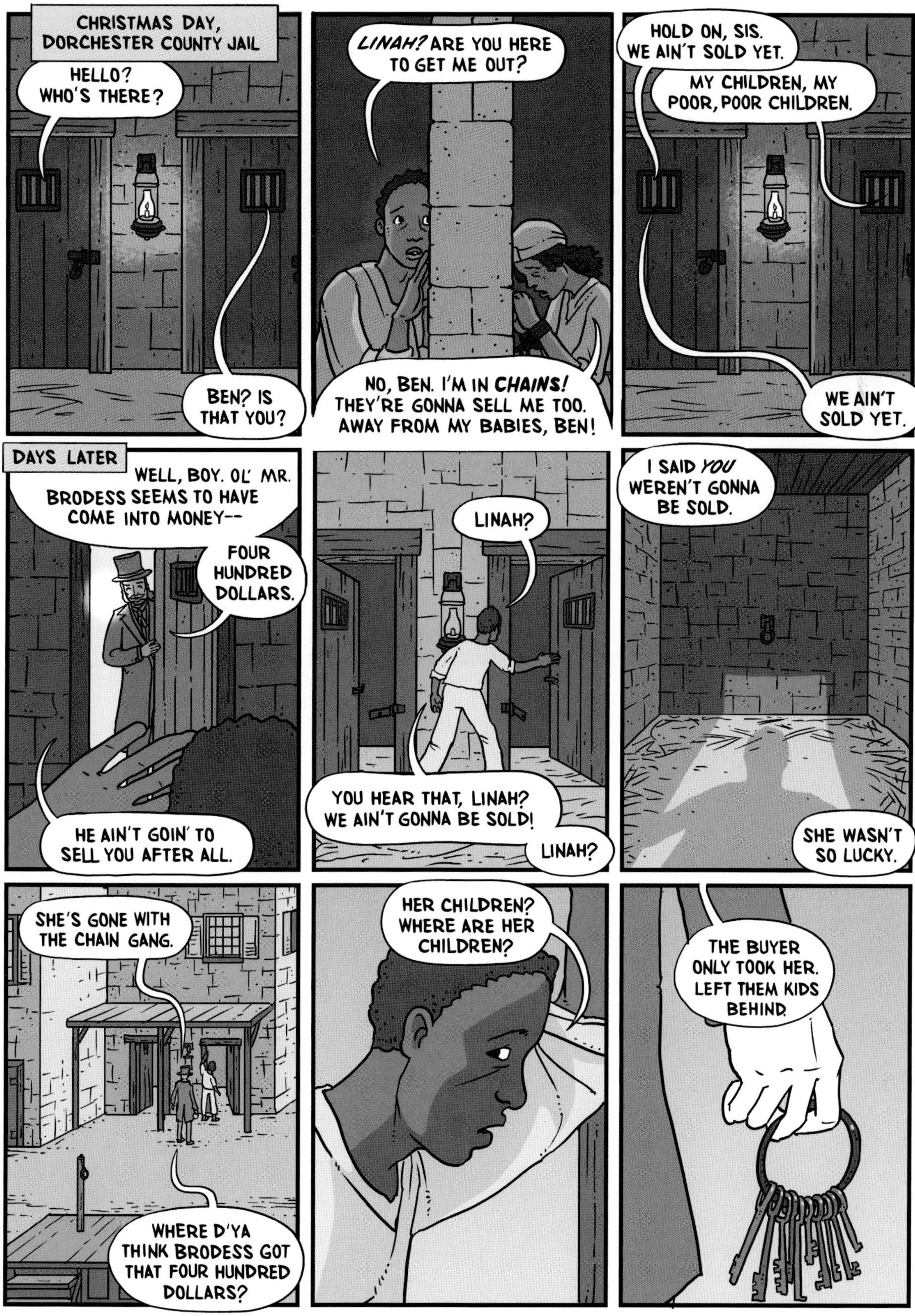
CHRISTMAS DAY, DORCHESTER COUNTY JAIL
HELLO? WHO'S THERE?
BEN? IS THAT YOU?
LINAH? ARE YOU HERE TO GET ME OUT?
NO, BEN. I'M IN CHAINS! THEY'RE GONNA SELL ME TOO. AWAY FROM MY BABIES, BEN!
HOLD ON, SIS. WE AIN'T SOLD YET.
MY CHILDREN, MY POOR, POOR CHILDREN.
WE AIN'T SOLD YET.
DAYS LATER
WELL, BOY. OL' MR. BRODESS SEEMS TO HAVE COME INTO MONEY--
FOUR HUNDRED DOLLARS.
HE AIN'T GOIN' TO SELL YOU AFTER ALL.
LINAH?
YOU HEAR THAT, LINAH? WE AIN'T GONNA BE SOLD!
LINAH?
I SAID YOU WEREN'T GONNA BE SOLD.
SHE WASN'T SO LUCKY.
SHE'S GONE WITH THE CHAIN GANG.
WHERE D'YA THINK BRODESS GOT THAT FOUR HUNDRED DOLLARS?
HER CHILDREN? WHERE ARE HER CHILDREN?
THE BUYER ONLY TOOK HER. LEFT THEM KIDS BEHIND.

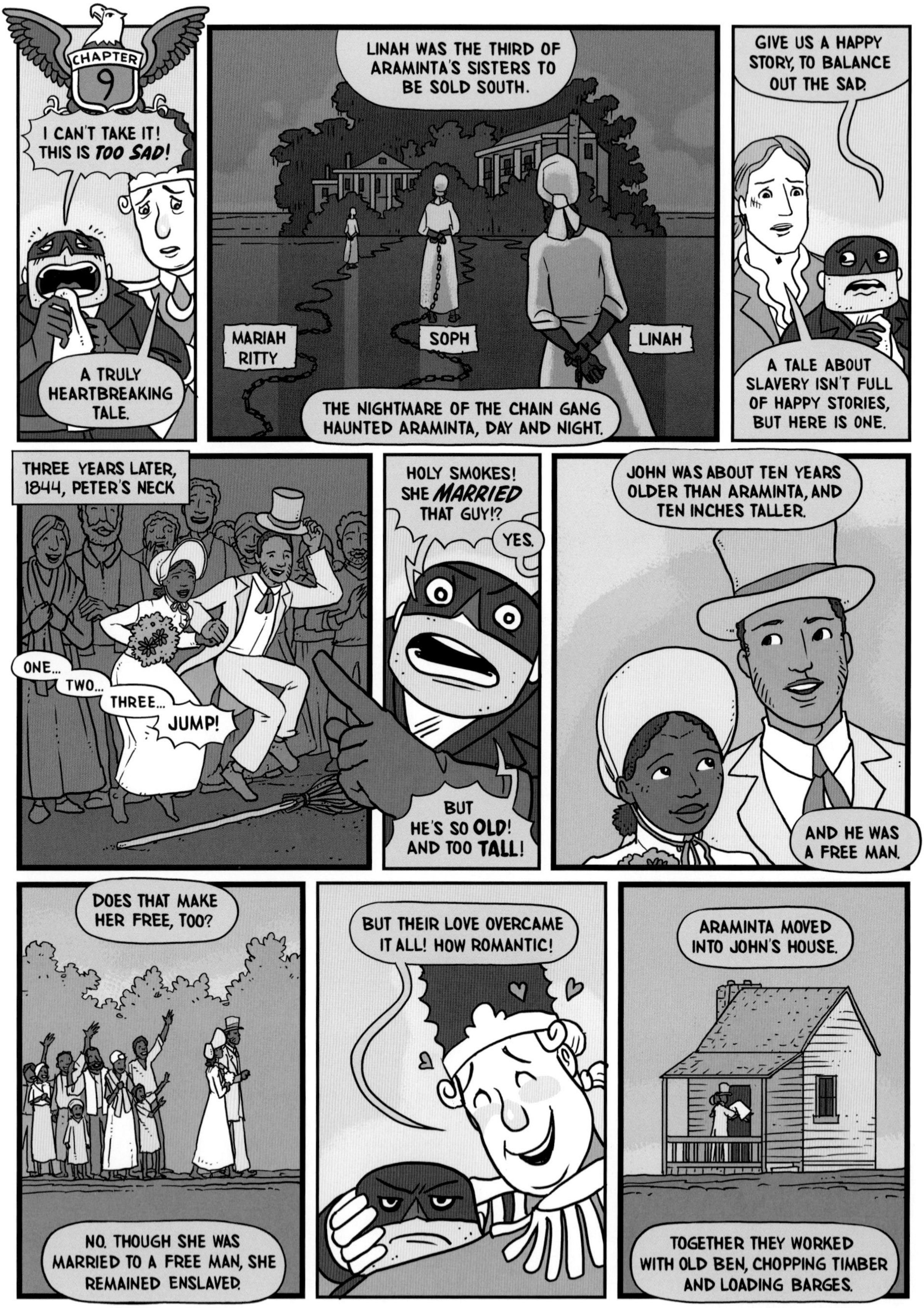
CHAPTER 9
I CAN'T TAKE IT! THIS IS TOO SAD!
A TRULY HEARTBREAKING TALE.
LINAH WAS THE THIRD OF ARAMINTA'S SISTERS TO BE SOLD SOUTH.
MARIAH RITTY
SOPH
LINAH
THE NIGHTMARE OF THE CHAIN GANG HAUNTED ARAMINTA, DAY AND NIGHT.
GIVE US A HAPPY STORY, TO BALANCE OUT THE SAD.
A TALE ABOUT SLAVERY ISN'T FULL OF HAPPY STORIES, BUT HERE IS ONE.
THREE YEARS LATER, 1844, PETER'S NECK
ONE...
TWO...
THREE...
JUMP!
HOLY SMOKES! SHE MARRIED THAT GUY!?
YES.
BUT HE'S SO OLD! AND TOO TALL!
JOHN WAS ABOUT TEN YEARS OLDER THAN ARAMINTA, AND TEN INCHES TALLER.
AND HE WAS A FREE MAN.
DOES THAT MAKE HER FREE, TOO?
NO. THOUGH SHE WAS MARRIED TO A FREE MAN, SHE REMAINED ENSLAVED.
BUT THEIR LOVE OVERCAME IT ALL! HOW ROMANTIC!
ARAMINTA MOVED INTO JOHN'S HOUSE.
TOGETHER THEY WORKED WITH OLD BEN, CHOPPING TIMBER AND LOADING BARGES.

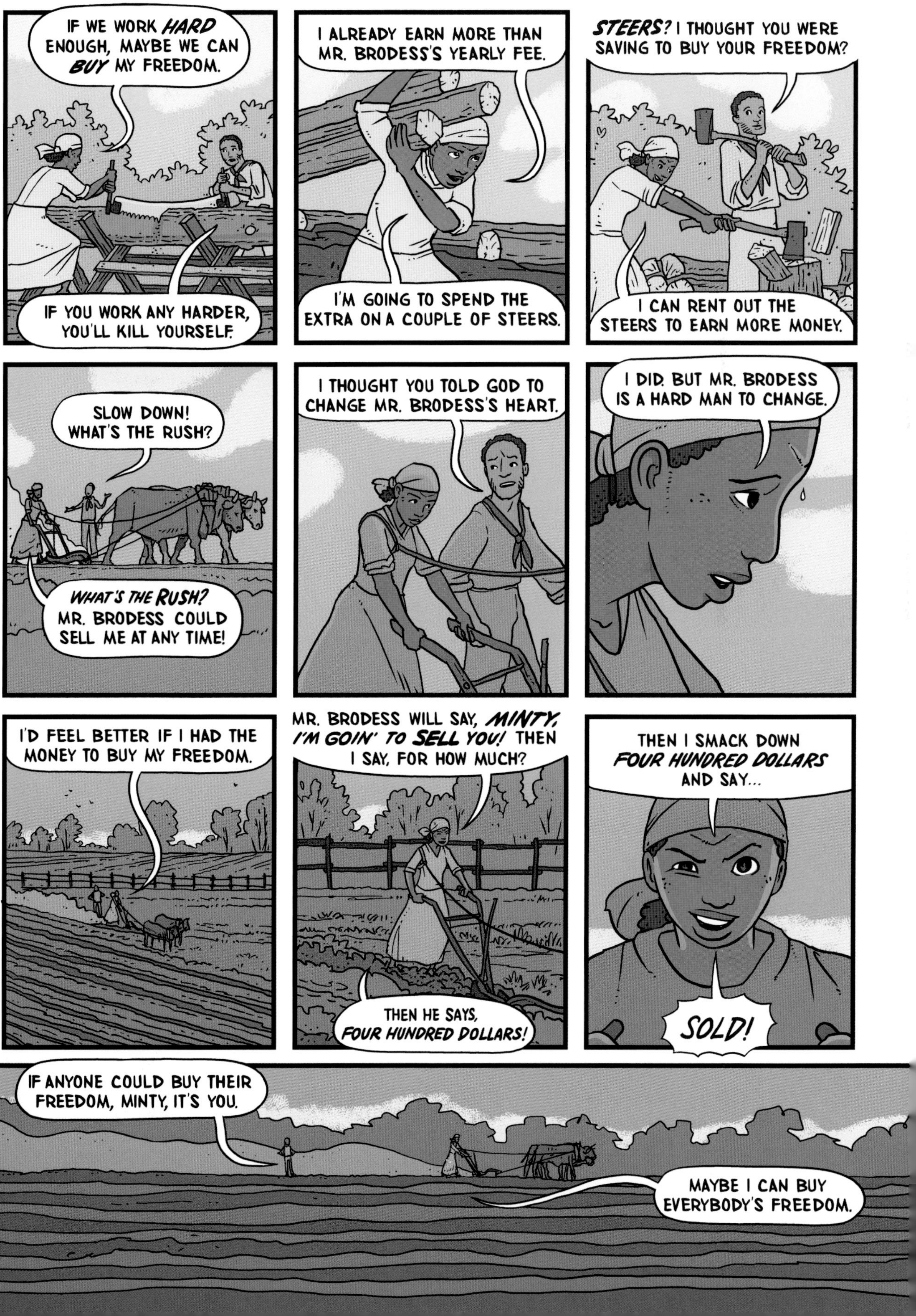
IF WE WORK HARD ENOUGH, MAYBE WE CAN BUY MY FREEDOM.
IF YOU WORK ANY HARDER, YOU'LL KILL YOURSELF.
I ALREADY EARN MORE THAN MR. BRODESS'S YEARLY FEE.
I'M GOING TO SPEND THE EXTRA ON A COUPLE OF STEERS.
STEERS? I THOUGHT YOU WERE SAVING TO BUY YOUR FREEDOM?
I CAN RENT OUT THE STEERS TO EARN MORE MONEY.
SLOW DOWN! WHAT'S THE RUSH?
WHAT'S THE RUSH? MR. BRODESS COULD SELL ME AT ANY TIME!
I THOUGHT YOU TOLD GOD TO CHANGE MR. BRODESS'S HEART.
I DID. BUT MR. BRODESS IS A HARD MAN TO CHANGE.
I'D FEEL BETTER IF I HAD THE MONEY TO BUY MY FREEDOM.
MR. BRODESS WILL SAY, MINTY, I'M GOIN' TO SELL YOU! THEN I SAY, FOR HOW MUCH?
THEN HE SAYS, FOUR HUNDRED DOLLARS!
THEN I SMACK DOWN FOUR HUNDRED DOLLARS AND SAY...
SOLD!
IF ANYONE COULD BUY THEIR FREEDOM, MINTY, IT'S YOU.
MAYBE I CAN BUY EVERYBODY'S FREEDOM.

A LAWYER'S OFFICE IN CAMBRIDGE, MARYLAND

YES?

I'D LIKE YOU TO READ ME THE WILL OF MR. ATTHOW PATTISON. I HAVE FIVE DOLLARS.

WHAT IS YOUR RELATION TO MR. PATTISON?

HE WAS MY MOTHER'S FIRST MASTER.

HMM. HOW LONG AGO WAS THIS?

'BOUT FIFTY YEARS?

I'LL TAKE A LOOK.

HOW LONG WILL THAT TAKE, SUH?

'BOUT A WEEK.

YES, SUH. I'LL BE BACK NEXT WEEK.

THERE YOU ARE. WHERE HAVE YOU BEEN?

I WAS AT A LAWYER'S.

A *LAWYER'S?* WHAT FOR?

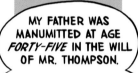

MY FATHER WAS MANUMITTED AT AGE *FORTY-FIVE* IN THE WILL OF MR. THOMPSON.

MY MOTHER'S GOIN' ON *SIXTY* YEARS OF LABOR. MAYBE SHE WAS SUPPOSED TO BE MANUMITTED TOO.

BY MR. BRODESS?

NO. BY MR. BRODESS'S GREAT-GRANDFATHER.

HUH?

MR. BRODESS INHERITED MY MOTHER FROM *HIS* MOTHER, WHO INHERITED HER FROM MR. ATTHOW PATTISON.

I'M CONFUSED. WHERE ARE YOU GOIN' NOW?

GOT TO EARN THAT MONEY!

LAWYER'S OFFICE, ONE WEEK LATER

IT WASN'T EASY TO FIND. I HAD TO GO ALL THE WAY BACK TO 1791.

CAN YOU READ IT? I CAN'T READ.

CONCERNING SLAVES: UNTO MY GRANDDAUGHTER MARY PATTISON, I BEQUEATH ONE NEGRO GIRL: RITTIA--

THAT'S HER!

...AND HER INCREASE UNTIL SHE AND THEY ARRIVE TO FORTY-FIVE YEARS OF AGE.

READ THAT LAST PART AGAIN.

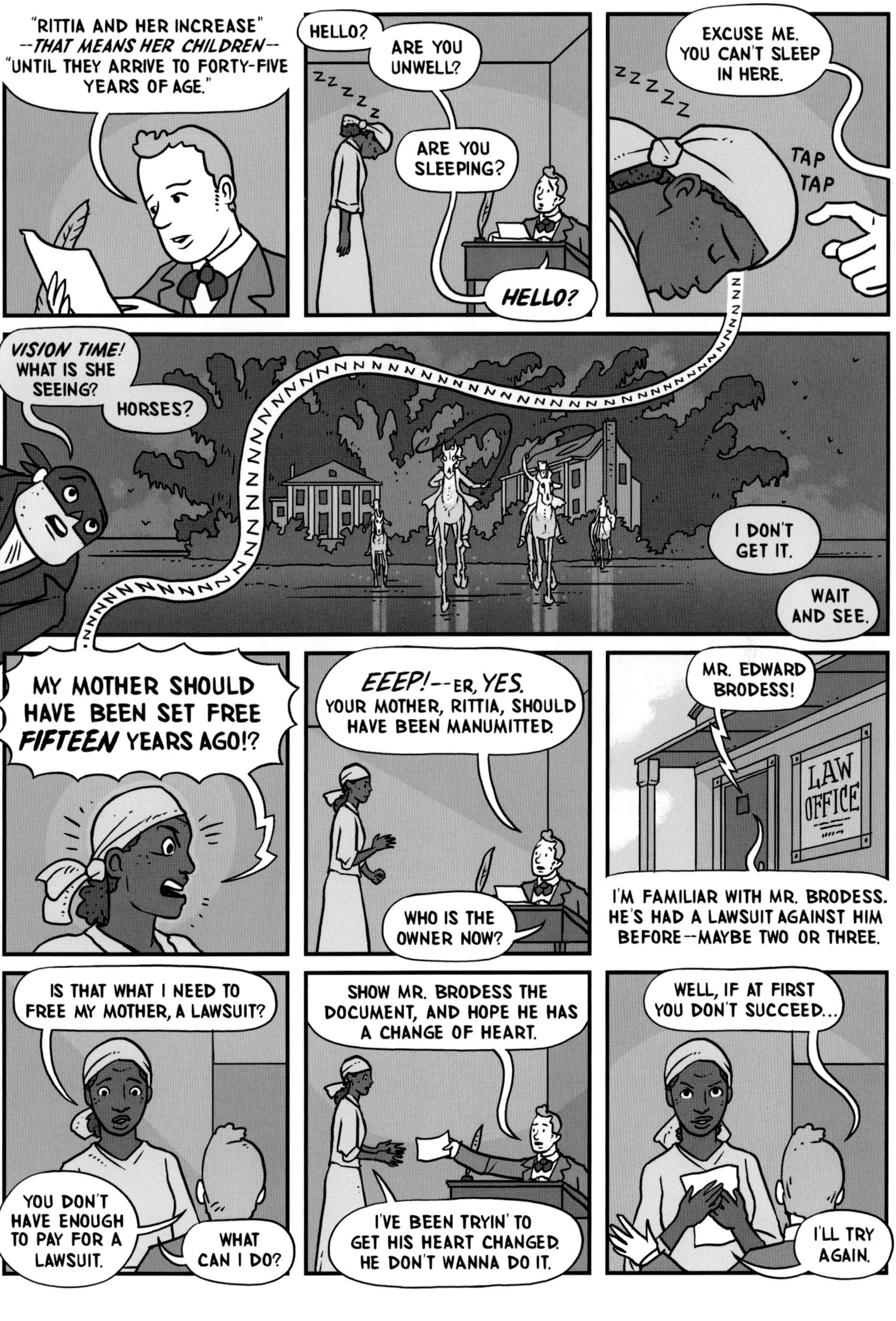
"RITTIA AND HER INCREASE" --THAT MEANS HER CHILDREN-- "UNTIL THEY ARRIVE TO FORTY-FIVE YEARS OF AGE."
HELLO?
ZZZZZ
ARE YOU UNWELL?
ARE YOU SLEEPING?
HELLO?
ZZZZZ
EXCUSE ME. YOU CAN'T SLEEP IN HERE.
TAP TAP
VISION TIME! WHAT IS SHE SEEING?
HORSES?
I DON'T GET IT.
WAIT AND SEE.
MY MOTHER SHOULD HAVE BEEN SET FREE FIFTEEN YEARS AGO!?
EEEP!--ER, YES. YOUR MOTHER, RITTIA, SHOULD HAVE BEEN MANUMITTED.
WHO IS THE OWNER NOW?
MR. EDWARD BRODESS!
LAW OFFICE
I'M FAMILIAR WITH MR. BRODESS. HE'S HAD A LAWSUIT AGAINST HIM BEFORE--MAYBE TWO OR THREE.
IS THAT WHAT I NEED TO FREE MY MOTHER, A LAWSUIT?
YOU DON'T HAVE ENOUGH TO PAY FOR A LAWSUIT.
WHAT CAN I DO?
SHOW MR. BRODESS THE DOCUMENT, AND HOPE HE HAS A CHANGE OF HEART.
I'VE BEEN TRYIN' TO GET HIS HEART CHANGED. HE DON'T WANNA DO IT.
WELL, IF AT FIRST YOU DON'T SUCCEED...
I'LL TRY AGAIN.

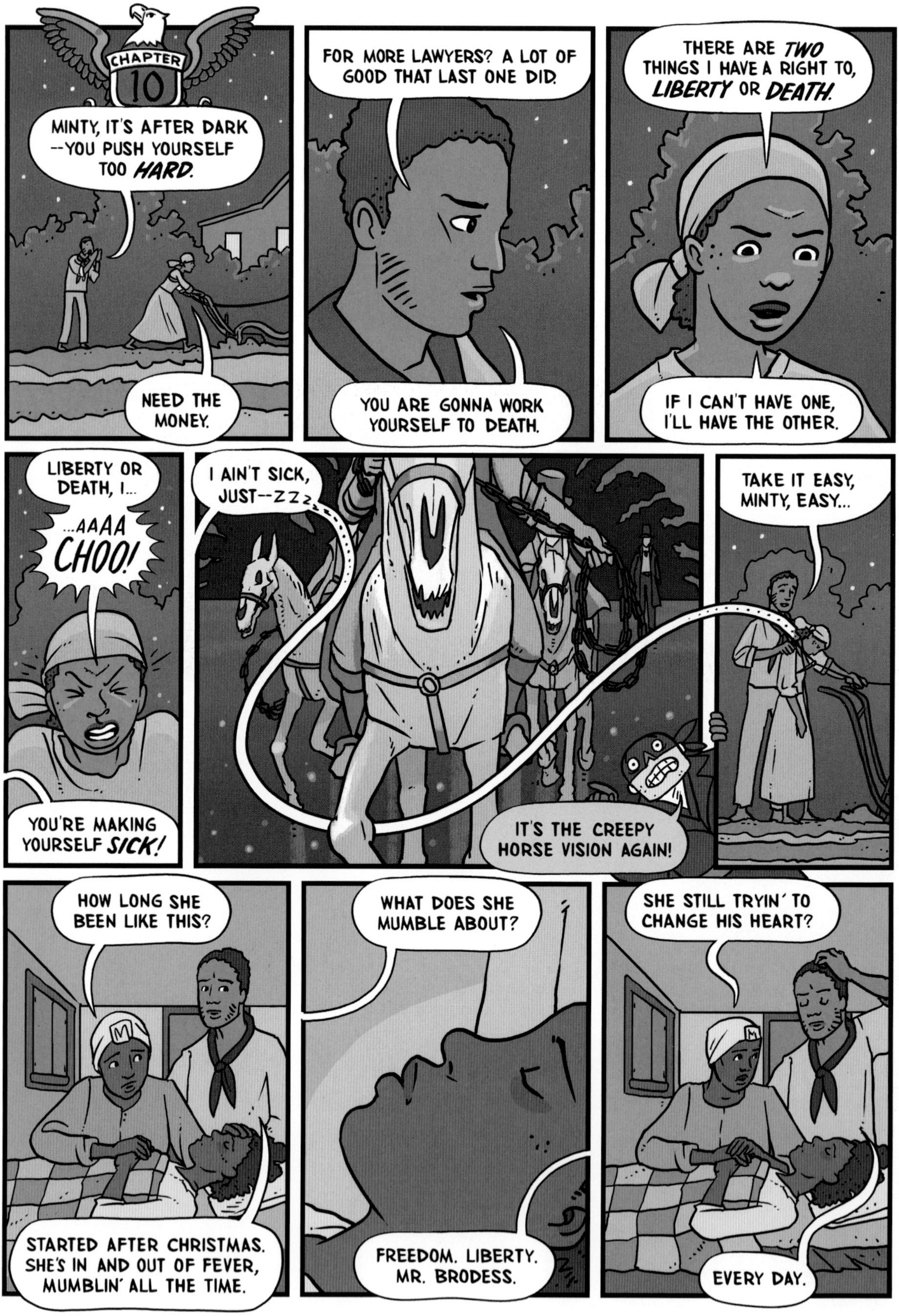
CHAPTER 10
MINTY, IT'S AFTER DARK --YOU PUSH YOURSELF TOO HARD.
NEED THE MONEY.
FOR MORE LAWYERS? A LOT OF GOOD THAT LAST ONE DID.
YOU ARE GONNA WORK YOURSELF TO DEATH.
THERE ARE TWO THINGS I HAVE A RIGHT TO, LIBERTY OR DEATH.
IF I CAN'T HAVE ONE, I'LL HAVE THE OTHER.
LIBERTY OR DEATH, I...
...AAAA CHOO!
YOU'RE MAKING YOURSELF SICK!
I AIN'T SICK, JUST--ZZZ
IT'S THE CREEPY HORSE VISION AGAIN!
TAKE IT EASY, MINTY, EASY...
HOW LONG SHE BEEN LIKE THIS?
STARTED AFTER CHRISTMAS. SHE'S IN AND OUT OF FEVER, MUMBLIN' ALL THE TIME.
WHAT DOES SHE MUMBLE ABOUT?
FREEDOM. LIBERTY. MR. BRODESS.
SHE STILL TRYIN' TO CHANGE HIS HEART?
EVERY DAY.

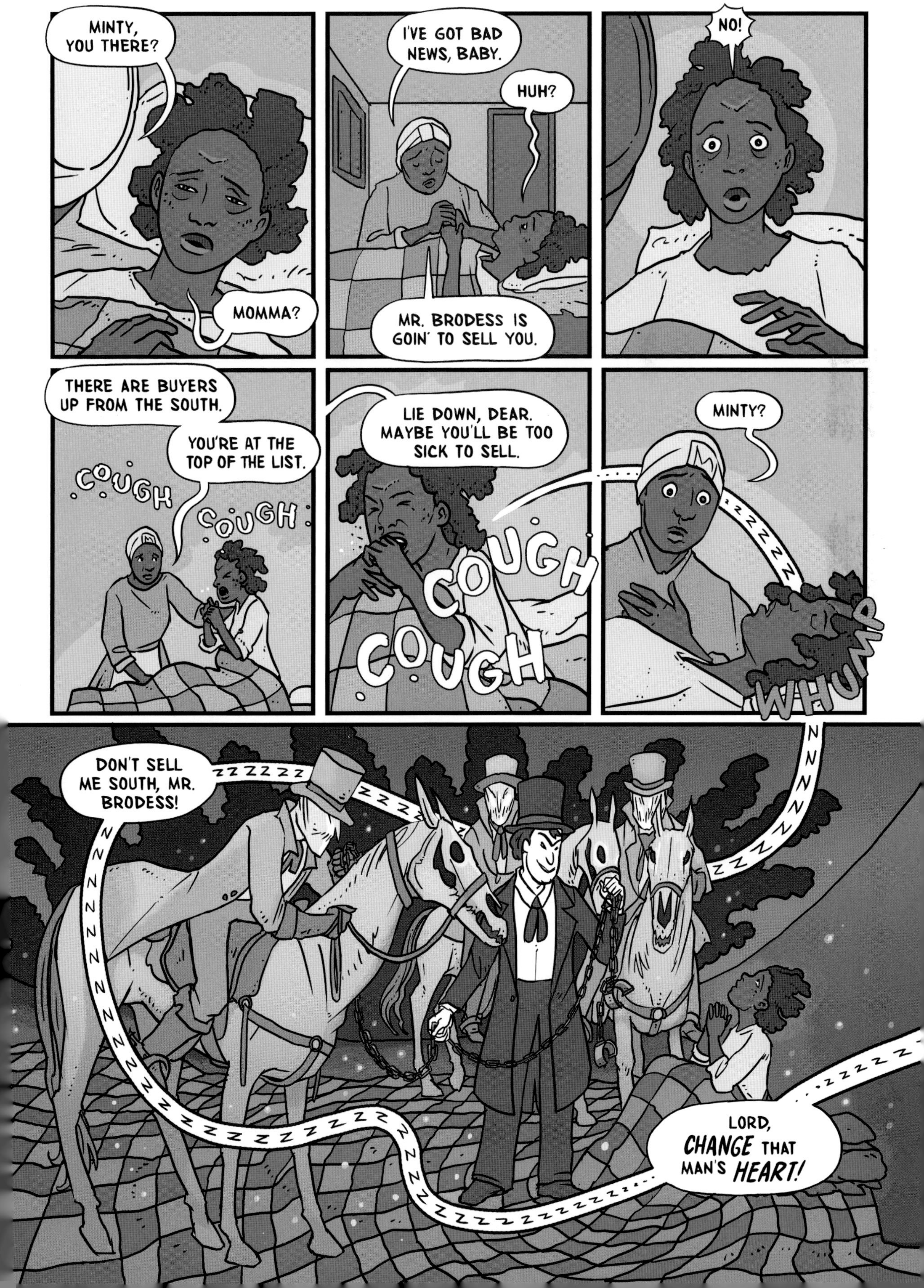
MINTY, YOU THERE?
MOMMA?
I'VE GOT BAD NEWS, BABY.
HUH?
MR. BRODESS IS GOIN' TO SELL YOU.
NO!
THERE ARE BUYERS UP FROM THE SOUTH.
YOU'RE AT THE TOP OF THE LIST.
COUGH
COUGH
LIE DOWN, DEAR. MAYBE YOU'LL BE TOO SICK TO SELL.
COUGH
COUGH
MINTY?
WHUMP
DON'T SELL ME SOUTH, MR. BRODESS!
LORD, CHANGE THAT MAN'S HEART!

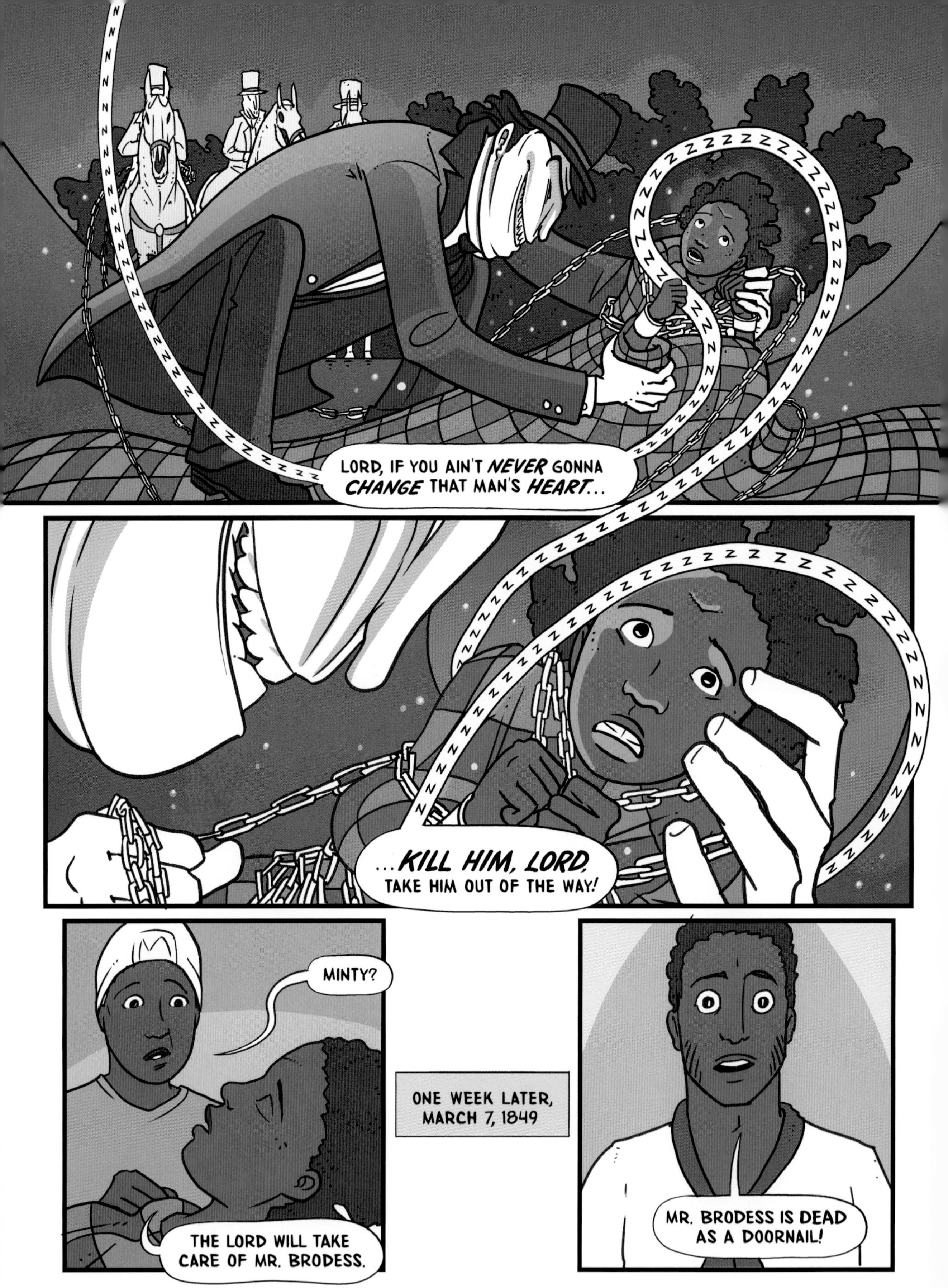
LORD, IF YOU AIN'T NEVER GONNA CHANGE THAT MAN'S HEART...
...KILL HIM, LORD. TAKE HIM OUT OF THE WAY!
MINTY?
THE LORD WILL TAKE CARE OF MR. BRODESS.
ONE WEEK LATER, MARCH 7, 1849
MR. BRODESS IS DEAD AS A DOORNAIL!

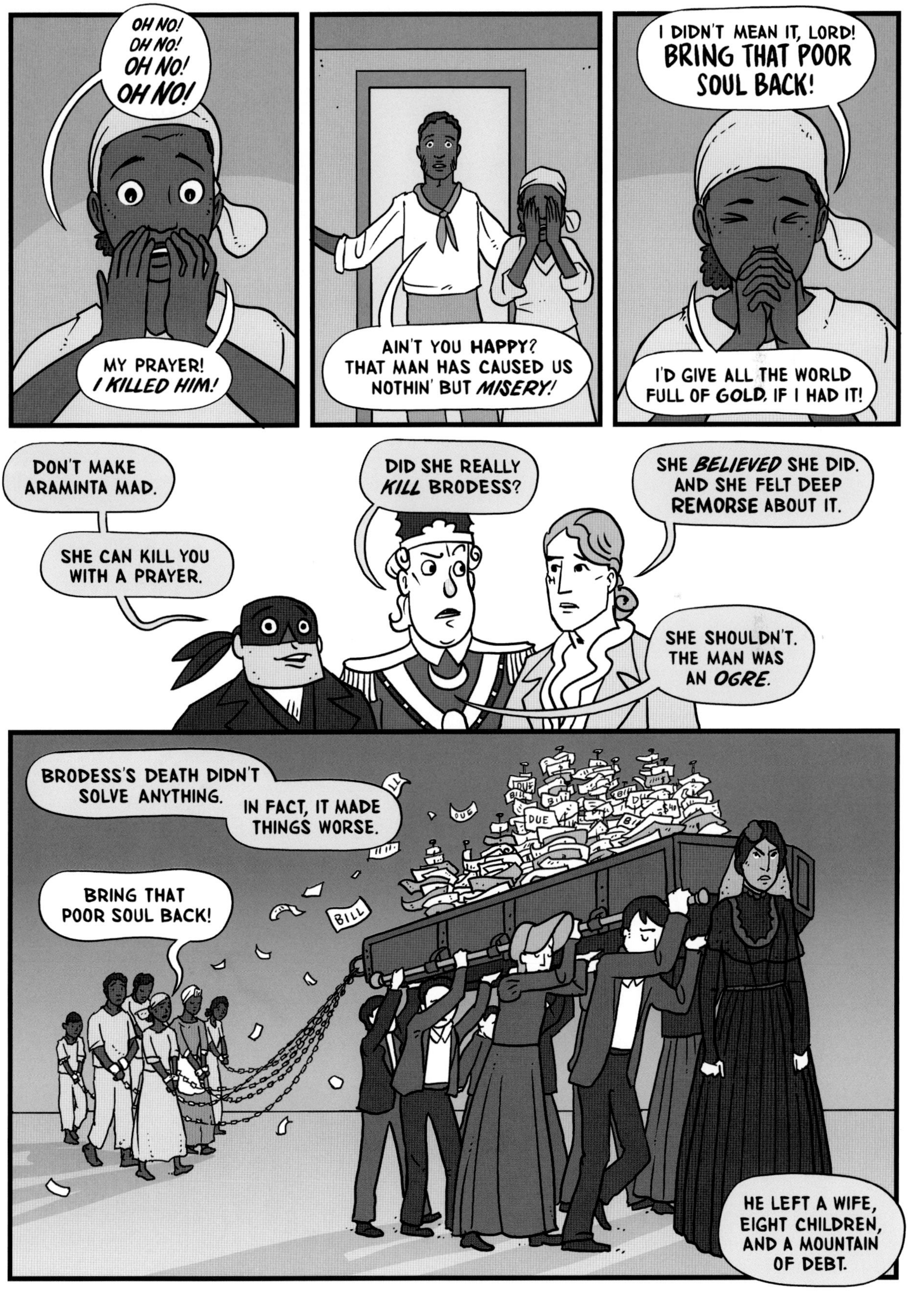
OH NO! OH NO! OH NO! OH NO!
MY PRAYER! I KILLED HIM!
AIN'T YOU HAPPY? THAT MAN HAS CAUSED US NOTHIN' BUT MISERY!
I DIDN'T MEAN IT, LORD! BRING THAT POOR SOUL BACK!
I'D GIVE ALL THE WORLD FULL OF GOLD, IF I HAD IT!
DON'T MAKE ARAMINTA MAD.
SHE CAN KILL YOU WITH A PRAYER.
DID SHE REALLY KILL BRODESS?
SHE BELIEVED SHE DID. AND SHE FELT DEEP REMORSE ABOUT IT.
SHE SHOULDN'T. THE MAN WAS AN OGRE.
BRODESS'S DEATH DIDN'T SOLVE ANYTHING.
IN FACT, IT MADE THINGS WORSE.
BRING THAT POOR SOUL BACK!
DUE
BILL
HE LEFT A WIFE, EIGHT CHILDREN, AND A MOUNTAIN OF DEBT.

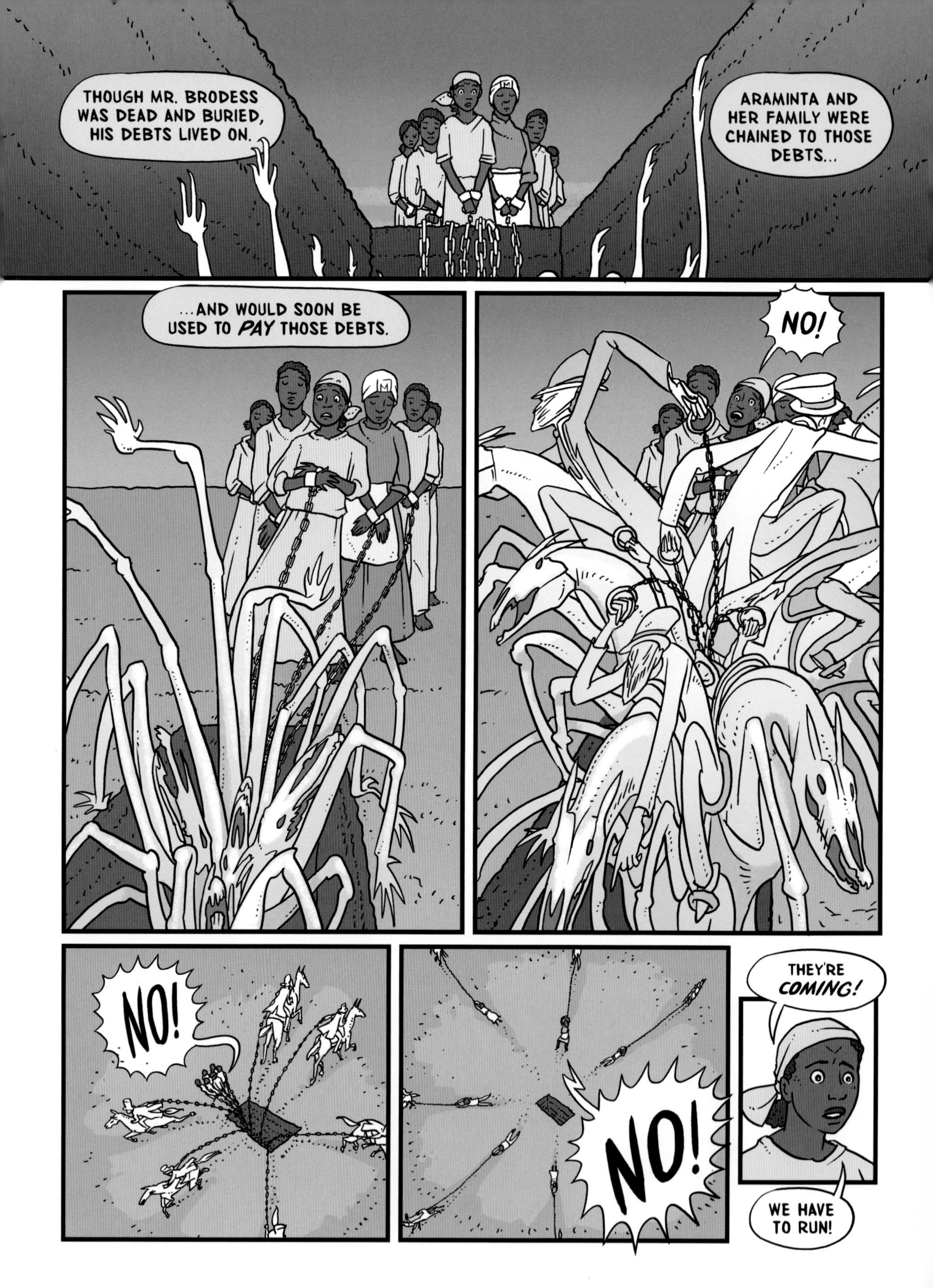
THOUGH MR. BRODESS WAS DEAD AND BURIED, HIS DEBTS LIVED ON.
ARAMINTA AND HER FAMILY WERE CHAINED TO THOSE DEBTS...
...AND WOULD SOON BE USED TO PAY THOSE DEBTS.
NO!
NO!
NO!
THEY'RE COMING!
WE HAVE TO RUN!

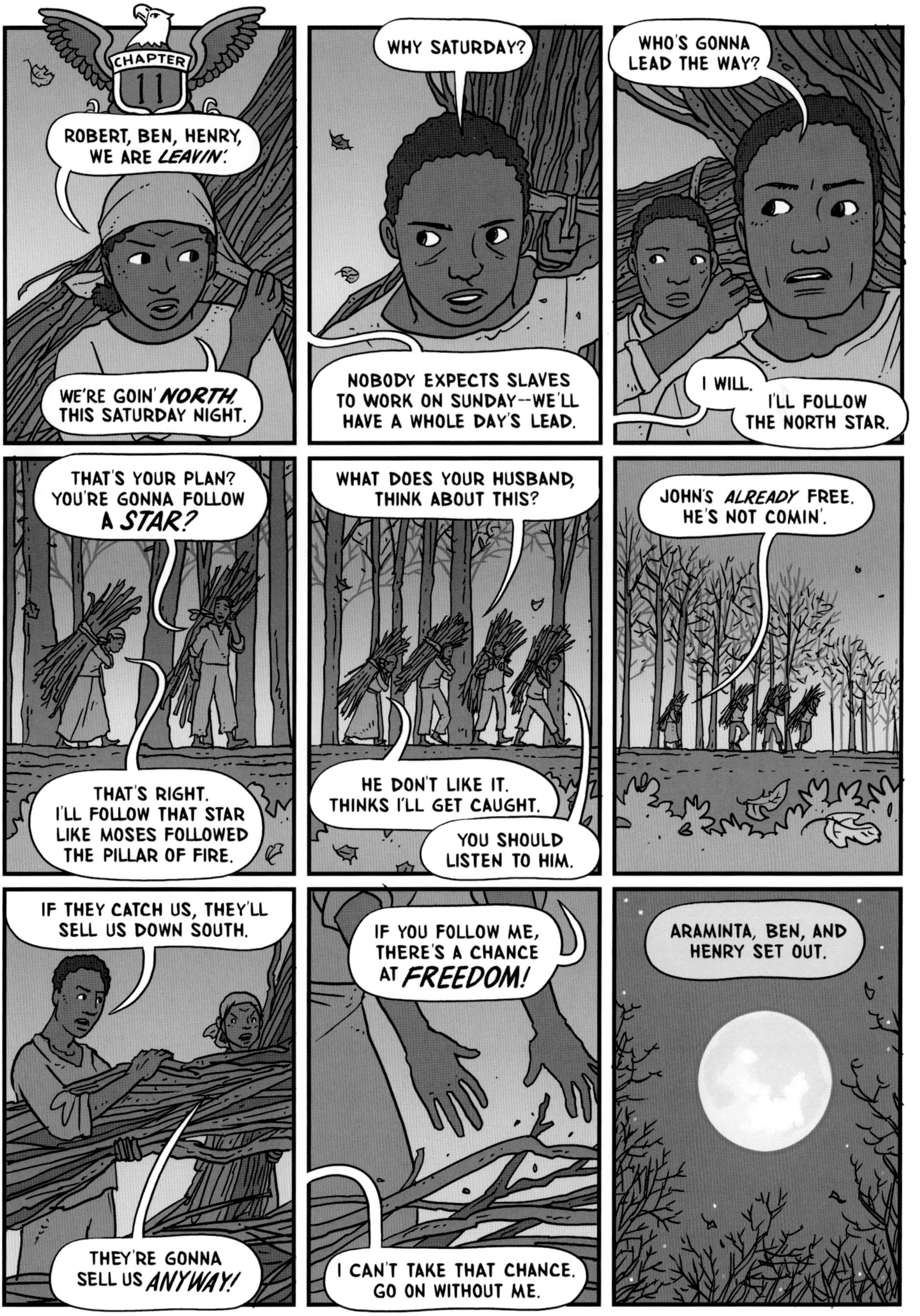
CHAPTER 11
ROBERT, BEN, HENRY, WE ARE LEAVIN'.
WE'RE GOIN' NORTH, THIS SATURDAY NIGHT.
WHY SATURDAY?
NOBODY EXPECTS SLAVES TO WORK ON SUNDAY--WE'LL HAVE A WHOLE DAY'S LEAD.
WHO'S GONNA LEAD THE WAY?
I WILL.
I'LL FOLLOW THE NORTH STAR.
THAT'S YOUR PLAN? YOU'RE GONNA FOLLOW A STAR?
THAT'S RIGHT. I'LL FOLLOW THAT STAR LIKE MOSES FOLLOWED THE PILLAR OF FIRE.
WHAT DOES YOUR HUSBAND, THINK ABOUT THIS?
HE DON'T LIKE IT. THINKS I'LL GET CAUGHT.
YOU SHOULD LISTEN TO HIM.
JOHN'S ALREADY FREE. HE'S NOT COMIN'.
IF THEY CATCH US, THEY'LL SELL US DOWN SOUTH.
THEY'RE GONNA SELL US ANYWAY!
IF YOU FOLLOW ME, THERE'S A CHANCE AT FREEDOM!
I CAN'T TAKE THAT CHANCE. GO ON WITHOUT ME.
ARAMINTA, BEN, AND HENRY SET OUT.

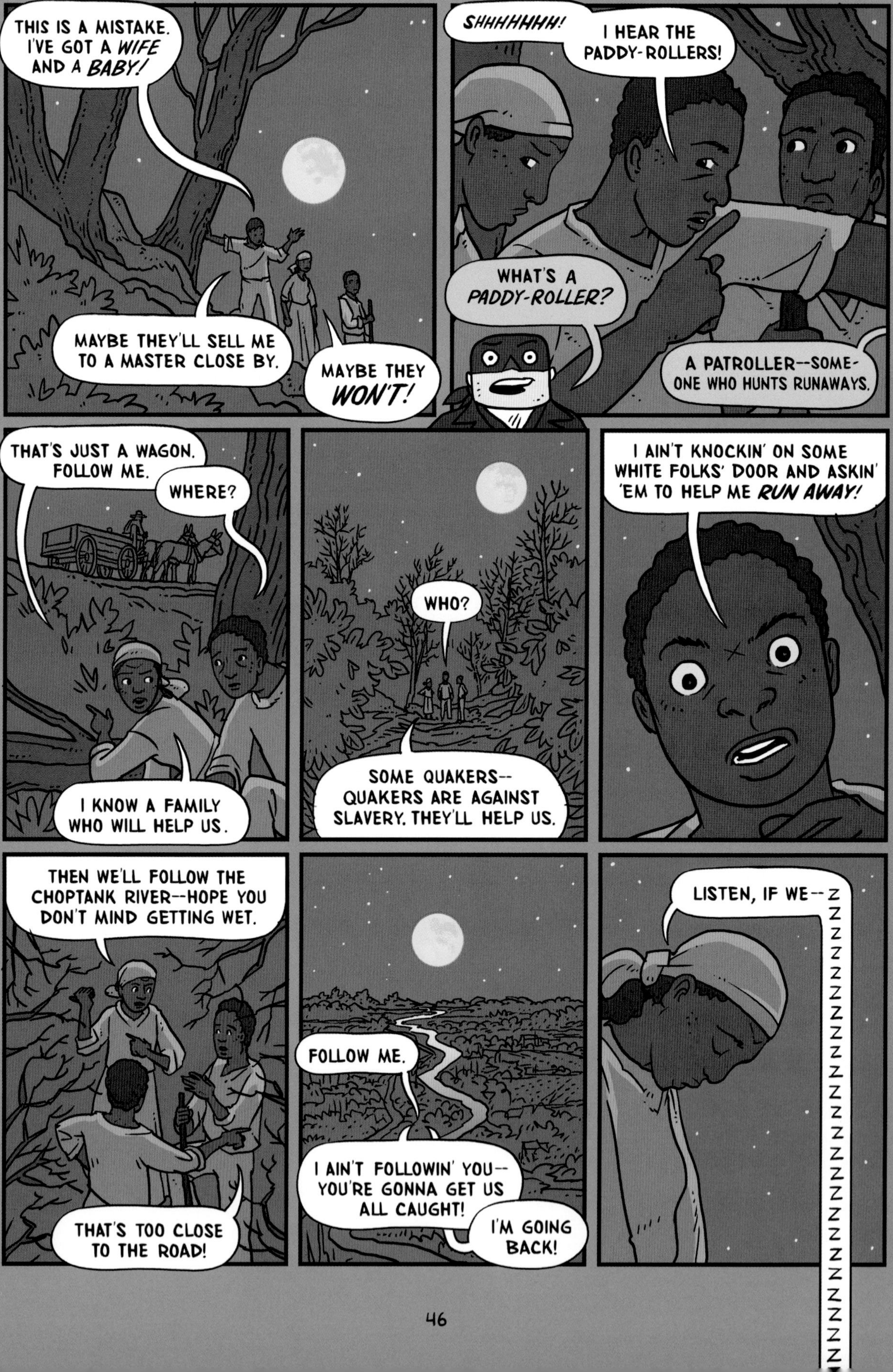

THIS IS A MISTAKE. I'VE GOT A *WIFE* AND A *BABY!*
MAYBE THEY'LL SELL ME TO A MASTER CLOSE BY.
MAYBE THEY *WON'T!*
SHHHHHHH!
I HEAR THE PADDY-ROLLERS!
WHAT'S A *PADDY-ROLLER?*
A PATROLLER--SOMEONE WHO HUNTS RUNAWAYS.
THAT'S JUST A WAGON. FOLLOW ME.
WHERE?
I KNOW A FAMILY WHO WILL HELP US.
WHO?
SOME QUAKERS--QUAKERS ARE AGAINST SLAVERY. THEY'LL HELP US.
I AIN'T KNOCKIN' ON SOME WHITE FOLKS' DOOR AND ASKIN' 'EM TO HELP ME *RUN AWAY!*
THEN WE'LL FOLLOW THE CHOPTANK RIVER--HOPE YOU DON'T MIND GETTING WET.
THAT'S TOO CLOSE TO THE ROAD!
FOLLOW ME.
I AIN'T FOLLOWIN' YOU--YOU'RE GONNA GET US ALL CAUGHT!
I'M GOING BACK!
LISTEN, IF WE--ZZZZZZZZZZZZZZZZZZZZZZZZZZZZZZZZZZZZZZZ

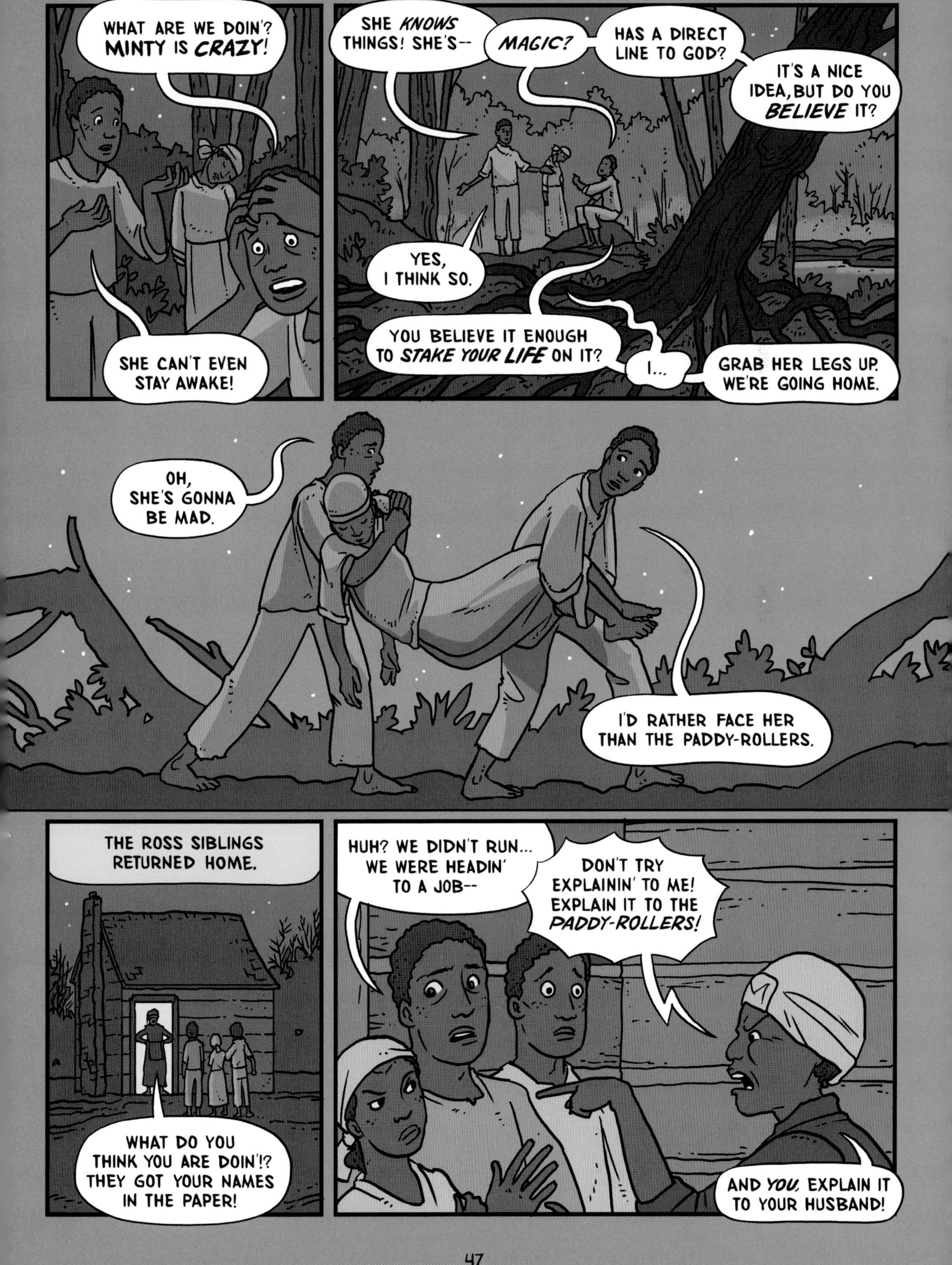
WHAT ARE WE DOIN'? MINTY IS CRAZY!
SHE CAN'T EVEN STAY AWAKE!
SHE KNOWS THINGS! SHE'S--
MAGIC?
HAS A DIRECT LINE TO GOD?
IT'S A NICE IDEA, BUT DO YOU BELIEVE IT?
YES, I THINK SO.
YOU BELIEVE IT ENOUGH TO STAKE YOUR LIFE ON IT?
I...
GRAB HER LEGS UP. WE'RE GOING HOME.
OH, SHE'S GONNA BE MAD.
I'D RATHER FACE HER THAN THE PADDY-ROLLERS.
THE ROSS SIBLINGS RETURNED HOME.
WHAT DO YOU THINK YOU ARE DOIN'!? THEY GOT YOUR NAMES IN THE PAPER!
HUH? WE DIDN'T RUN... WE WERE HEADIN' TO A JOB--
DON'T TRY EXPLAININ' TO ME! EXPLAIN IT TO THE PADDY-ROLLERS!
AND YOU, EXPLAIN IT TO YOUR HUSBAND!

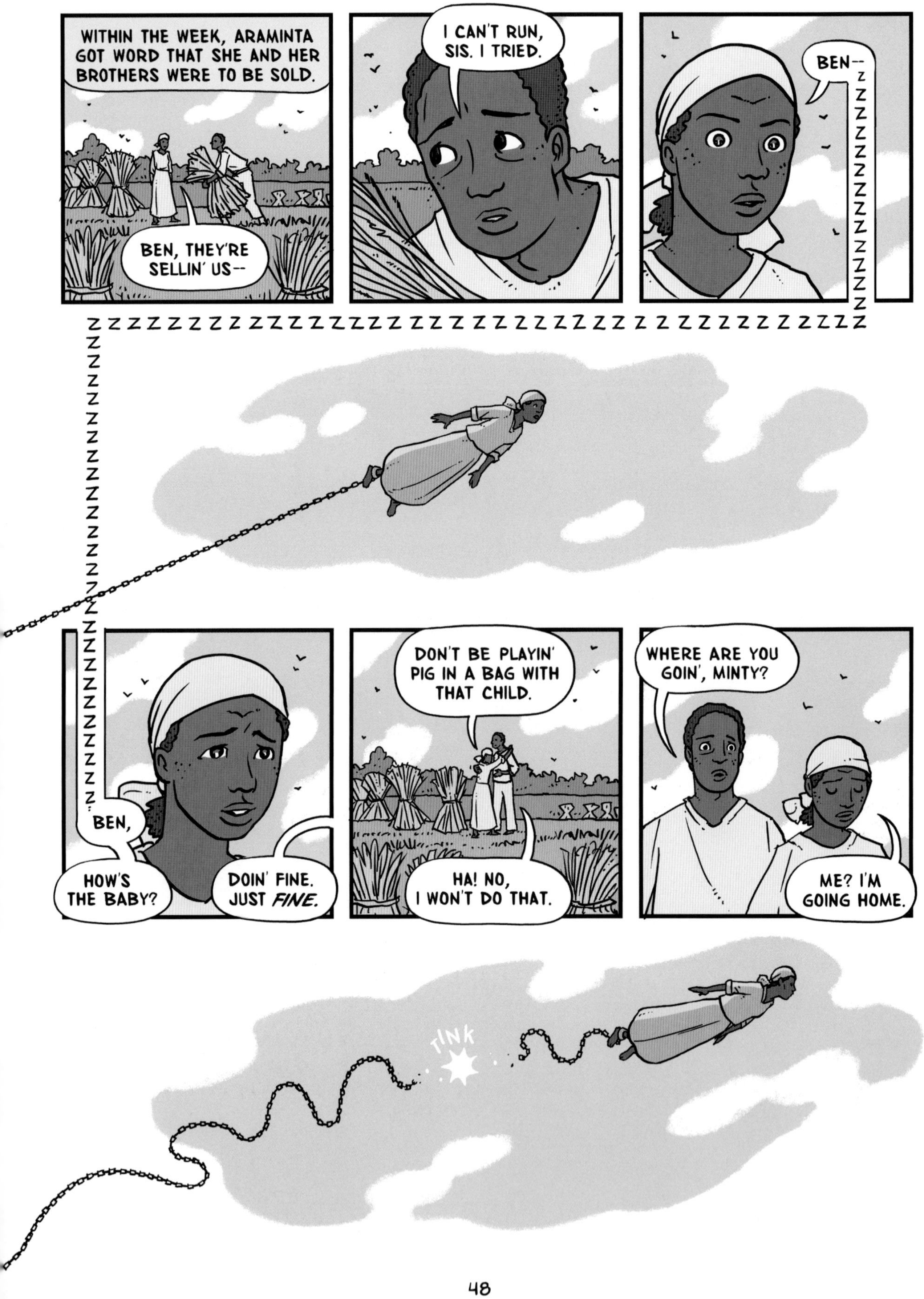
WITHIN THE WEEK, ARAMINTA GOT WORD THAT SHE AND HER BROTHERS WERE TO BE SOLD.
BEN, THEY'RE SELLIN' US--
I CAN'T RUN, SIS. I TRIED.
BEN--
ZZZZZZZZZZZZZZZZZZZZZZZZZZZZZZZZZZZZZZZZZZZZZZZZZZZZZZZZZZZZZZZZZZZZZZZZZ
BEN,
HOW'S THE BABY?
DOIN' FINE. JUST *FINE.*
DON'T BE PLAYIN' PIG IN A BAG WITH THAT CHILD.
HA! NO, I WON'T DO THAT.
WHERE ARE YOU GOIN', MINTY?
ME? I'M GOING HOME.
TINK

THIS IS ANOTHER *VISION*, RIGHT?

MINTY CAN'T *REALLY* FLY, CAN SHE?

IN HER VISIONS, ARAMINTA FLEW LIKE A BIRD...

...OVER HOUSES, FIELDS, AND FORESTS.

BUT THERE WAS ALWAYS ONE LAST OBSTACLE SHE COULDN'T FLY OVER.

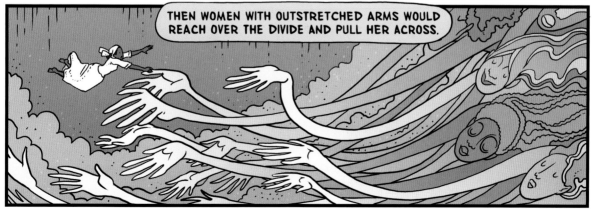

THEN WOMEN WITH OUTSTRETCHED ARMS WOULD REACH OVER THE DIVIDE AND PULL HER ACROSS.

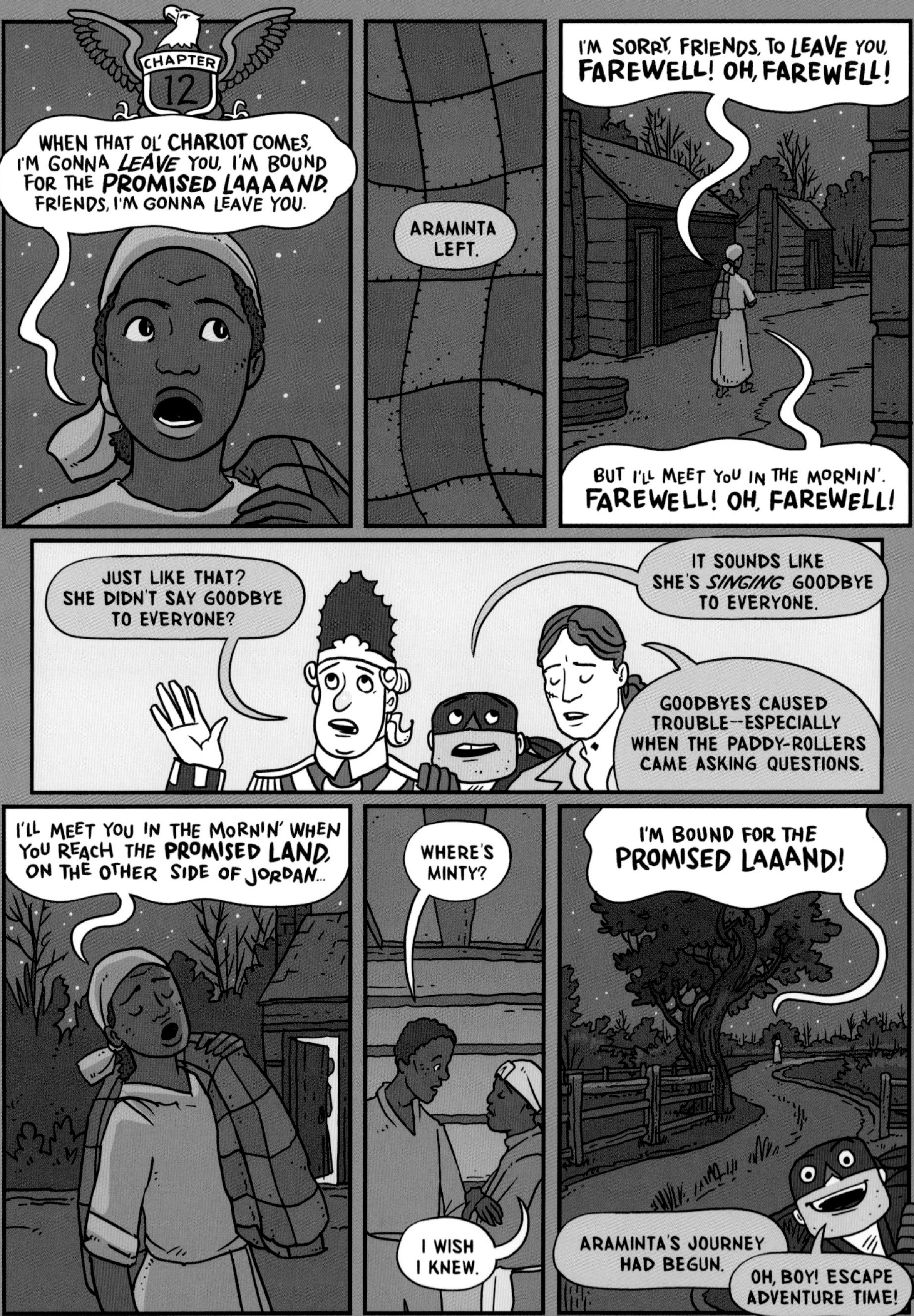
CHAPTER 12
WHEN THAT OL' CHARIOT COMES, I'M GONNA LEAVE YOU, I'M BOUND FOR THE PROMISED LAAAAND. FRIENDS, I'M GONNA LEAVE YOU.
ARAMINTA LEFT.
I'M SORRY, FRIENDS, TO LEAVE YOU, FAREWELL! OH, FAREWELL!
BUT I'LL MEET YOU IN THE MORNIN'. FAREWELL! OH, FAREWELL!
JUST LIKE THAT? SHE DIDN'T SAY GOODBYE TO EVERYONE?
IT SOUNDS LIKE SHE'S SINGING GOODBYE TO EVERYONE.
GOODBYES CAUSED TROUBLE--ESPECIALLY WHEN THE PADDY-ROLLERS CAME ASKING QUESTIONS.
I'LL MEET YOU IN THE MORNIN' WHEN YOU REACH THE PROMISED LAND, ON THE OTHER SIDE OF JORDAN...
WHERE'S MINTY?
I WISH I KNEW.
I'M BOUND FOR THE PROMISED LAAAND!
ARAMINTA'S JOURNEY HAD BEGUN.
OH, BOY! ESCAPE ADVENTURE TIME!

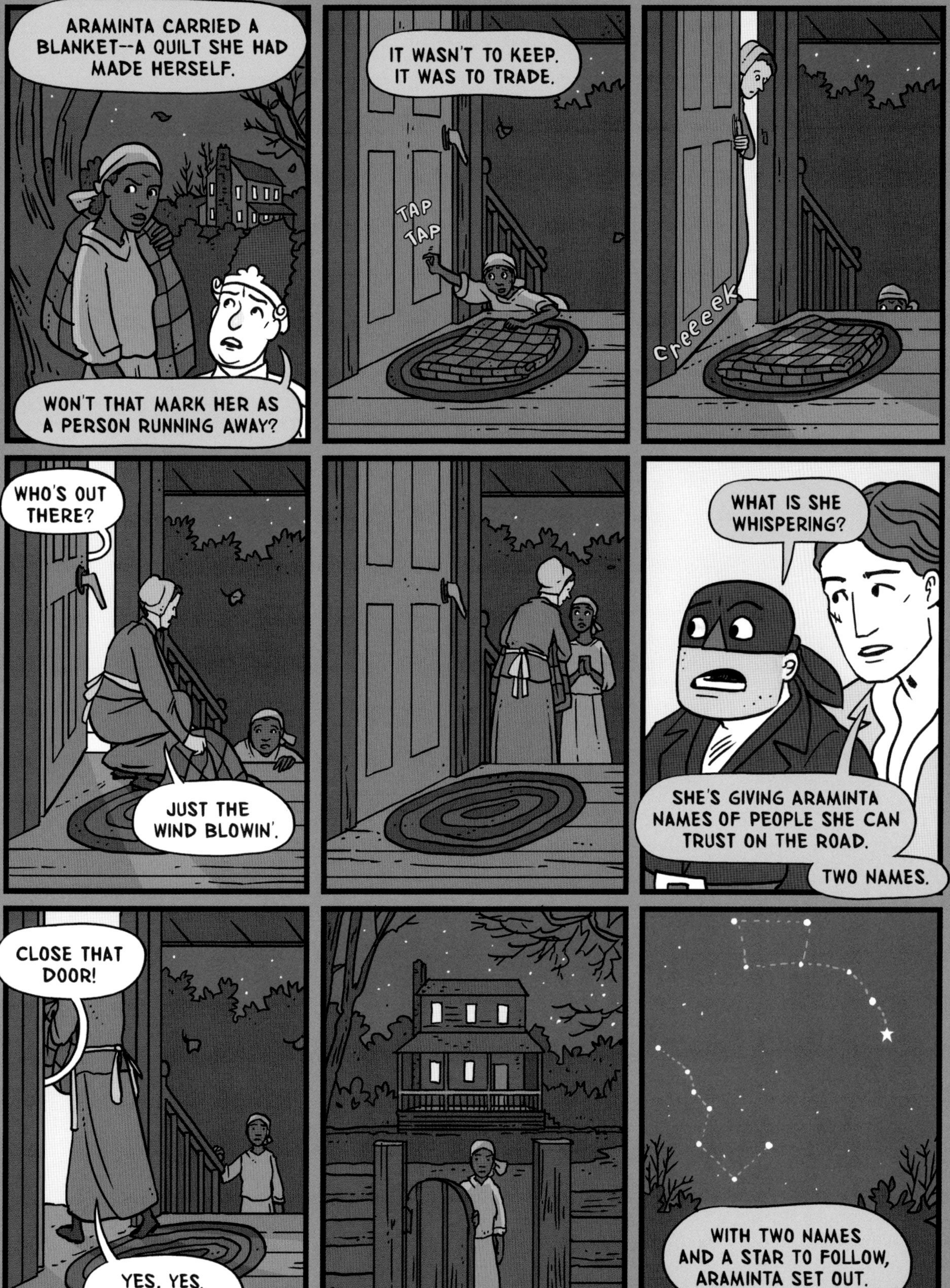
ARAMINTA CARRIED A BLANKET--A QUILT SHE HAD MADE HERSELF.
WON'T THAT MARK HER AS A PERSON RUNNING AWAY?
IT WASN'T TO KEEP. IT WAS TO TRADE.
TAP TAP
CREEEEK
WHO'S OUT THERE?
JUST THE WIND BLOWIN'.
WHAT IS SHE WHISPERING?
SHE'S GIVING ARAMINTA NAMES OF PEOPLE SHE CAN TRUST ON THE ROAD.
TWO NAMES.
CLOSE THAT DOOR!
YES, YES, HERE I COME.
WITH TWO NAMES AND A STAR TO FOLLOW, ARAMINTA SET OUT.

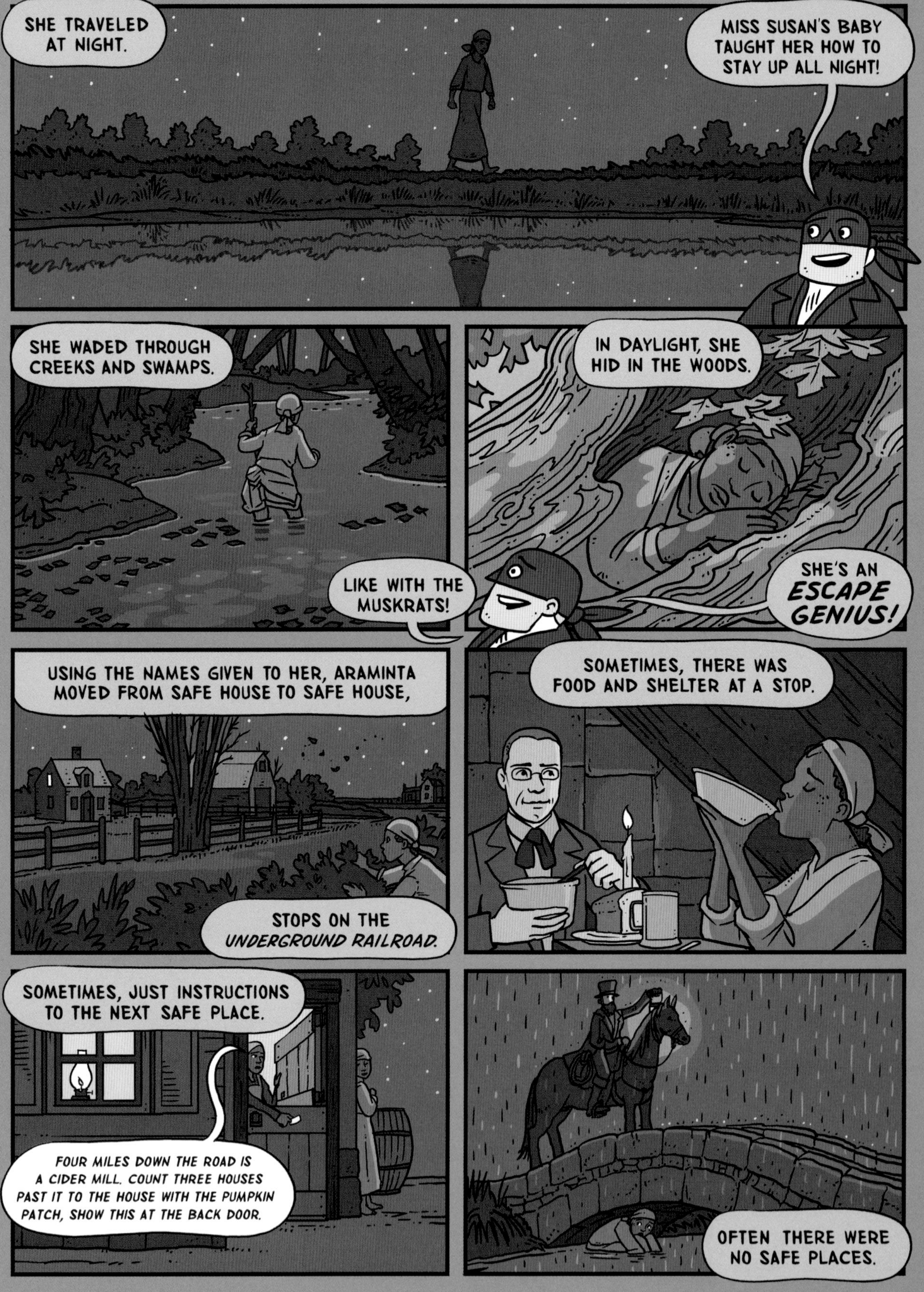
SHE TRAVELED AT NIGHT.
MISS SUSAN'S BABY TAUGHT HER HOW TO STAY UP ALL NIGHT!
SHE WADED THROUGH CREEKS AND SWAMPS.
IN DAYLIGHT, SHE HID IN THE WOODS.
LIKE WITH THE MUSKRATS!
SHE'S AN *ESCAPE GENIUS!*
USING THE NAMES GIVEN TO HER, ARAMINTA MOVED FROM SAFE HOUSE TO SAFE HOUSE,
STOPS ON THE *UNDERGROUND RAILROAD.*
SOMETIMES, THERE WAS FOOD AND SHELTER AT A STOP.
SOMETIMES, JUST INSTRUCTIONS TO THE NEXT SAFE PLACE.
FOUR MILES DOWN THE ROAD IS A CIDER MILL. COUNT THREE HOUSES PAST IT TO THE HOUSE WITH THE PUMPKIN PATCH, SHOW THIS AT THE BACK DOOR.
OFTEN THERE WERE NO SAFE PLACES.

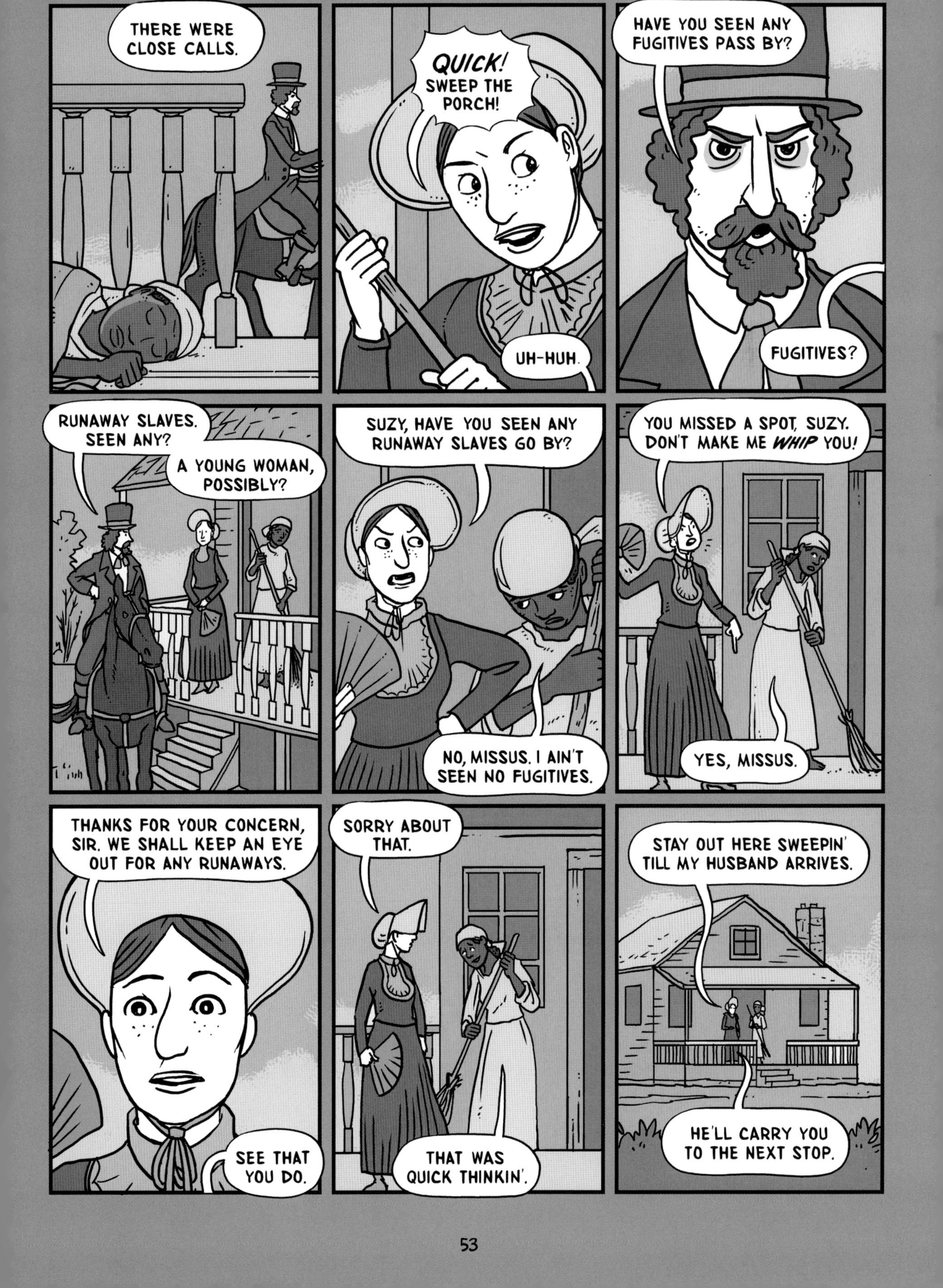
THERE WERE CLOSE CALLS.
QUICK! SWEEP THE PORCH!
UH-HUH.
HAVE YOU SEEN ANY FUGITIVES PASS BY?
FUGITIVES?
RUNAWAY SLAVES. SEEN ANY?
A YOUNG WOMAN, POSSIBLY?
SUZY, HAVE YOU SEEN ANY RUNAWAY SLAVES GO BY?
NO, MISSUS. I AIN'T SEEN NO FUGITIVES.
YOU MISSED A SPOT, SUZY. DON'T MAKE ME *WHIP* YOU!
YES, MISSUS.
THANKS FOR YOUR CONCERN, SIR. WE SHALL KEEP AN EYE OUT FOR ANY RUNAWAYS.
SEE THAT YOU DO.
SORRY ABOUT THAT.
THAT WAS QUICK THINKIN'.
STAY OUT HERE SWEEPIN' TILL MY HUSBAND ARRIVES.
HE'LL CARRY YOU TO THE NEXT STOP.

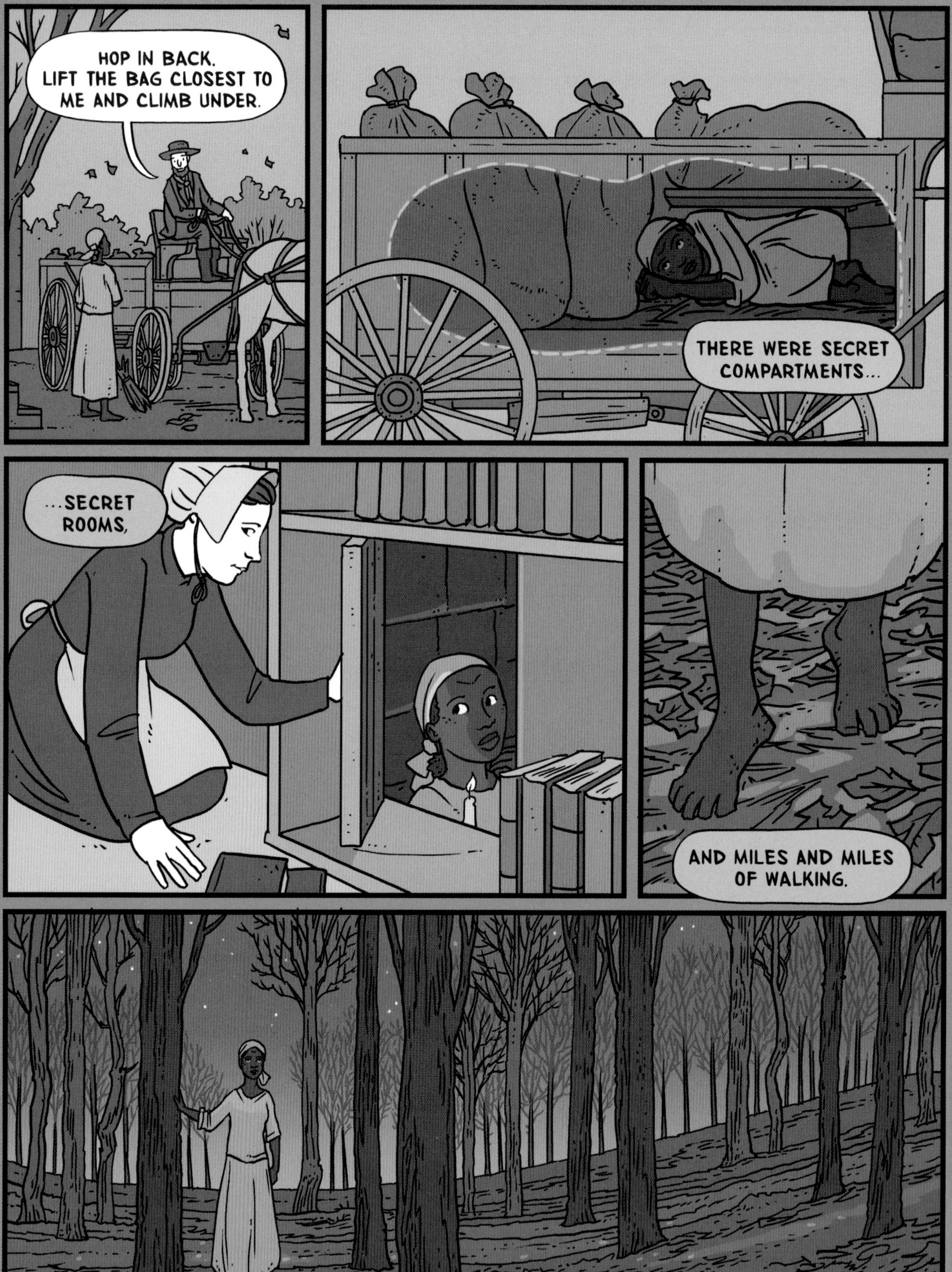
HOP IN BACK. LIFT THE BAG CLOSEST TO ME AND CLIMB UNDER.
THERE WERE SECRET COMPARTMENTS...
...SECRET ROOMS,
AND MILES AND MILES OF WALKING.
ARAMINTA MADE HER WAY NEARLY ONE HUNDRED MILES NORTH.

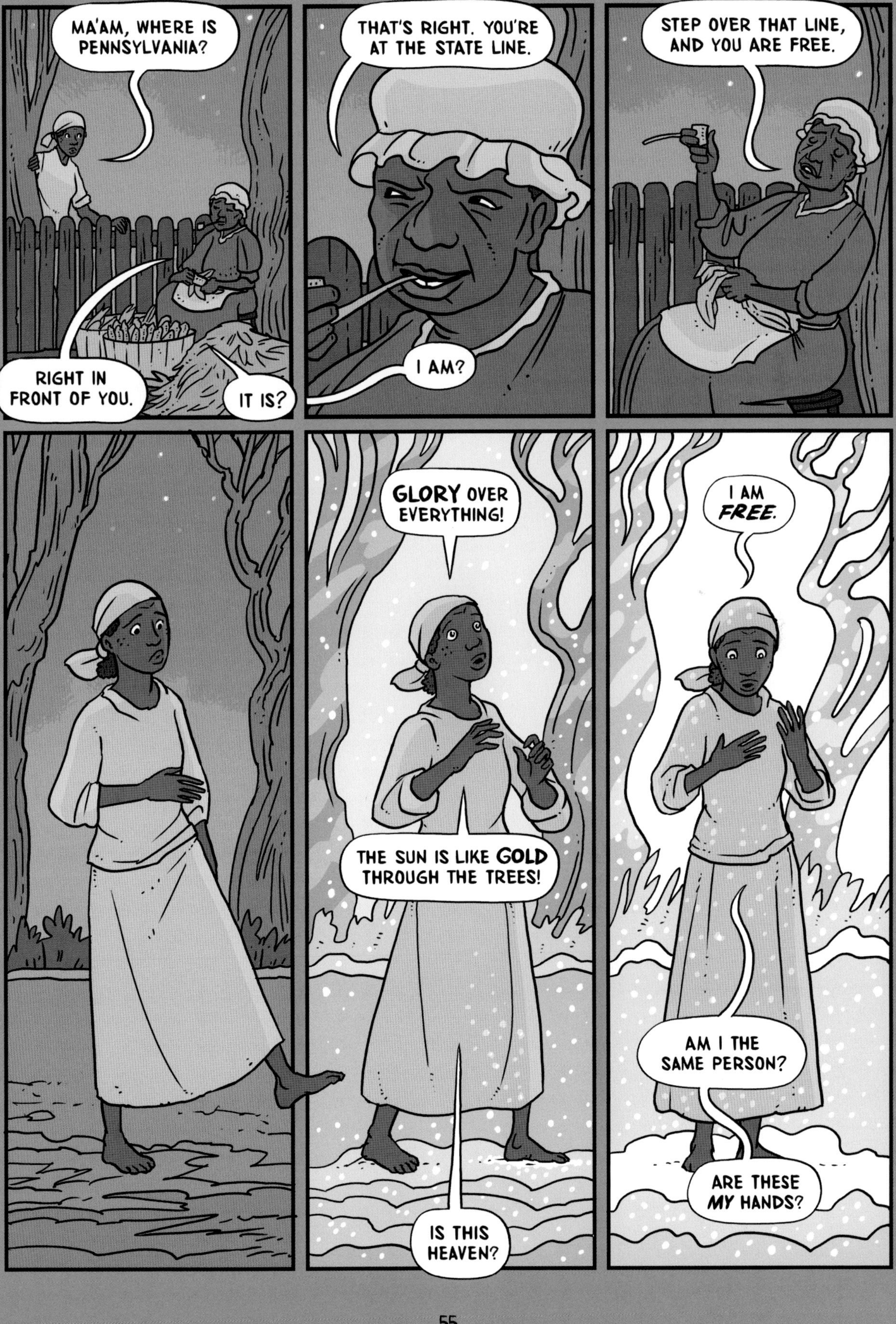
MA'AM, WHERE IS PENNSYLVANIA?
RIGHT IN FRONT OF YOU.
IT IS?
THAT'S RIGHT. YOU'RE AT THE STATE LINE.
I AM?
STEP OVER THAT LINE, AND YOU ARE FREE.
GLORY OVER EVERYTHING!
THE SUN IS LIKE GOLD THROUGH THE TREES!
IS THIS HEAVEN?
I AM FREE.
AM I THE SAME PERSON?
ARE THESE MY HANDS?

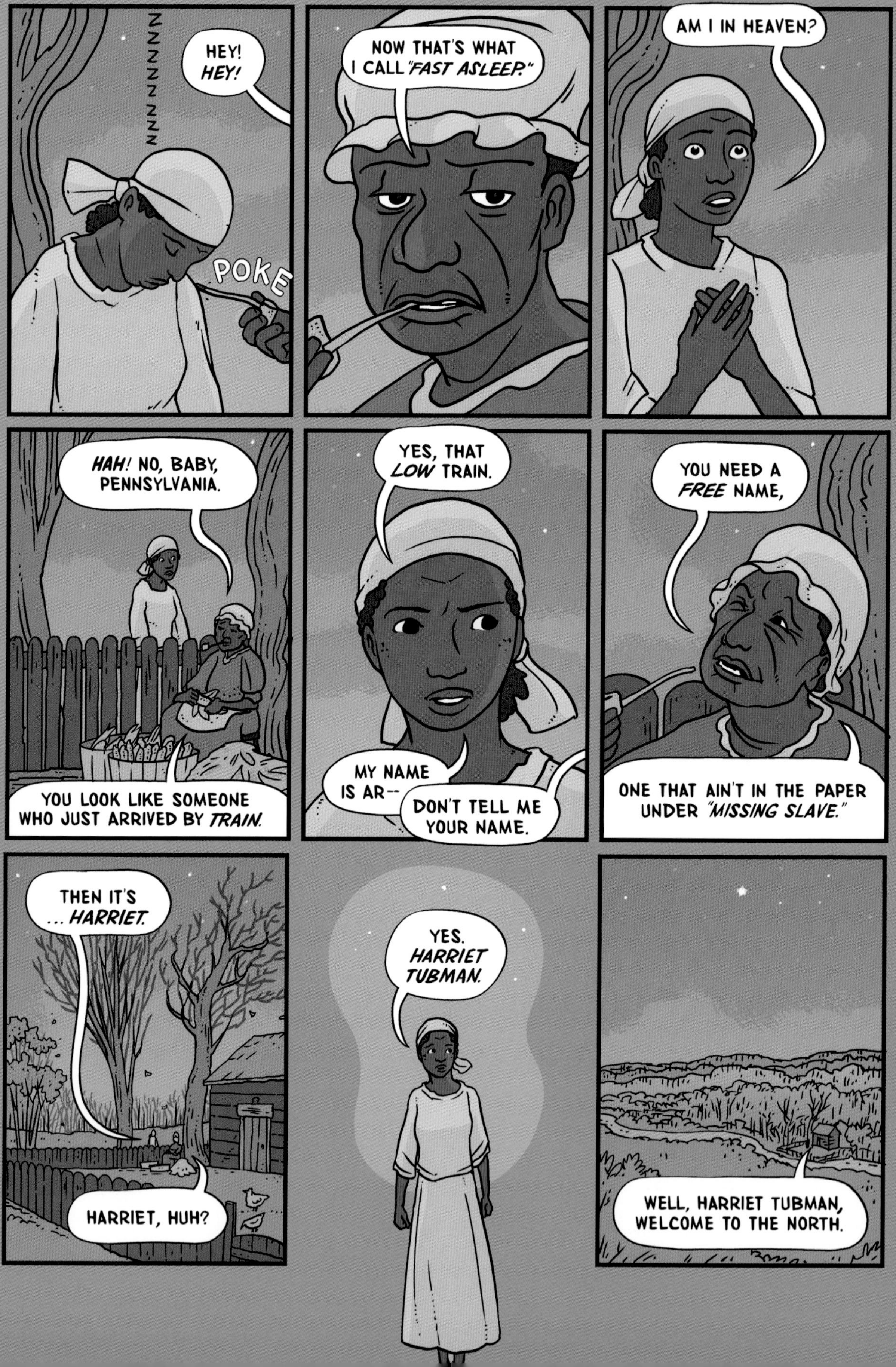
ZZZZZZZZ
HEY! HEY!
POKE
NOW THAT'S WHAT I CALL "FAST ASLEEP."
AM I IN HEAVEN?
HAH! NO, BABY, PENNSYLVANIA.
YOU LOOK LIKE SOMEONE WHO JUST ARRIVED BY TRAIN.
YES, THAT LOW TRAIN.
MY NAME IS AR--
DON'T TELL ME YOUR NAME.
YOU NEED A FREE NAME,
ONE THAT AIN'T IN THE PAPER UNDER "MISSING SLAVE."
THEN IT'S ... HARRIET.
HARRIET, HUH?
YES. HARRIET TUBMAN.
WELL, HARRIET TUBMAN, WELCOME TO THE NORTH.

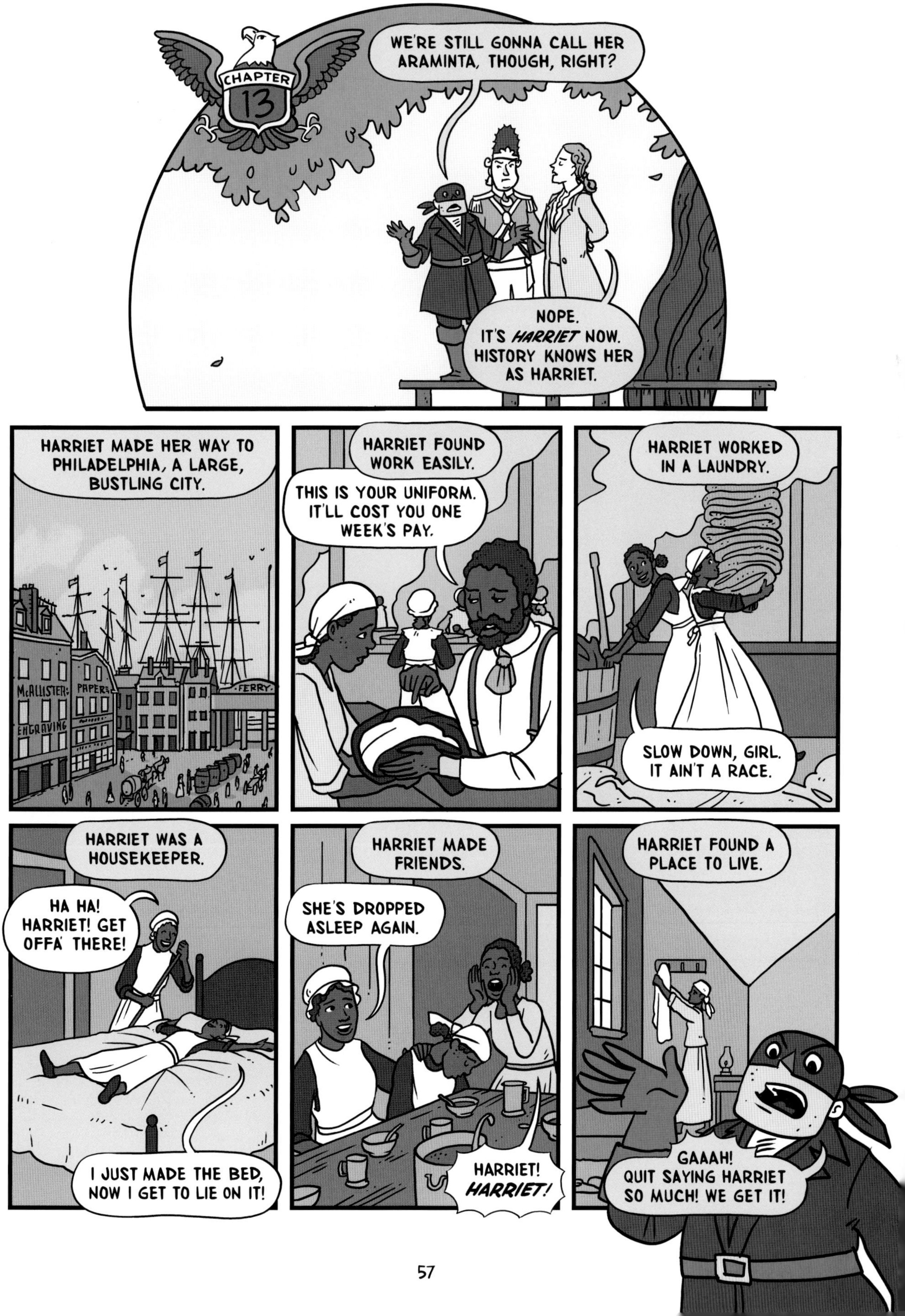
CHAPTER 13
WE'RE STILL GONNA CALL HER ARAMINTA, THOUGH, RIGHT?
NOPE. IT'S HARRIET NOW. HISTORY KNOWS HER AS HARRIET.
HARRIET MADE HER WAY TO PHILADELPHIA, A LARGE, BUSTLING CITY.
McALLISTER ENGRAVING
PAPER
FERRY
HARRIET FOUND WORK EASILY.
THIS IS YOUR UNIFORM. IT'LL COST YOU ONE WEEK'S PAY.
HARRIET WORKED IN A LAUNDRY.
SLOW DOWN, GIRL. IT AIN'T A RACE.
HARRIET WAS A HOUSEKEEPER.
HA HA! HARRIET! GET OFFA' THERE!
I JUST MADE THE BED, NOW I GET TO LIE ON IT!
HARRIET MADE FRIENDS.
SHE'S DROPPED ASLEEP AGAIN.
HARRIET! HARRIET!
HARRIET FOUND A PLACE TO LIVE.
GAAAH! QUIT SAYING HARRIET SO MUCH! WE GET IT!

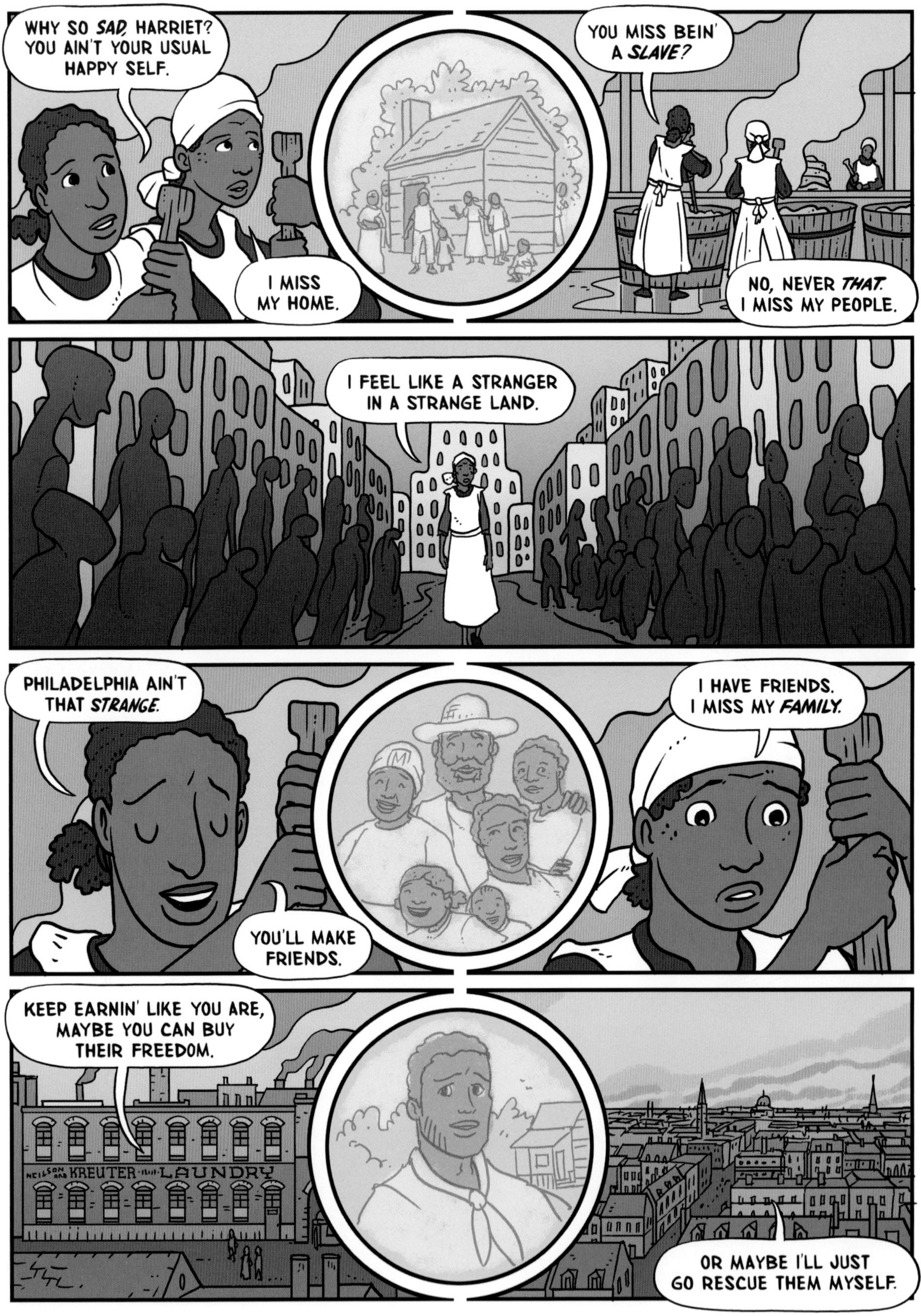
WHY SO SAD, HARRIET? YOU AIN'T YOUR USUAL HAPPY SELF.
I MISS MY HOME.
YOU MISS BEIN' A SLAVE?
NO, NEVER THAT. I MISS MY PEOPLE.
I FEEL LIKE A STRANGER IN A STRANGE LAND.
PHILADELPHIA AIN'T THAT STRANGE.
YOU'LL MAKE FRIENDS.
I HAVE FRIENDS. I MISS MY FAMILY.
KEEP EARNIN' LIKE YOU ARE, MAYBE YOU CAN BUY THEIR FREEDOM.
NEILSON AND KREUTER LAUNDRY
OR MAYBE I'LL JUST GO RESCUE THEM MYSELF.

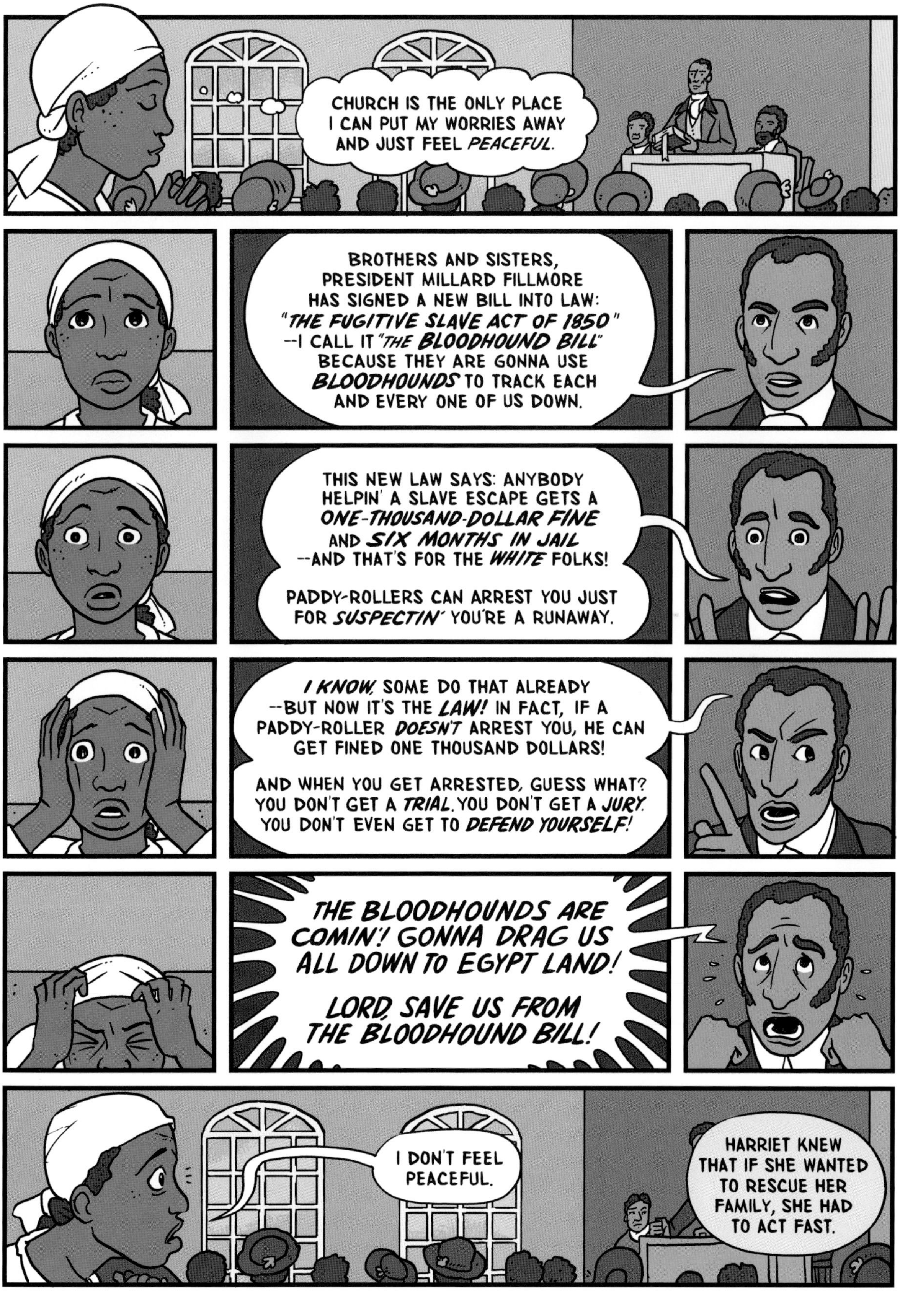
CHURCH IS THE ONLY PLACE I CAN PUT MY WORRIES AWAY AND JUST FEEL *PEACEFUL.*
BROTHERS AND SISTERS, PRESIDENT MILLARD FILLMORE HAS SIGNED A NEW BILL INTO LAW: "*THE FUGITIVE SLAVE ACT OF 1850*" --I CALL IT "*THE BLOODHOUND BILL*" BECAUSE THEY ARE GONNA USE *BLOODHOUNDS* TO TRACK EACH AND EVERY ONE OF US DOWN.
THIS NEW LAW SAYS: ANYBODY HELPIN' A SLAVE ESCAPE GETS A *ONE-THOUSAND-DOLLAR FINE* AND *SIX MONTHS IN JAIL* --AND THAT'S FOR THE *WHITE* FOLKS!
PADDY-ROLLERS CAN ARREST YOU JUST FOR *SUSPECTIN'* YOU'RE A RUNAWAY.
I KNOW, SOME DO THAT ALREADY --BUT NOW IT'S THE *LAW!* IN FACT, IF A PADDY-ROLLER *DOESN'T* ARREST YOU, HE CAN GET FINED ONE THOUSAND DOLLARS!
AND WHEN YOU GET ARRESTED, GUESS WHAT? YOU DON'T GET A *TRIAL.* YOU DON'T GET A *JURY.* YOU DON'T EVEN GET TO *DEFEND YOURSELF!*
THE BLOODHOUNDS ARE COMIN'! GONNA DRAG US ALL DOWN TO EGYPT LAND!
LORD, SAVE US FROM THE BLOODHOUND BILL!
I DON'T FEEL PEACEFUL.
HARRIET KNEW THAT IF SHE WANTED TO RESCUE HER FAMILY, SHE HAD TO ACT FAST.

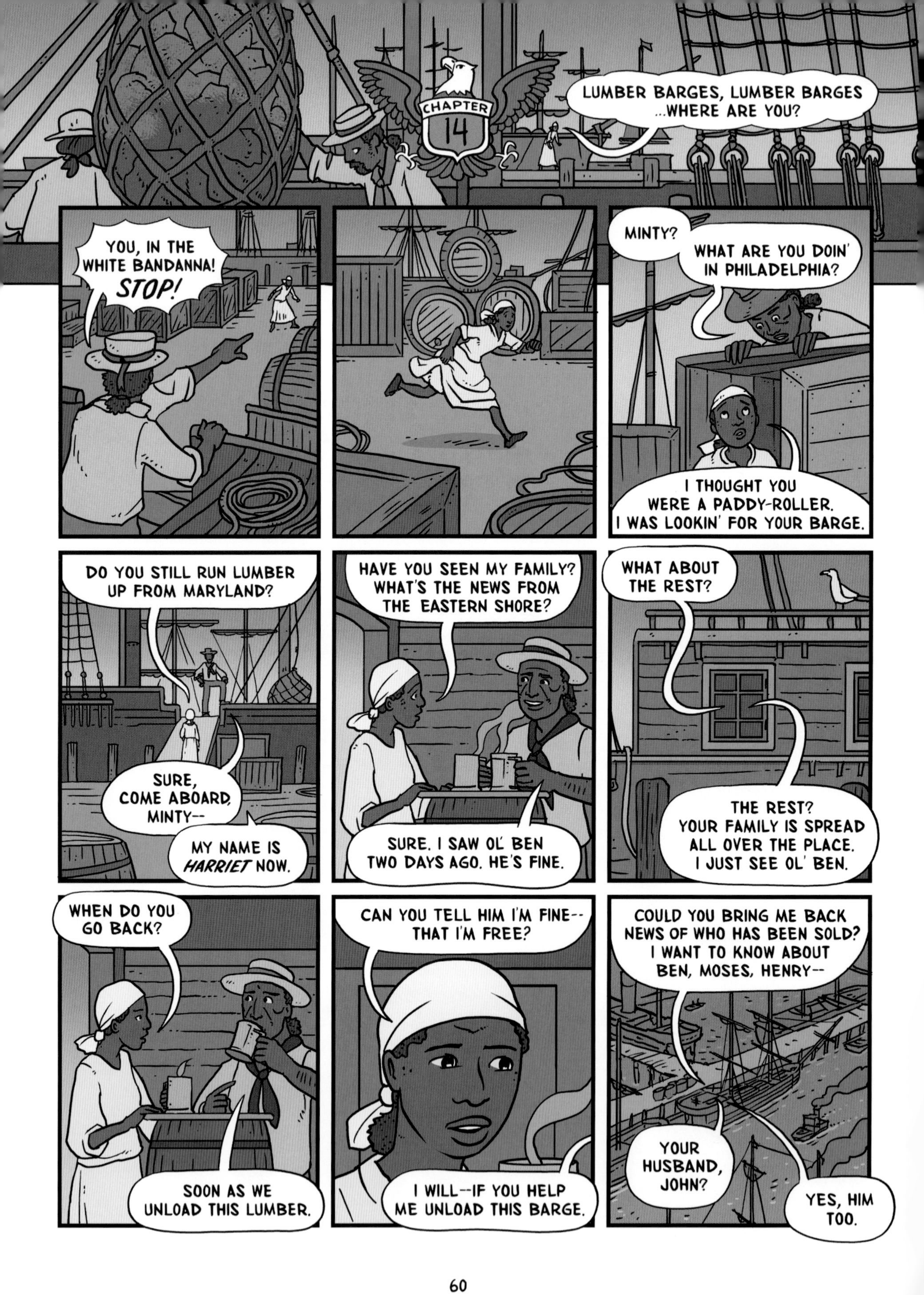
CHAPTER 14
LUMBER BARGES, LUMBER BARGES ...WHERE ARE YOU?
YOU, IN THE WHITE BANDANNA! STOP!
MINTY?
WHAT ARE YOU DOIN' IN PHILADELPHIA?
I THOUGHT YOU WERE A PADDY-ROLLER. I WAS LOOKIN' FOR YOUR BARGE.
DO YOU STILL RUN LUMBER UP FROM MARYLAND?
SURE, COME ABOARD, MINTY--
MY NAME IS HARRIET NOW.
HAVE YOU SEEN MY FAMILY? WHAT'S THE NEWS FROM THE EASTERN SHORE?
SURE. I SAW OL' BEN TWO DAYS AGO. HE'S FINE.
WHAT ABOUT THE REST?
THE REST? YOUR FAMILY IS SPREAD ALL OVER THE PLACE. I JUST SEE OL' BEN.
WHEN DO YOU GO BACK?
SOON AS WE UNLOAD THIS LUMBER.
CAN YOU TELL HIM I'M FINE-- THAT I'M FREE?
I WILL--IF YOU HELP ME UNLOAD THIS BARGE.
COULD YOU BRING ME BACK NEWS OF WHO HAS BEEN SOLD? I WANT TO KNOW ABOUT BEN, MOSES, HENRY--
YOUR HUSBAND, JOHN?
YES, HIM TOO.

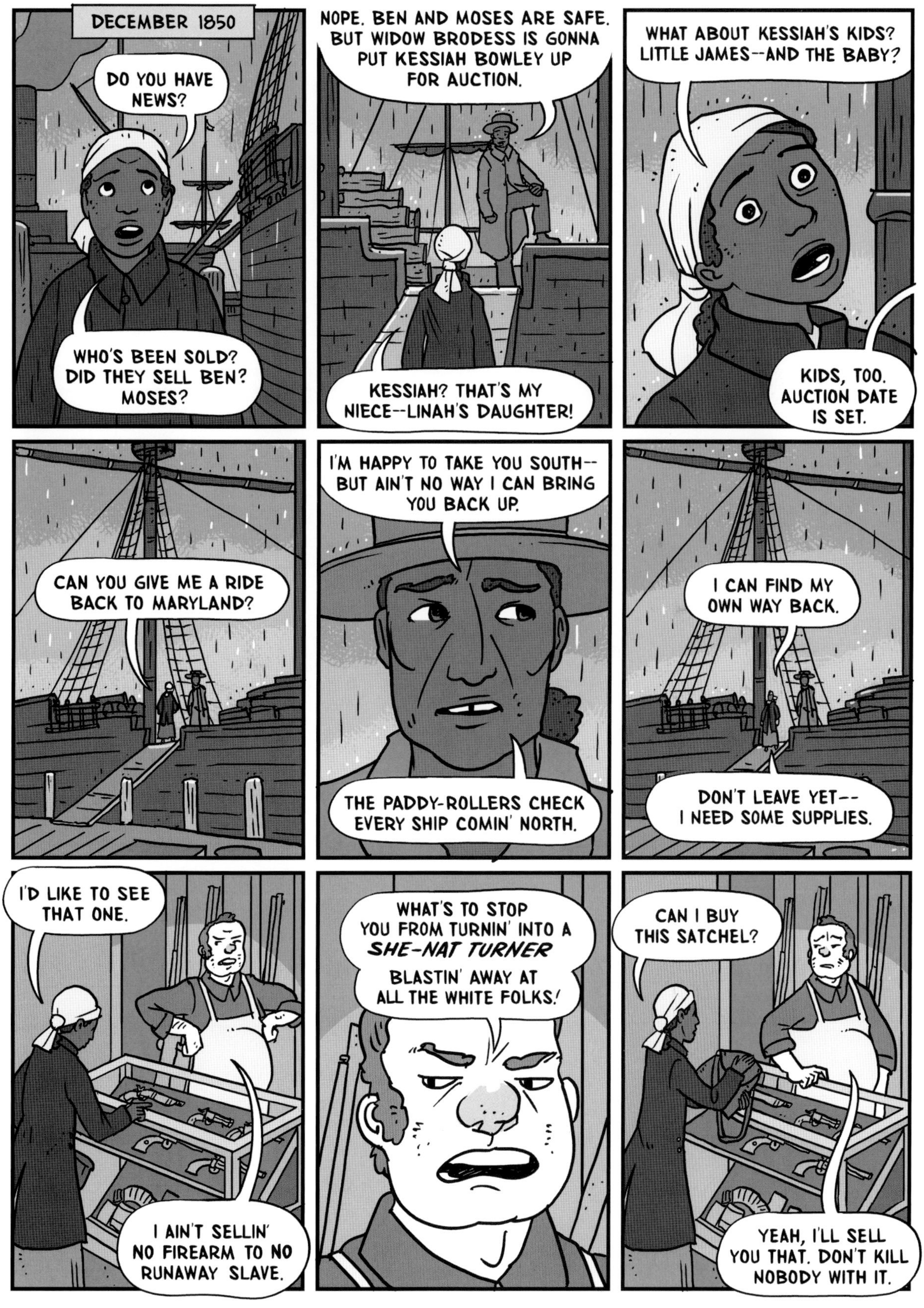
DECEMBER 1850
DO YOU HAVE NEWS?
WHO'S BEEN SOLD? DID THEY SELL BEN? MOSES?
NOPE. BEN AND MOSES ARE SAFE. BUT WIDOW BRODESS IS GONNA PUT KESSIAH BOWLEY UP FOR AUCTION.
KESSIAH? THAT'S MY NIECE--LINAH'S DAUGHTER!
WHAT ABOUT KESSIAH'S KIDS? LITTLE JAMES--AND THE BABY?
KIDS, TOO. AUCTION DATE IS SET.
CAN YOU GIVE ME A RIDE BACK TO MARYLAND?
I'M HAPPY TO TAKE YOU SOUTH--BUT AIN'T NO WAY I CAN BRING YOU BACK UP.
THE PADDY-ROLLERS CHECK EVERY SHIP COMIN' NORTH.
I CAN FIND MY OWN WAY BACK.
DON'T LEAVE YET--I NEED SOME SUPPLIES.
I'D LIKE TO SEE THAT ONE.
I AIN'T SELLIN' NO FIREARM TO NO RUNAWAY SLAVE.
WHAT'S TO STOP YOU FROM TURNIN' INTO A *SHE-NAT TURNER* BLASTIN' AWAY AT ALL THE WHITE FOLKS!
CAN I BUY THIS SATCHEL?
YEAH, I'LL SELL YOU THAT. DON'T KILL NOBODY WITH IT.

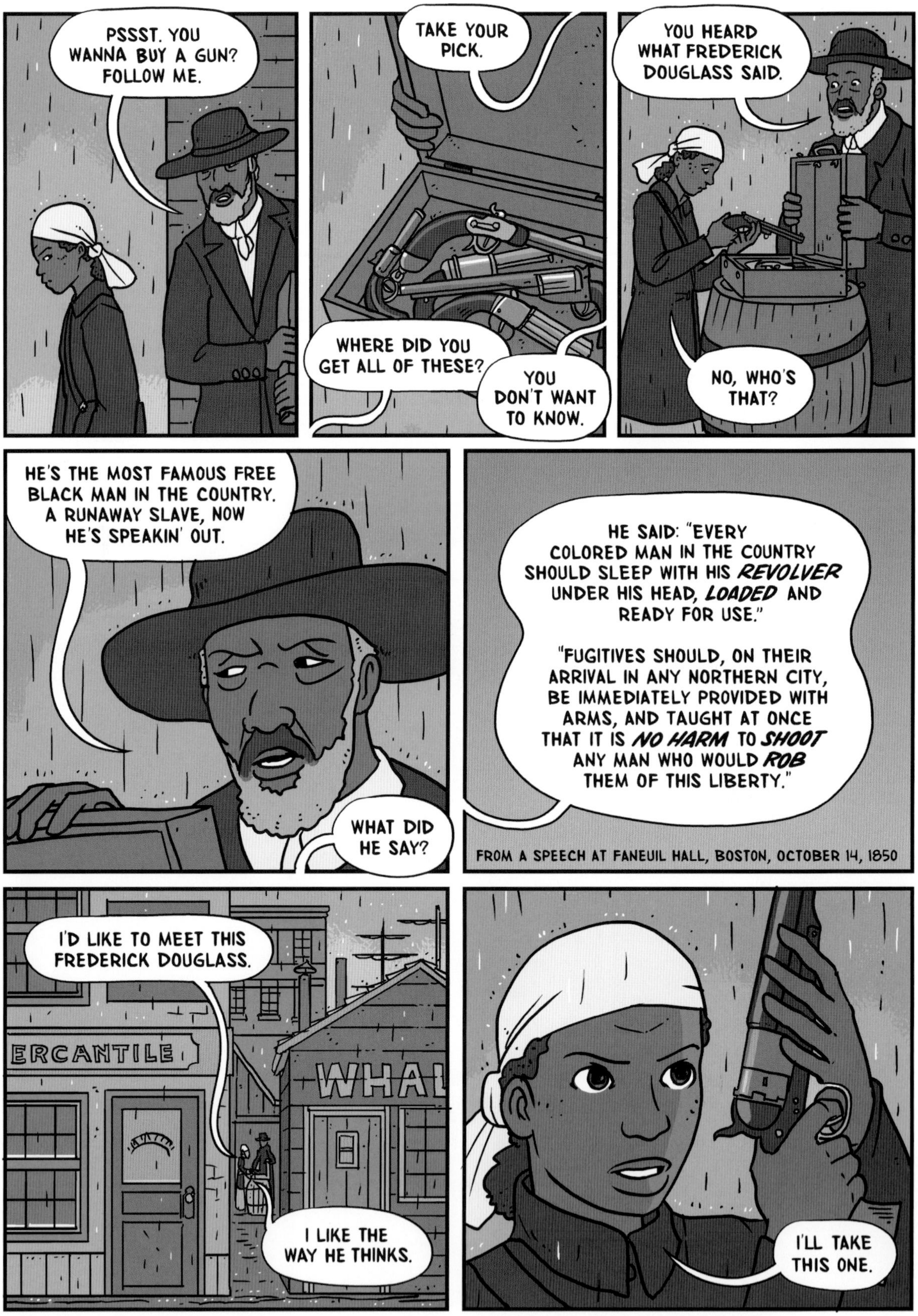
PSSST. YOU WANNA BUY A GUN? FOLLOW ME.
TAKE YOUR PICK.
WHERE DID YOU GET ALL OF THESE?
YOU DON'T WANT TO KNOW.
YOU HEARD WHAT FREDERICK DOUGLASS SAID.
NO, WHO'S THAT?
HE'S THE MOST FAMOUS FREE BLACK MAN IN THE COUNTRY. A RUNAWAY SLAVE, NOW HE'S SPEAKIN' OUT.
WHAT DID HE SAY?
HE SAID: "EVERY COLORED MAN IN THE COUNTRY SHOULD SLEEP WITH HIS *REVOLVER* UNDER HIS HEAD, *LOADED* AND READY FOR USE."
"FUGITIVES SHOULD, ON THEIR ARRIVAL IN ANY NORTHERN CITY, BE IMMEDIATELY PROVIDED WITH ARMS, AND TAUGHT AT ONCE THAT IT IS *NO HARM* TO *SHOOT* ANY MAN WHO WOULD *ROB* THEM OF THIS LIBERTY."
FROM A SPEECH AT FANEUIL HALL, BOSTON, OCTOBER 14, 1850
I'D LIKE TO MEET THIS FREDERICK DOUGLASS.
ERCANTILE
WHAL
I LIKE THE WAY HE THINKS.
I'LL TAKE THIS ONE.

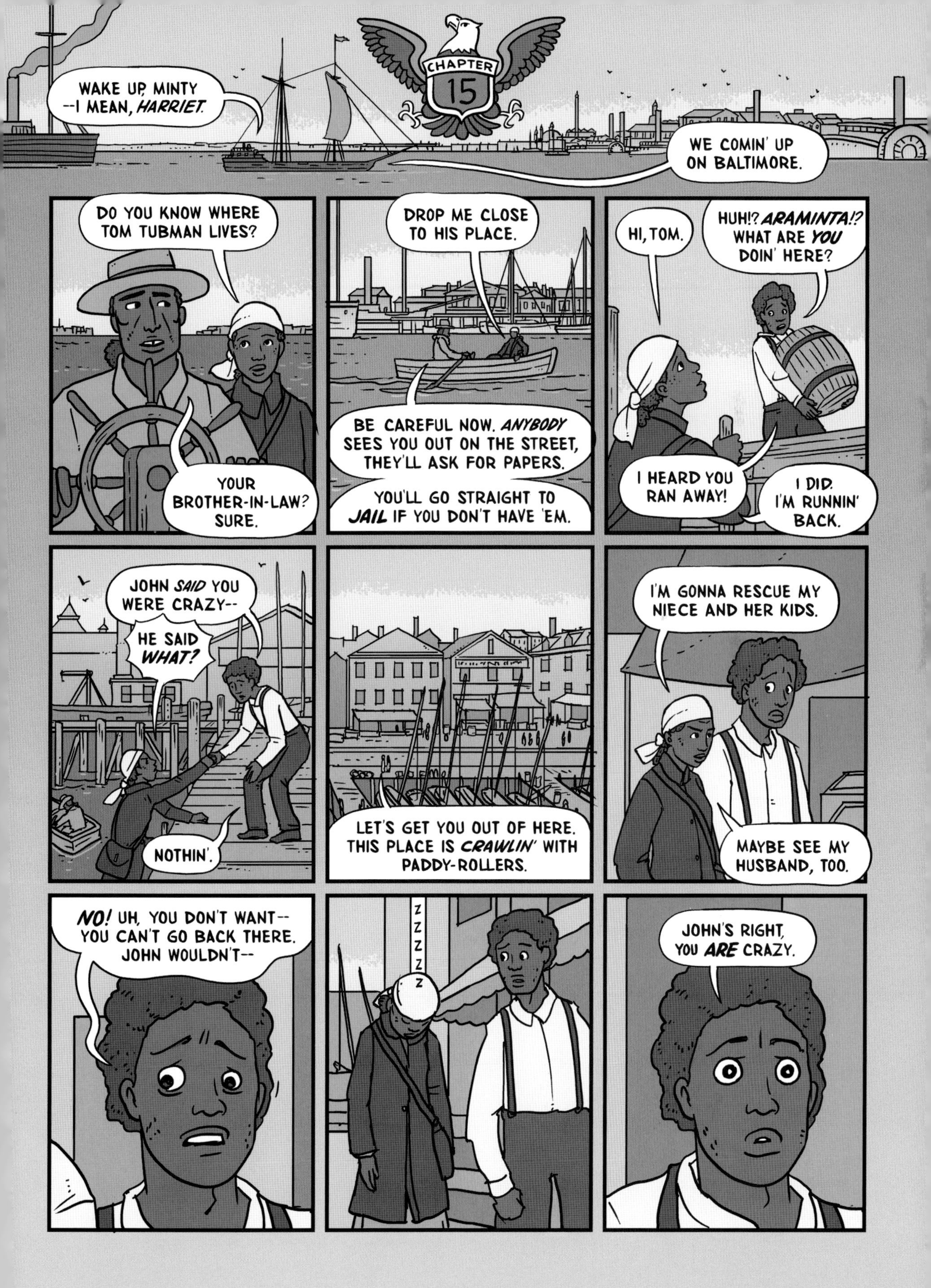
CHAPTER
15
WAKE UP, MINTY --I MEAN, *HARRIET.*
WE COMIN' UP ON BALTIMORE.
DO YOU KNOW WHERE TOM TUBMAN LIVES?
YOUR BROTHER-IN-LAW? SURE.
DROP ME CLOSE TO HIS PLACE.
BE CAREFUL NOW. *ANYBODY* SEES YOU OUT ON THE STREET, THEY'LL ASK FOR PAPERS.
YOU'LL GO STRAIGHT TO *JAIL* IF YOU DON'T HAVE 'EM.
HI, TOM.
HUH!? *ARAMINTA!?* WHAT ARE *YOU* DOIN' HERE?
I HEARD YOU RAN AWAY!
I DID. I'M RUNNIN' BACK.
JOHN *SAID* YOU WERE CRAZY--
HE SAID *WHAT?*
NOTHIN'.
LET'S GET YOU OUT OF HERE. THIS PLACE IS *CRAWLIN'* WITH PADDY-ROLLERS.
I'M GONNA RESCUE MY NIECE AND HER KIDS.
MAYBE SEE MY HUSBAND, TOO.
NO! UH, YOU DON'T WANT-- YOU CAN'T GO BACK THERE. JOHN WOULDN'T--
ZZZZZ
JOHN'S RIGHT, YOU *ARE* CRAZY.

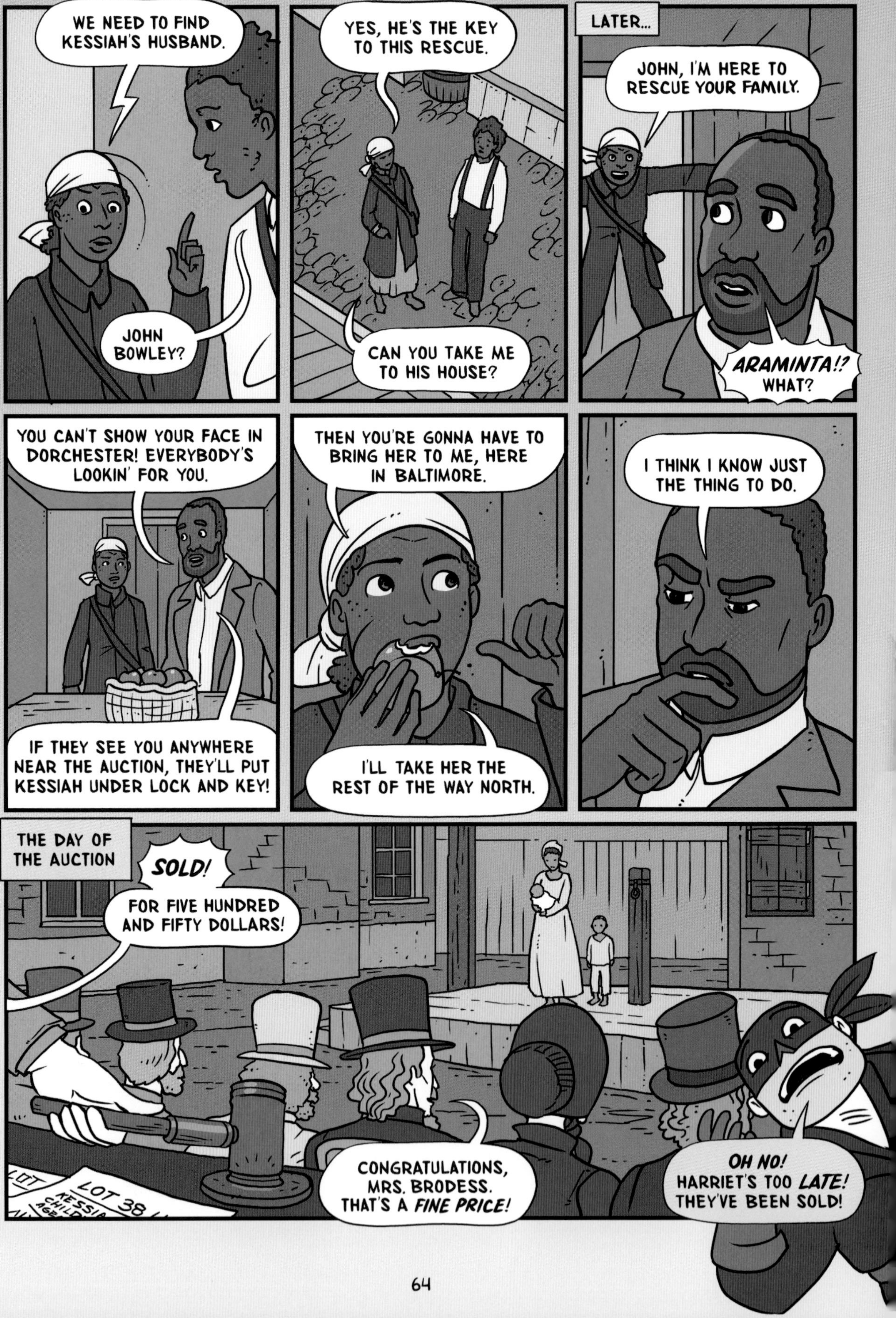
WE NEED TO FIND KESSIAH'S HUSBAND.
JOHN BOWLEY?
YES, HE'S THE KEY TO THIS RESCUE.
CAN YOU TAKE ME TO HIS HOUSE?
LATER...
JOHN, I'M HERE TO RESCUE YOUR FAMILY.
ARAMINTA!? WHAT?
YOU CAN'T SHOW YOUR FACE IN DORCHESTER! EVERYBODY'S LOOKIN' FOR YOU.
IF THEY SEE YOU ANYWHERE NEAR THE AUCTION, THEY'LL PUT KESSIAH UNDER LOCK AND KEY!
THEN YOU'RE GONNA HAVE TO BRING HER TO ME, HERE IN BALTIMORE.
I'LL TAKE HER THE REST OF THE WAY NORTH.
I THINK I KNOW JUST THE THING TO DO.
THE DAY OF THE AUCTION
SOLD!
FOR FIVE HUNDRED AND FIFTY DOLLARS!
LOT 38
CONGRATULATIONS, MRS. BRODESS. THAT'S A FINE PRICE!
OH NO! HARRIET'S TOO LATE! THEY'VE BEEN SOLD!

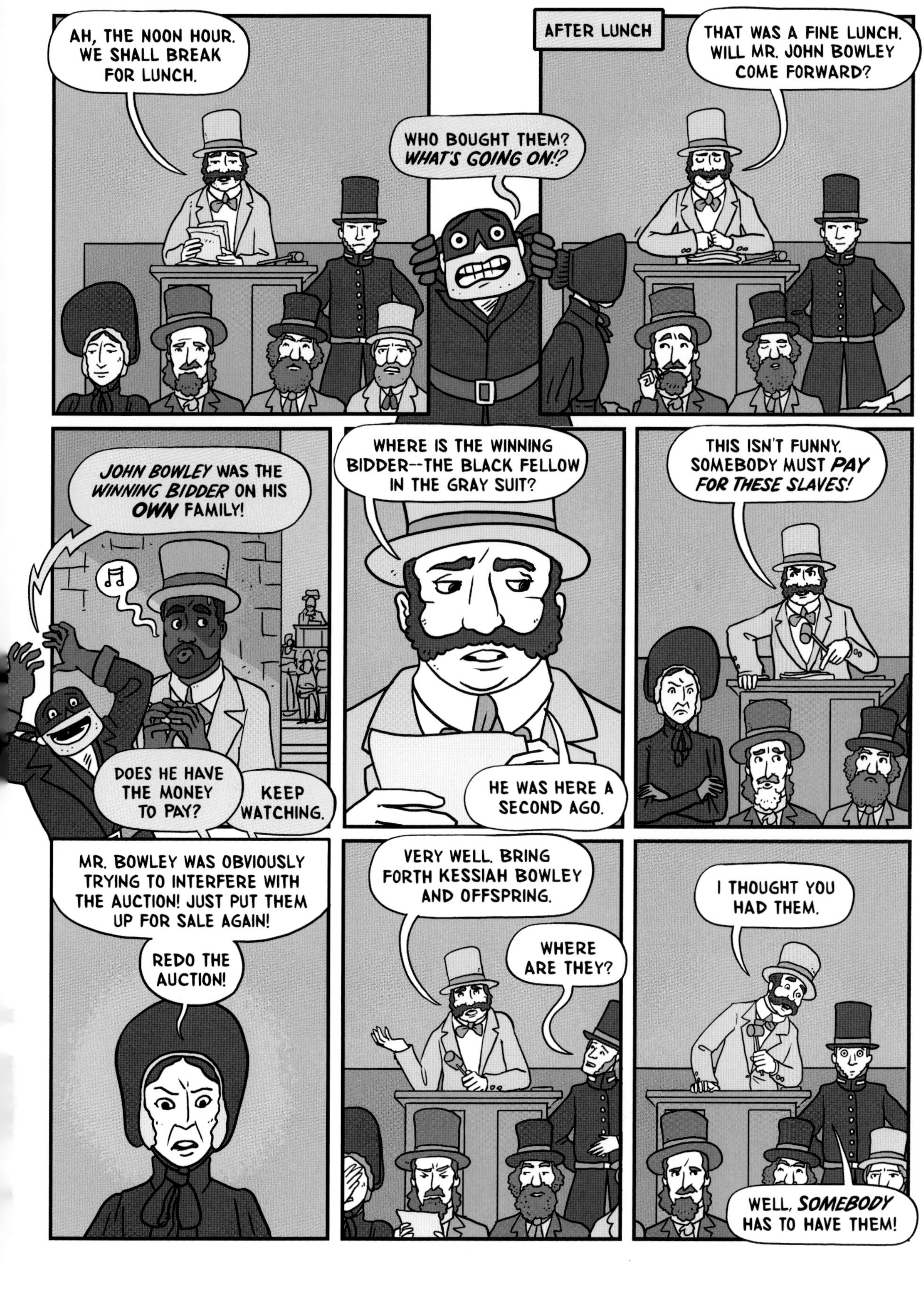
AH, THE NOON HOUR. WE SHALL BREAK FOR LUNCH.
WHO BOUGHT THEM? WHAT'S GOING ON!?
AFTER LUNCH
THAT WAS A FINE LUNCH. WILL MR. JOHN BOWLEY COME FORWARD?
JOHN BOWLEY WAS THE WINNING BIDDER ON HIS OWN FAMILY!
DOES HE HAVE THE MONEY TO PAY?
KEEP WATCHING.
WHERE IS THE WINNING BIDDER--THE BLACK FELLOW IN THE GRAY SUIT?
HE WAS HERE A SECOND AGO.
THIS ISN'T FUNNY. SOMEBODY MUST PAY FOR THESE SLAVES!
MR. BOWLEY WAS OBVIOUSLY TRYING TO INTERFERE WITH THE AUCTION! JUST PUT THEM UP FOR SALE AGAIN!
REDO THE AUCTION!
VERY WELL. BRING FORTH KESSIAH BOWLEY AND OFFSPRING.
WHERE ARE THEY?
I THOUGHT YOU HAD THEM.
WELL, SOMEBODY HAS TO HAVE THEM!

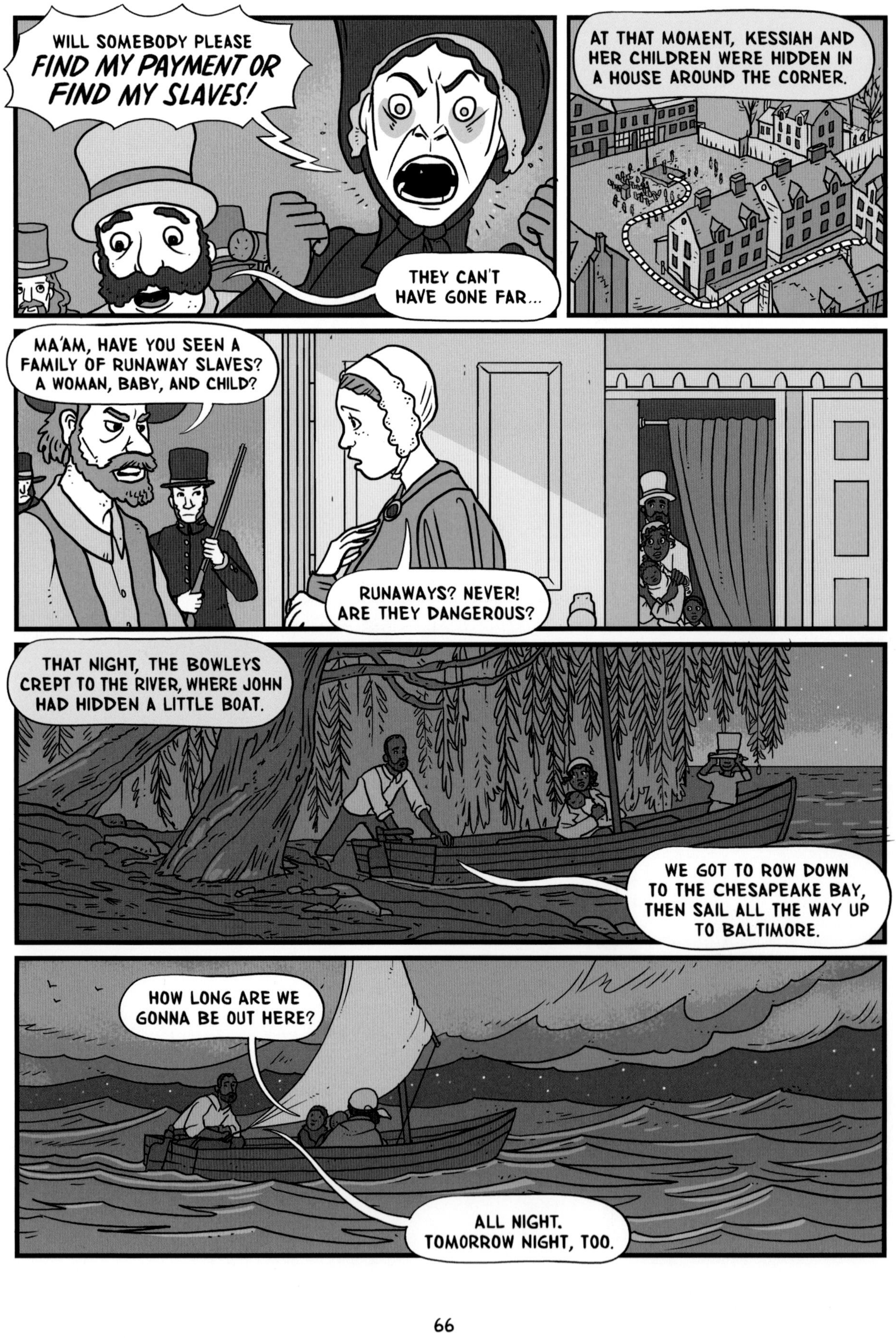
WILL SOMEBODY PLEASE FIND MY PAYMENT OR FIND MY SLAVES!
THEY CAN'T HAVE GONE FAR...
AT THAT MOMENT, KESSIAH AND HER CHILDREN WERE HIDDEN IN A HOUSE AROUND THE CORNER.
MA'AM, HAVE YOU SEEN A FAMILY OF RUNAWAY SLAVES? A WOMAN, BABY, AND CHILD?
RUNAWAYS? NEVER! ARE THEY DANGEROUS?
THAT NIGHT, THE BOWLEYS CREPT TO THE RIVER, WHERE JOHN HAD HIDDEN A LITTLE BOAT.
WE GOT TO ROW DOWN TO THE CHESAPEAKE BAY, THEN SAIL ALL THE WAY UP TO BALTIMORE.
HOW LONG ARE WE GONNA BE OUT HERE?
ALL NIGHT. TOMORROW NIGHT, TOO.

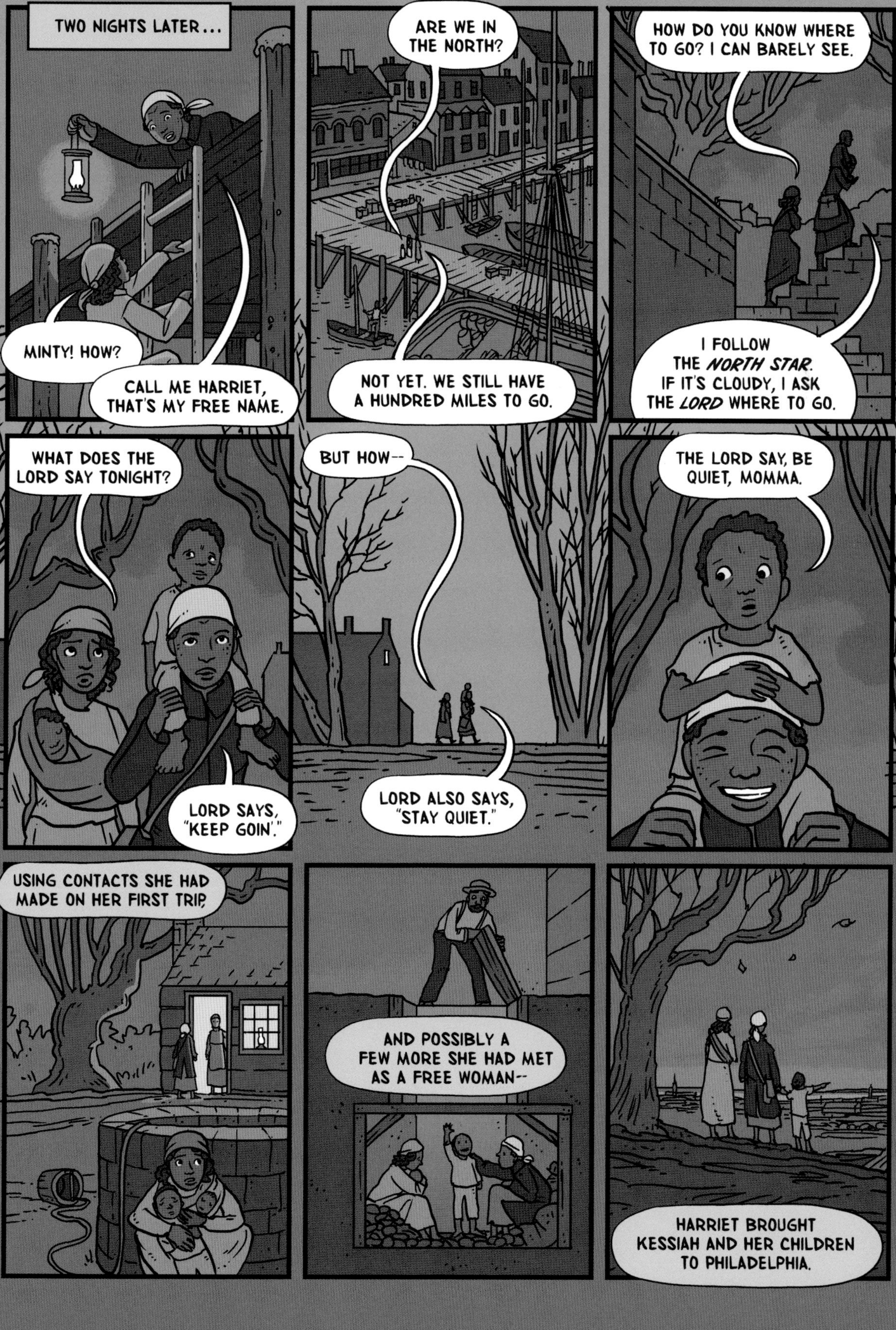
TWO NIGHTS LATER...
MINTY! HOW?
CALL ME HARRIET, THAT'S MY FREE NAME.
ARE WE IN THE NORTH?
NOT YET. WE STILL HAVE A HUNDRED MILES TO GO.
HOW DO YOU KNOW WHERE TO GO? I CAN BARELY SEE.
I FOLLOW THE *NORTH STAR*. IF IT'S CLOUDY, I ASK THE *LORD* WHERE TO GO.
WHAT DOES THE LORD SAY TONIGHT?
LORD SAYS, "KEEP GOIN'."
BUT HOW--
LORD ALSO SAYS, "STAY QUIET."
THE LORD SAY, BE QUIET, MOMMA.
USING CONTACTS SHE HAD MADE ON HER FIRST TRIP,
AND POSSIBLY A FEW MORE SHE HAD MET AS A FREE WOMAN--
HARRIET BROUGHT KESSIAH AND HER CHILDREN TO PHILADELPHIA.

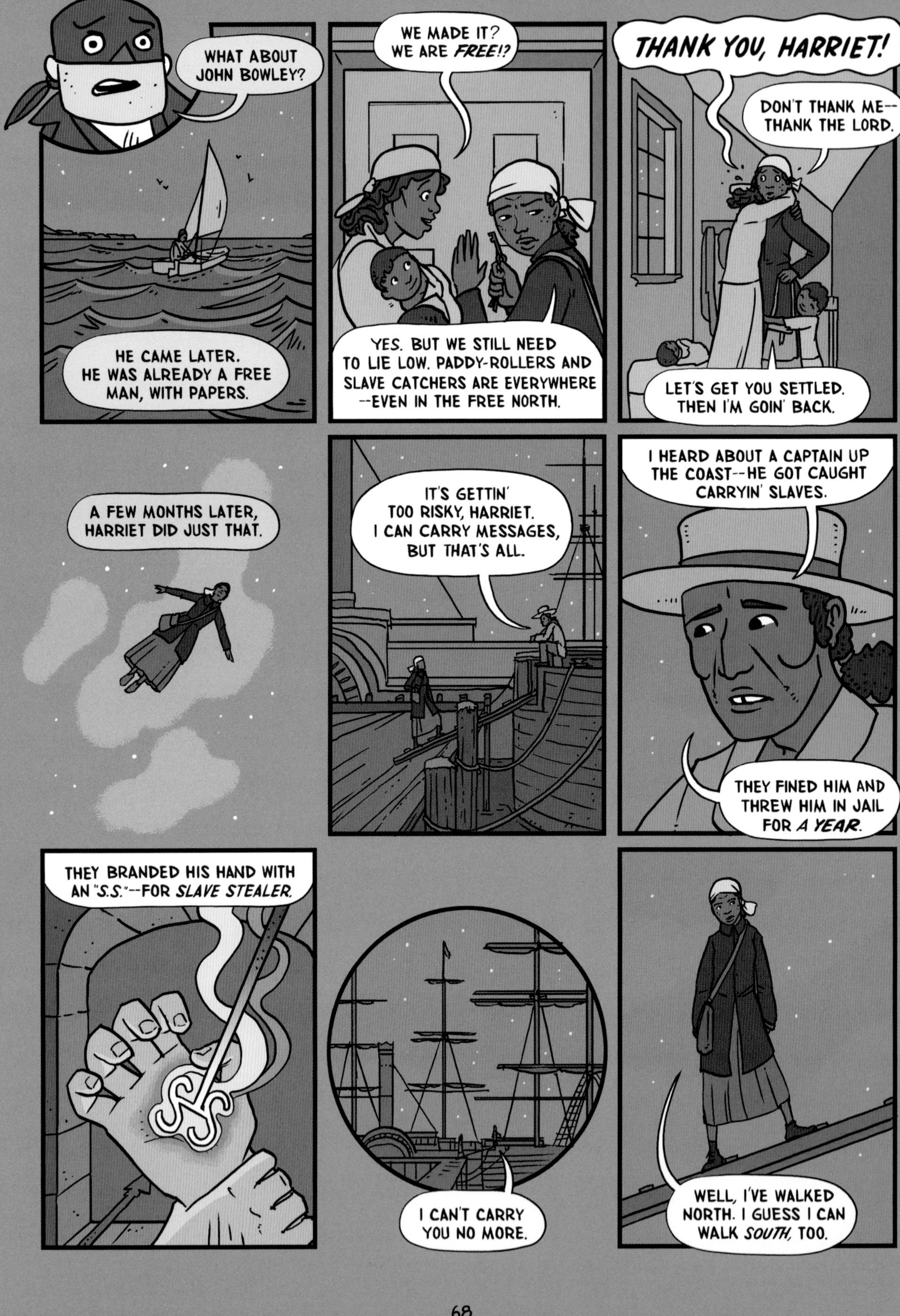
WHAT ABOUT JOHN BOWLEY?
HE CAME LATER. HE WAS ALREADY A FREE MAN, WITH PAPERS.
WE MADE IT? WE ARE *FREE*!?
YES. BUT WE STILL NEED TO LIE LOW. PADDY-ROLLERS AND SLAVE CATCHERS ARE EVERYWHERE --EVEN IN THE FREE NORTH.
THANK YOU, HARRIET!
DON'T THANK ME--THANK THE LORD.
LET'S GET YOU SETTLED. THEN I'M GOIN' BACK.
A FEW MONTHS LATER, HARRIET DID JUST THAT.
IT'S GETTIN' TOO RISKY, HARRIET. I CAN CARRY MESSAGES, BUT THAT'S ALL.
I HEARD ABOUT A CAPTAIN UP THE COAST--HE GOT CAUGHT CARRYIN' SLAVES.
THEY FINED HIM AND THREW HIM IN JAIL FOR *A YEAR*.
THEY BRANDED HIS HAND WITH AN "*S.S.*"--FOR *SLAVE STEALER*.
I CAN'T CARRY YOU NO MORE.
WELL, I'VE WALKED NORTH. I GUESS I CAN WALK *SOUTH*, TOO.

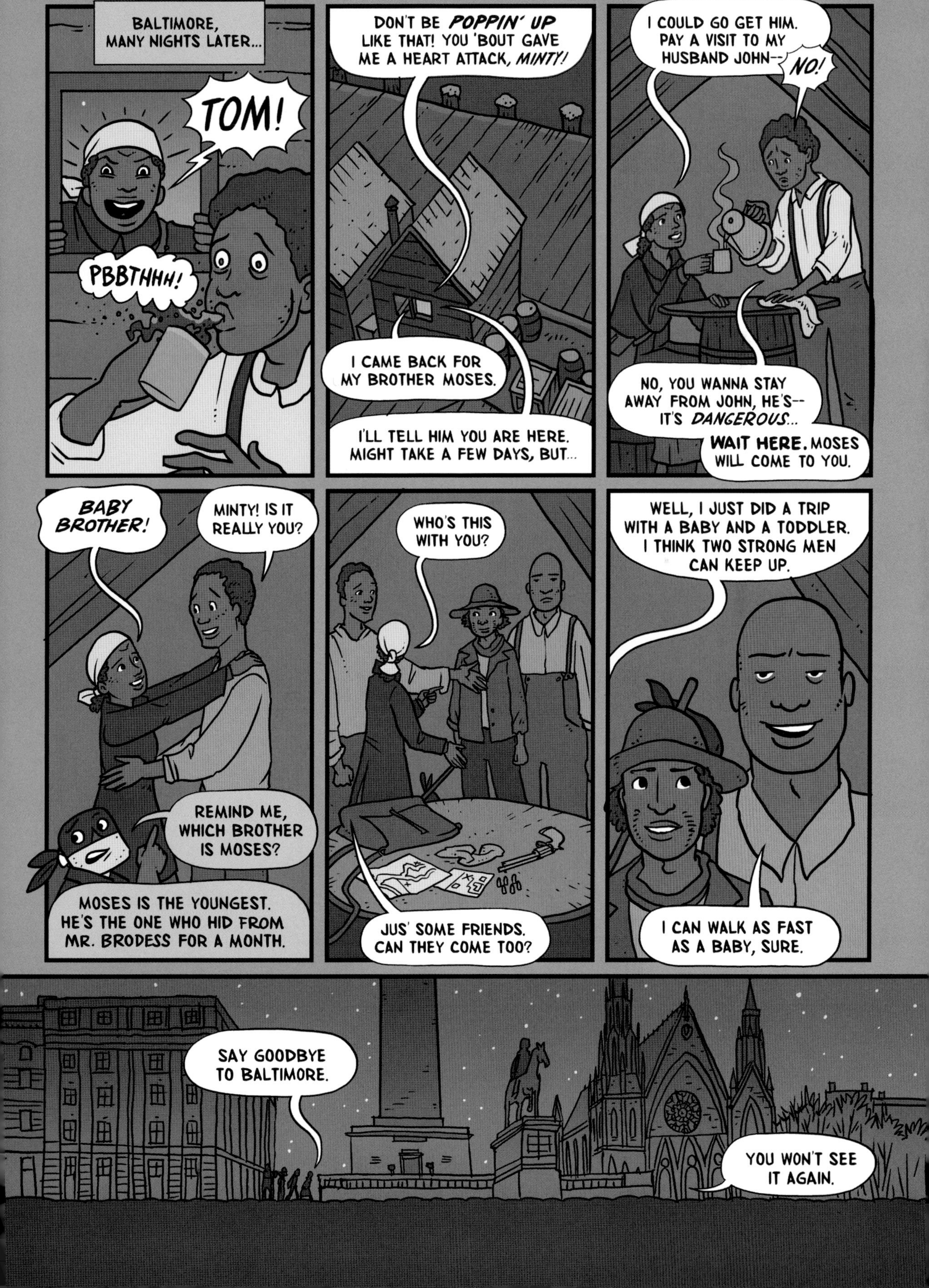
BALTIMORE, MANY NIGHTS LATER...
TOM!
PBBTHHH!
DON'T BE POPPIN' UP LIKE THAT! YOU 'BOUT GAVE ME A HEART ATTACK, MINTY!
I CAME BACK FOR MY BROTHER MOSES.
I'LL TELL HIM YOU ARE HERE. MIGHT TAKE A FEW DAYS, BUT...
I COULD GO GET HIM. PAY A VISIT TO MY HUSBAND JOHN--
NO!
NO, YOU WANNA STAY AWAY FROM JOHN, HE'S-- IT'S DANGEROUS...
WAIT HERE. MOSES WILL COME TO YOU.
BABY BROTHER!
MINTY! IS IT REALLY YOU?
REMIND ME, WHICH BROTHER IS MOSES?
MOSES IS THE YOUNGEST. HE'S THE ONE WHO HID FROM MR. BRODESS FOR A MONTH.
WHO'S THIS WITH YOU?
JUS' SOME FRIENDS. CAN THEY COME TOO?
WELL, I JUST DID A TRIP WITH A BABY AND A TODDLER. I THINK TWO STRONG MEN CAN KEEP UP.
I CAN WALK AS FAST AS A BABY, SURE.
SAY GOODBYE TO BALTIMORE.
YOU WON'T SEE IT AGAIN.

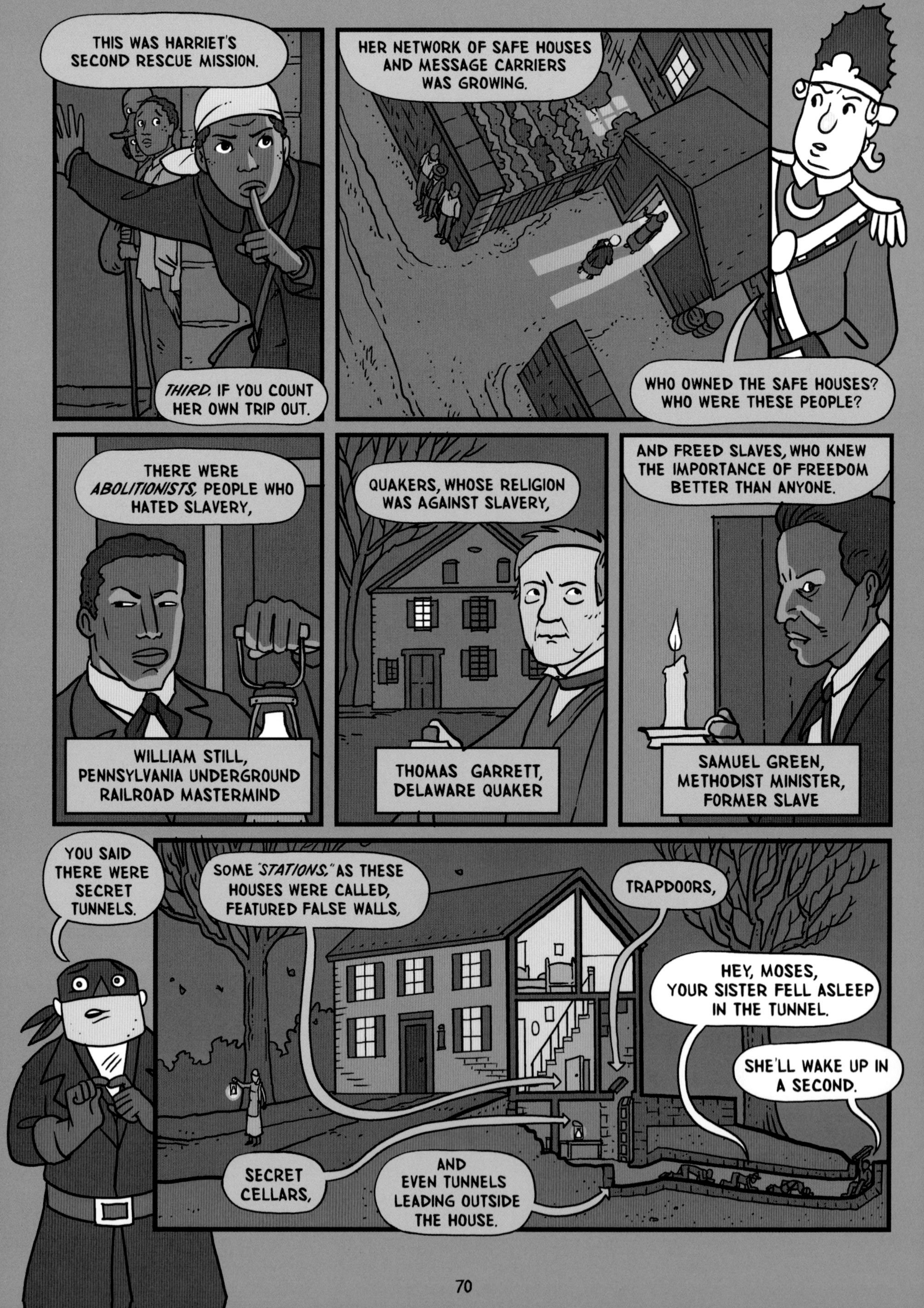
THIS WAS HARRIET'S SECOND RESCUE MISSION.
THIRD, IF YOU COUNT HER OWN TRIP OUT.
HER NETWORK OF SAFE HOUSES AND MESSAGE CARRIERS WAS GROWING.
WHO OWNED THE SAFE HOUSES? WHO WERE THESE PEOPLE?
THERE WERE *ABOLITIONISTS,* PEOPLE WHO HATED SLAVERY,
WILLIAM STILL, PENNSYLVANIA UNDERGROUND RAILROAD MASTERMIND
QUAKERS, WHOSE RELIGION WAS AGAINST SLAVERY,
THOMAS GARRETT, DELAWARE QUAKER
AND FREED SLAVES, WHO KNEW THE IMPORTANCE OF FREEDOM BETTER THAN ANYONE.
SAMUEL GREEN, METHODIST MINISTER, FORMER SLAVE
YOU SAID THERE WERE SECRET TUNNELS.
SOME *"STATIONS,"* AS THESE HOUSES WERE CALLED, FEATURED FALSE WALLS,
TRAPDOORS,
SECRET CELLARS,
AND EVEN TUNNELS LEADING OUTSIDE THE HOUSE.
HEY, MOSES, YOUR SISTER FELL ASLEEP IN THE TUNNEL.
SHE'LL WAKE UP IN A SECOND.

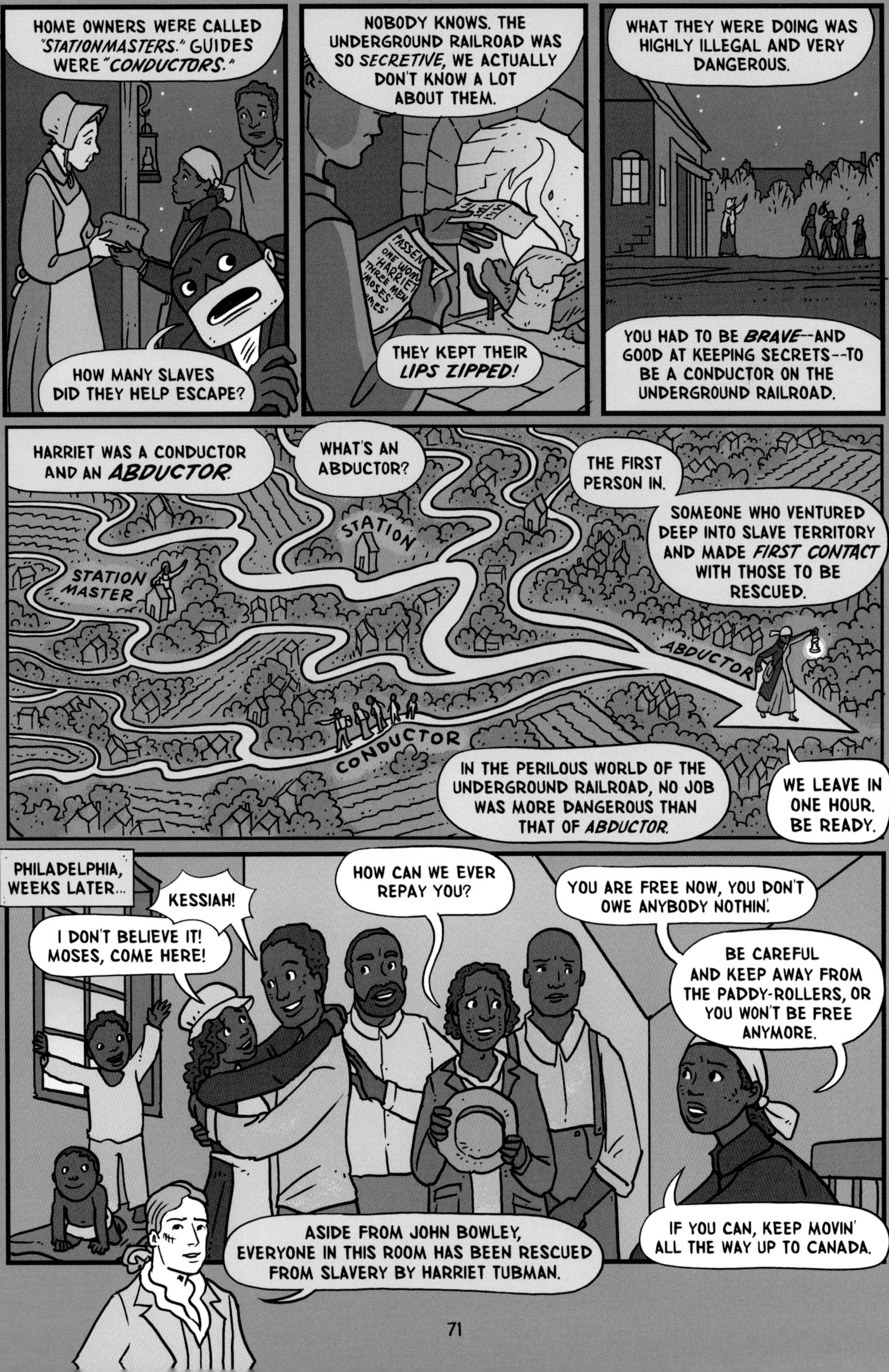
HOME OWNERS WERE CALLED "STATIONMASTERS." GUIDES WERE "CONDUCTORS."
HOW MANY SLAVES DID THEY HELP ESCAPE?
NOBODY KNOWS. THE UNDERGROUND RAILROAD WAS SO SECRETIVE, WE ACTUALLY DON'T KNOW A LOT ABOUT THEM.
THEY KEPT THEIR LIPS ZIPPED!
WHAT THEY WERE DOING WAS HIGHLY ILLEGAL AND VERY DANGEROUS.
YOU HAD TO BE BRAVE--AND GOOD AT KEEPING SECRETS--TO BE A CONDUCTOR ON THE UNDERGROUND RAILROAD.
HARRIET WAS A CONDUCTOR AND AN ABDUCTOR.
WHAT'S AN ABDUCTOR?
THE FIRST PERSON IN.
SOMEONE WHO VENTURED DEEP INTO SLAVE TERRITORY AND MADE FIRST CONTACT WITH THOSE TO BE RESCUED.
STATION
STATION MASTER
ABDUCTOR
CONDUCTOR
IN THE PERILOUS WORLD OF THE UNDERGROUND RAILROAD, NO JOB WAS MORE DANGEROUS THAN THAT OF ABDUCTOR.
WE LEAVE IN ONE HOUR. BE READY.
PHILADELPHIA, WEEKS LATER...
KESSIAH!
I DON'T BELIEVE IT! MOSES, COME HERE!
HOW CAN WE EVER REPAY YOU?
YOU ARE FREE NOW, YOU DON'T OWE ANYBODY NOTHIN'.
BE CAREFUL AND KEEP AWAY FROM THE PADDY-ROLLERS, OR YOU WON'T BE FREE ANYMORE.
ASIDE FROM JOHN BOWLEY, EVERYONE IN THIS ROOM HAS BEEN RESCUED FROM SLAVERY BY HARRIET TUBMAN.
IF YOU CAN, KEEP MOVIN' ALL THE WAY UP TO CANADA.

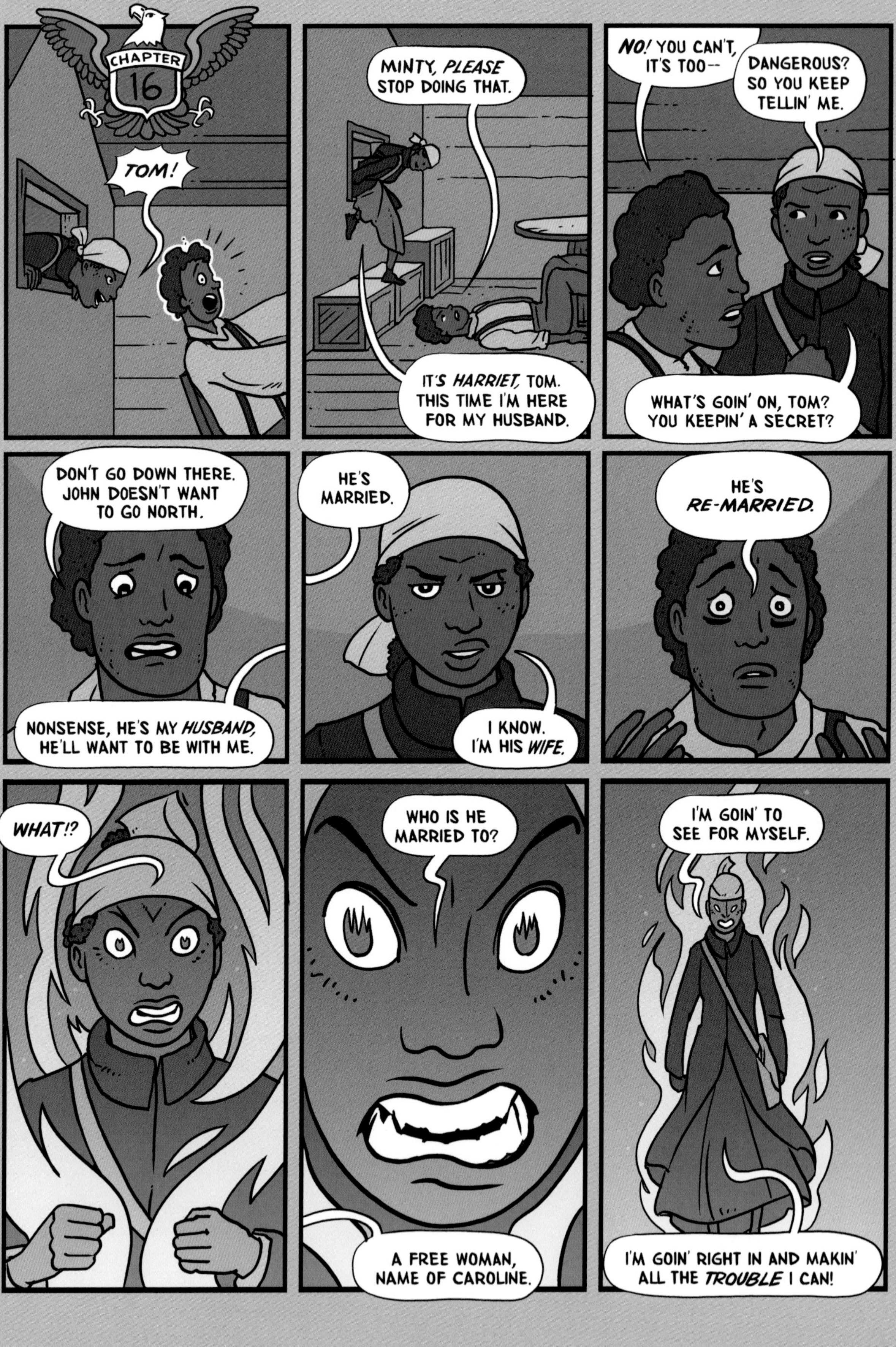
CHAPTER 16
TOM!
MINTY, PLEASE STOP DOING THAT.
IT'S HARRIET, TOM. THIS TIME I'M HERE FOR MY HUSBAND.
NO! YOU CAN'T, IT'S TOO--
DANGEROUS? SO YOU KEEP TELLIN' ME.
WHAT'S GOIN' ON, TOM? YOU KEEPIN' A SECRET?
DON'T GO DOWN THERE. JOHN DOESN'T WANT TO GO NORTH.
NONSENSE, HE'S MY HUSBAND, HE'LL WANT TO BE WITH ME.
HE'S MARRIED.
I KNOW. I'M HIS WIFE.
HE'S RE-MARRIED.
WHAT!?
WHO IS HE MARRIED TO?
A FREE WOMAN, NAME OF CAROLINE.
I'M GOIN' TO SEE FOR MYSELF.
I'M GOIN' RIGHT IN AND MAKIN' ALL THE TROUBLE I CAN!

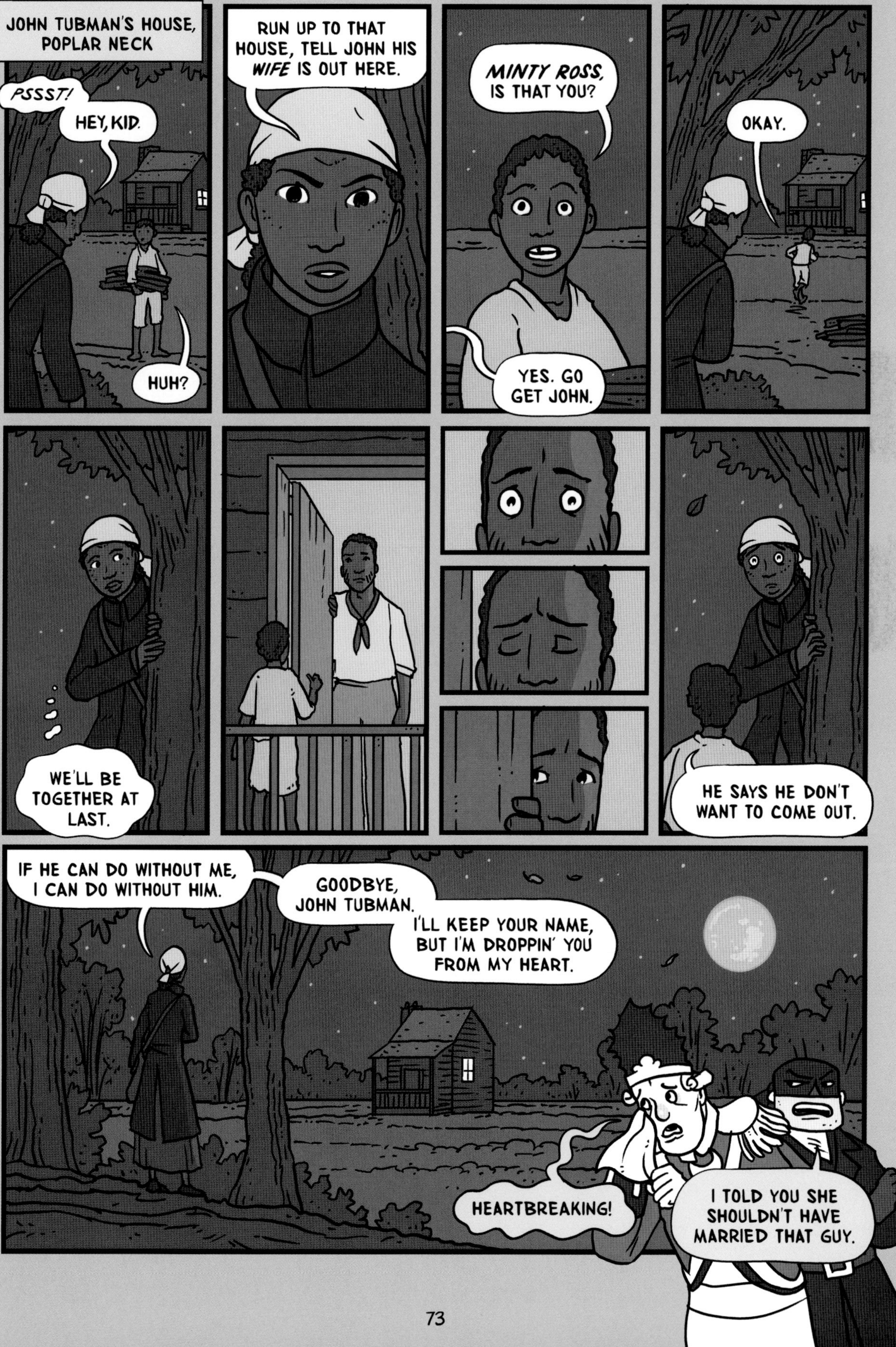
JOHN TUBMAN'S HOUSE, POPLAR NECK
PSSST!
HEY, KID.
HUH?
RUN UP TO THAT HOUSE, TELL JOHN HIS *WIFE* IS OUT HERE.
MINTY ROSS, IS THAT YOU?
YES. GO GET JOHN.
OKAY.
WE'LL BE TOGETHER AT LAST.
HE SAYS HE DON'T WANT TO COME OUT.
IF HE CAN DO WITHOUT ME, I CAN DO WITHOUT HIM.
GOODBYE, JOHN TUBMAN.
I'LL KEEP YOUR NAME, BUT I'M DROPPIN' YOU FROM MY HEART.
HEARTBREAKING!
I TOLD YOU SHE SHOULDN'T HAVE MARRIED THAT GUY.

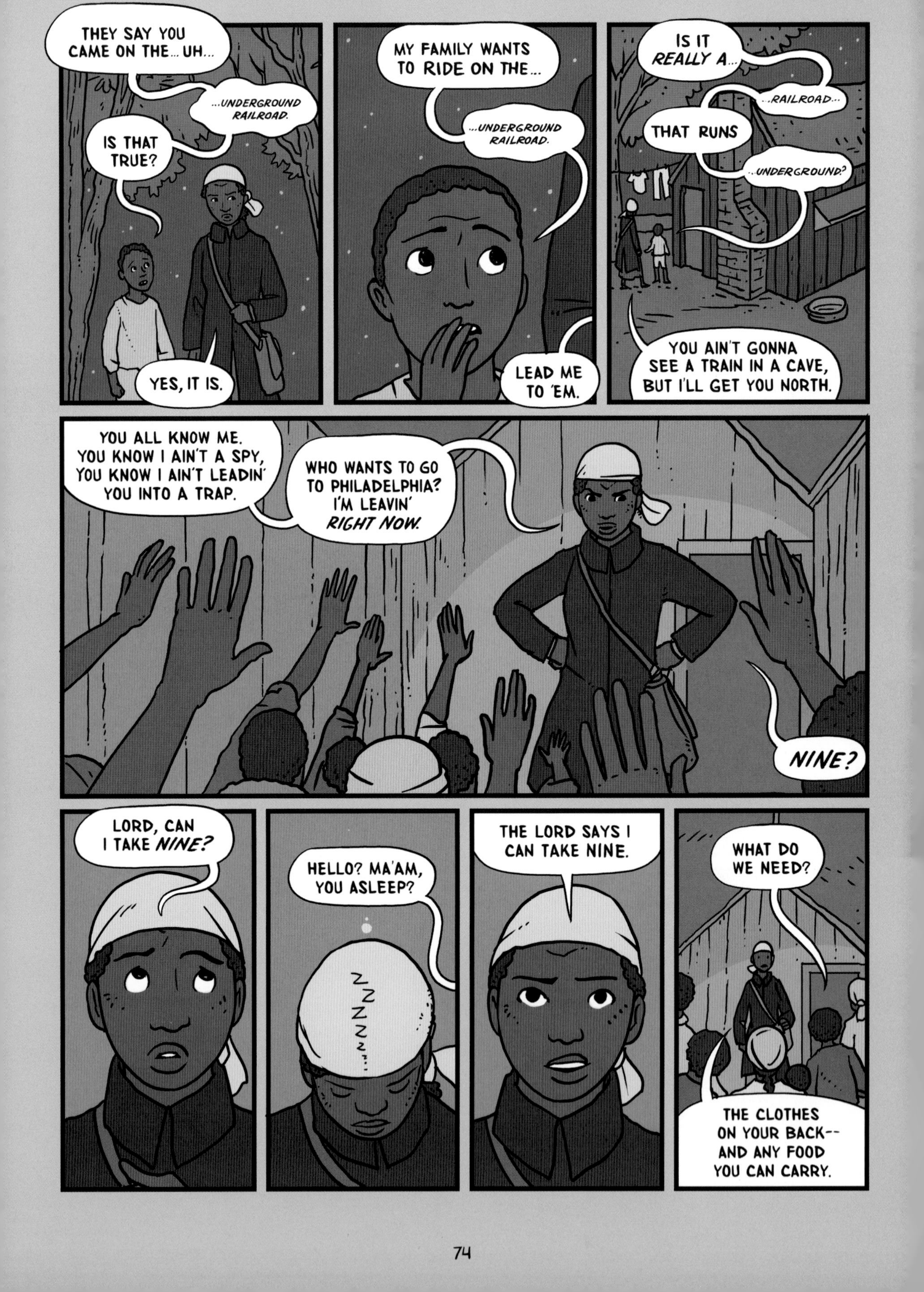
THEY SAY YOU CAME ON THE... UH...
...UNDERGROUND RAILROAD.
IS THAT TRUE?
YES, IT IS.
MY FAMILY WANTS TO RIDE ON THE...
...UNDERGROUND RAILROAD.
LEAD ME TO 'EM.
IS IT REALLY A...
...RAILROAD...
THAT RUNS
...UNDERGROUND?
YOU AIN'T GONNA SEE A TRAIN IN A CAVE, BUT I'LL GET YOU NORTH.
YOU ALL KNOW ME. YOU KNOW I AIN'T A SPY, YOU KNOW I AIN'T LEADIN' YOU INTO A TRAP.
WHO WANTS TO GO TO PHILADELPHIA? I'M LEAVIN' RIGHT NOW.
NINE?
LORD, CAN I TAKE NINE?
HELLO? MA'AM, YOU ASLEEP?
ZZZZZ...
THE LORD SAYS I CAN TAKE NINE.
WHAT DO WE NEED?
THE CLOTHES ON YOUR BACK-- AND ANY FOOD YOU CAN CARRY.

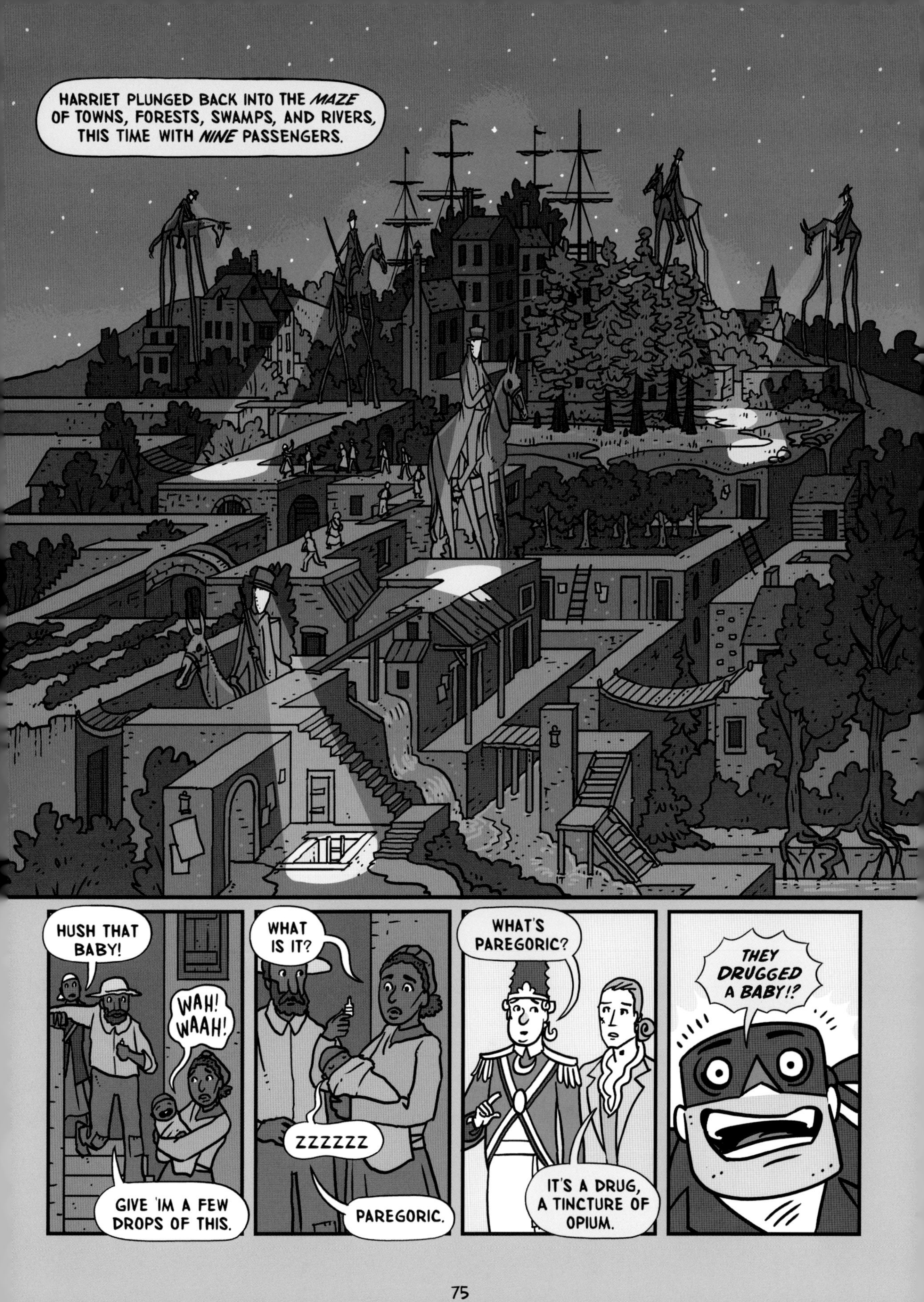
HARRIET PLUNGED BACK INTO THE *MAZE* OF TOWNS, FORESTS, SWAMPS, AND RIVERS, THIS TIME WITH *NINE* PASSENGERS.
HUSH THAT BABY!
WAH! WAAH!
GIVE 'IM A FEW DROPS OF THIS.
WHAT IS IT?
ZZZZZZ
PAREGORIC.
WHAT'S PAREGORIC?
IT'S A DRUG, A TINCTURE OF OPIUM.
THEY DRUGGED A BABY!?

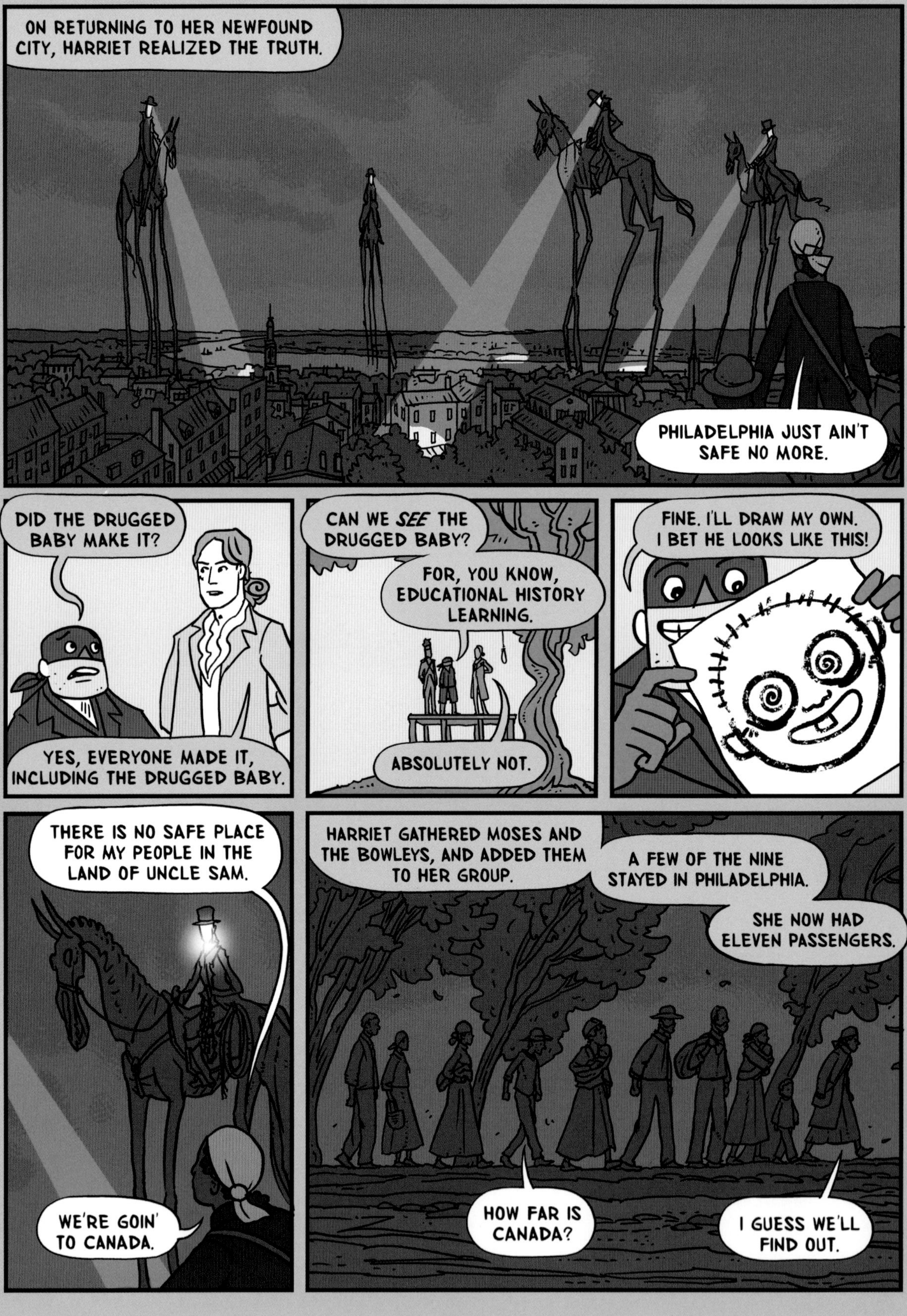
ON RETURNING TO HER NEWFOUND CITY, HARRIET REALIZED THE TRUTH.
PHILADELPHIA JUST AIN'T SAFE NO MORE.
DID THE DRUGGED BABY MAKE IT?
YES, EVERYONE MADE IT, INCLUDING THE DRUGGED BABY.
CAN WE *SEE* THE DRUGGED BABY?
FOR, YOU KNOW, EDUCATIONAL HISTORY LEARNING.
ABSOLUTELY NOT.
FINE. I'LL DRAW MY OWN. I BET HE LOOKS LIKE THIS!
THERE IS NO SAFE PLACE FOR MY PEOPLE IN THE LAND OF UNCLE SAM.
WE'RE GOIN' TO CANADA.
HARRIET GATHERED MOSES AND THE BOWLEYS, AND ADDED THEM TO HER GROUP.
A FEW OF THE NINE STAYED IN PHILADELPHIA.
SHE NOW HAD ELEVEN PASSENGERS.
HOW FAR IS CANADA?
I GUESS WE'LL FIND OUT.

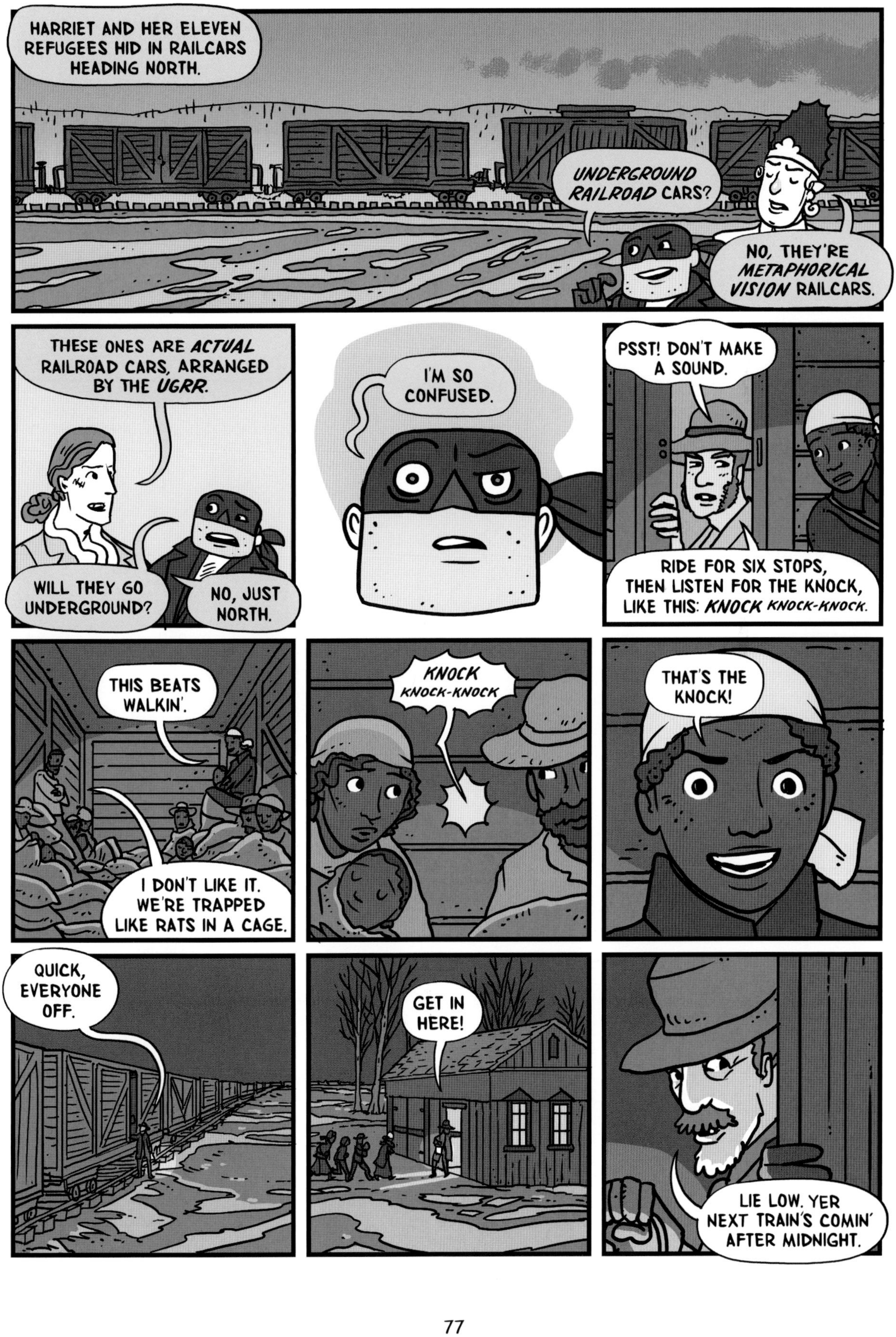
HARRIET AND HER ELEVEN REFUGEES HID IN RAILCARS HEADING NORTH.
UNDERGROUND RAILROAD CARS?
NO, THEY'RE METAPHORICAL VISION RAILCARS.
THESE ONES ARE ACTUAL RAILROAD CARS, ARRANGED BY THE UGRR.
WILL THEY GO UNDERGROUND?
NO, JUST NORTH.
I'M SO CONFUSED.
PSST! DON'T MAKE A SOUND.
RIDE FOR SIX STOPS, THEN LISTEN FOR THE KNOCK, LIKE THIS: KNOCK KNOCK-KNOCK.
THIS BEATS WALKIN'.
I DON'T LIKE IT. WE'RE TRAPPED LIKE RATS IN A CAGE.
KNOCK KNOCK-KNOCK
THAT'S THE KNOCK!
QUICK, EVERYONE OFF.
GET IN HERE!
LIE LOW. YER NEXT TRAIN'S COMIN' AFTER MIDNIGHT.

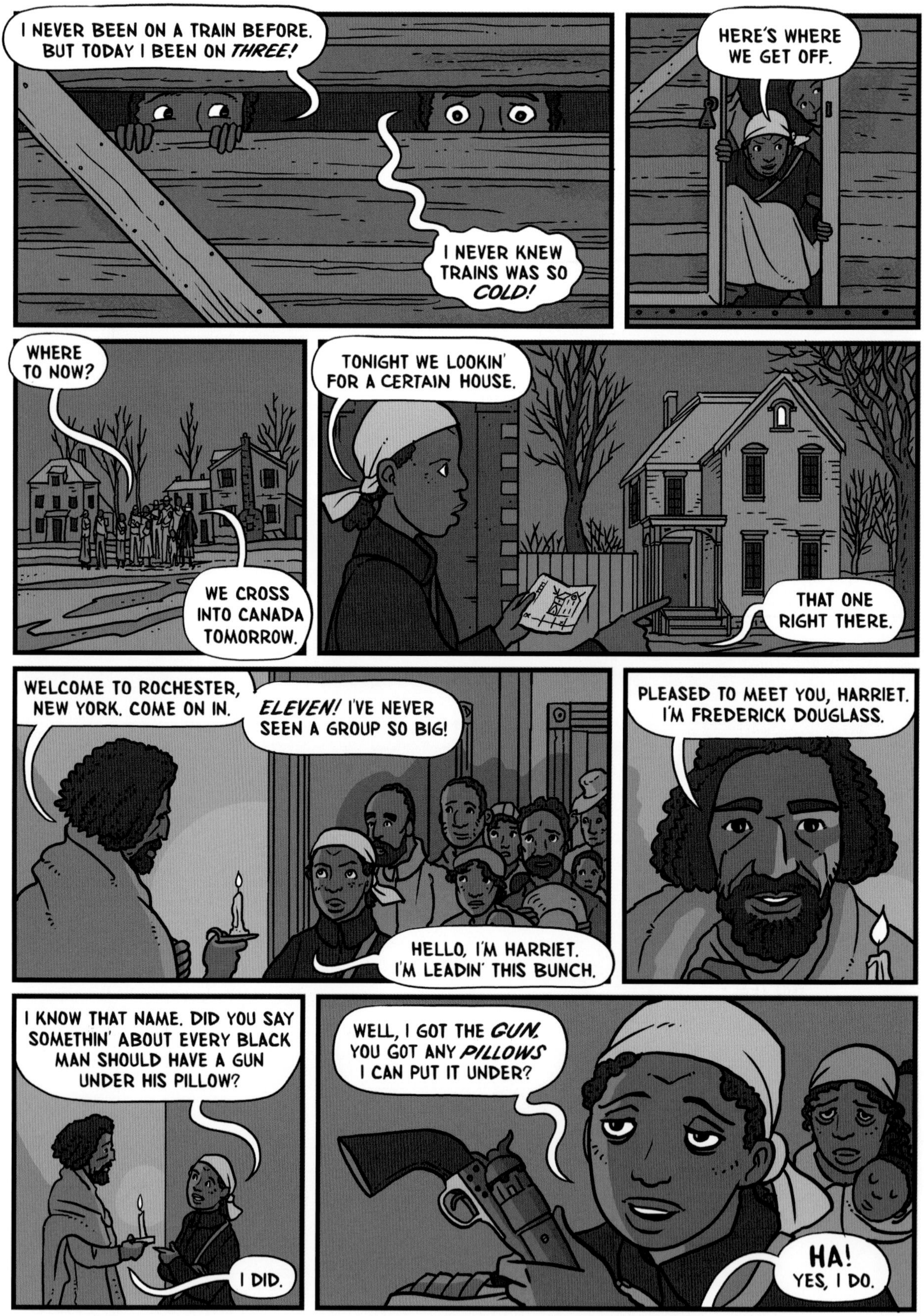
I NEVER BEEN ON A TRAIN BEFORE. BUT TODAY I BEEN ON *THREE!*
I NEVER KNEW TRAINS WAS SO *COLD!*
HERE'S WHERE WE GET OFF.
WHERE TO NOW?
WE CROSS INTO CANADA TOMORROW.
TONIGHT WE LOOKIN' FOR A CERTAIN HOUSE.
THAT ONE RIGHT THERE.
WELCOME TO ROCHESTER, NEW YORK. COME ON IN.
ELEVEN! I'VE NEVER SEEN A GROUP SO BIG!
HELLO, I'M HARRIET. I'M LEADIN' THIS BUNCH.
PLEASED TO MEET YOU, HARRIET. I'M FREDERICK DOUGLASS.
I KNOW THAT NAME. DID YOU SAY SOMETHIN' ABOUT EVERY BLACK MAN SHOULD HAVE A GUN UNDER HIS PILLOW?
I DID.
WELL, I GOT THE *GUN.* YOU GOT ANY *PILLOWS* I CAN PUT IT UNDER?
HA! YES, I DO.

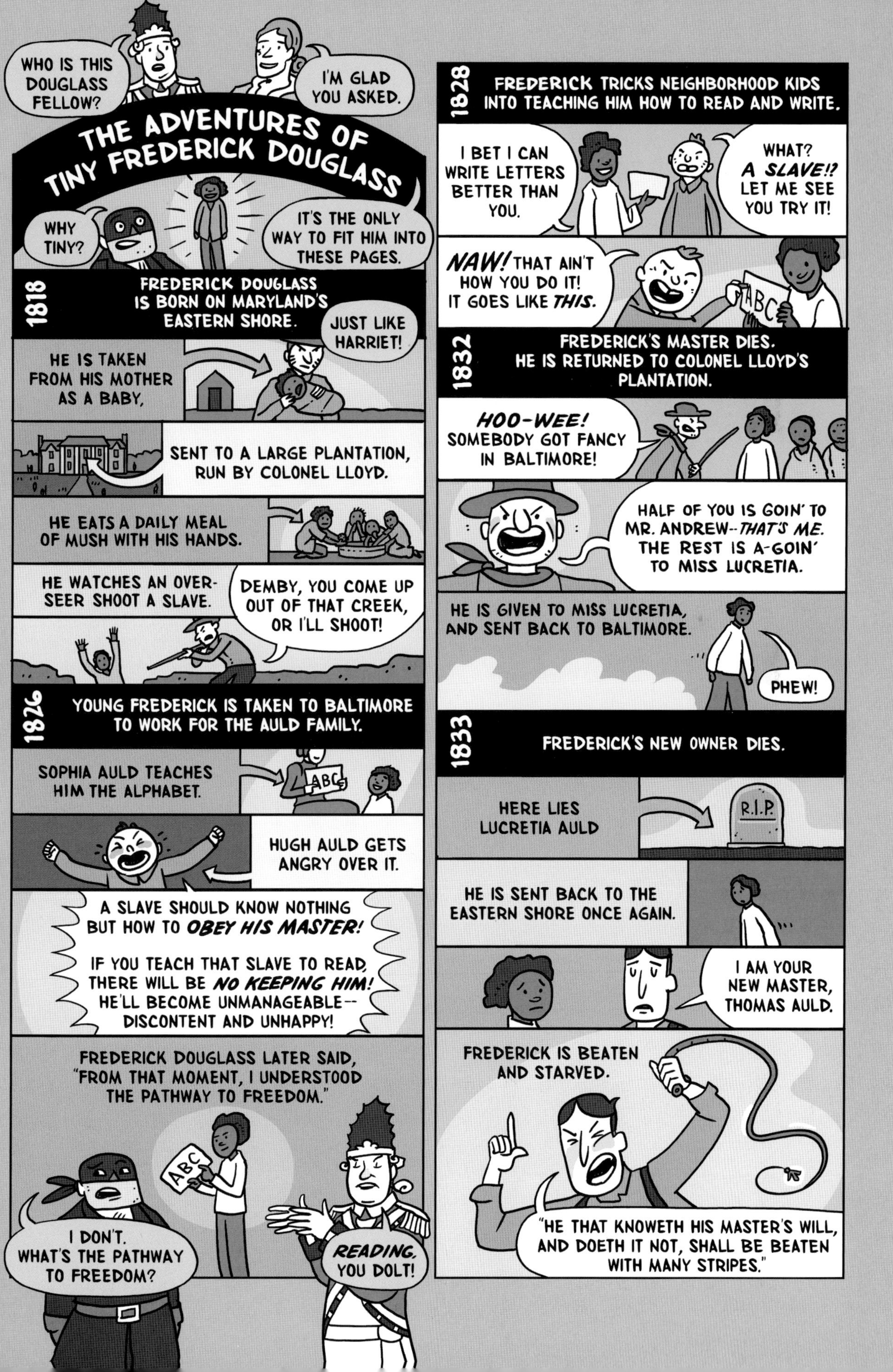

WHO IS THIS DOUGLASS FELLOW?
I'M GLAD YOU ASKED.
THE ADVENTURES OF TINY FREDERICK DOUGLASS
WHY TINY?
IT'S THE ONLY WAY TO FIT HIM INTO THESE PAGES.
1818
FREDERICK DOUGLASS IS BORN ON MARYLAND'S EASTERN SHORE.
JUST LIKE HARRIET!
HE IS TAKEN FROM HIS MOTHER AS A BABY,
SENT TO A LARGE PLANTATION, RUN BY COLONEL LLOYD.
HE EATS A DAILY MEAL OF MUSH WITH HIS HANDS.
HE WATCHES AN OVER-SEER SHOOT A SLAVE.
DEMBY, YOU COME UP OUT OF THAT CREEK, OR I'LL SHOOT!
1826
YOUNG FREDERICK IS TAKEN TO BALTIMORE TO WORK FOR THE AULD FAMILY.
SOPHIA AULD TEACHES HIM THE ALPHABET.
ABC
HUGH AULD GETS ANGRY OVER IT.
A SLAVE SHOULD KNOW NOTHING BUT HOW TO OBEY HIS MASTER!
IF YOU TEACH THAT SLAVE TO READ, THERE WILL BE NO KEEPING HIM! HE'LL BECOME UNMANAGEABLE-- DISCONTENT AND UNHAPPY!
FREDERICK DOUGLASS LATER SAID, "FROM THAT MOMENT, I UNDERSTOOD THE PATHWAY TO FREEDOM."
ABC
I DON'T. WHAT'S THE PATHWAY TO FREEDOM?
READING, YOU DOLT!
1828
FREDERICK TRICKS NEIGHBORHOOD KIDS INTO TEACHING HIM HOW TO READ AND WRITE.
I BET I CAN WRITE LETTERS BETTER THAN YOU.
WHAT? A SLAVE!? LET ME SEE YOU TRY IT!
NAW! THAT AIN'T HOW YOU DO IT! IT GOES LIKE THIS.
ABC
1832
FREDERICK'S MASTER DIES. HE IS RETURNED TO COLONEL LLOYD'S PLANTATION.
HOO-WEE! SOMEBODY GOT FANCY IN BALTIMORE!
HALF OF YOU IS GOIN' TO MR. ANDREW--THAT'S ME. THE REST IS A-GOIN' TO MISS LUCRETIA.
HE IS GIVEN TO MISS LUCRETIA, AND SENT BACK TO BALTIMORE.
PHEW!
1833
FREDERICK'S NEW OWNER DIES.
HERE LIES LUCRETIA AULD
R.I.P.
HE IS SENT BACK TO THE EASTERN SHORE ONCE AGAIN.
I AM YOUR NEW MASTER, THOMAS AULD.
FREDERICK IS BEATEN AND STARVED.
"HE THAT KNOWETH HIS MASTER'S WILL, AND DOETH IT NOT, SHALL BE BEATEN WITH MANY STRIPES."

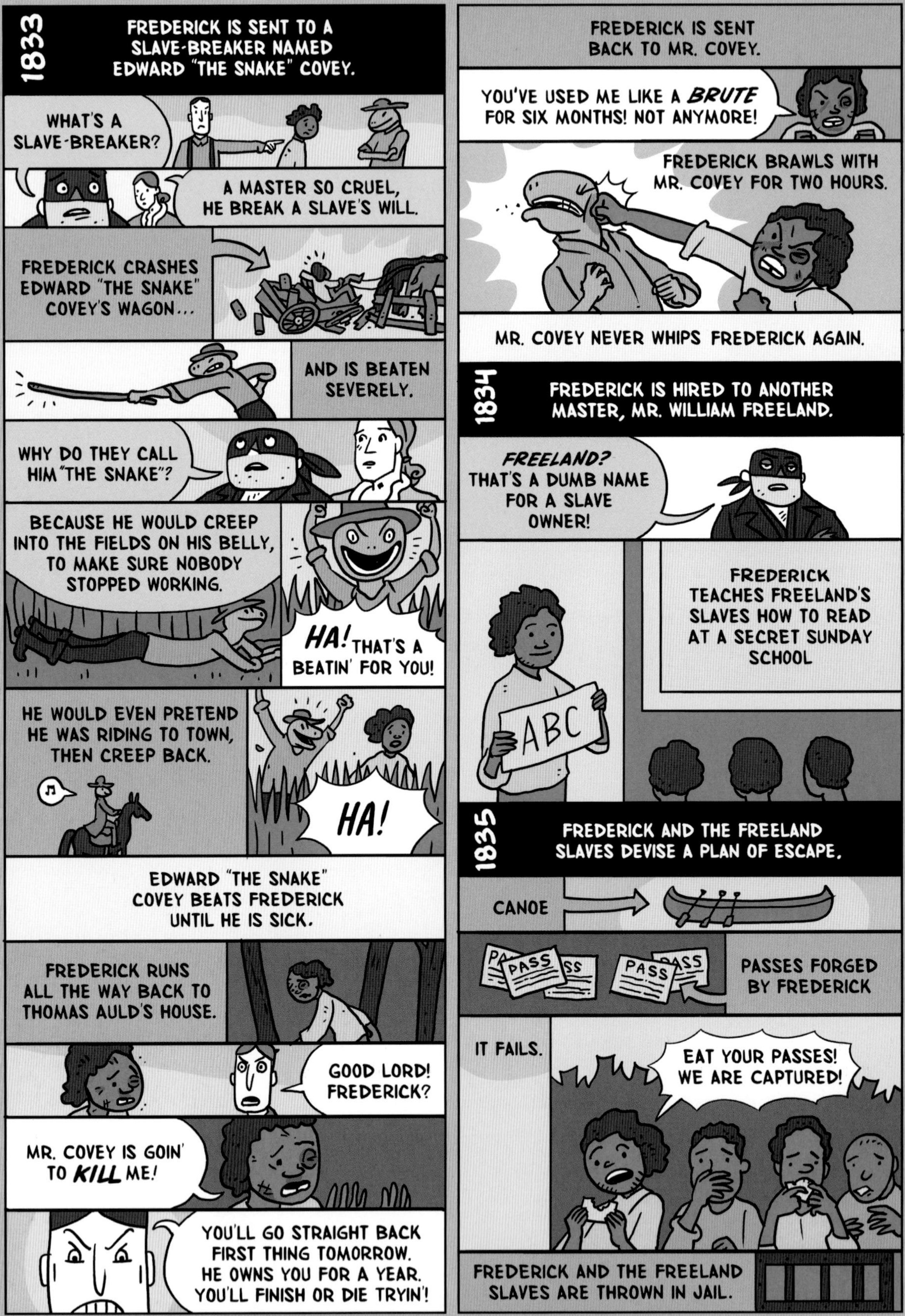
1833
FREDERICK IS SENT TO A SLAVE-BREAKER NAMED EDWARD "THE SNAKE" COVEY.
WHAT'S A SLAVE-BREAKER?
A MASTER SO CRUEL, HE BREAK A SLAVE'S WILL.
FREDERICK CRASHES EDWARD "THE SNAKE" COVEY'S WAGON...
AND IS BEATEN SEVERELY.
WHY DO THEY CALL HIM "THE SNAKE"?
BECAUSE HE WOULD CREEP INTO THE FIELDS ON HIS BELLY, TO MAKE SURE NOBODY STOPPED WORKING.
HA! THAT'S A BEATIN' FOR YOU!
HE WOULD EVEN PRETEND HE WAS RIDING TO TOWN, THEN CREEP BACK.
♫
HA!
EDWARD "THE SNAKE" COVEY BEATS FREDERICK UNTIL HE IS SICK.
FREDERICK RUNS ALL THE WAY BACK TO THOMAS AULD'S HOUSE.
GOOD LORD! FREDERICK?
MR. COVEY IS GOIN' TO KILL ME!
YOU'LL GO STRAIGHT BACK FIRST THING TOMORROW. HE OWNS YOU FOR A YEAR. YOU'LL FINISH OR DIE TRYIN'!
FREDERICK IS SENT BACK TO MR. COVEY.
YOU'VE USED ME LIKE A BRUTE FOR SIX MONTHS! NOT ANYMORE!
FREDERICK BRAWLS WITH MR. COVEY FOR TWO HOURS.
MR. COVEY NEVER WHIPS FREDERICK AGAIN.
1834
FREDERICK IS HIRED TO ANOTHER MASTER, MR. WILLIAM FREELAND.
FREELAND? THAT'S A DUMB NAME FOR A SLAVE OWNER!
FREDERICK TEACHES FREELAND'S SLAVES HOW TO READ AT A SECRET SUNDAY SCHOOL
ABC
1835
FREDERICK AND THE FREELAND SLAVES DEVISE A PLAN OF ESCAPE.
CANOE
PASS
PASS
PASSES FORGED BY FREDERICK
IT FAILS.
EAT YOUR PASSES! WE ARE CAPTURED!
FREDERICK AND THE FREELAND SLAVES ARE THROWN IN JAIL.

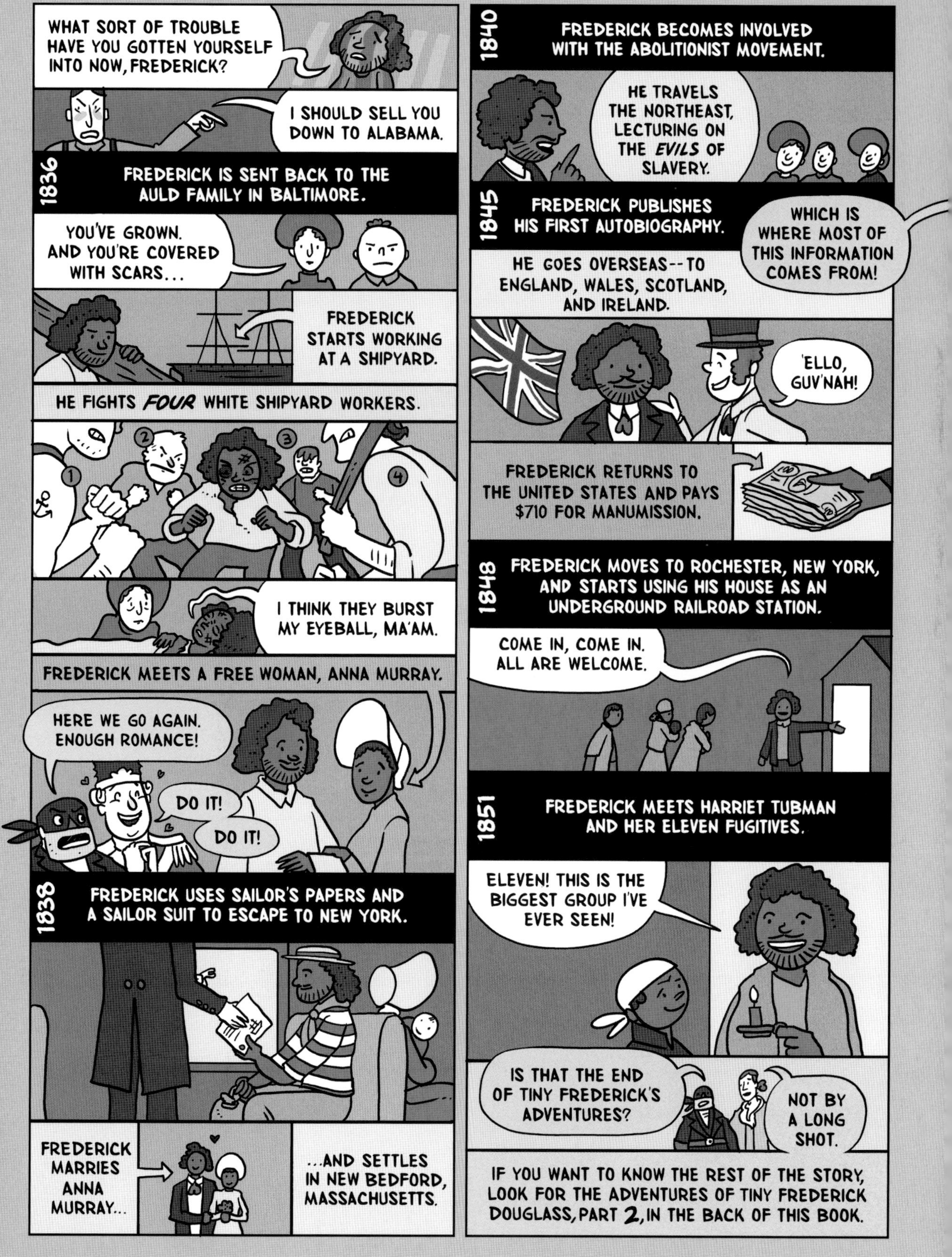
WHAT SORT OF TROUBLE HAVE YOU GOTTEN YOURSELF INTO NOW, FREDERICK?
I SHOULD SELL YOU DOWN TO ALABAMA.
1836
FREDERICK IS SENT BACK TO THE AULD FAMILY IN BALTIMORE.
YOU'VE GROWN. AND YOU'RE COVERED WITH SCARS...
FREDERICK STARTS WORKING AT A SHIPYARD.
HE FIGHTS *FOUR* WHITE SHIPYARD WORKERS.
1
2
3
4
I THINK THEY BURST MY EYEBALL, MA'AM.
FREDERICK MEETS A FREE WOMAN, ANNA MURRAY.
HERE WE GO AGAIN. ENOUGH ROMANCE!
DO IT!
DO IT!
1838
FREDERICK USES SAILOR'S PAPERS AND A SAILOR SUIT TO ESCAPE TO NEW YORK.
FREDERICK MARRIES ANNA MURRAY...
...AND SETTLES IN NEW BEDFORD, MASSACHUSETTS.
1840
FREDERICK BECOMES INVOLVED WITH THE ABOLITIONIST MOVEMENT.
HE TRAVELS THE NORTHEAST, LECTURING ON THE *EVILS* OF SLAVERY.
1845
FREDERICK PUBLISHES HIS FIRST AUTOBIOGRAPHY.
WHICH IS WHERE MOST OF THIS INFORMATION COMES FROM!
HE GOES OVERSEAS--TO ENGLAND, WALES, SCOTLAND, AND IRELAND.
'ELLO, GUV'NAH!
FREDERICK RETURNS TO THE UNITED STATES AND PAYS $710 FOR MANUMISSION.
1848
FREDERICK MOVES TO ROCHESTER, NEW YORK, AND STARTS USING HIS HOUSE AS AN UNDERGROUND RAILROAD STATION.
COME IN, COME IN. ALL ARE WELCOME.
1851
FREDERICK MEETS HARRIET TUBMAN AND HER ELEVEN FUGITIVES.
ELEVEN! THIS IS THE BIGGEST GROUP I'VE EVER SEEN!
IS THAT THE END OF TINY FREDERICK'S ADVENTURES?
NOT BY A LONG SHOT.
IF YOU WANT TO KNOW THE REST OF THE STORY, LOOK FOR THE ADVENTURES OF TINY FREDERICK DOUGLASS, PART 2, IN THE BACK OF THIS BOOK.

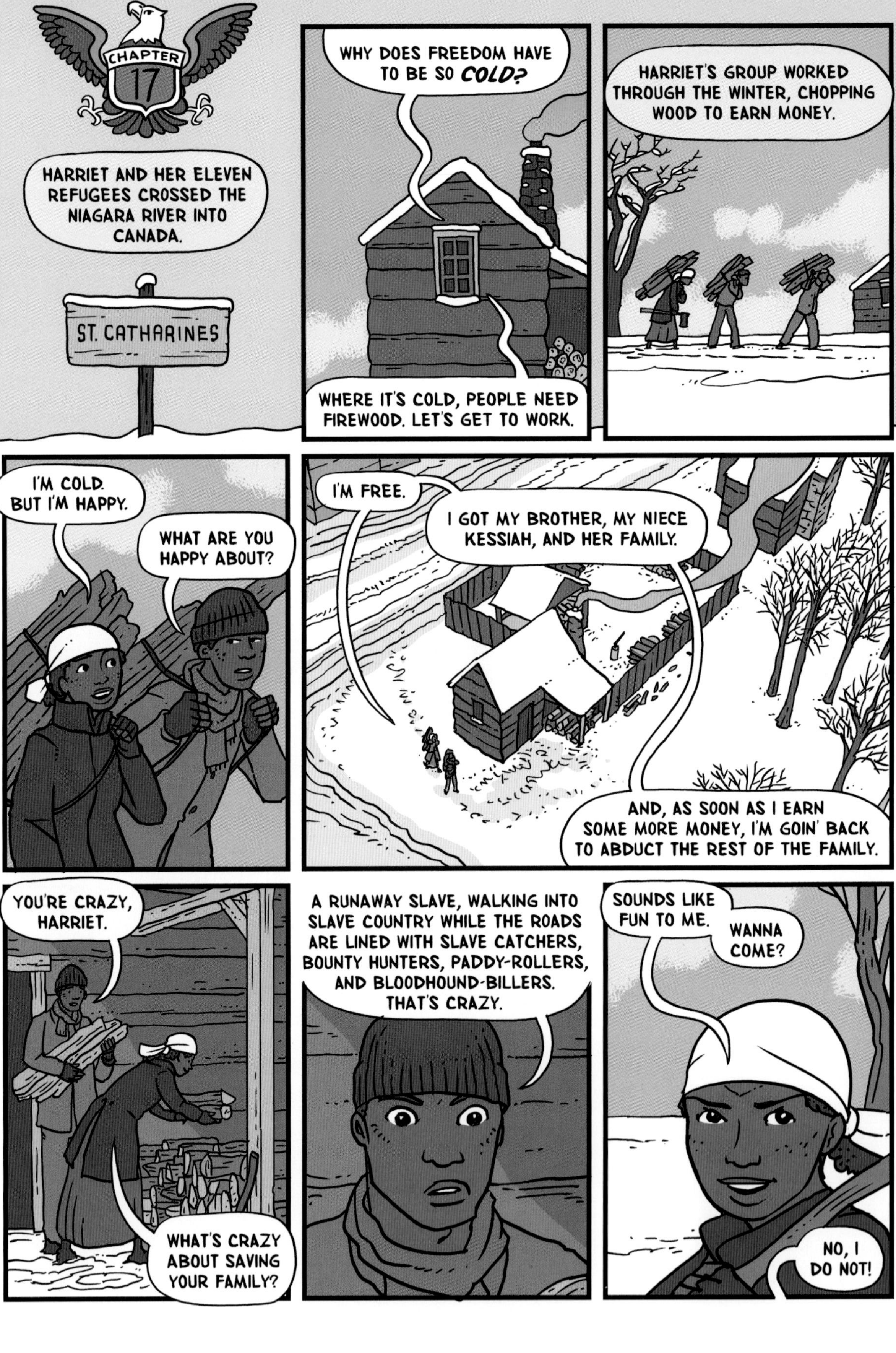
CHAPTER
17
HARRIET AND HER ELEVEN REFUGEES CROSSED THE NIAGARA RIVER INTO CANADA.
ST. CATHARINES
WHY DOES FREEDOM HAVE TO BE SO COLD?
WHERE IT'S COLD, PEOPLE NEED FIREWOOD. LET'S GET TO WORK.
HARRIET'S GROUP WORKED THROUGH THE WINTER, CHOPPING WOOD TO EARN MONEY.
I'M COLD. BUT I'M HAPPY.
WHAT ARE YOU HAPPY ABOUT?
I'M FREE.
I GOT MY BROTHER, MY NIECE KESSIAH, AND HER FAMILY.
AND, AS SOON AS I EARN SOME MORE MONEY, I'M GOIN' BACK TO ABDUCT THE REST OF THE FAMILY.
YOU'RE CRAZY, HARRIET.
WHAT'S CRAZY ABOUT SAVING YOUR FAMILY?
A RUNAWAY SLAVE, WALKING INTO SLAVE COUNTRY WHILE THE ROADS ARE LINED WITH SLAVE CATCHERS, BOUNTY HUNTERS, PADDY-ROLLERS, AND BLOODHOUND-BILLERS. THAT'S CRAZY.
SOUNDS LIKE FUN TO ME.
WANNA COME?
NO, I DO NOT!

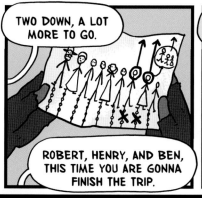

TWO DOWN, A LOT MORE TO GO.

ROBERT, HENRY, AND BEN, THIS TIME YOU ARE GONNA FINISH THE TRIP.

WEREN'T THEY ABOUT TO BE SOLD WHEN THEY FIRST TRIED TO ESCAPE?

SURELY THEY'VE ALL BEEN SOLD BY NOW.

DO YOU REMEMBER WHEN HARRIET WENT TO SEE THAT LAWYER?

YEAH, THAT WAS THE MOST *BORING* PART IN THIS BOOK.

WELL, THE INFORMATION HARRIET'S LAWYER UNCOVERED STARTED A *FEUD* BETWEEN THE BRODESSES AND THE PATTISONS, THE FORMER OWNERS OF HARRIET'S MOTHER.

THE WILL STATES MR. BRODESS ONLY HAD OWNERSHIP *UNTIL* RIT REACHED AGE FORTY-FIVE. *AFTER* THAT, RIGHTS REVERT TO US!

THAT'S *ABSURD!*

WE SHOULD *OWN* RIT AND *ANY* OF HER CHILDREN OVER FORTY-FIVE!

WHAT!?

IF YOU CAN'T DELIVER THE SLAVES, YOU MUST PAY THE *WAGES* THEIR LABOR *WOULD* HAVE EARNED US!

WE WILL DO NO SUCH THING!

GOURNEY PATTISON (EDWARD BRODESS'S UNCLE)

ELIZA BRODESS (EDWARD BRODESS'S WIDOW)

THINGS GOT EVEN MORE CONFUSING WHEN THE DORCHESTER COUNTY COURTHOUSE *BURNED DOWN*...

...WITH ALL OF THE COURT RECORDS INSIDE.

I BET MRS. BRODESS BURNED IT DOWN.

THE LEGAL BATTLE BETWEEN THE TWO FAMILIES *FROZE* THE SALE OF ANY SLAVES IN HARRIET'S FAMILY.

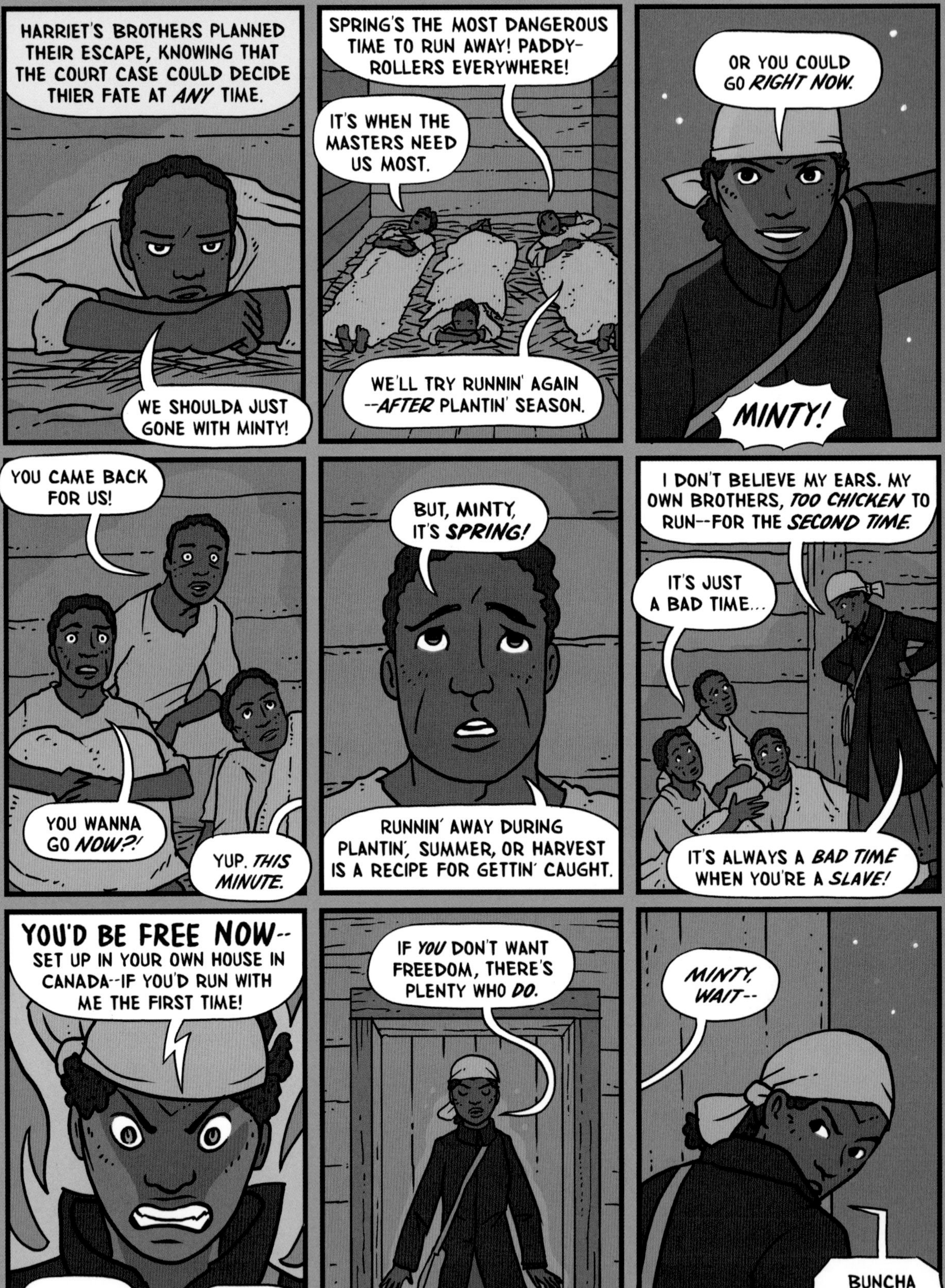
HARRIET'S BROTHERS PLANNED THEIR ESCAPE, KNOWING THAT THE COURT CASE COULD DECIDE THIER FATE AT ANY TIME.
WE SHOULDA JUST GONE WITH MINTY!
SPRING'S THE MOST DANGEROUS TIME TO RUN AWAY! PADDY-ROLLERS EVERYWHERE!
IT'S WHEN THE MASTERS NEED US MOST.
WE'LL TRY RUNNIN' AGAIN --AFTER PLANTIN' SEASON.
OR YOU COULD GO RIGHT NOW.
MINTY!
YOU CAME BACK FOR US!
YOU WANNA GO NOW?!
YUP. THIS MINUTE.
BUT, MINTY, IT'S SPRING!
RUNNIN' AWAY DURING PLANTIN', SUMMER, OR HARVEST IS A RECIPE FOR GETTIN' CAUGHT.
I DON'T BELIEVE MY EARS. MY OWN BROTHERS, TOO CHICKEN TO RUN--FOR THE SECOND TIME.
IT'S JUST A BAD TIME...
IT'S ALWAYS A BAD TIME WHEN YOU'RE A SLAVE!
YOU'D BE FREE NOW-- SET UP IN YOUR OWN HOUSE IN CANADA--IF YOU'D RUN WITH ME THE FIRST TIME!
NEXT TIME.
NEXT TIME FOR SURE.
IF YOU DON'T WANT FREEDOM, THERE'S PLENTY WHO DO.
MINTY, WAIT--
BUNCHA SPRING CHICKENS!

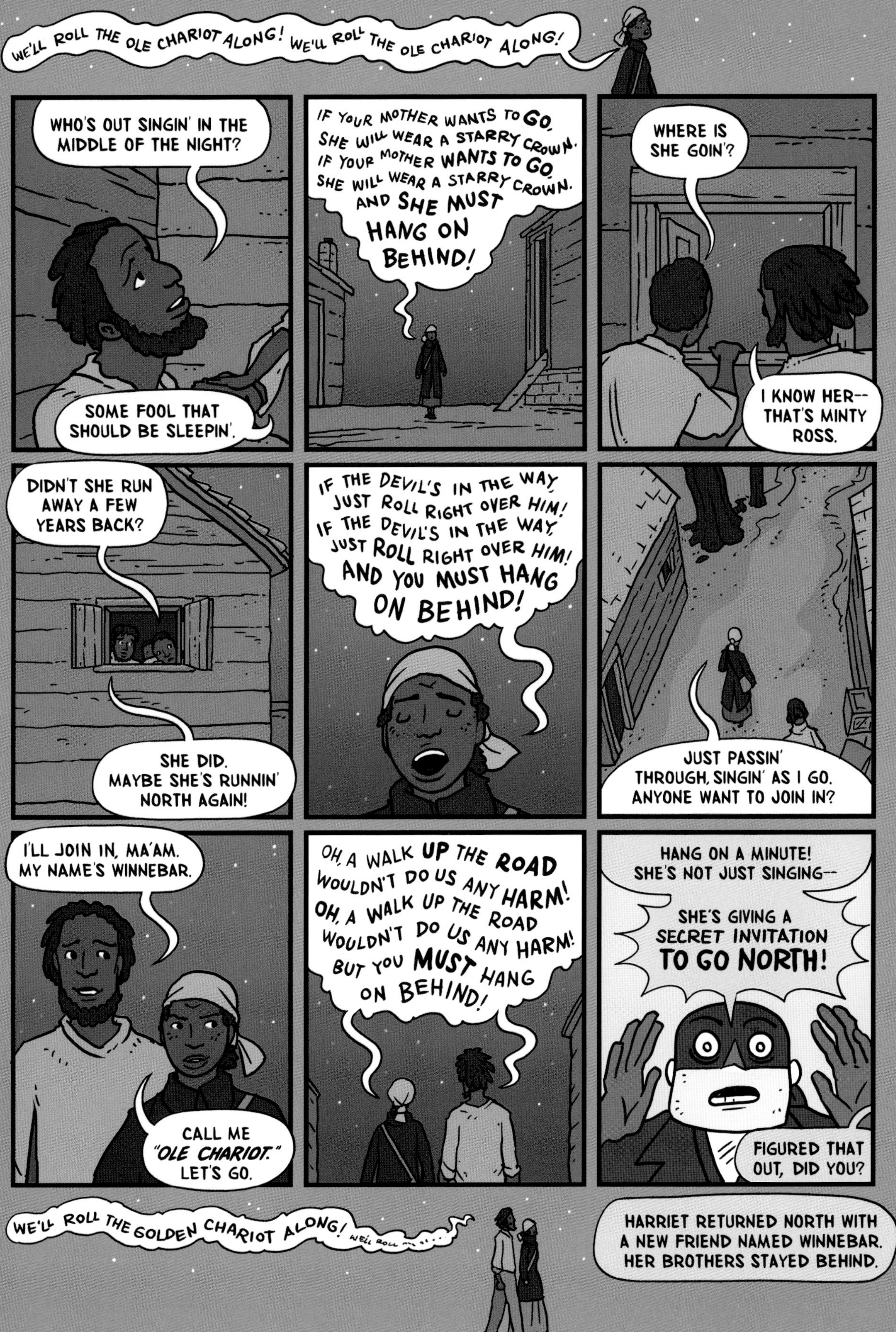
WE'LL ROLL THE OLE CHARIOT ALONG! WE'LL ROLL THE OLE CHARIOT ALONG!
WHO'S OUT SINGIN' IN THE MIDDLE OF THE NIGHT?
SOME FOOL THAT SHOULD BE SLEEPIN'.
IF YOUR MOTHER WANTS TO GO, SHE WILL WEAR A STARRY CROWN. IF YOUR MOTHER WANTS TO GO, SHE WILL WEAR A STARRY CROWN. AND SHE MUST HANG ON BEHIND!
WHERE IS SHE GOIN'?
I KNOW HER-- THAT'S MINTY ROSS.
DIDN'T SHE RUN AWAY A FEW YEARS BACK?
SHE DID. MAYBE SHE'S RUNNIN' NORTH AGAIN!
IF THE DEVIL'S IN THE WAY, JUST ROLL RIGHT OVER HIM! IF THE DEVIL'S IN THE WAY, JUST ROLL RIGHT OVER HIM! AND YOU MUST HANG ON BEHIND!
JUST PASSIN' THROUGH, SINGIN' AS I GO. ANYONE WANT TO JOIN IN?
I'LL JOIN IN, MA'AM. MY NAME'S WINNEBAR.
CALL ME "OLE CHARIOT." LET'S GO.
OH, A WALK UP THE ROAD WOULDN'T DO US ANY HARM! OH, A WALK UP THE ROAD WOULDN'T DO US ANY HARM! BUT YOU MUST HANG ON BEHIND!
HANG ON A MINUTE! SHE'S NOT JUST SINGING--
SHE'S GIVING A SECRET INVITATION TO GO NORTH!
FIGURED THAT OUT, DID YOU?
WE'LL ROLL THE GOLDEN CHARIOT ALONG! WE'LL ROLL...
HARRIET RETURNED NORTH WITH A NEW FRIEND NAMED WINNEBAR. HER BROTHERS STAYED BEHIND.

FORGIVE ME IF THIS SOUNDS *RUDE*--

THAT MEANS HE'S ABOUT TO SAY SOMETHING RUDE.

BUT, THIS JOURNEY ALONG THE UNDERGROUND RAILROAD SEEMS, WELL...

EASY.

HARRIET JUST MAKES IT *LOOK* EASY.

ASIDE FROM THE SLAVE-HUNTERS AND PADDY-ROLLERS, THERE WERE CONSTANT DANGERS.

FUGITIVES DROWNED,

DIED OF FEVER,

FROZE TO DEATH,

LOST LIMBS TO FROSTBITE,

SUFFERED GANGRENOUS INFECTIONS, AND MORE.

ESCAPEES HOPPING TRAINS LOST LIMBS IF THEY JUMPED WRONG.

STOWAWAYS ON NORTH-BOUND SHIPS WERE SMOKED OUT OR SUFFOCATED LIKE RATS.

THOSE WHO WERE CAPTURED WEREN'T JUST RETURNED TO THIER OWNERS.

THEY WERE WHIPPED, BEATEN,

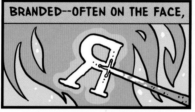

BRANDED--OFTEN ON THE FACE,

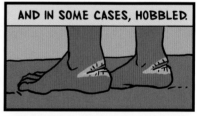

AND IN SOME CASES, HOBBLED.

UGRR AGENTS WHO WEREN'T AS LUCKY AS HARRIET:

ABDUCTOR CHARLES TORREY WAS CAUGHT HELPING A RUN-AWAY FAMILY IN VIRGINIA.

HE WAS SENTENCED TO FIVE YEARS OF HARD LABOR.

HE DIED AFTER TWO.

THOMAS GARRET, A UGRR STATIONMASTER WAS BEATEN AND THROWN FROM A TRAIN WHILE TRYING TO RESCUE AN ENSLAVED PERSON.

HE WAS THEN FINED $5,000.

ABDUCTOR CALVIN FAIRBANK WAS ARRESTED FOR AIDING SLAVES TWICE. HE SERVED SEVENTEEN YEARS IN PRISON--DURING WHICH, HE CLAIMED TO HAVE RECIEVED 35,000 LASHES.

THAT'S A LOT OF LASHES.

AND KEEP IN MIND, THESE ABDUCTORS WERE *WHITE MEN*, FREE, AND ABLE TO TRAVEL OPENLY ON HORSE-BACK, IN WAGONS, TRAINS, AND CARRIAGES. THEY COULD ALSO READ, WRITE, AND PROVIDE PAPERS.

HARRIET HAD NONE OF THESE ADVANTAGES. SHE WAS ILLITERATE, HAD A DEBILITATING INJURY, AND WAS HERSELF A RUNAWAY. THAT SHE TRAVELED WITHOUT CAPTURE OR LOSS IS *ASTOUNDING!*

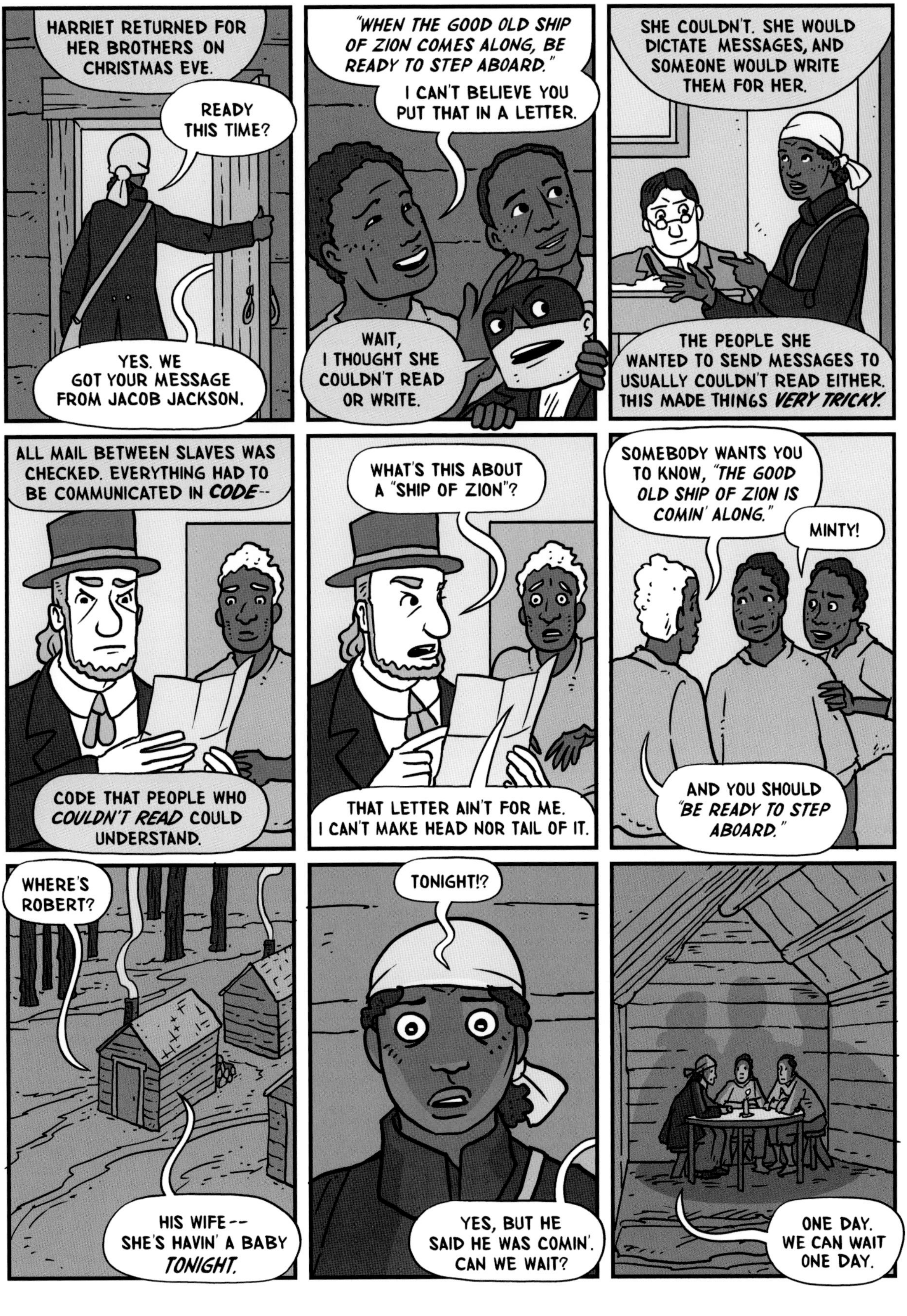
HARRIET RETURNED FOR HER BROTHERS ON CHRISTMAS EVE.
READY THIS TIME?
YES. WE GOT YOUR MESSAGE FROM JACOB JACKSON.
"WHEN THE GOOD OLD SHIP OF ZION COMES ALONG, BE READY TO STEP ABOARD."
I CAN'T BELIEVE YOU PUT THAT IN A LETTER.
WAIT, I THOUGHT SHE COULDN'T READ OR WRITE.
SHE COULDN'T. SHE WOULD DICTATE MESSAGES, AND SOMEONE WOULD WRITE THEM FOR HER.
THE PEOPLE SHE WANTED TO SEND MESSAGES TO USUALLY COULDN'T READ EITHER. THIS MADE THINGS VERY TRICKY.
ALL MAIL BETWEEN SLAVES WAS CHECKED. EVERYTHING HAD TO BE COMMUNICATED IN CODE--
CODE THAT PEOPLE WHO COULDN'T READ COULD UNDERSTAND.
WHAT'S THIS ABOUT A "SHIP OF ZION"?
THAT LETTER AIN'T FOR ME. I CAN'T MAKE HEAD NOR TAIL OF IT.
SOMEBODY WANTS YOU TO KNOW, "THE GOOD OLD SHIP OF ZION IS COMIN' ALONG."
MINTY!
AND YOU SHOULD "BE READY TO STEP ABOARD."
WHERE'S ROBERT?
HIS WIFE-- SHE'S HAVIN' A BABY TONIGHT.
TONIGHT!?
YES, BUT HE SAID HE WAS COMIN'. CAN WE WAIT?
ONE DAY. WE CAN WAIT ONE DAY.

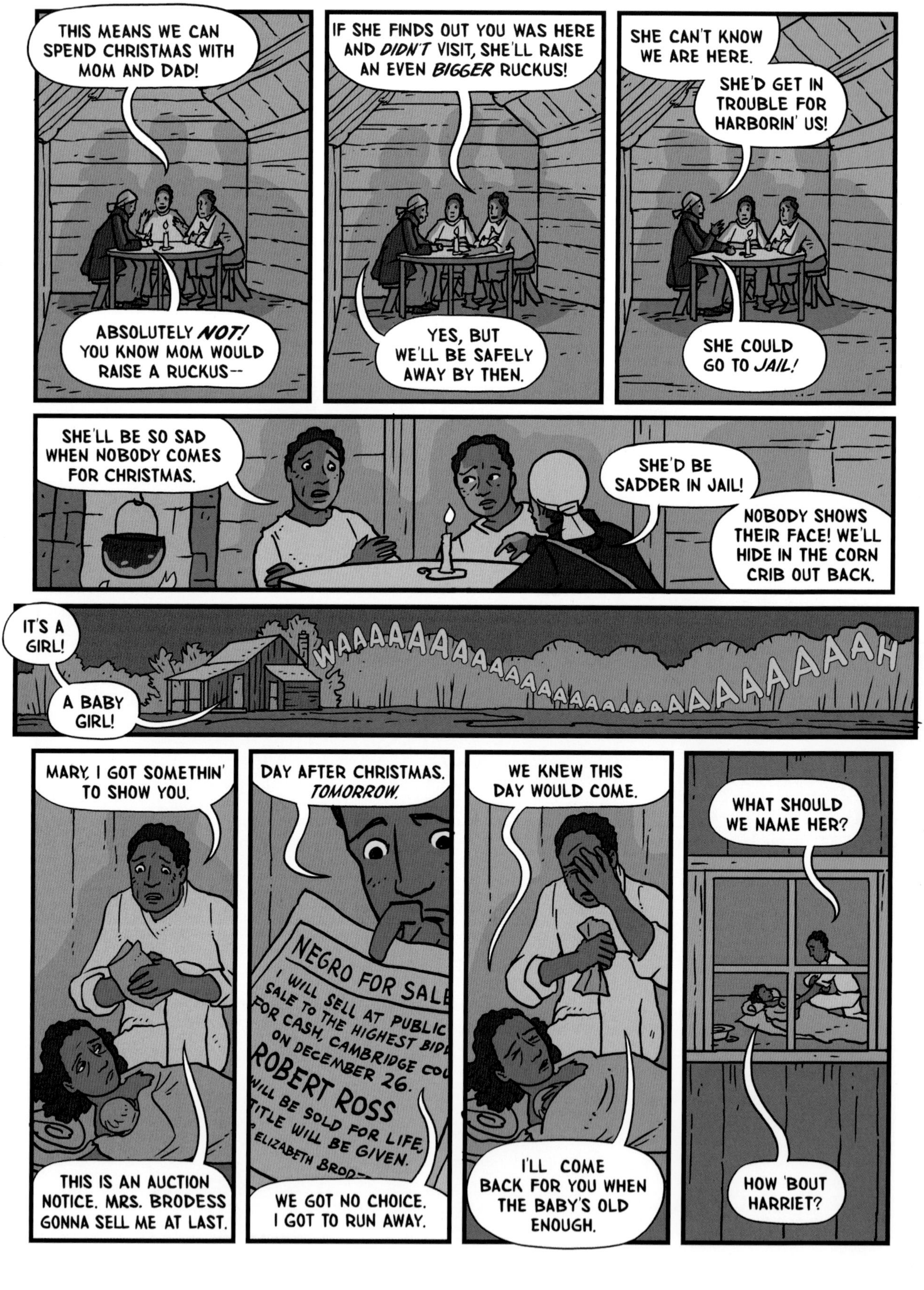

THIS MEANS WE CAN SPEND CHRISTMAS WITH MOM AND DAD!
ABSOLUTELY *NOT!* YOU KNOW MOM WOULD RAISE A RUCKUS--
IF SHE FINDS OUT YOU WAS HERE AND *DIDN'T* VISIT, SHE'LL RAISE AN EVEN *BIGGER* RUCKUS!
YES, BUT WE'LL BE SAFELY AWAY BY THEN.
SHE CAN'T KNOW WE ARE HERE.
SHE'D GET IN TROUBLE FOR HARBORIN' US!
SHE COULD GO TO *JAIL!*
SHE'LL BE SO SAD WHEN NOBODY COMES FOR CHRISTMAS.
SHE'D BE SADDER IN JAIL!
NOBODY SHOWS THEIR FACE! WE'LL HIDE IN THE CORN CRIB OUT BACK.
IT'S A GIRL!
A BABY GIRL!
WAAAAAAAAAAAAAAAAAAAAAAAAAAAAAAH
MARY, I GOT SOMETHIN' TO SHOW YOU.
THIS IS AN AUCTION NOTICE. MRS. BRODESS GONNA SELL ME AT LAST.
DAY AFTER CHRISTMAS. *TOMORROW.*
NEGRO FOR SALE
I WILL SELL AT PUBLIC SALE TO THE HIGHEST BID FOR CASH, CAMBRIDGE CO ON DECEMBER 26.
ROBERT ROSS
WILL BE SOLD FOR LIFE, TITLE WILL BE GIVEN.
ELIZABETH BROD
WE GOT NO CHOICE. I GOT TO RUN AWAY.
WE KNEW THIS DAY WOULD COME.
I'LL COME BACK FOR YOU WHEN THE BABY'S OLD ENOUGH.
WHAT SHOULD WE NAME HER?
HOW 'BOUT HARRIET?

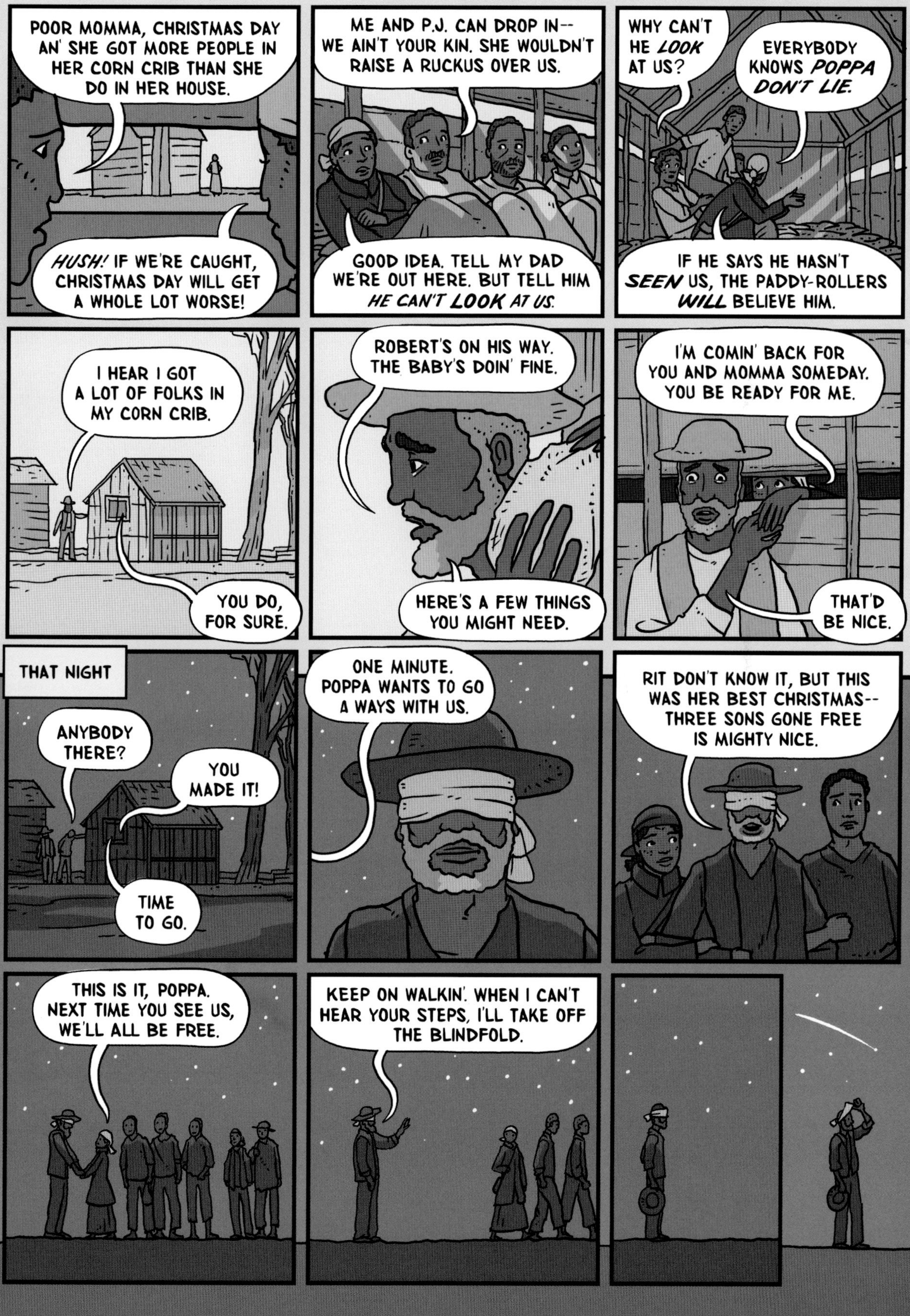
POOR MOMMA, CHRISTMAS DAY AN' SHE GOT MORE PEOPLE IN HER CORN CRIB THAN SHE DO IN HER HOUSE.
HUSH! IF WE'RE CAUGHT, CHRISTMAS DAY WILL GET A WHOLE LOT WORSE!
ME AND P.J. CAN DROP IN-- WE AIN'T YOUR KIN. SHE WOULDN'T RAISE A RUCKUS OVER US.
GOOD IDEA. TELL MY DAD WE'RE OUT HERE. BUT TELL HIM HE CAN'T LOOK AT US.
WHY CAN'T HE LOOK AT US?
EVERYBODY KNOWS POPPA DON'T LIE.
IF HE SAYS HE HASN'T SEEN US, THE PADDY-ROLLERS WILL BELIEVE HIM.
I HEAR I GOT A LOT OF FOLKS IN MY CORN CRIB.
YOU DO, FOR SURE.
ROBERT'S ON HIS WAY. THE BABY'S DOIN' FINE.
HERE'S A FEW THINGS YOU MIGHT NEED.
I'M COMIN' BACK FOR YOU AND MOMMA SOMEDAY. YOU BE READY FOR ME.
THAT'D BE NICE.
THAT NIGHT
ANYBODY THERE?
YOU MADE IT!
TIME TO GO.
ONE MINUTE. POPPA WANTS TO GO A WAYS WITH US.
RIT DON'T KNOW IT, BUT THIS WAS HER BEST CHRISTMAS-- THREE SONS GONE FREE IS MIGHTY NICE.
THIS IS IT, POPPA. NEXT TIME YOU SEE US, WE'LL ALL BE FREE.
KEEP ON WALKIN'. WHEN I CAN'T HEAR YOUR STEPS, I'LL TAKE OFF THE BLINDFOLD.

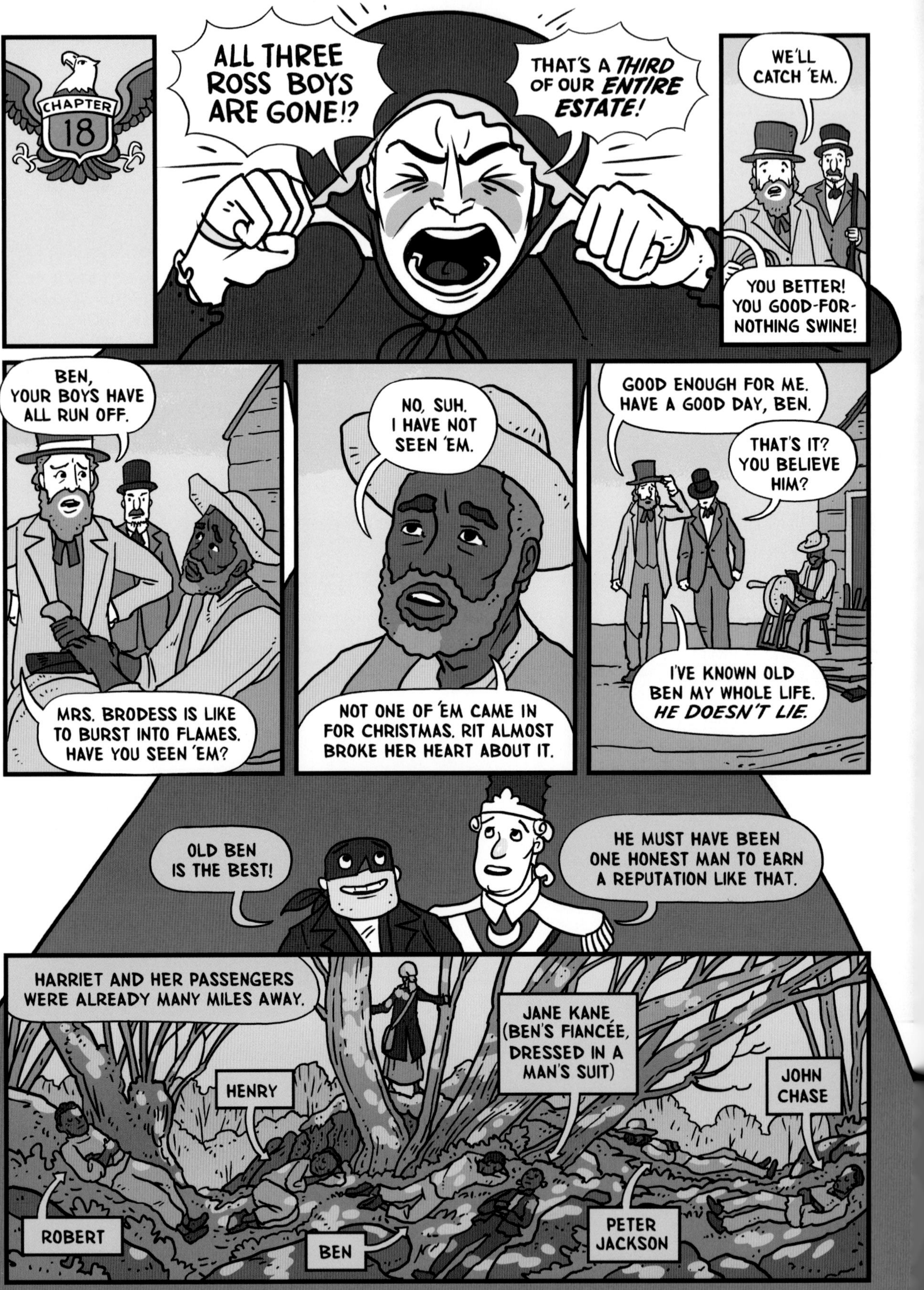
CHAPTER 18
ALL THREE ROSS BOYS ARE GONE!?
THAT'S A THIRD OF OUR ENTIRE ESTATE!
WE'LL CATCH 'EM.
YOU BETTER! YOU GOOD-FOR-NOTHING SWINE!
BEN, YOUR BOYS HAVE ALL RUN OFF.
MRS. BRODESS IS LIKE TO BURST INTO FLAMES. HAVE YOU SEEN 'EM?
NO, SUH. I HAVE NOT SEEN 'EM.
NOT ONE OF 'EM CAME IN FOR CHRISTMAS. RIT ALMOST BROKE HER HEART ABOUT IT.
GOOD ENOUGH FOR ME. HAVE A GOOD DAY, BEN.
THAT'S IT? YOU BELIEVE HIM?
I'VE KNOWN OLD BEN MY WHOLE LIFE. HE DOESN'T LIE.
OLD BEN IS THE BEST!
HE MUST HAVE BEEN ONE HONEST MAN TO EARN A REPUTATION LIKE THAT.
HARRIET AND HER PASSENGERS WERE ALREADY MANY MILES AWAY.
HENRY
JANE KANE (BEN'S FIANCÉE, DRESSED IN A MAN'S SUIT)
JOHN CHASE
ROBERT
BEN
PETER JACKSON

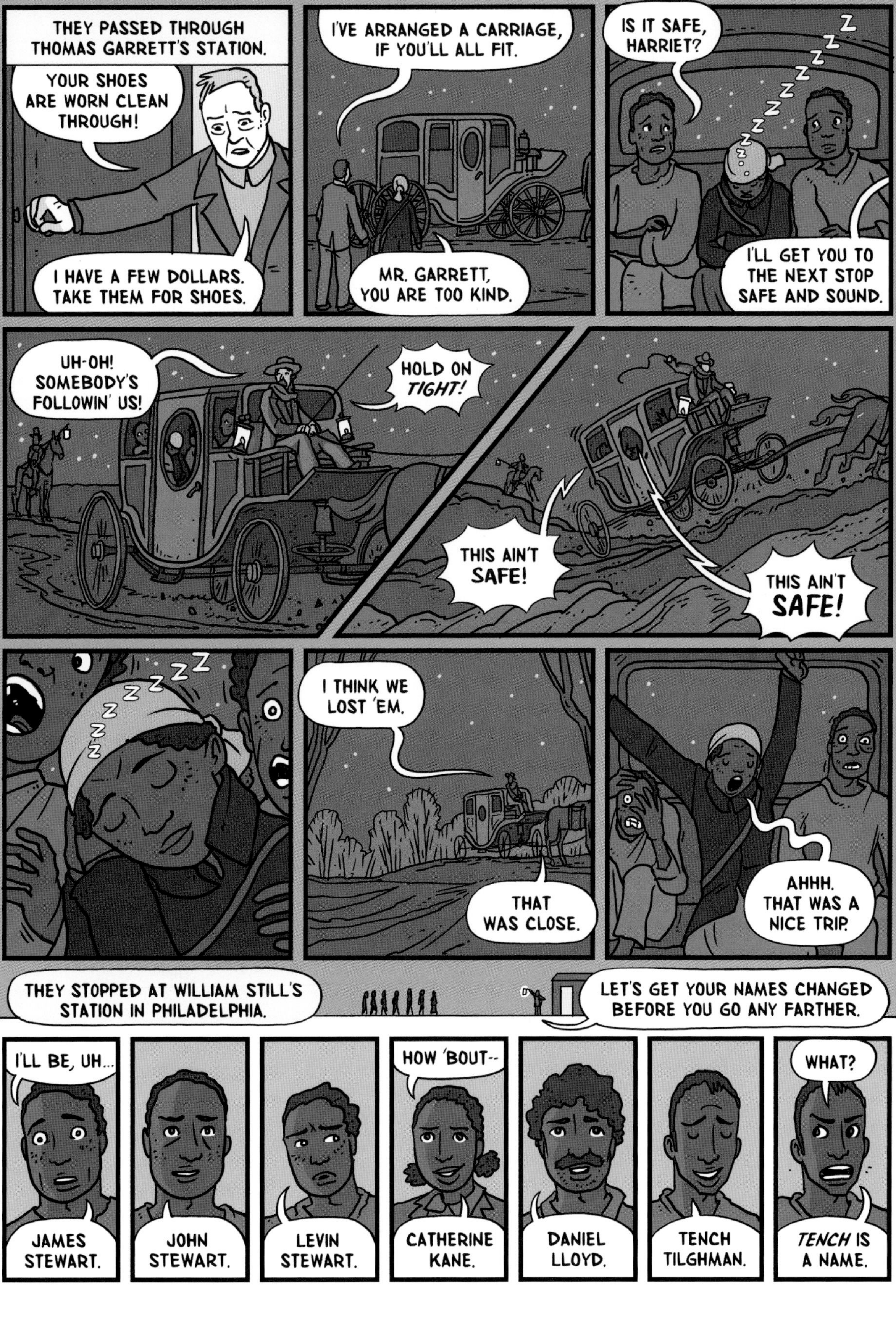
THEY PASSED THROUGH THOMAS GARRETT'S STATION.
YOUR SHOES ARE WORN CLEAN THROUGH!
I HAVE A FEW DOLLARS. TAKE THEM FOR SHOES.
I'VE ARRANGED A CARRIAGE, IF YOU'LL ALL FIT.
MR. GARRETT, YOU ARE TOO KIND.
IS IT SAFE, HARRIET?
ZZZZZZZZZ
I'LL GET YOU TO THE NEXT STOP SAFE AND SOUND.
UH-OH! SOMEBODY'S FOLLOWIN' US!
HOLD ON *TIGHT!*
THIS AIN'T SAFE!
THIS AIN'T SAFE!
ZZZZZZZ
I THINK WE LOST 'EM.
THAT WAS CLOSE.
AHHH. THAT WAS A NICE TRIP.
THEY STOPPED AT WILLIAM STILL'S STATION IN PHILADELPHIA.
LET'S GET YOUR NAMES CHANGED BEFORE YOU GO ANY FARTHER.
I'LL BE, UH...
JAMES STEWART.
JOHN STEWART.
LEVIN STEWART.
HOW 'BOUT--
CATHERINE KANE.
DANIEL LLOYD.
TENCH TILGHMAN.
WHAT?
TENCH IS A NAME.

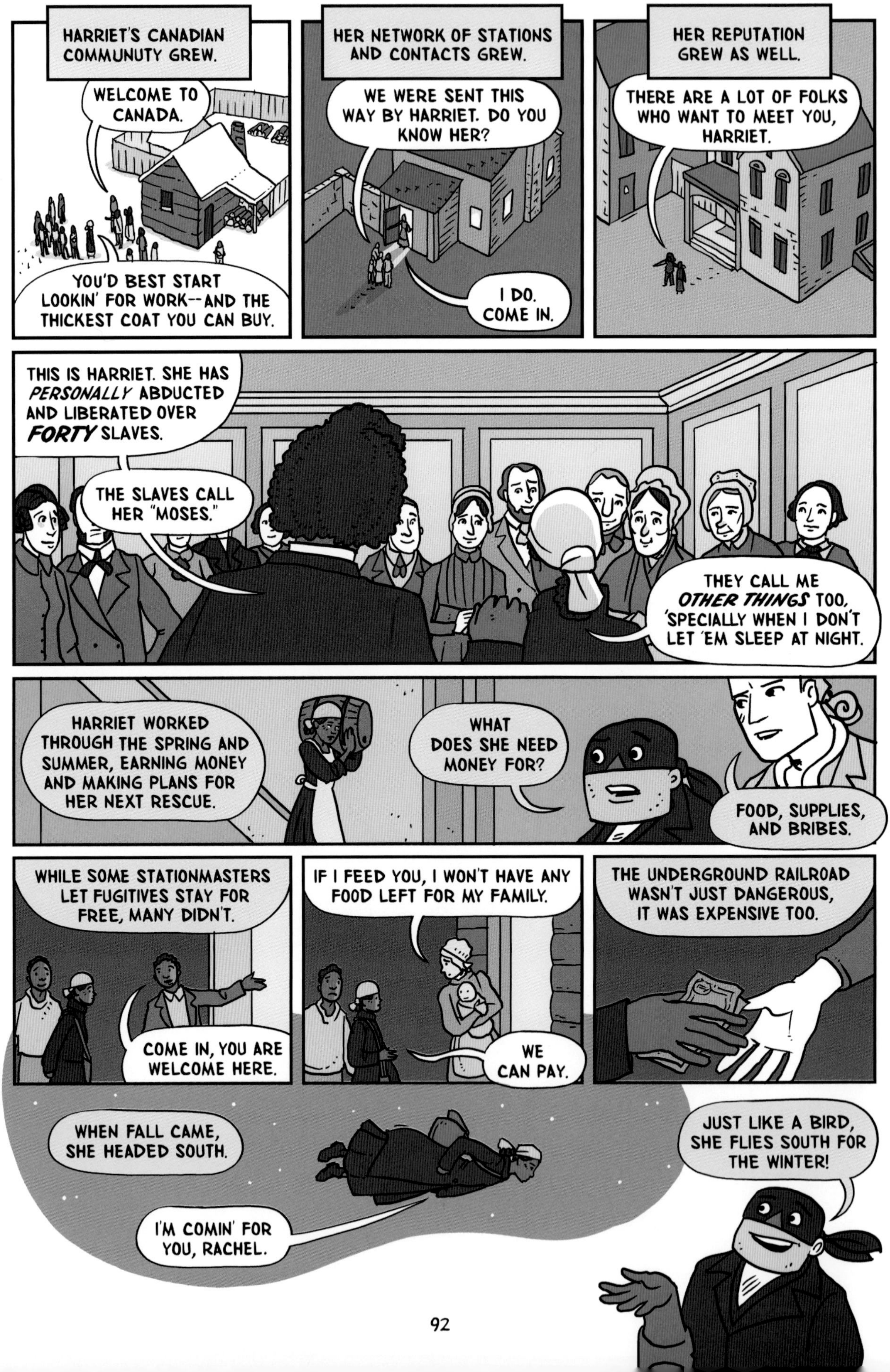
HARRIET'S CANADIAN COMMUNUTY GREW.
WELCOME TO CANADA.
YOU'D BEST START LOOKIN' FOR WORK--AND THE THICKEST COAT YOU CAN BUY.
HER NETWORK OF STATIONS AND CONTACTS GREW.
WE WERE SENT THIS WAY BY HARRIET. DO YOU KNOW HER?
I DO. COME IN.
HER REPUTATION GREW AS WELL.
THERE ARE A LOT OF FOLKS WHO WANT TO MEET YOU, HARRIET.
THIS IS HARRIET. SHE HAS PERSONALLY ABDUCTED AND LIBERATED OVER FORTY SLAVES.
THE SLAVES CALL HER "MOSES."
THEY CALL ME OTHER THINGS TOO, 'SPECIALLY WHEN I DON'T LET 'EM SLEEP AT NIGHT.
HARRIET WORKED THROUGH THE SPRING AND SUMMER, EARNING MONEY AND MAKING PLANS FOR HER NEXT RESCUE.
WHAT DOES SHE NEED MONEY FOR?
FOOD, SUPPLIES, AND BRIBES.
WHILE SOME STATIONMASTERS LET FUGITIVES STAY FOR FREE, MANY DIDN'T.
COME IN, YOU ARE WELCOME HERE.
IF I FEED YOU, I WON'T HAVE ANY FOOD LEFT FOR MY FAMILY.
WE CAN PAY.
THE UNDERGROUND RAILROAD WASN'T JUST DANGEROUS, IT WAS EXPENSIVE TOO.
WHEN FALL CAME, SHE HEADED SOUTH.
I'M COMIN' FOR YOU, RACHEL.
JUST LIKE A BIRD, SHE FLIES SOUTH FOR THE WINTER!

THE RACHEL RESCUE

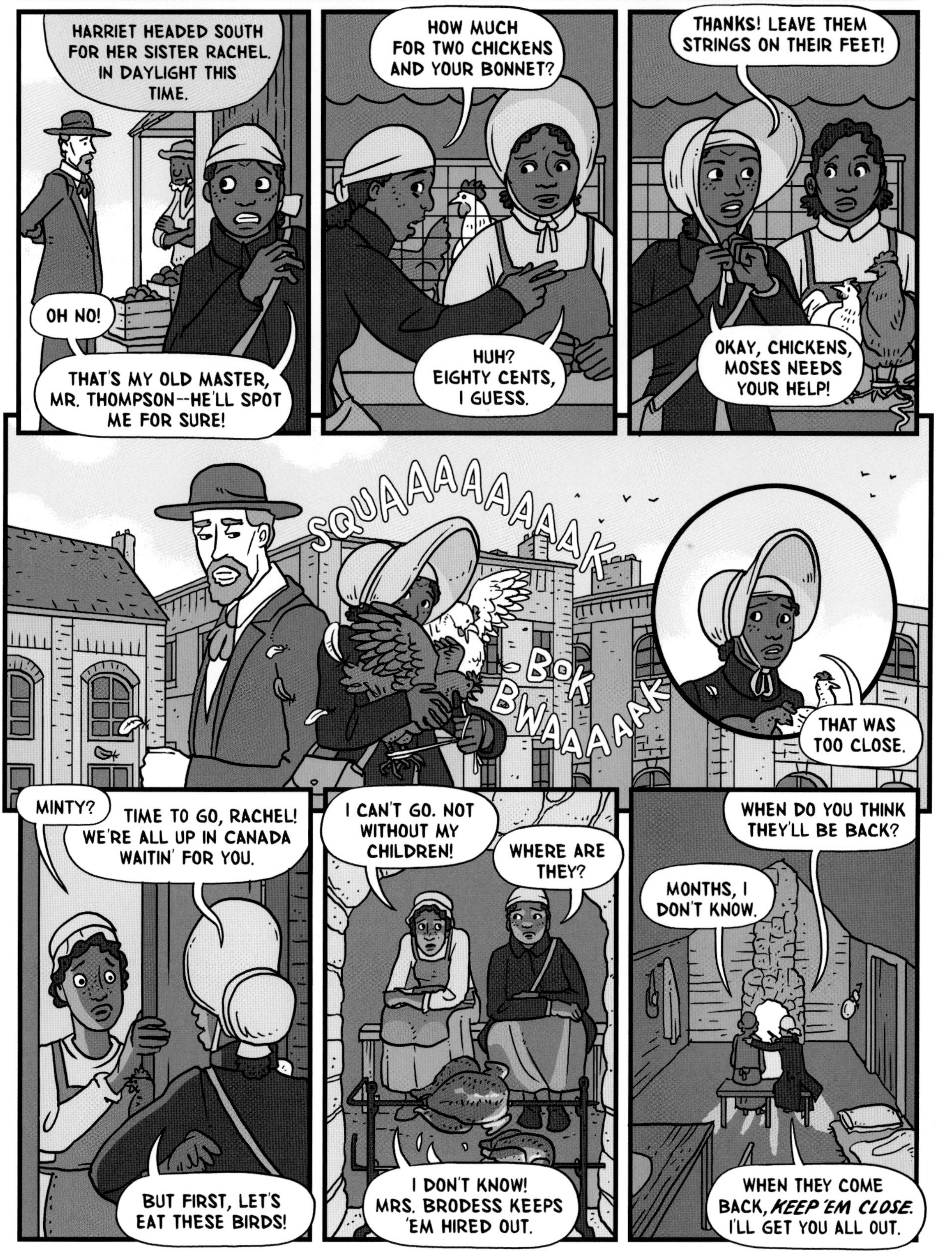

HARRIET HEADED SOUTH FOR HER SISTER RACHEL. IN DAYLIGHT THIS TIME.
OH NO!
THAT'S MY OLD MASTER, MR. THOMPSON--HE'LL SPOT ME FOR SURE!
HOW MUCH FOR TWO CHICKENS AND YOUR BONNET?
HUH? EIGHTY CENTS, I GUESS.
THANKS! LEAVE THEM STRINGS ON THEIR FEET!
OKAY, CHICKENS, MOSES NEEDS YOUR HELP!
SQUAAAAAAAAAK
BOK
BWAAAAAK
THAT WAS TOO CLOSE.
MINTY?
TIME TO GO, RACHEL! WE'RE ALL UP IN CANADA WAITIN' FOR YOU.
BUT FIRST, LET'S EAT THESE BIRDS!
I CAN'T GO. NOT WITHOUT MY CHILDREN!
WHERE ARE THEY?
I DON'T KNOW! MRS. BRODESS KEEPS 'EM HIRED OUT.
WHEN DO YOU THINK THEY'LL BE BACK?
MONTHS, I DON'T KNOW.
WHEN THEY COME BACK, *KEEP 'EM CLOSE.* I'LL GET YOU ALL OUT.

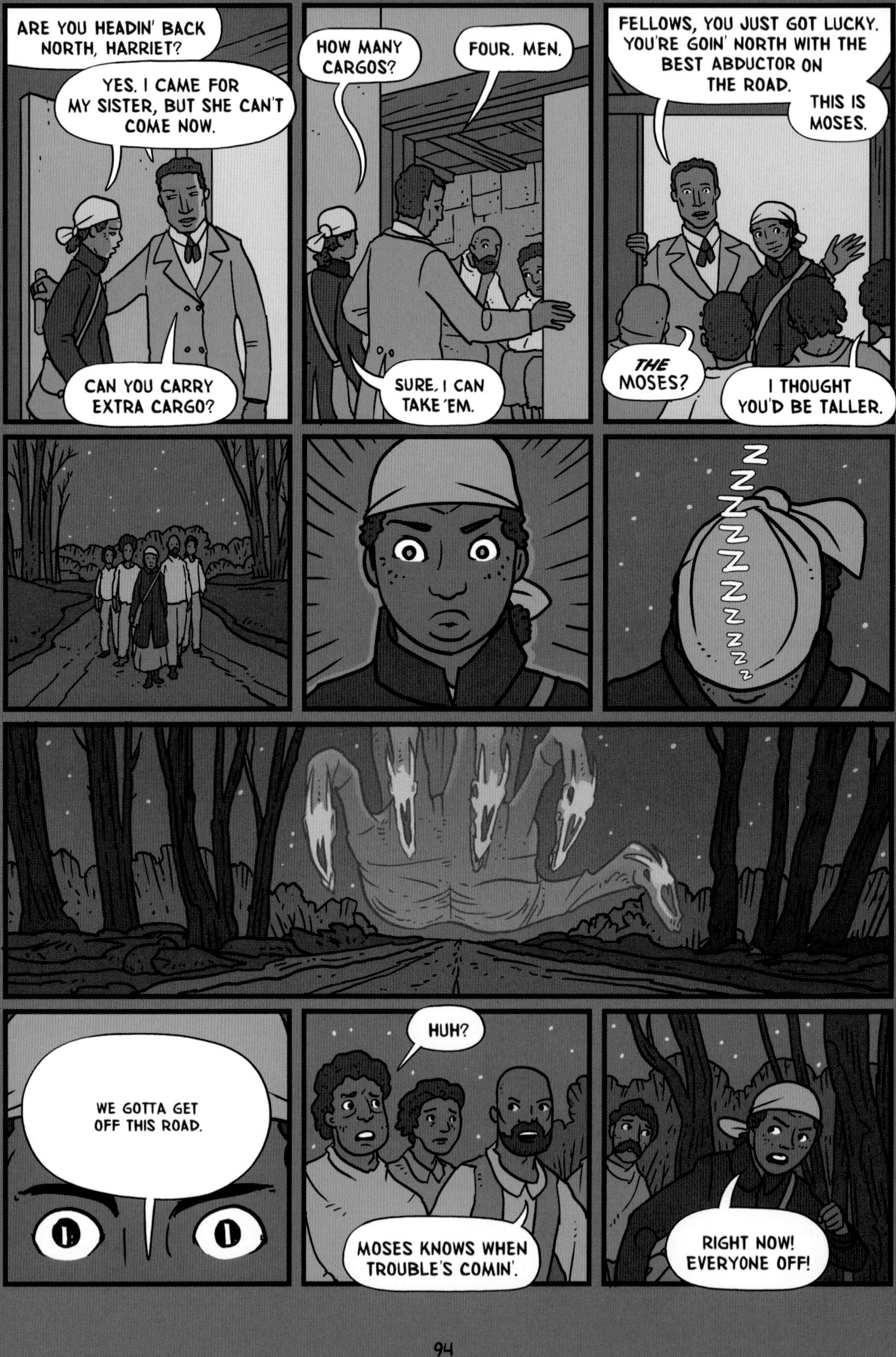
ARE YOU HEADIN' BACK NORTH, HARRIET?
YES. I CAME FOR MY SISTER, BUT SHE CAN'T COME NOW.
CAN YOU CARRY EXTRA CARGO?
HOW MANY CARGOS?
FOUR. MEN.
SURE, I CAN TAKE 'EM.
FELLOWS, YOU JUST GOT LUCKY. YOU'RE GOIN' NORTH WITH THE BEST ABDUCTOR ON THE ROAD.
THIS IS MOSES.
THE MOSES?
I THOUGHT YOU'D BE TALLER.
ZZZZZZZZZZZ
WE GOTTA GET OFF THIS ROAD.
HUH?
MOSES KNOWS WHEN TROUBLE'S COMIN'.
RIGHT NOW! EVERYONE OFF!

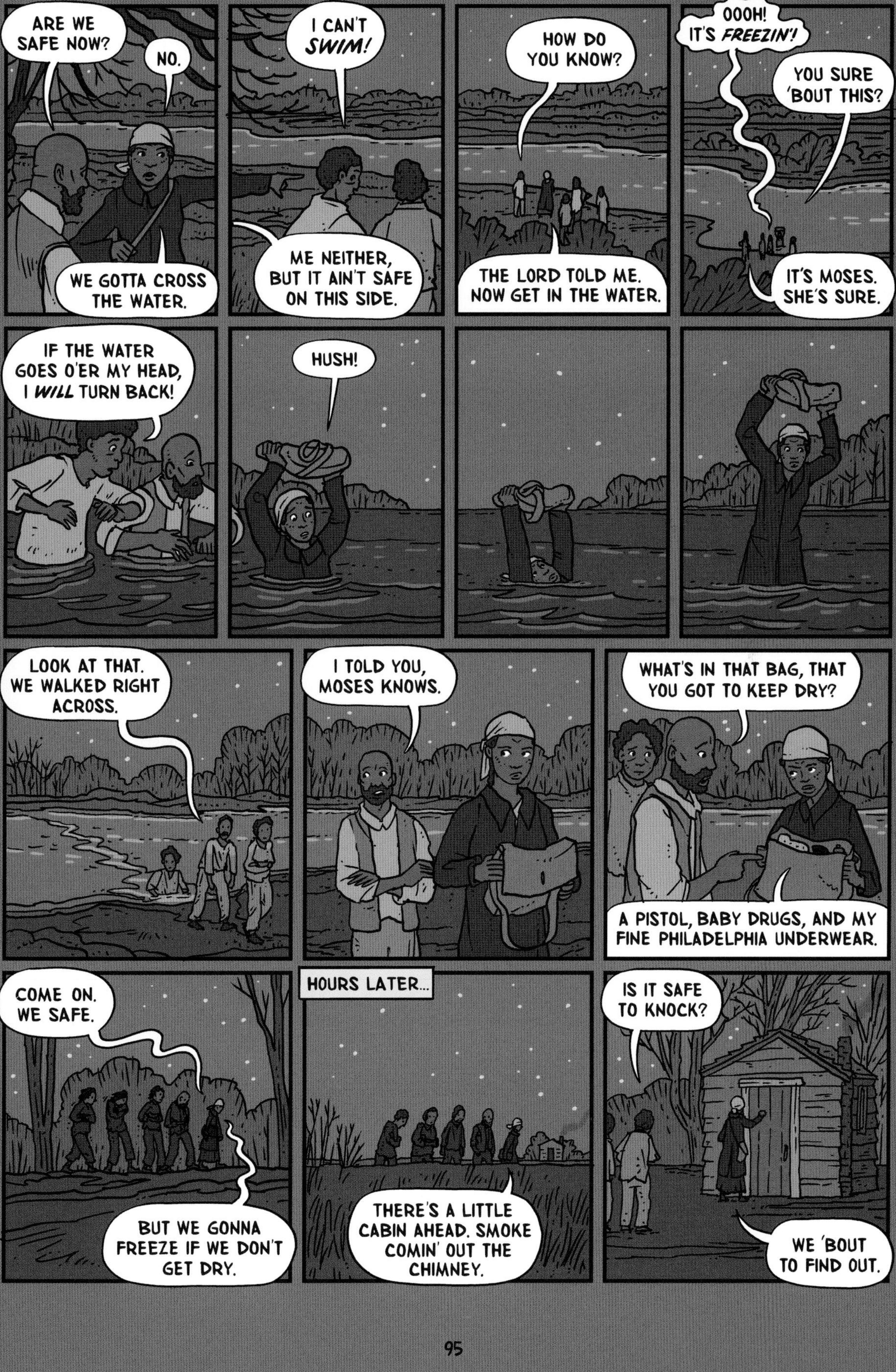
ARE WE SAFE NOW?
NO.
WE GOTTA CROSS THE WATER.
I CAN'T *SWIM!*
ME NEITHER, BUT IT AIN'T SAFE ON THIS SIDE.
HOW DO YOU KNOW?
THE LORD TOLD ME. NOW GET IN THE WATER.
OOOH! IT'S *FREEZIN'!*
YOU SURE 'BOUT THIS?
IT'S MOSES. SHE'S SURE.
IF THE WATER GOES O'ER MY HEAD, I *WILL* TURN BACK!
HUSH!
LOOK AT THAT. WE WALKED RIGHT ACROSS.
I TOLD YOU, MOSES KNOWS.
WHAT'S IN THAT BAG, THAT YOU GOT TO KEEP DRY?
A PISTOL, BABY DRUGS, AND MY FINE PHILADELPHIA UNDERWEAR.
COME ON. WE SAFE.
BUT WE GONNA FREEZE IF WE DON'T GET DRY.
HOURS LATER...
THERE'S A LITTLE CABIN AHEAD. SMOKE COMIN' OUT THE CHIMNEY.
IS IT SAFE TO KNOCK?
WE 'BOUT TO FIND OUT.

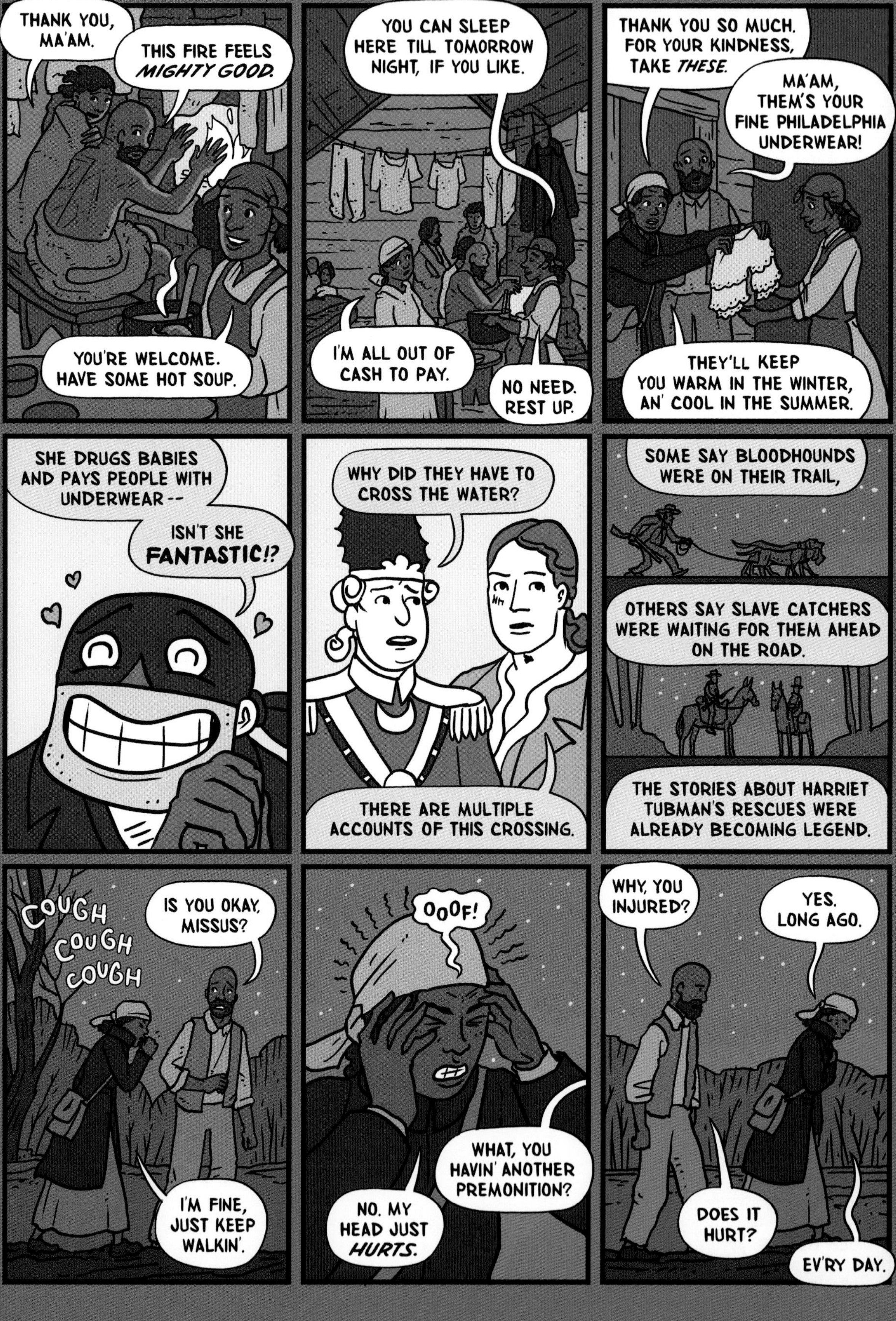
THANK YOU, MA'AM.
THIS FIRE FEELS *MIGHTY GOOD.*
YOU'RE WELCOME. HAVE SOME HOT SOUP.
YOU CAN SLEEP HERE TILL TOMORROW NIGHT, IF YOU LIKE.
I'M ALL OUT OF CASH TO PAY.
NO NEED. REST UP.
THANK YOU SO MUCH. FOR YOUR KINDNESS, TAKE *THESE.*
MA'AM, THEM'S YOUR FINE PHILADELPHIA UNDERWEAR!
THEY'LL KEEP YOU WARM IN THE WINTER, AN' COOL IN THE SUMMER.
SHE DRUGS BABIES AND PAYS PEOPLE WITH UNDERWEAR--
ISN'T SHE **FANTASTIC!?**
WHY DID THEY HAVE TO CROSS THE WATER?
THERE ARE MULTIPLE ACCOUNTS OF THIS CROSSING.
SOME SAY BLOODHOUNDS WERE ON THEIR TRAIL,
OTHERS SAY SLAVE CATCHERS WERE WAITING FOR THEM AHEAD ON THE ROAD.
THE STORIES ABOUT HARRIET TUBMAN'S RESCUES WERE ALREADY BECOMING LEGEND.
COUGH COUGH COUGH
IS YOU OKAY, MISSUS?
I'M FINE, JUST KEEP WALKIN'.
OOOF!
WHAT, YOU HAVIN' ANOTHER PREMONITION?
NO. MY HEAD JUST *HURTS.*
WHY, YOU INJURED?
YES. LONG AGO.
DOES IT HURT?
EV'RY DAY.

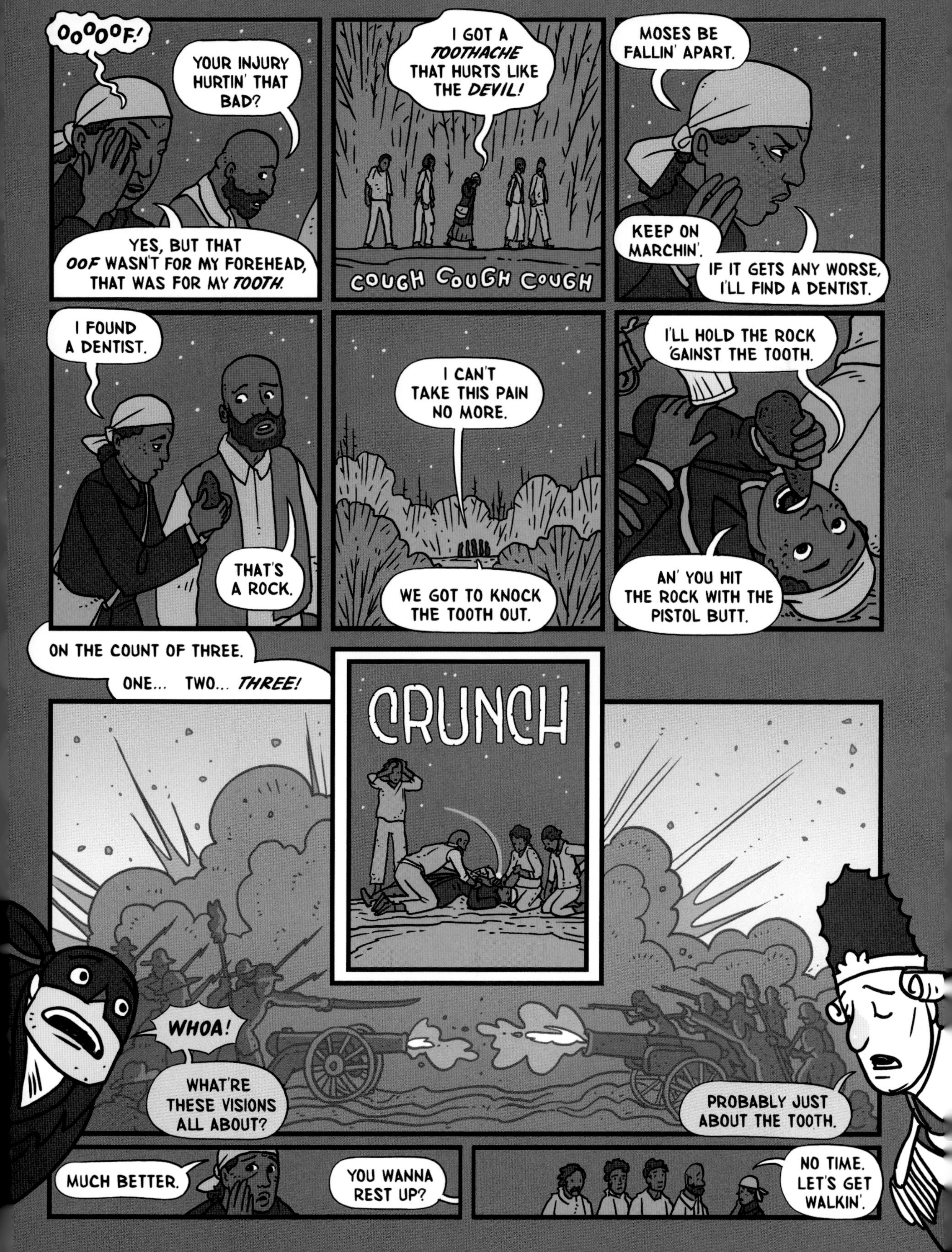

OOOOOF!
YOUR INJURY HURTIN' THAT BAD?
YES, BUT THAT OOF WASN'T FOR MY FOREHEAD, THAT WAS FOR MY TOOTH.
I GOT A TOOTHACHE THAT HURTS LIKE THE DEVIL!
COUGH COUGH COUGH
MOSES BE FALLIN' APART.
KEEP ON MARCHIN'.
IF IT GETS ANY WORSE, I'LL FIND A DENTIST.
I FOUND A DENTIST.
THAT'S A ROCK.
I CAN'T TAKE THIS PAIN NO MORE.
WE GOT TO KNOCK THE TOOTH OUT.
I'LL HOLD THE ROCK 'GAINST THE TOOTH.
AN' YOU HIT THE ROCK WITH THE PISTOL BUTT.
ON THE COUNT OF THREE.
ONE... TWO... THREE!
CRUNCH
WHOA!
WHAT'RE THESE VISIONS ALL ABOUT?
PROBABLY JUST ABOUT THE TOOTH.
MUCH BETTER.
YOU WANNA REST UP?
NO TIME. LET'S GET WALKIN'.

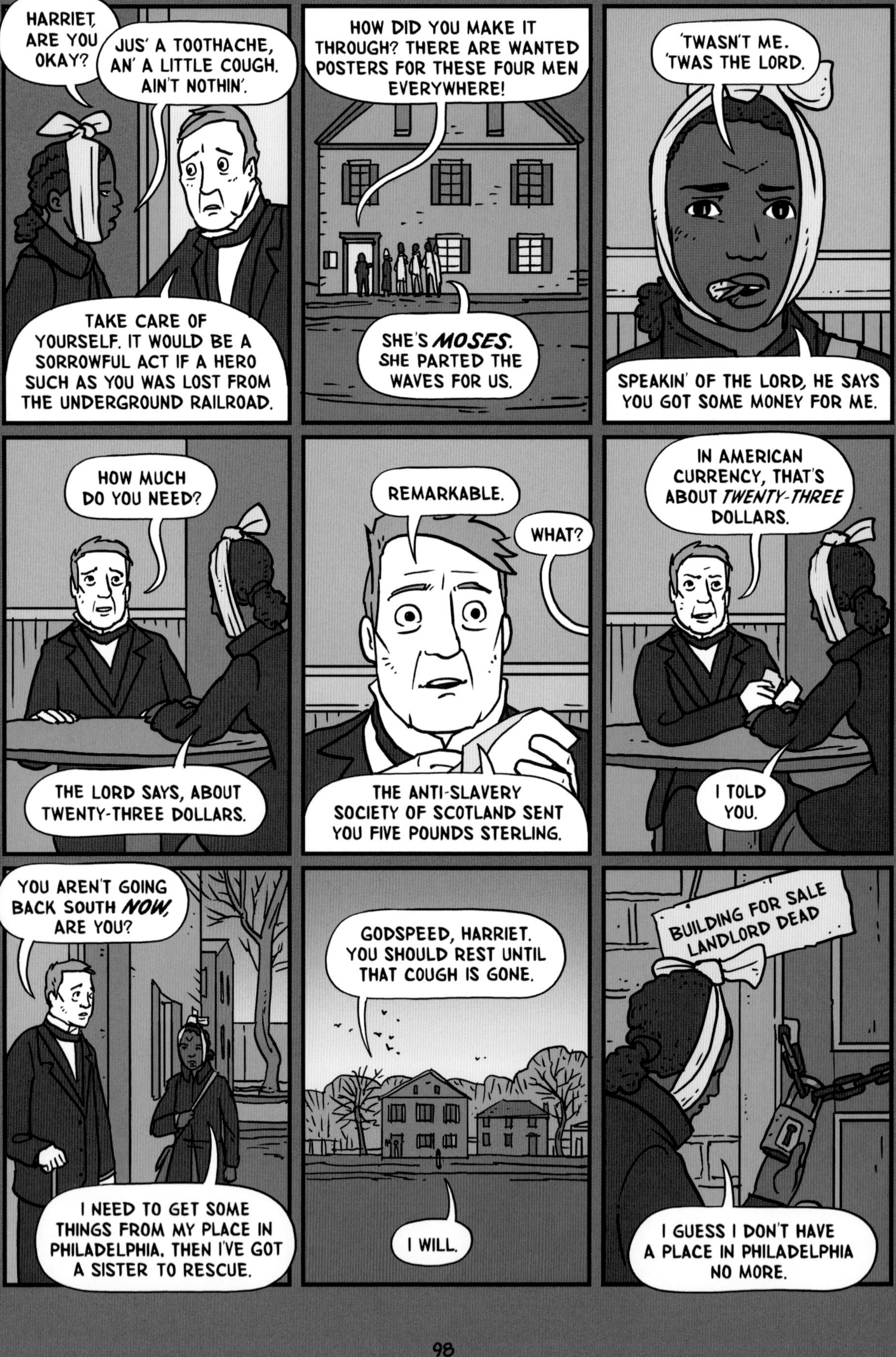
HARRIET, ARE YOU OKAY?
JUS' A TOOTHACHE, AN' A LITTLE COUGH. AIN'T NOTHIN'.
TAKE CARE OF YOURSELF. IT WOULD BE A SORROWFUL ACT IF A HERO SUCH AS YOU WAS LOST FROM THE UNDERGROUND RAILROAD.
HOW DID YOU MAKE IT THROUGH? THERE ARE WANTED POSTERS FOR THESE FOUR MEN EVERYWHERE!
SHE'S *MOSES*. SHE PARTED THE WAVES FOR US.
'TWASN'T ME. 'TWAS THE LORD.
SPEAKIN' OF THE LORD, HE SAYS YOU GOT SOME MONEY FOR ME.
HOW MUCH DO YOU NEED?
THE LORD SAYS, ABOUT TWENTY-THREE DOLLARS.
REMARKABLE.
WHAT?
THE ANTI-SLAVERY SOCIETY OF SCOTLAND SENT YOU FIVE POUNDS STERLING.
IN AMERICAN CURRENCY, THAT'S ABOUT *TWENTY-THREE* DOLLARS.
I TOLD YOU.
YOU AREN'T GOING BACK SOUTH *NOW*, ARE YOU?
I NEED TO GET SOME THINGS FROM MY PLACE IN PHILADELPHIA. THEN I'VE GOT A SISTER TO RESCUE.
GODSPEED, HARRIET. YOU SHOULD REST UNTIL THAT COUGH IS GONE.
I WILL.
BUILDING FOR SALE
LANDLORD DEAD
I GUESS I DON'T HAVE A PLACE IN PHILADELPHIA NO MORE.

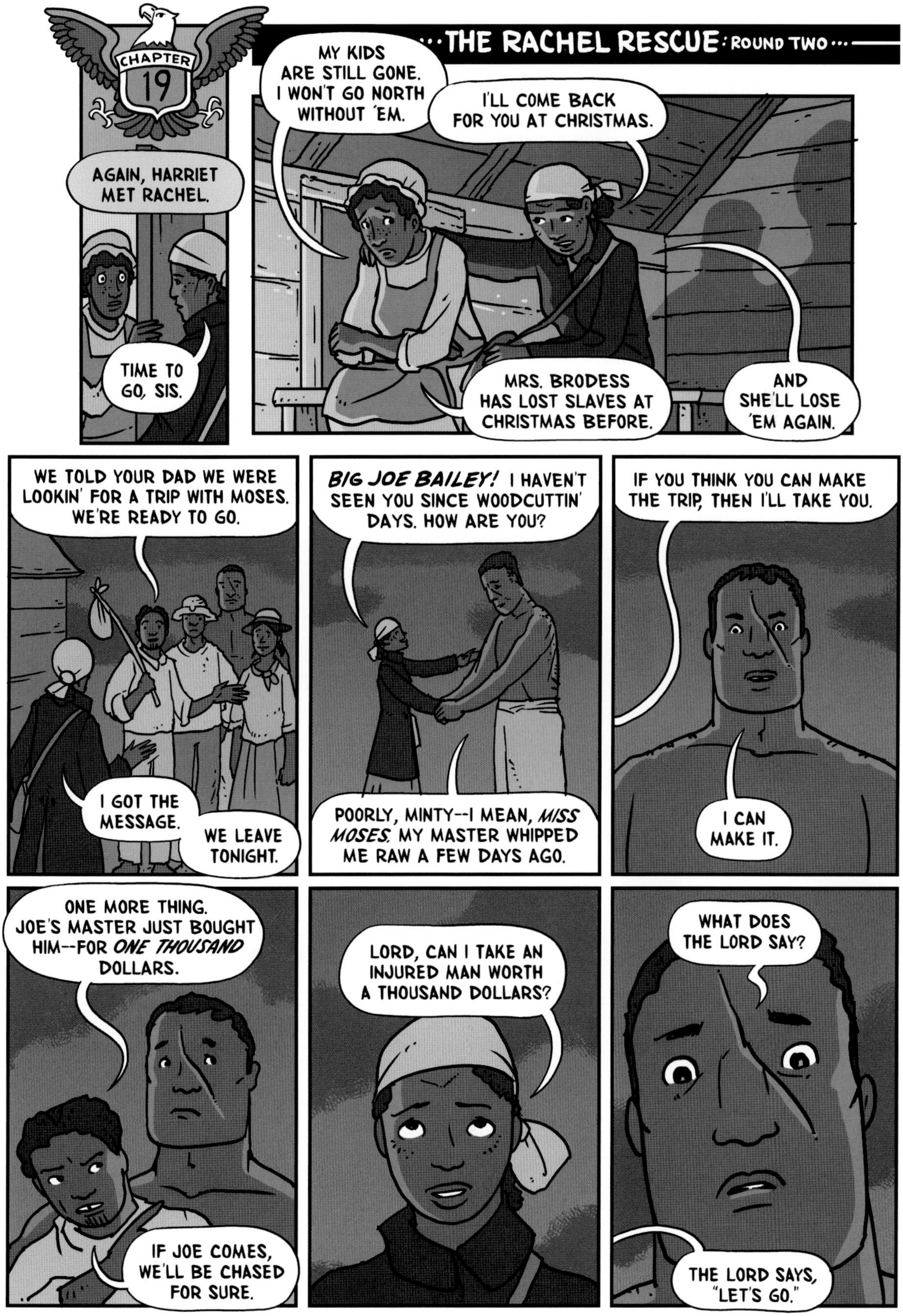
CHAPTER 19
...THE RACHEL RESCUE: ROUND TWO...
AGAIN, HARRIET MET RACHEL.
TIME TO GO, SIS.
MY KIDS ARE STILL GONE. I WON'T GO NORTH WITHOUT 'EM.
I'LL COME BACK FOR YOU AT CHRISTMAS.
MRS. BRODESS HAS LOST SLAVES AT CHRISTMAS BEFORE.
AND SHE'LL LOSE 'EM AGAIN.
WE TOLD YOUR DAD WE WERE LOOKIN' FOR A TRIP WITH MOSES. WE'RE READY TO GO.
I GOT THE MESSAGE.
WE LEAVE TONIGHT.
BIG JOE BAILEY! I HAVEN'T SEEN YOU SINCE WOODCUTTIN' DAYS. HOW ARE YOU?
POORLY, MINTY--I MEAN, MISS MOSES. MY MASTER WHIPPED ME RAW A FEW DAYS AGO.
IF YOU THINK YOU CAN MAKE THE TRIP, THEN I'LL TAKE YOU.
I CAN MAKE IT.
ONE MORE THING. JOE'S MASTER JUST BOUGHT HIM--FOR ONE THOUSAND DOLLARS.
IF JOE COMES, WE'LL BE CHASED FOR SURE.
LORD, CAN I TAKE AN INJURED MAN WORTH A THOUSAND DOLLARS?
WHAT DOES THE LORD SAY?
THE LORD SAYS, "LET'S GO."

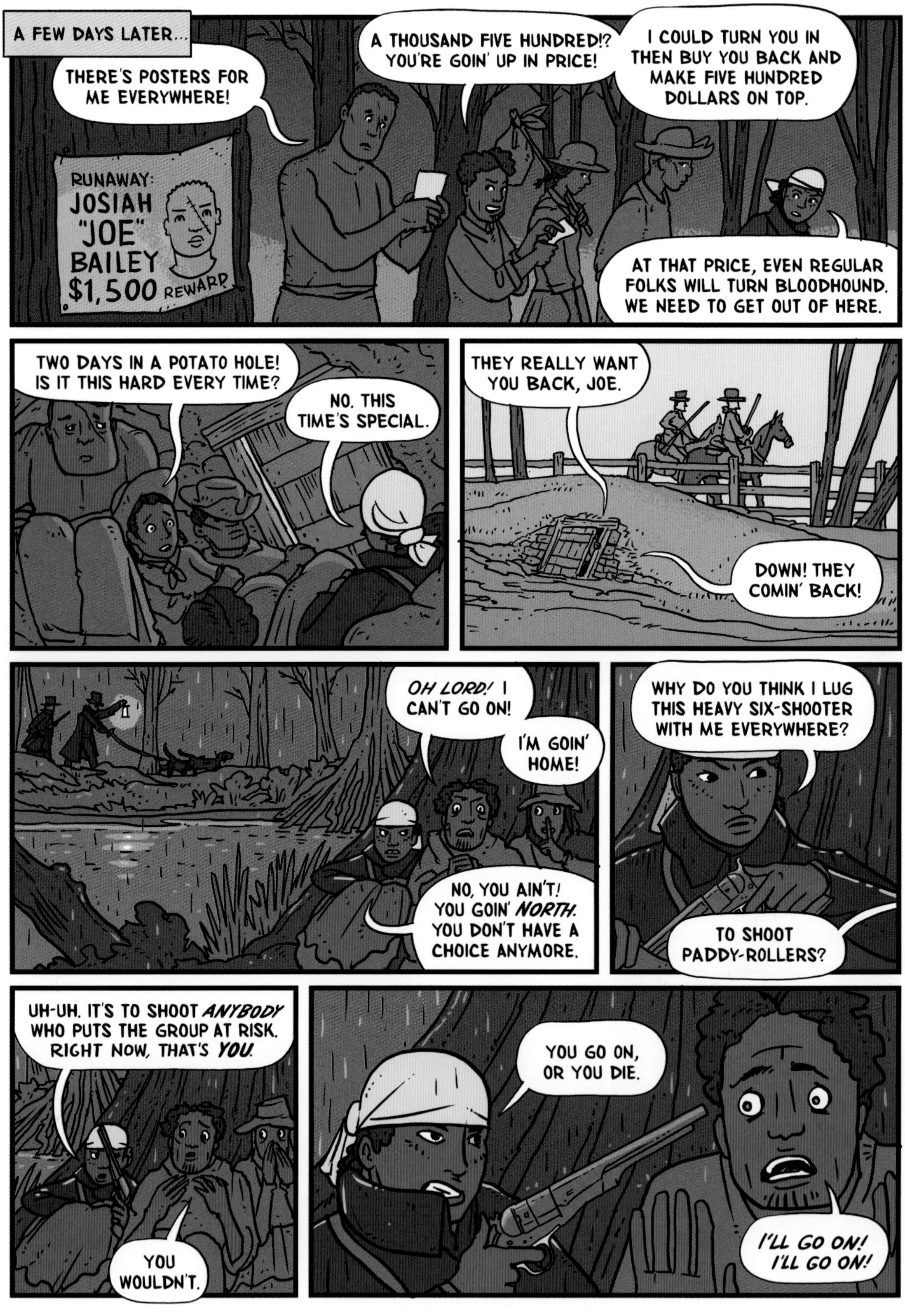
A FEW DAYS LATER...
THERE'S POSTERS FOR ME EVERYWHERE!
RUNAWAY: JOSIAH "JOE" BAILEY $1,500 REWARD
A THOUSAND FIVE HUNDRED!? YOU'RE GOIN' UP IN PRICE!
I COULD TURN YOU IN THEN BUY YOU BACK AND MAKE FIVE HUNDRED DOLLARS ON TOP.
AT THAT PRICE, EVEN REGULAR FOLKS WILL TURN BLOODHOUND. WE NEED TO GET OUT OF HERE.
TWO DAYS IN A POTATO HOLE! IS IT THIS HARD EVERY TIME?
NO. THIS TIME'S SPECIAL.
THEY REALLY WANT YOU BACK, JOE.
DOWN! THEY COMIN' BACK!
OH LORD! I CAN'T GO ON!
I'M GOIN' HOME!
NO, YOU AIN'T! YOU GOIN' NORTH. YOU DON'T HAVE A CHOICE ANYMORE.
WHY DO YOU THINK I LUG THIS HEAVY SIX-SHOOTER WITH ME EVERYWHERE?
TO SHOOT PADDY-ROLLERS?
UH-UH. IT'S TO SHOOT ANYBODY WHO PUTS THE GROUP AT RISK. RIGHT NOW, THAT'S YOU.
YOU WOULDN'T.
YOU GO ON, OR YOU DIE.
I'LL GO ON! I'LL GO ON!

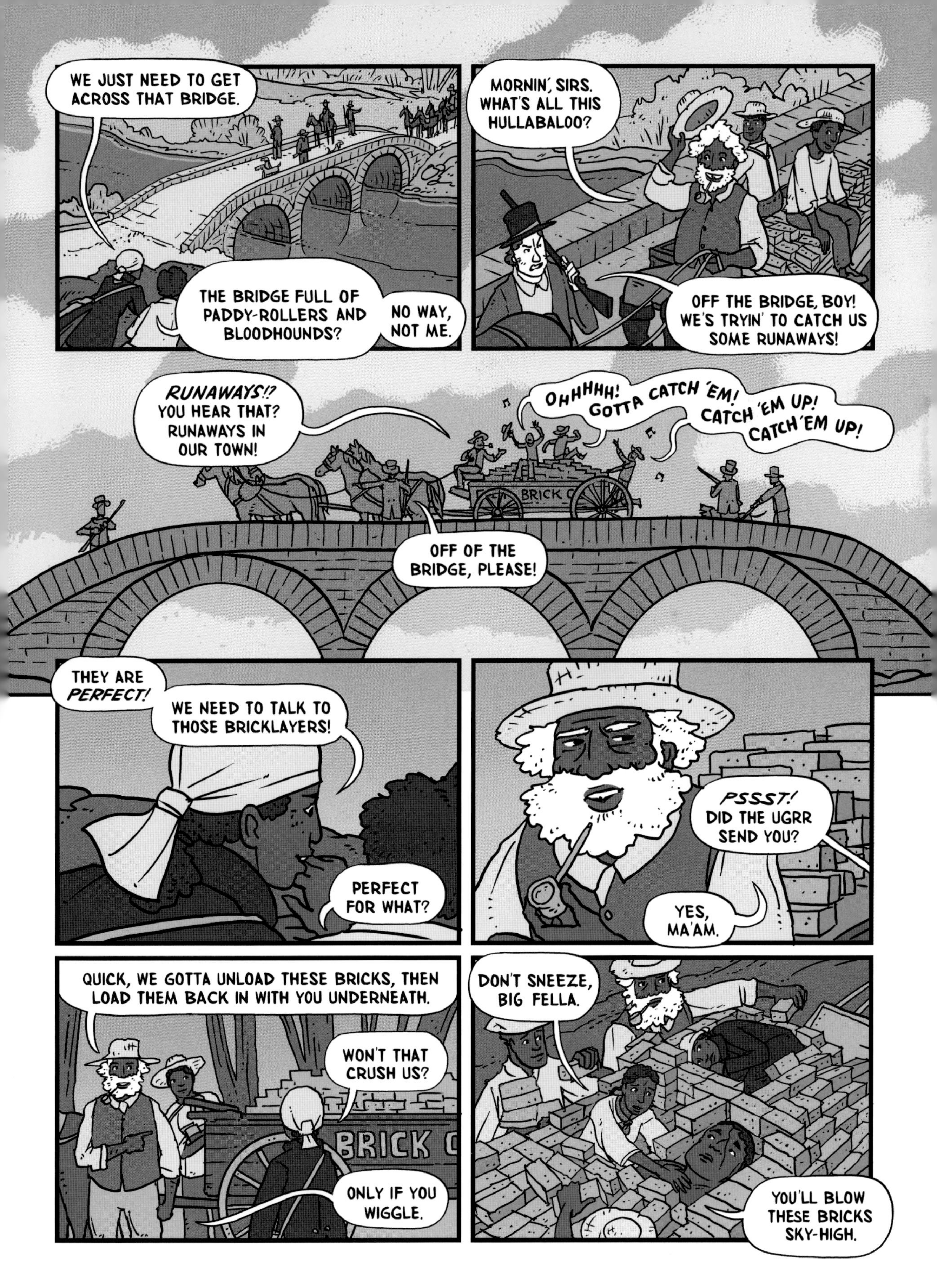

WE JUST NEED TO GET ACROSS THAT BRIDGE.
THE BRIDGE FULL OF PADDY-ROLLERS AND BLOODHOUNDS?
NO WAY, NOT ME.
MORNIN', SIRS. WHAT'S ALL THIS HULLABALOO?
OFF THE BRIDGE, BOY! WE'S TRYIN' TO CATCH US SOME RUNAWAYS!
RUNAWAYS!? YOU HEAR THAT? RUNAWAYS IN OUR TOWN!
OHHHHH! GOTTA CATCH 'EM! CATCH 'EM UP! CATCH 'EM UP!
BRICK C
OFF OF THE BRIDGE, PLEASE!
THEY ARE PERFECT!
WE NEED TO TALK TO THOSE BRICKLAYERS!
PERFECT FOR WHAT?
PSSST! DID THE UGRR SEND YOU?
YES, MA'AM.
QUICK, WE GOTTA UNLOAD THESE BRICKS, THEN LOAD THEM BACK IN WITH YOU UNDERNEATH.
WON'T THAT CRUSH US?
BRICK C
ONLY IF YOU WIGGLE.
DON'T SNEEZE, BIG FELLA.
YOU'LL BLOW THESE BRICKS SKY-HIGH.

DID YOU CATCH 'EM, OFFICERS? DID YOU CATCH UP THEM RUNAWAYS?
BRICK
CATCH 'EM UP! CATCH 'EM UP!
GET OFF THIS BRIDGE, YOU *FOOLS!*
YOU NEED SOME BRICKS?
NO! I DON'T NEED *NO BRICKS!* MOVE ALONG!
YOU COULD *THROW* THEM AT THE RUNAWAYS.
NO! PLEASE *MOVE* THIS WAGON!
I'M GOIN' TO GIVE YOU SOME *FREE* SAMPLE BRICKS.
GET OFF THIS BRIDGE!
YOU *SURE* YOU DON'T WANT THE FREE SAMPLES?
GET OFF!
YES, SUH. YES, SUH. GETTIN' OFF THE BRIDGE.
THANK YOU.
BRICK
ANYTHING FOR YOU, MOSES.
I CAN'T TAKE ANY MORE RUNNIN' AND HIDIN'. MY MIND IS GONNA CRACK!
JOE, LOOK AT THAT WATERFALL.
I DON'T WANNA LOOK AT NOTHIN'!
THAT'S NIAGARA FALLS.
DON'T CARE!
JOE, YOU ARE FREE. WE MADE IT.
FREE?
THAT'S CANADA.
GLORY TO GOD AND JESUS TOO. ONE MORE SOUL IS SAFE!

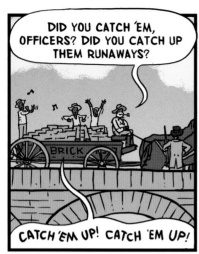

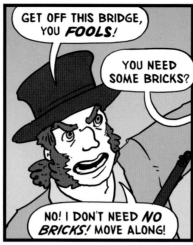

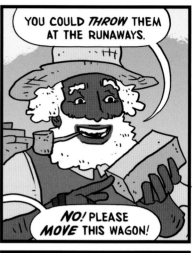

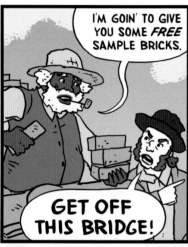

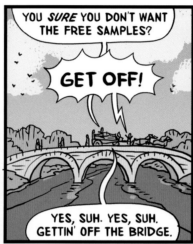

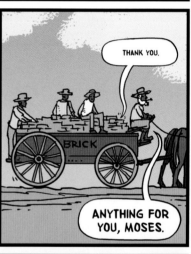

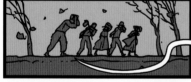

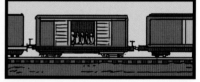

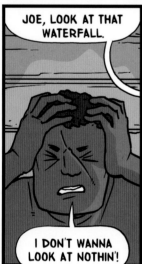

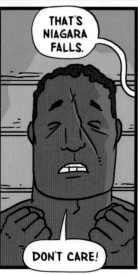

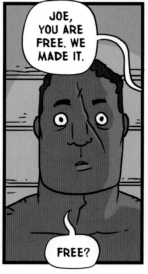

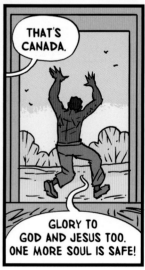

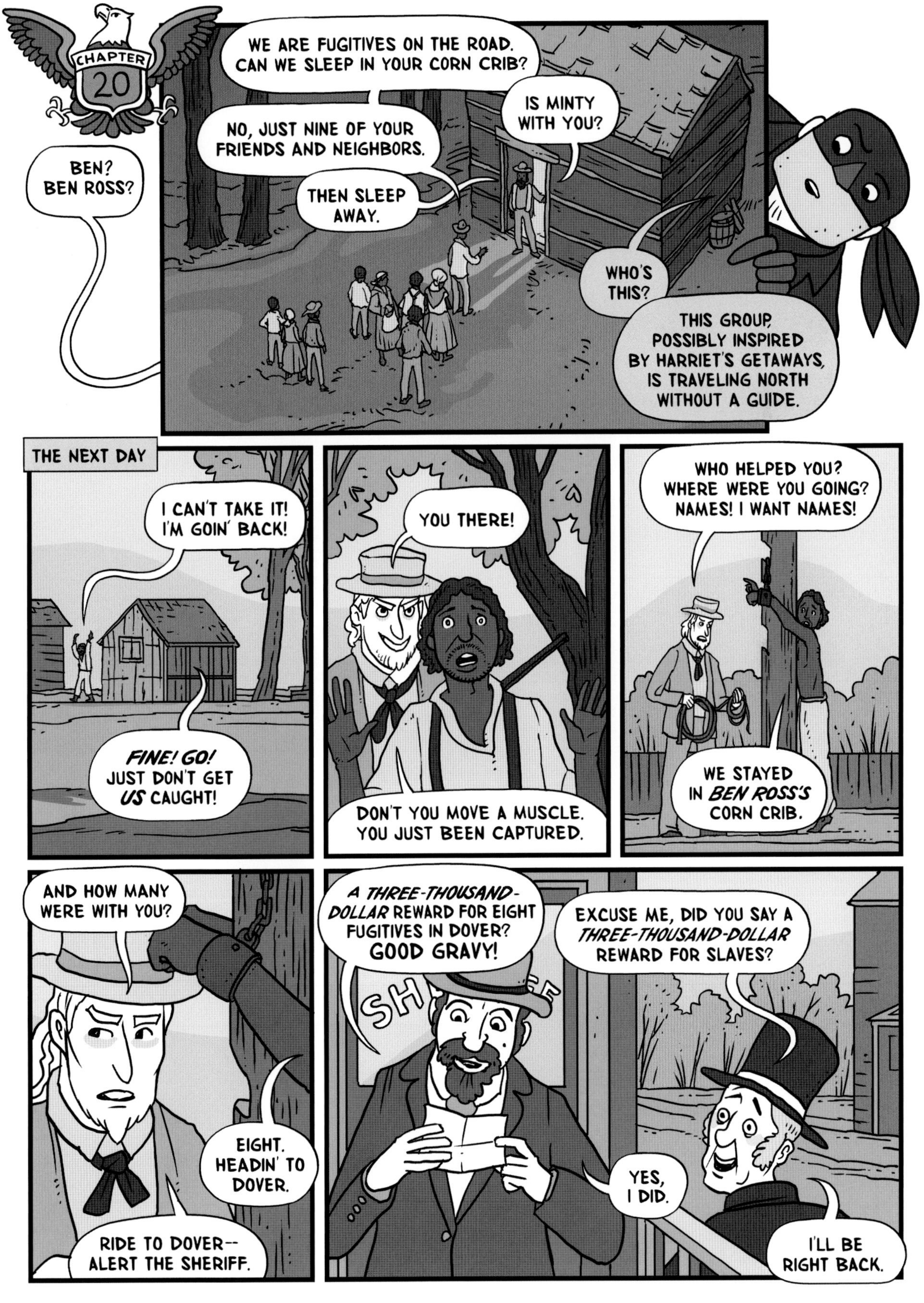

CHAPTER 20
BEN? BEN ROSS?
WE ARE FUGITIVES ON THE ROAD. CAN WE SLEEP IN YOUR CORN CRIB?
IS MINTY WITH YOU?
NO, JUST NINE OF YOUR FRIENDS AND NEIGHBORS.
THEN SLEEP AWAY.
WHO'S THIS?
THIS GROUP, POSSIBLY INSPIRED BY HARRIET'S GETAWAYS, IS TRAVELING NORTH WITHOUT A GUIDE.
THE NEXT DAY
I CAN'T TAKE IT! I'M GOIN' BACK!
FINE! GO! JUST DON'T GET *US* CAUGHT!
YOU THERE!
DON'T YOU MOVE A MUSCLE. YOU JUST BEEN CAPTURED.
WHO HELPED YOU? WHERE WERE YOU GOING? NAMES! I WANT NAMES!
WE STAYED IN *BEN ROSS'S* CORN CRIB.
AND HOW MANY WERE WITH YOU?
EIGHT. HEADIN' TO DOVER.
RIDE TO DOVER-- ALERT THE SHERIFF.
A THREE-THOUSAND-DOLLAR REWARD FOR EIGHT FUGITIVES IN DOVER? **GOOD GRAVY!**
EXCUSE ME, DID YOU SAY A *THREE-THOUSAND-DOLLAR* REWARD FOR SLAVES?
YES, I DID.
I'LL BE RIGHT BACK.

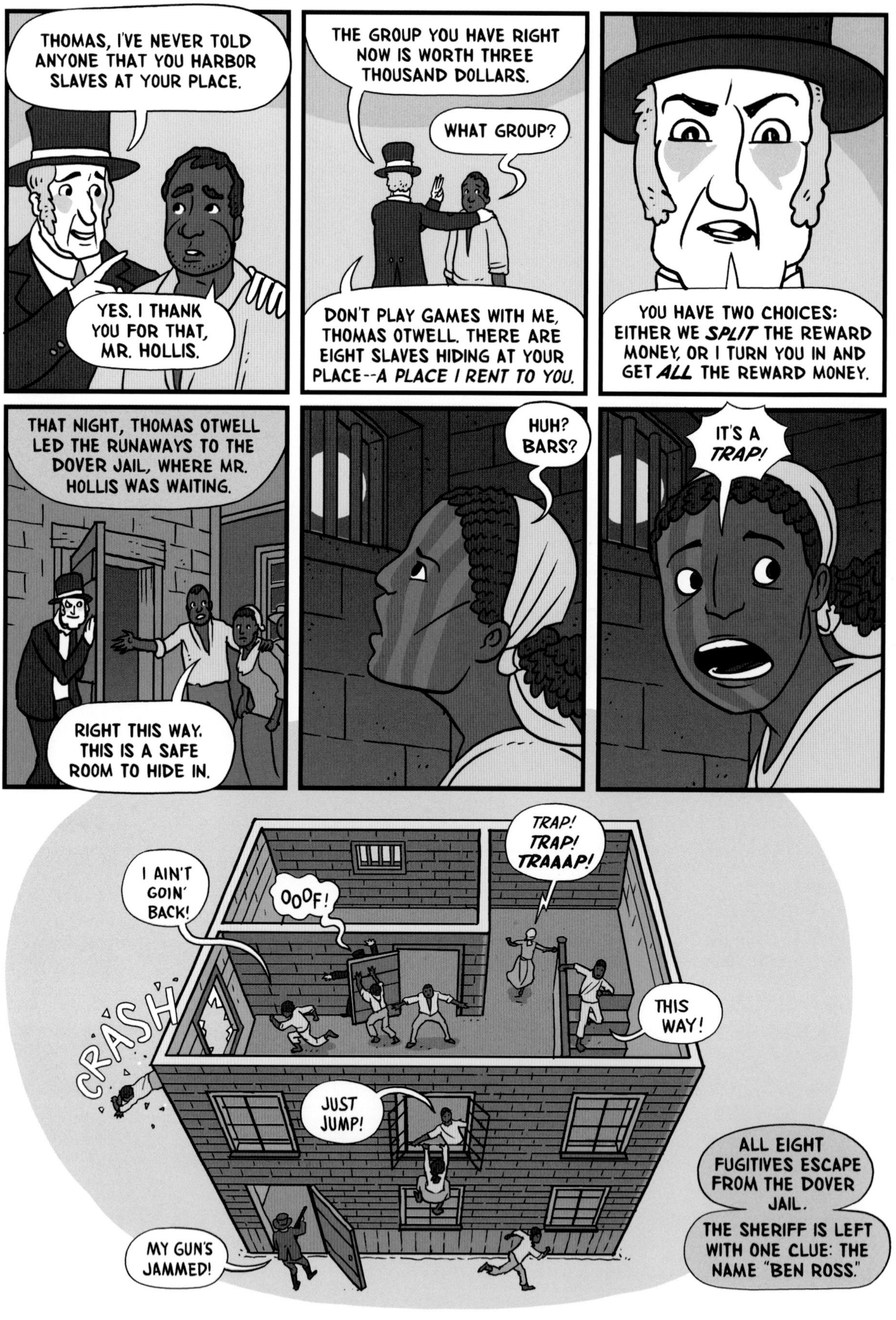
THOMAS, I'VE NEVER TOLD ANYONE THAT YOU HARBOR SLAVES AT YOUR PLACE.
YES. I THANK YOU FOR THAT, MR. HOLLIS.
THE GROUP YOU HAVE RIGHT NOW IS WORTH THREE THOUSAND DOLLARS.
WHAT GROUP?
DON'T PLAY GAMES WITH ME, THOMAS OTWELL. THERE ARE EIGHT SLAVES HIDING AT YOUR PLACE--A PLACE I RENT TO YOU.
YOU HAVE TWO CHOICES: EITHER WE SPLIT THE REWARD MONEY, OR I TURN YOU IN AND GET ALL THE REWARD MONEY.
THAT NIGHT, THOMAS OTWELL LED THE RUNAWAYS TO THE DOVER JAIL, WHERE MR. HOLLIS WAS WAITING.
RIGHT THIS WAY. THIS IS A SAFE ROOM TO HIDE IN.
HUH? BARS?
IT'S A TRAP!
I AIN'T GOIN' BACK!
OOOF!
TRAP! TRAP! TRAAAP!
CRASH
THIS WAY!
JUST JUMP!
MY GUN'S JAMMED!
ALL EIGHT FUGITIVES ESCAPE FROM THE DOVER JAIL.
THE SHERIFF IS LEFT WITH ONE CLUE: THE NAME "BEN ROSS."

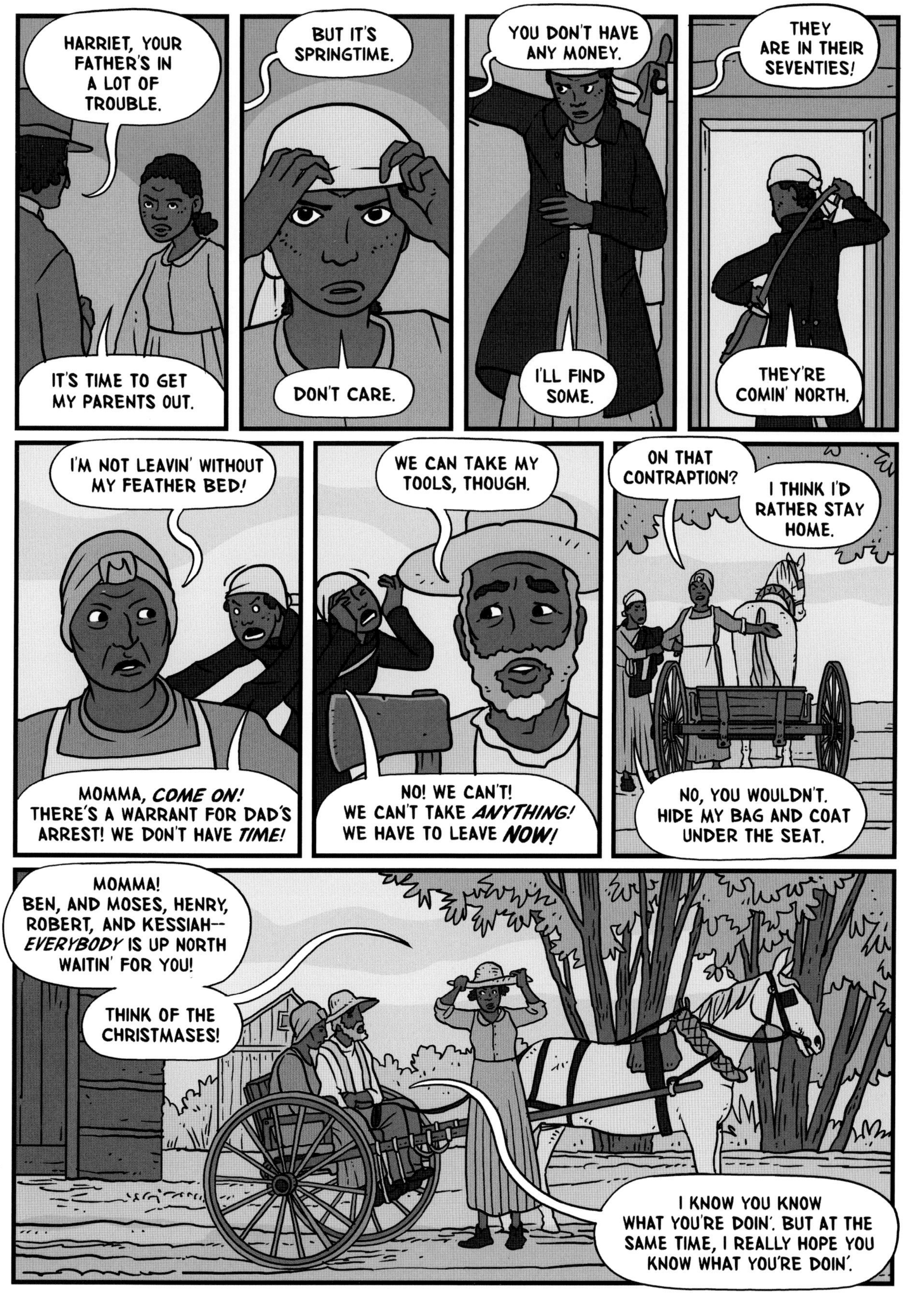
HARRIET, YOUR FATHER'S IN A LOT OF TROUBLE.
IT'S TIME TO GET MY PARENTS OUT.
BUT IT'S SPRINGTIME.
DON'T CARE.
YOU DON'T HAVE ANY MONEY.
I'LL FIND SOME.
THEY ARE IN THEIR SEVENTIES!
THEY'RE COMIN' NORTH.
I'M NOT LEAVIN' WITHOUT MY FEATHER BED!
MOMMA, *COME ON!* THERE'S A WARRANT FOR DAD'S ARREST! WE DON'T HAVE *TIME!*
WE CAN TAKE MY TOOLS, THOUGH.
NO! WE CAN'T! WE CAN'T TAKE *ANYTHING!* WE HAVE TO LEAVE ***NOW!***
ON THAT CONTRAPTION?
I THINK I'D RATHER STAY HOME.
NO, YOU WOULDN'T. HIDE MY BAG AND COAT UNDER THE SEAT.
MOMMA! BEN, AND MOSES, HENRY, ROBERT, AND KESSIAH-- *EVERYBODY* IS UP NORTH WAITIN' FOR YOU!
THINK OF THE CHRISTMASES!
I KNOW YOU KNOW WHAT YOU'RE DOIN'. BUT AT THE SAME TIME, I REALLY HOPE YOU KNOW WHAT YOU'RE DOIN'.

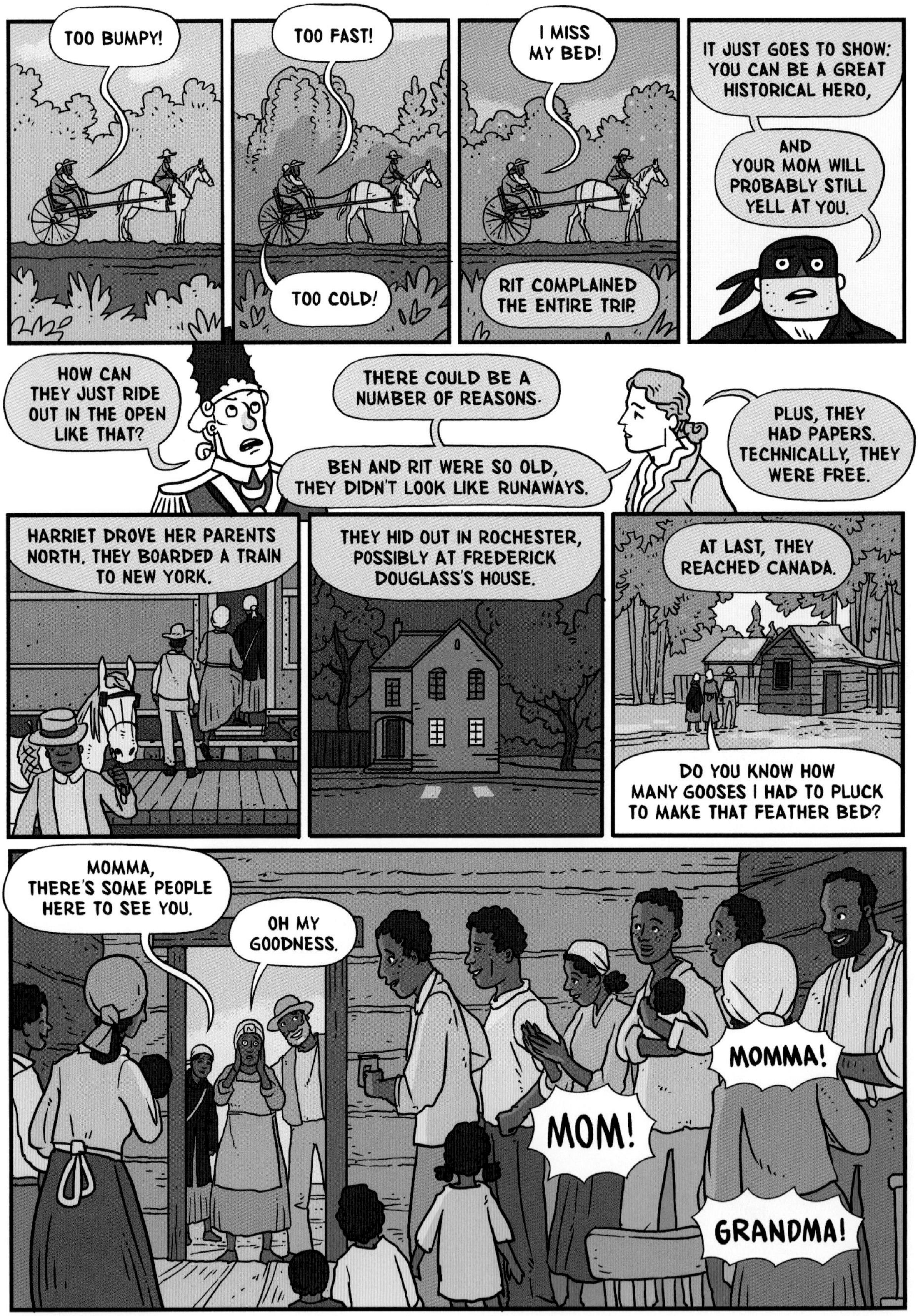
TOO BUMPY!
TOO FAST!
TOO COLD!
I MISS MY BED!
RIT COMPLAINED THE ENTIRE TRIP.
IT JUST GOES TO SHOW: YOU CAN BE A GREAT HISTORICAL HERO,
AND YOUR MOM WILL PROBABLY STILL YELL AT YOU.
HOW CAN THEY JUST RIDE OUT IN THE OPEN LIKE THAT?
THERE COULD BE A NUMBER OF REASONS.
BEN AND RIT WERE SO OLD, THEY DIDN'T LOOK LIKE RUNAWAYS.
PLUS, THEY HAD PAPERS. TECHNICALLY, THEY WERE FREE.
HARRIET DROVE HER PARENTS NORTH. THEY BOARDED A TRAIN TO NEW YORK.
THEY HID OUT IN ROCHESTER, POSSIBLY AT FREDERICK DOUGLASS'S HOUSE.
AT LAST, THEY REACHED CANADA.
DO YOU KNOW HOW MANY GOOSES I HAD TO PLUCK TO MAKE THAT FEATHER BED?
MOMMA, THERE'S SOME PEOPLE HERE TO SEE YOU.
OH MY GOODNESS.
MOMMA!
MOM!
GRANDMA!

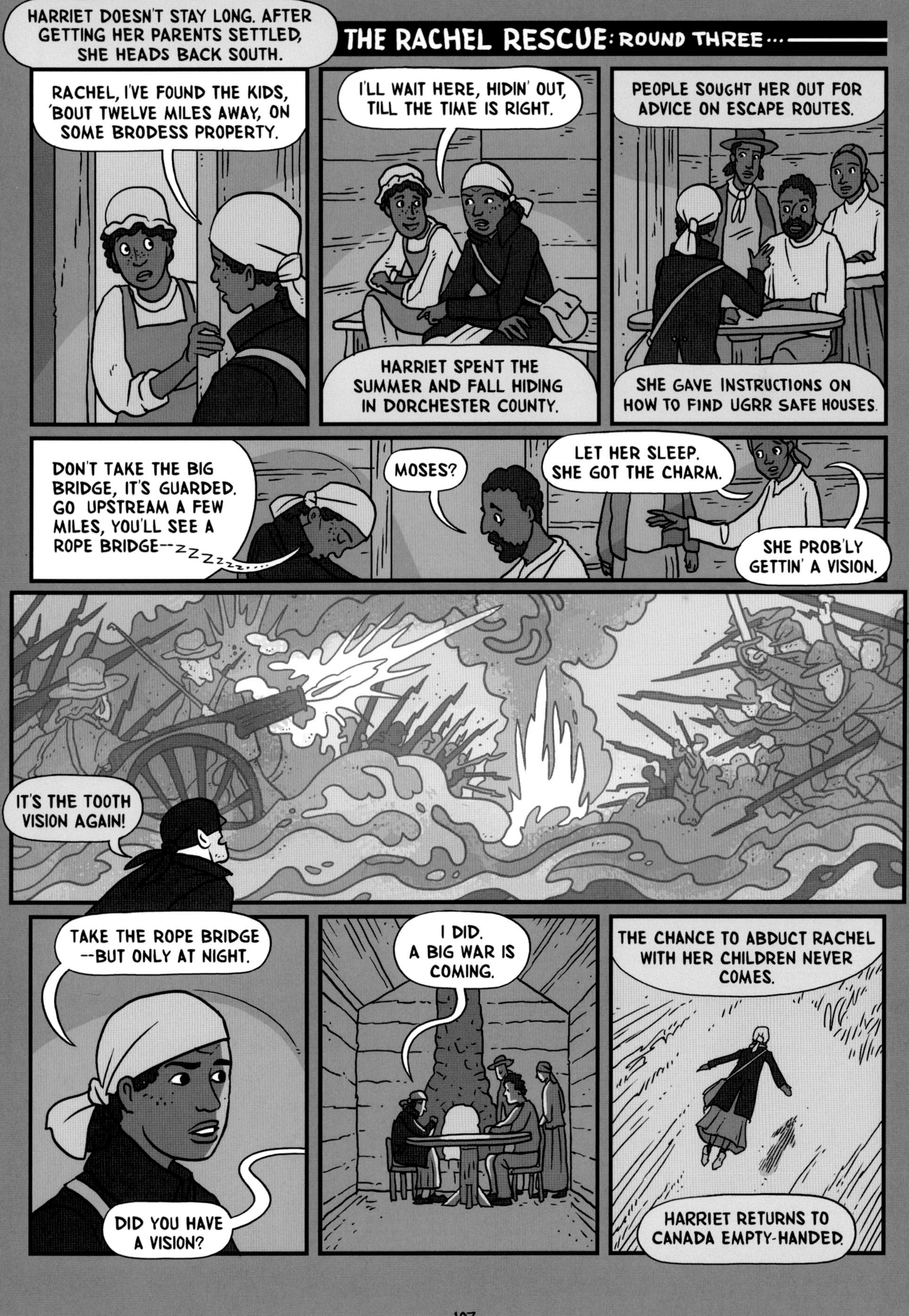

HARRIET DOESN'T STAY LONG. AFTER GETTING HER PARENTS SETTLED, SHE HEADS BACK SOUTH.
THE RACHEL RESCUE: ROUND THREE...
RACHEL, I'VE FOUND THE KIDS, 'BOUT TWELVE MILES AWAY, ON SOME BRODESS PROPERTY.
I'LL WAIT HERE, HIDIN' OUT, TILL THE TIME IS RIGHT.
HARRIET SPENT THE SUMMER AND FALL HIDING IN DORCHESTER COUNTY.
PEOPLE SOUGHT HER OUT FOR ADVICE ON ESCAPE ROUTES.
SHE GAVE INSTRUCTIONS ON HOW TO FIND UGRR SAFE HOUSES.
DON'T TAKE THE BIG BRIDGE, IT'S GUARDED. GO UPSTREAM A FEW MILES, YOU'LL SEE A ROPE BRIDGE--ZZZZZZ...
MOSES?
LET HER SLEEP. SHE GOT THE CHARM.
SHE PROB'LY GETTIN' A VISION.
IT'S THE TOOTH VISION AGAIN!
TAKE THE ROPE BRIDGE --BUT ONLY AT NIGHT.
DID YOU HAVE A VISION?
I DID. A BIG WAR IS COMING.
THE CHANCE TO ABDUCT RACHEL WITH HER CHILDREN NEVER COMES.
HARRIET RETURNS TO CANADA EMPTY-HANDED.

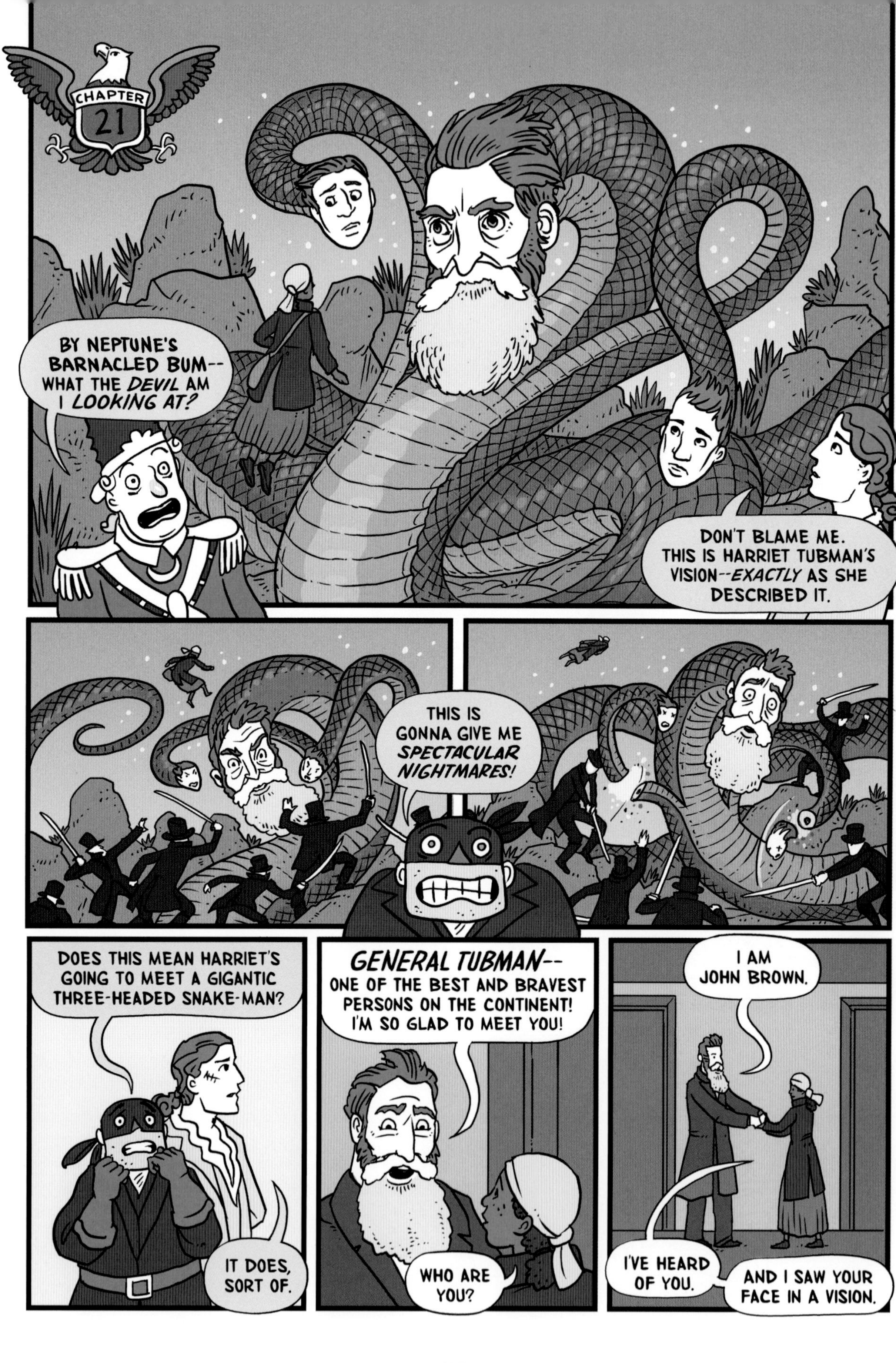
CHAPTER 21
BY NEPTUNE'S BARNACLED BUM-- WHAT THE DEVIL AM I LOOKING AT?
DON'T BLAME ME. THIS IS HARRIET TUBMAN'S VISION--EXACTLY AS SHE DESCRIBED IT.
THIS IS GONNA GIVE ME SPECTACULAR NIGHTMARES!
DOES THIS MEAN HARRIET'S GOING TO MEET A GIGANTIC THREE-HEADED SNAKE-MAN?
IT DOES, SORT OF.
GENERAL TUBMAN-- ONE OF THE BEST AND BRAVEST PERSONS ON THE CONTINENT! I'M SO GLAD TO MEET YOU!
WHO ARE YOU?
I AM JOHN BROWN.
I'VE HEARD OF YOU.
AND I SAW YOUR FACE IN A VISION.

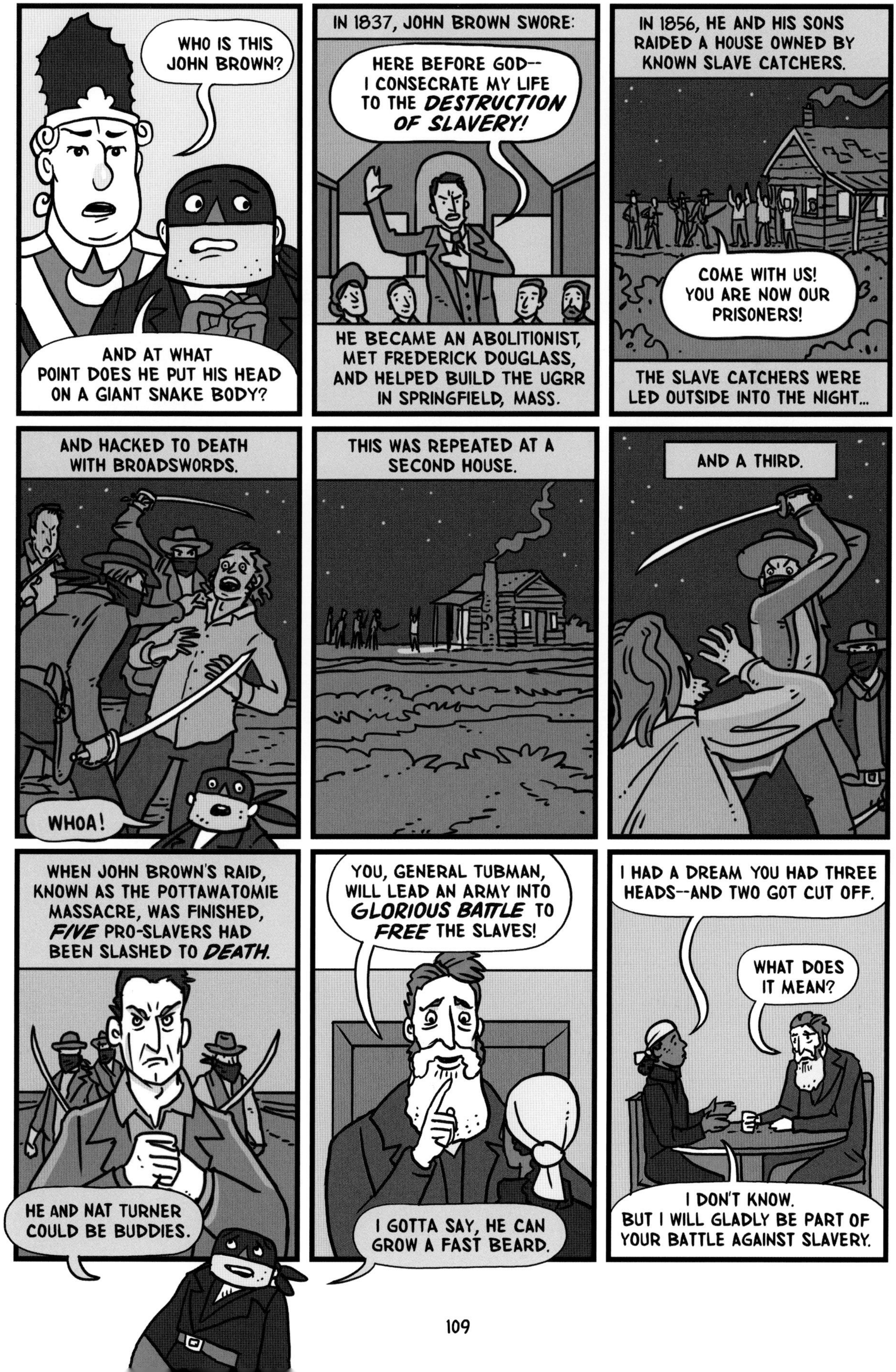

WHO IS THIS JOHN BROWN?
AND AT WHAT POINT DOES HE PUT HIS HEAD ON A GIANT SNAKE BODY?
IN 1837, JOHN BROWN SWORE:
HERE BEFORE GOD-- I CONSECRATE MY LIFE TO THE DESTRUCTION OF SLAVERY!
HE BECAME AN ABOLITIONIST, MET FREDERICK DOUGLASS, AND HELPED BUILD THE UGRR IN SPRINGFIELD, MASS.
IN 1856, HE AND HIS SONS RAIDED A HOUSE OWNED BY KNOWN SLAVE CATCHERS.
COME WITH US! YOU ARE NOW OUR PRISONERS!
THE SLAVE CATCHERS WERE LED OUTSIDE INTO THE NIGHT...
AND HACKED TO DEATH WITH BROADSWORDS.
WHOA!
THIS WAS REPEATED AT A SECOND HOUSE.
AND A THIRD.
WHEN JOHN BROWN'S RAID, KNOWN AS THE POTTAWATOMIE MASSACRE, WAS FINISHED, FIVE PRO-SLAVERS HAD BEEN SLASHED TO DEATH.
HE AND NAT TURNER COULD BE BUDDIES.
YOU, GENERAL TUBMAN, WILL LEAD AN ARMY INTO GLORIOUS BATTLE TO FREE THE SLAVES!
I GOTTA SAY, HE CAN GROW A FAST BEARD.
I HAD A DREAM YOU HAD THREE HEADS--AND TWO GOT CUT OFF.
WHAT DOES IT MEAN?
I DON'T KNOW. BUT I WILL GLADLY BE PART OF YOUR BATTLE AGAINST SLAVERY.

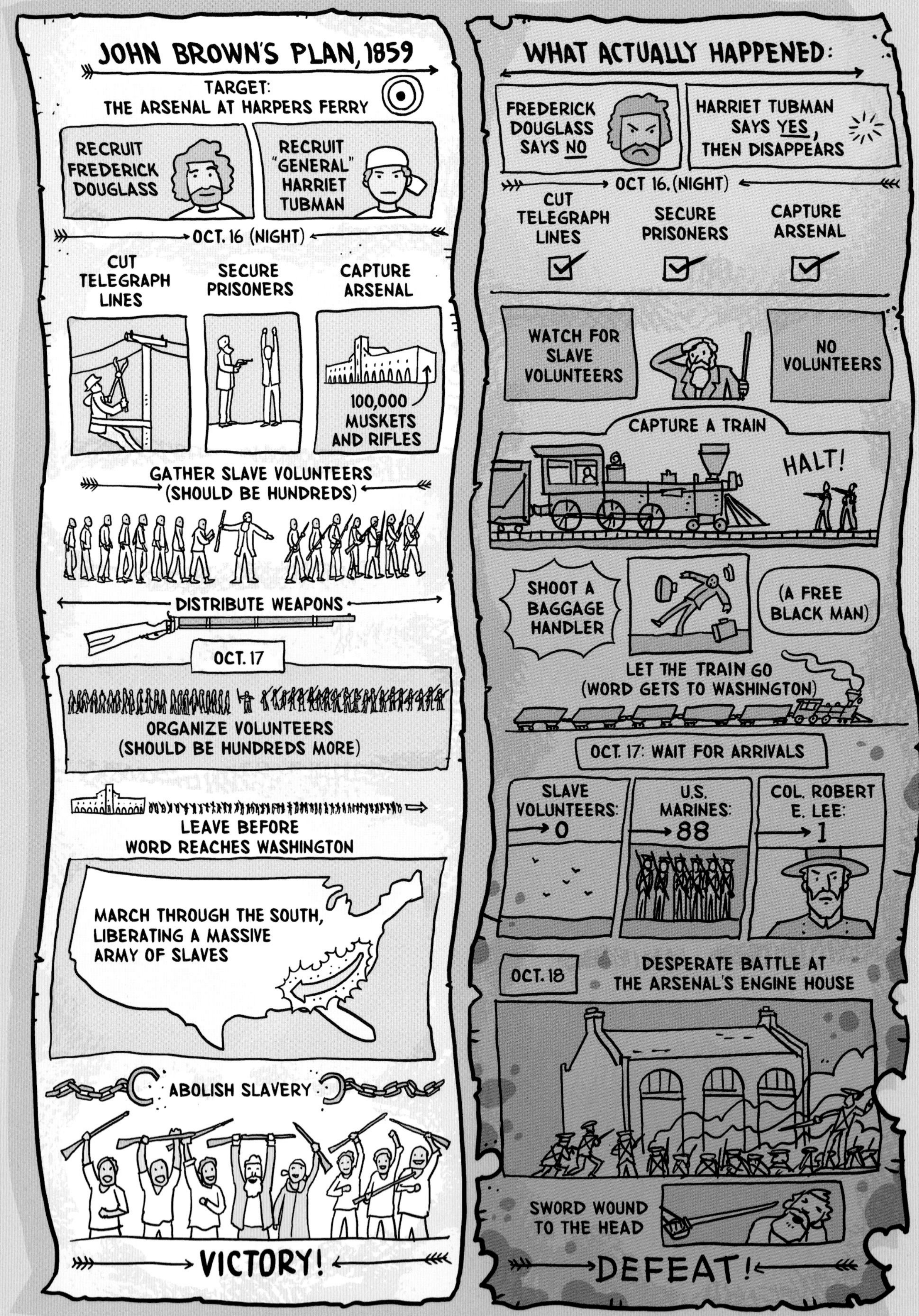

JOHN BROWN'S PLAN, 1859
TARGET:
THE ARSENAL AT HARPERS FERRY
RECRUIT FREDERICK DOUGLASS
RECRUIT "GENERAL" HARRIET TUBMAN
OCT. 16 (NIGHT)
CUT TELEGRAPH LINES
SECURE PRISONERS
CAPTURE ARSENAL
100,000 MUSKETS AND RIFLES
GATHER SLAVE VOLUNTEERS (SHOULD BE HUNDREDS)
DISTRIBUTE WEAPONS
OCT. 17
ORGANIZE VOLUNTEERS (SHOULD BE HUNDREDS MORE)
LEAVE BEFORE WORD REACHES WASHINGTON
MARCH THROUGH THE SOUTH, LIBERATING A MASSIVE ARMY OF SLAVES
ABOLISH SLAVERY
VICTORY!
WHAT ACTUALLY HAPPENED:
FREDERICK DOUGLASS SAYS NO
HARRIET TUBMAN SAYS YES, THEN DISAPPEARS
OCT 16. (NIGHT)
CUT TELEGRAPH LINES
SECURE PRISONERS
CAPTURE ARSENAL
WATCH FOR SLAVE VOLUNTEERS
NO VOLUNTEERS
CAPTURE A TRAIN
HALT!
SHOOT A BAGGAGE HANDLER
(A FREE BLACK MAN)
LET THE TRAIN GO (WORD GETS TO WASHINGTON)
OCT. 17: WAIT FOR ARRIVALS
SLAVE VOLUNTEERS: 0
U.S. MARINES: 88
COL. ROBERT E. LEE: 1
OCT. 18
DESPERATE BATTLE AT THE ARSENAL'S ENGINE HOUSE
SWORD WOUND TO THE HEAD
DEFEAT!

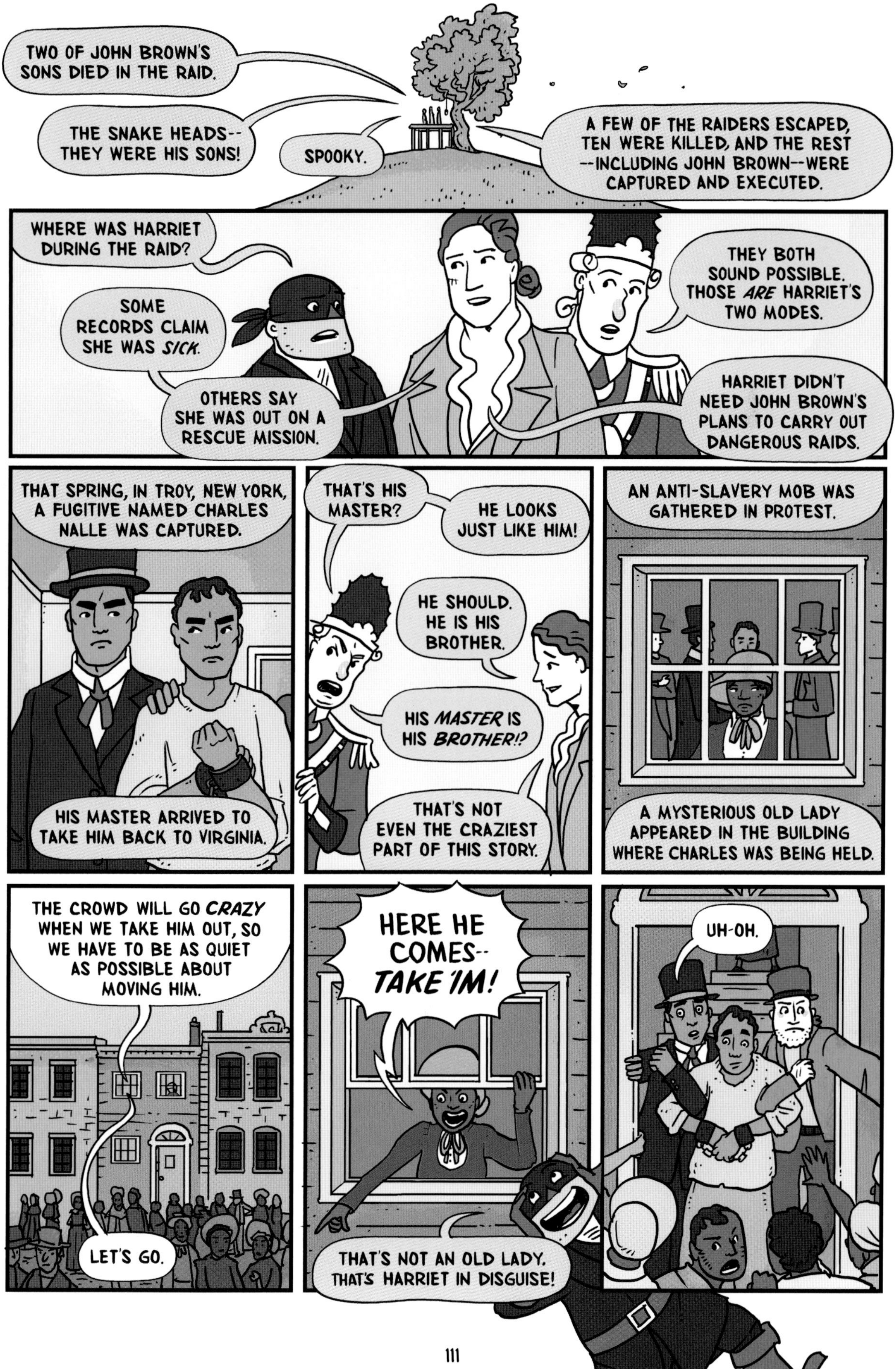
TWO OF JOHN BROWN'S SONS DIED IN THE RAID.
THE SNAKE HEADS-- THEY WERE HIS SONS!
SPOOKY.
A FEW OF THE RAIDERS ESCAPED, TEN WERE KILLED, AND THE REST --INCLUDING JOHN BROWN--WERE CAPTURED AND EXECUTED.
WHERE WAS HARRIET DURING THE RAID?
SOME RECORDS CLAIM SHE WAS *SICK*.
OTHERS SAY SHE WAS OUT ON A RESCUE MISSION.
THEY BOTH SOUND POSSIBLE. THOSE *ARE* HARRIET'S TWO MODES.
HARRIET DIDN'T NEED JOHN BROWN'S PLANS TO CARRY OUT DANGEROUS RAIDS.
THAT SPRING, IN TROY, NEW YORK, A FUGITIVE NAMED CHARLES NALLE WAS CAPTURED.
HIS MASTER ARRIVED TO TAKE HIM BACK TO VIRGINIA.
THAT'S HIS MASTER?
HE LOOKS JUST LIKE HIM!
HE SHOULD. HE IS HIS BROTHER.
HIS *MASTER* IS HIS *BROTHER!?*
THAT'S NOT EVEN THE CRAZIEST PART OF THIS STORY.
AN ANTI-SLAVERY MOB WAS GATHERED IN PROTEST.
A MYSTERIOUS OLD LADY APPEARED IN THE BUILDING WHERE CHARLES WAS BEING HELD.
THE CROWD WILL GO *CRAZY* WHEN WE TAKE HIM OUT, SO WE HAVE TO BE AS QUIET AS POSSIBLE ABOUT MOVING HIM.
LET'S GO.
HERE HE COMES-- *TAKE 'IM!*
THAT'S NOT AN OLD LADY. THAT'S HARRIET IN DISGUISE!
UH-OH.

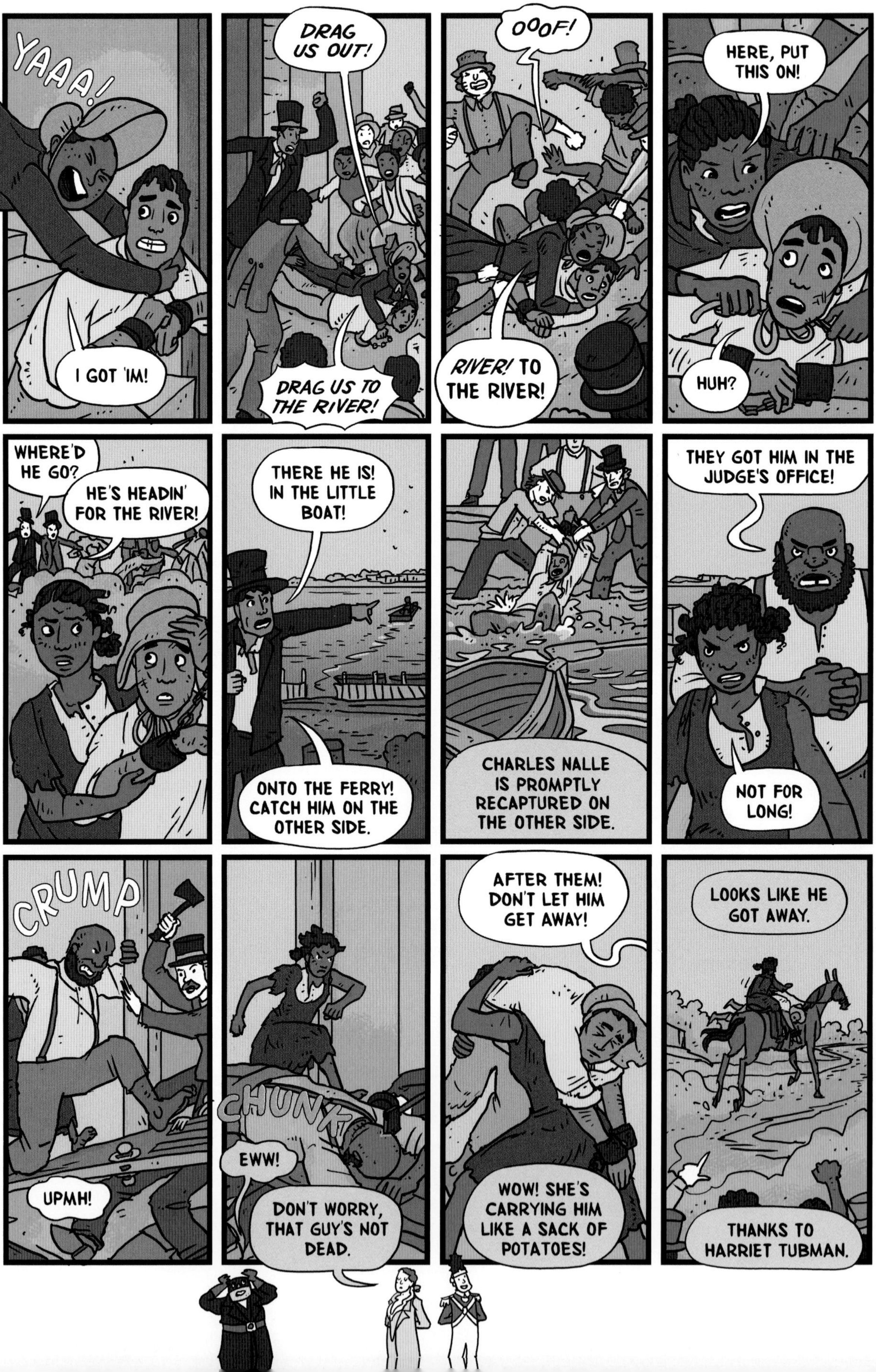
YAAAA!
I GOT 'IM!
DRAG US OUT!
DRAG US TO THE RIVER!
OOOF!
RIVER! TO THE RIVER!
HERE, PUT THIS ON!
HUH?
WHERE'D HE GO?
HE'S HEADIN' FOR THE RIVER!
THERE HE IS! IN THE LITTLE BOAT!
ONTO THE FERRY! CATCH HIM ON THE OTHER SIDE.
CHARLES NALLE IS PROMPTLY RECAPTURED ON THE OTHER SIDE.
THEY GOT HIM IN THE JUDGE'S OFFICE!
NOT FOR LONG!
CRUMP
UPMH!
CHUNK
EWW!
DON'T WORRY, THAT GUY'S NOT DEAD.
AFTER THEM! DON'T LET HIM GET AWAY!
WOW! SHE'S CARRYING HIM LIKE A SACK OF POTATOES!
LOOKS LIKE HE GOT AWAY.
THANKS TO HARRIET TUBMAN.

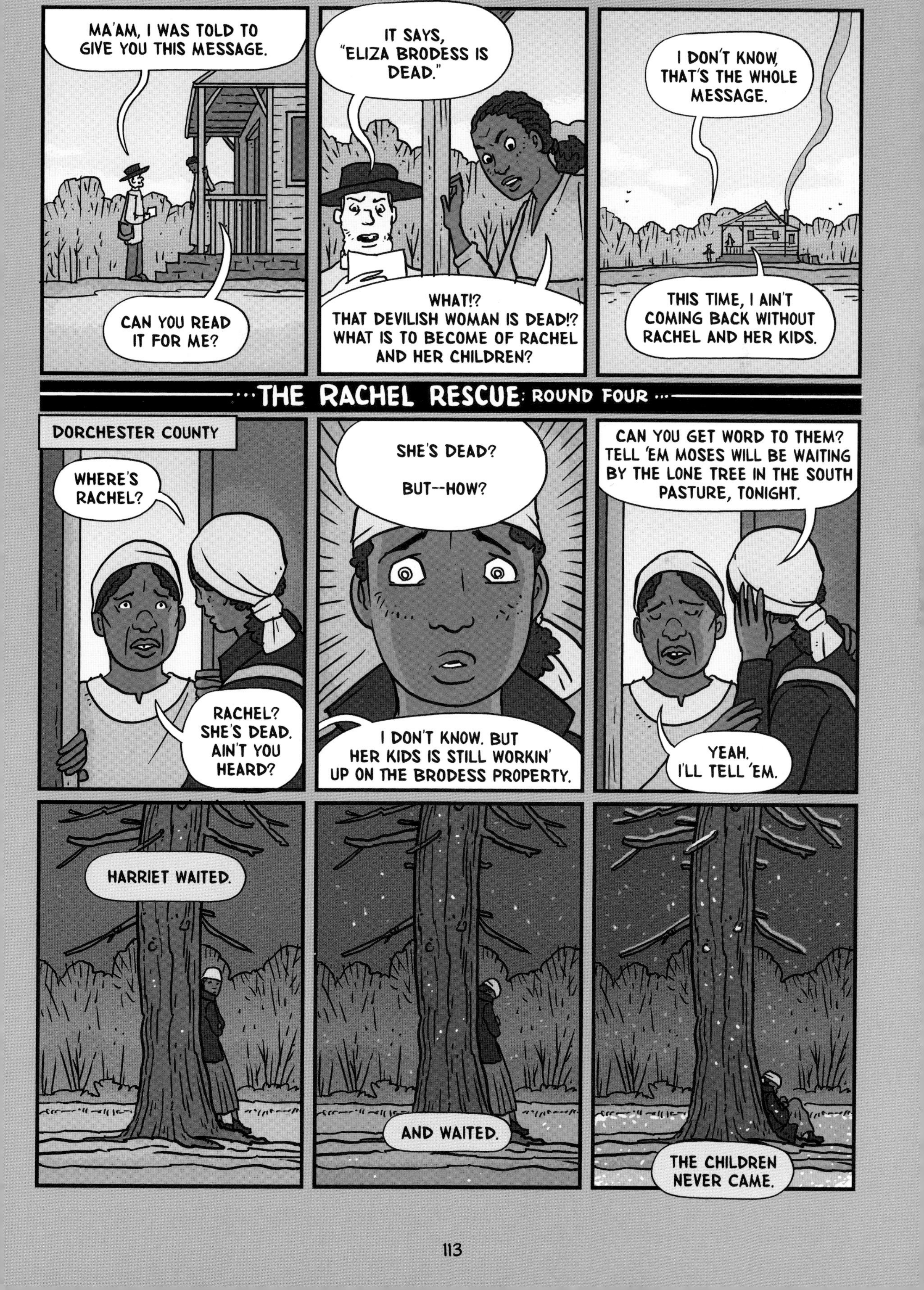
MA'AM, I WAS TOLD TO GIVE YOU THIS MESSAGE.
CAN YOU READ IT FOR ME?
IT SAYS, "ELIZA BRODESS IS DEAD."
WHAT!? THAT DEVILISH WOMAN IS DEAD!? WHAT IS TO BECOME OF RACHEL AND HER CHILDREN?
I DON'T KNOW, THAT'S THE WHOLE MESSAGE.
THIS TIME, I AIN'T COMING BACK WITHOUT RACHEL AND HER KIDS.
THE RACHEL RESCUE: ROUND FOUR
DORCHESTER COUNTY
WHERE'S RACHEL?
RACHEL? SHE'S DEAD. AIN'T YOU HEARD?
SHE'S DEAD?
BUT--HOW?
I DON'T KNOW. BUT HER KIDS IS STILL WORKIN' UP ON THE BRODESS PROPERTY.
CAN YOU GET WORD TO THEM? TELL 'EM MOSES WILL BE WAITING BY THE LONE TREE IN THE SOUTH PASTURE, TONIGHT.
YEAH. I'LL TELL 'EM.
HARRIET WAITED.
AND WAITED.
THE CHILDREN NEVER CAME.

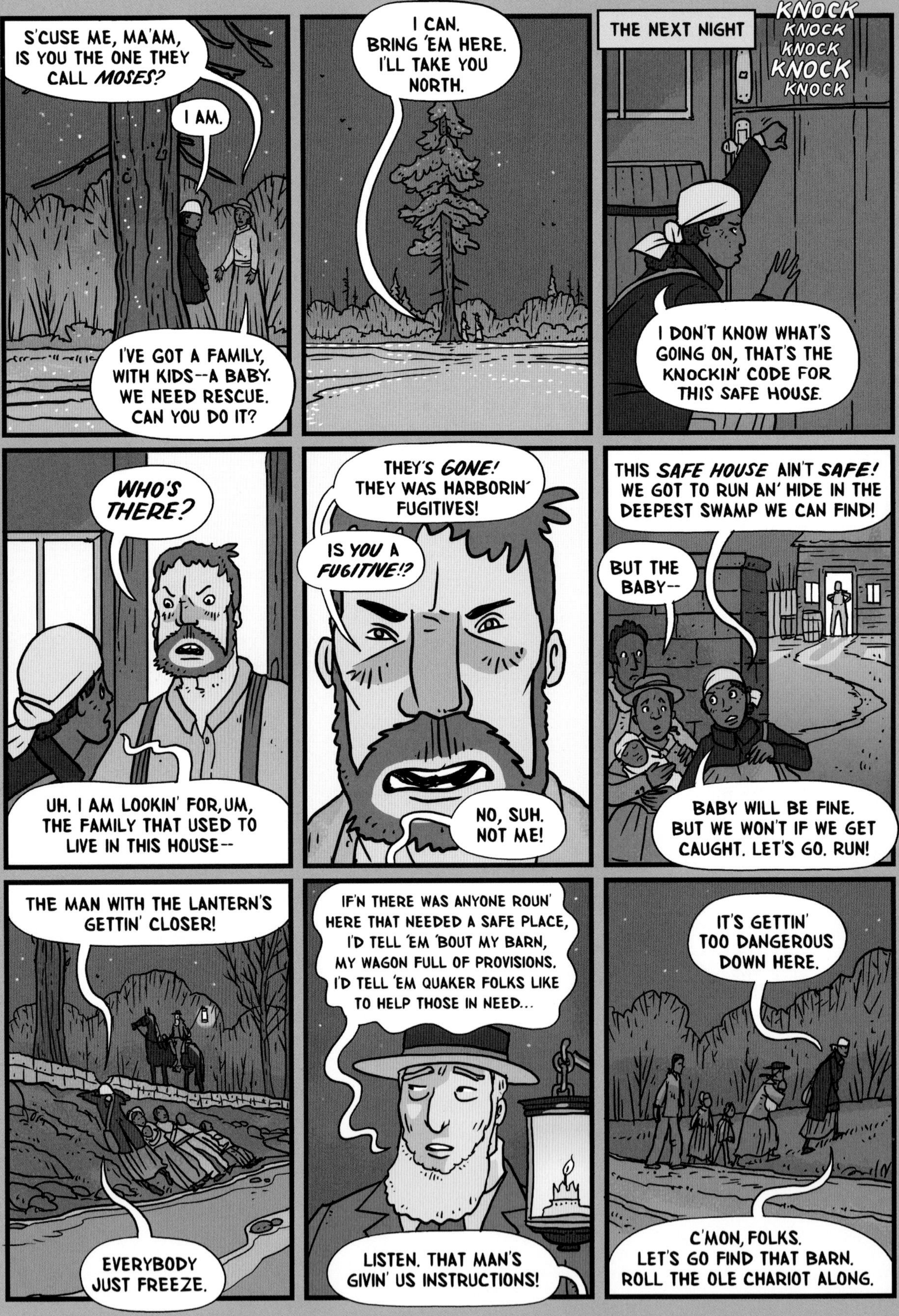
S'CUSE ME, MA'AM, IS YOU THE ONE THEY CALL *MOSES?*
I AM.
I'VE GOT A FAMILY, WITH KIDS--A BABY. WE NEED RESCUE. CAN YOU DO IT?
I CAN. BRING 'EM HERE. I'LL TAKE YOU NORTH.
THE NEXT NIGHT
KNOCK KNOCK KNOCK KNOCK KNOCK
I DON'T KNOW WHAT'S GOING ON, THAT'S THE KNOCKIN' CODE FOR THIS SAFE HOUSE.
WHO'S THERE?
UH. I AM LOOKIN' FOR, UM, THE FAMILY THAT USED TO LIVE IN THIS HOUSE--
THEY'S *GONE!* THEY WAS HARBORIN' FUGITIVES!
IS *YOU* A *FUGITIVE!?*
NO, SUH. NOT ME!
THIS *SAFE HOUSE* AIN'T *SAFE!* WE GOT TO RUN AN' HIDE IN THE DEEPEST SWAMP WE CAN FIND!
BUT THE BABY--
BABY WILL BE FINE. BUT WE WON'T IF WE GET CAUGHT. LET'S GO. RUN!
THE MAN WITH THE LANTERN'S GETTIN' CLOSER!
EVERYBODY JUST FREEZE.
IF'N THERE WAS ANYONE ROUN' HERE THAT NEEDED A SAFE PLACE, I'D TELL 'EM 'BOUT MY BARN, MY WAGON FULL OF PROVISIONS. I'D TELL 'EM QUAKER FOLKS LIKE TO HELP THOSE IN NEED...
LISTEN. THAT MAN'S GIVIN' US INSTRUCTIONS!
IT'S GETTIN' TOO DANGEROUS DOWN HERE.
C'MON, FOLKS. LET'S GO FIND THAT BARN. ROLL THE OLE CHARIOT ALONG.

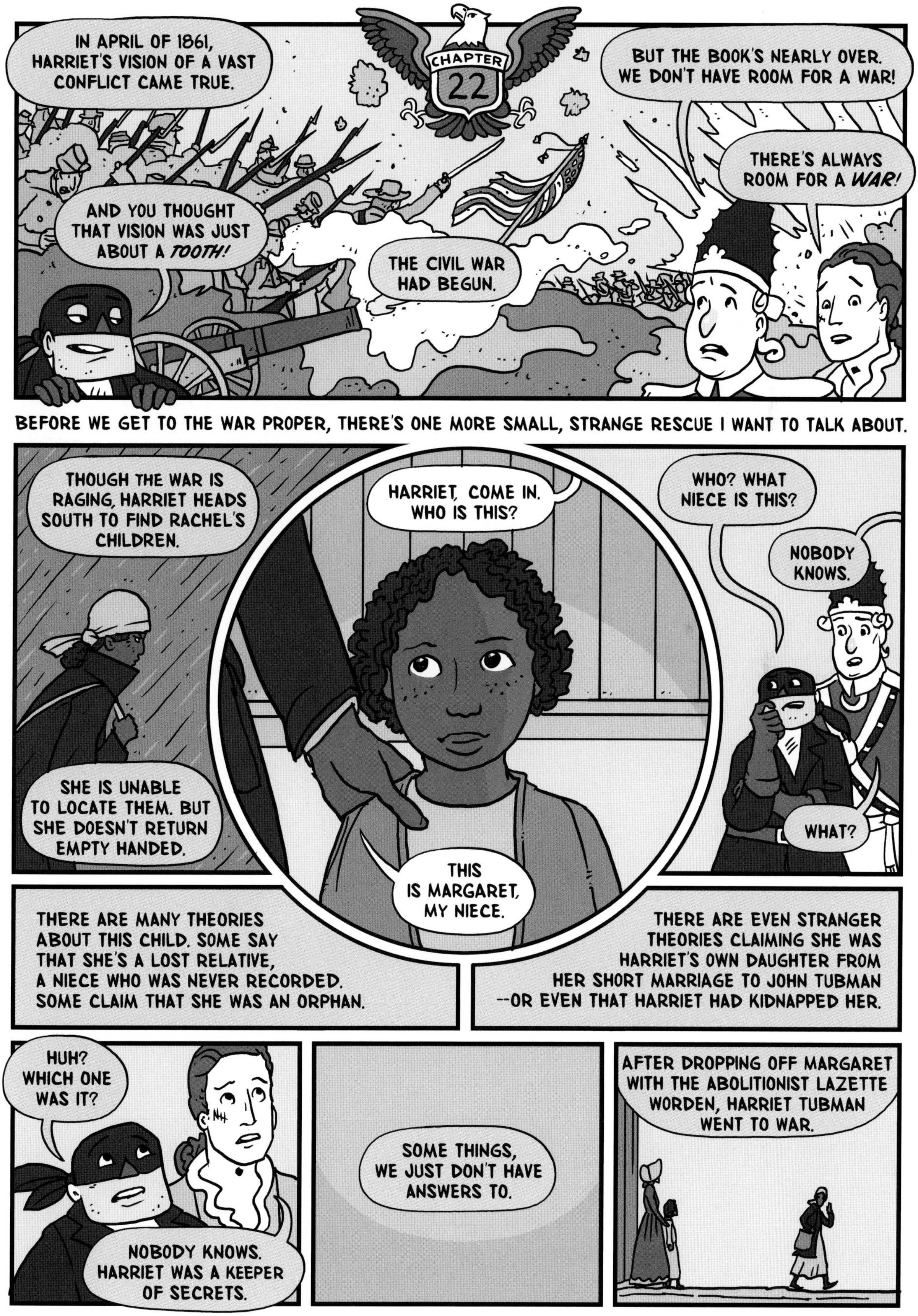
CHAPTER 22
IN APRIL OF 1861, HARRIET'S VISION OF A VAST CONFLICT CAME TRUE.
AND YOU THOUGHT THAT VISION WAS JUST ABOUT A *TOOTH!*
THE CIVIL WAR HAD BEGUN.
BUT THE BOOK'S NEARLY OVER. WE DON'T HAVE ROOM FOR A WAR!
THERE'S ALWAYS ROOM FOR A *WAR!*
BEFORE WE GET TO THE WAR PROPER, THERE'S ONE MORE SMALL, STRANGE RESCUE I WANT TO TALK ABOUT.
THOUGH THE WAR IS RAGING, HARRIET HEADS SOUTH TO FIND RACHEL'S CHILDREN.
SHE IS UNABLE TO LOCATE THEM. BUT SHE DOESN'T RETURN EMPTY HANDED.
HARRIET, COME IN. WHO IS THIS?
THIS IS MARGARET, MY NIECE.
WHO? WHAT NIECE IS THIS?
NOBODY KNOWS.
WHAT?
THERE ARE MANY THEORIES ABOUT THIS CHILD. SOME SAY THAT SHE'S A LOST RELATIVE, A NIECE WHO WAS NEVER RECORDED. SOME CLAIM THAT SHE WAS AN ORPHAN.
THERE ARE EVEN STRANGER THEORIES CLAIMING SHE WAS HARRIET'S OWN DAUGHTER FROM HER SHORT MARRIAGE TO JOHN TUBMAN --OR EVEN THAT HARRIET HAD KIDNAPPED HER.
HUH? WHICH ONE WAS IT?
NOBODY KNOWS. HARRIET WAS A KEEPER OF SECRETS.
SOME THINGS, WE JUST DON'T HAVE ANSWERS TO.
AFTER DROPPING OFF MARGARET WITH THE ABOLITIONIST LAZETTE WORDEN, HARRIET TUBMAN WENT TO WAR.

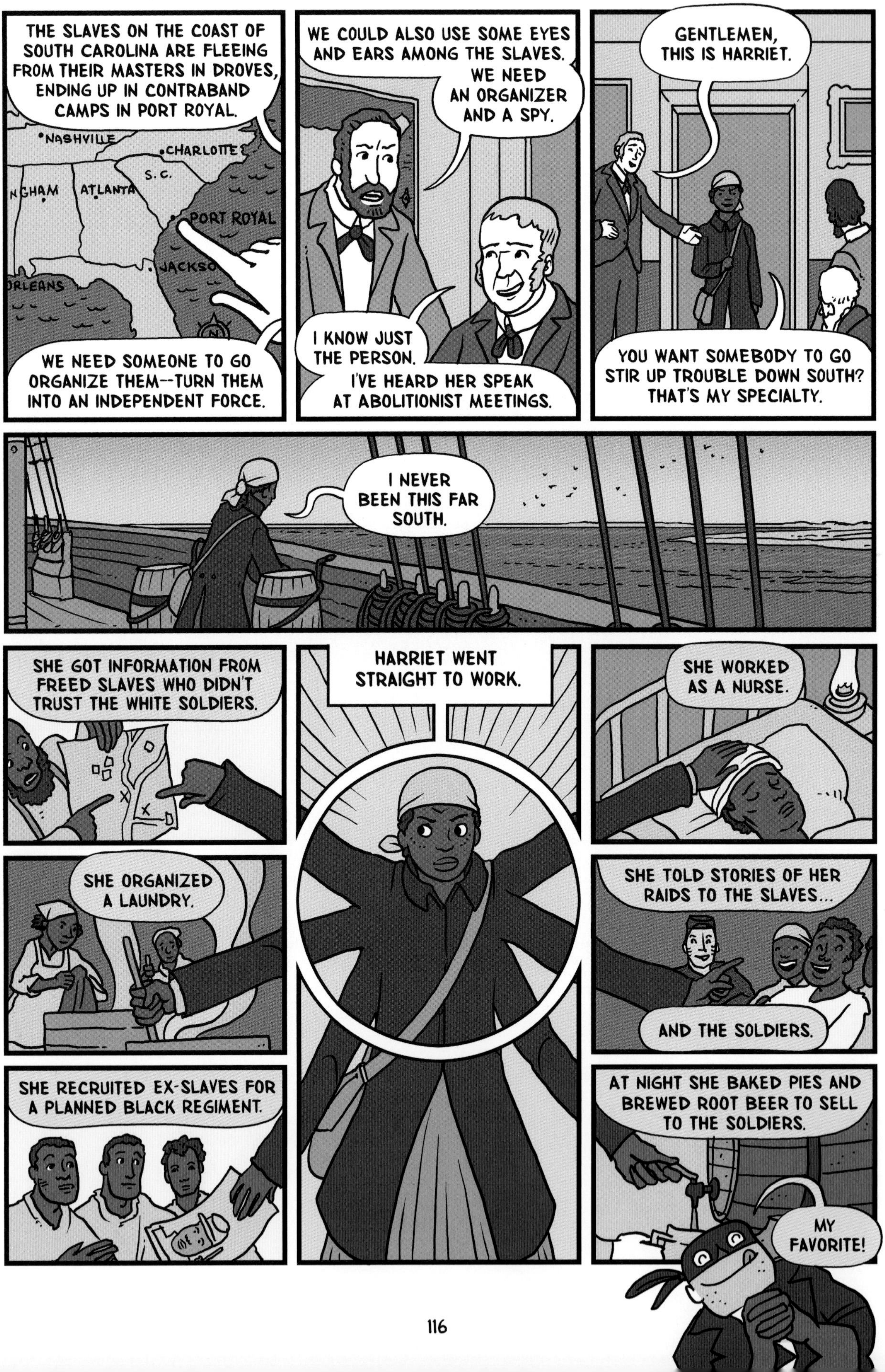
THE SLAVES ON THE COAST OF SOUTH CAROLINA ARE FLEEING FROM THEIR MASTERS IN DROVES, ENDING UP IN CONTRABAND CAMPS IN PORT ROYAL.
NASHVILLE
CHARLOTTE
S.C.
NGHAM
ATLANTA
PORT ROYAL
JACKSO
ORLEANS
WE NEED SOMEONE TO GO ORGANIZE THEM--TURN THEM INTO AN INDEPENDENT FORCE.
WE COULD ALSO USE SOME EYES AND EARS AMONG THE SLAVES.
WE NEED AN ORGANIZER AND A SPY.
I KNOW JUST THE PERSON.
I'VE HEARD HER SPEAK AT ABOLITIONIST MEETINGS.
GENTLEMEN, THIS IS HARRIET.
YOU WANT SOMEBODY TO GO STIR UP TROUBLE DOWN SOUTH? THAT'S MY SPECIALTY.
I NEVER BEEN THIS FAR SOUTH.
HARRIET WENT STRAIGHT TO WORK.
SHE GOT INFORMATION FROM FREED SLAVES WHO DIDN'T TRUST THE WHITE SOLDIERS.
SHE WORKED AS A NURSE.
SHE ORGANIZED A LAUNDRY.
SHE TOLD STORIES OF HER RAIDS TO THE SLAVES...
AND THE SOLDIERS.
SHE RECRUITED EX-SLAVES FOR A PLANNED BLACK REGIMENT.
AT NIGHT SHE BAKED PIES AND BREWED ROOT BEER TO SELL TO THE SOLDIERS.
MY FAVORITE!

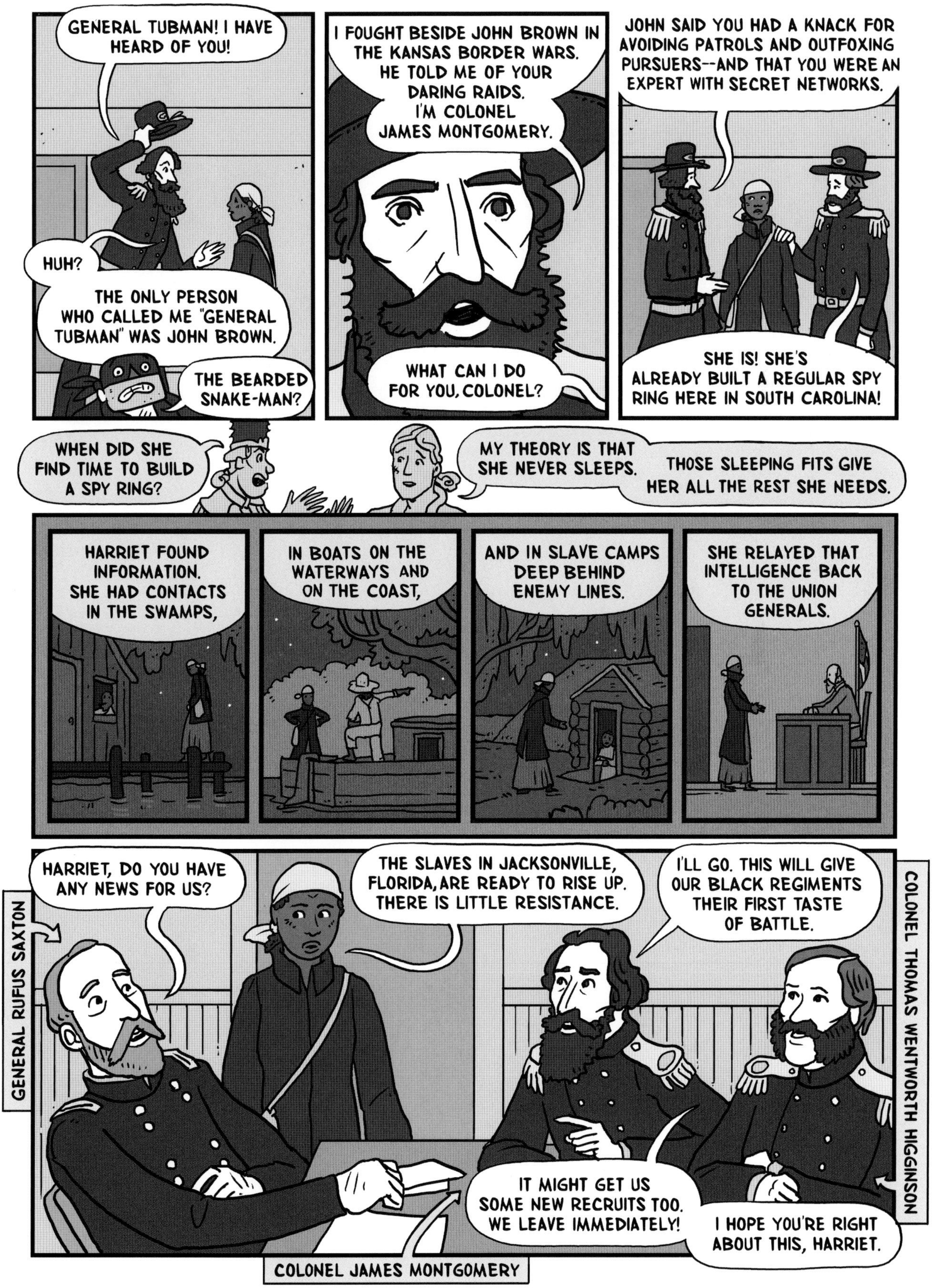
GENERAL TUBMAN! I HAVE HEARD OF YOU!
HUH?
THE ONLY PERSON WHO CALLED ME "GENERAL TUBMAN" WAS JOHN BROWN.
THE BEARDED SNAKE-MAN?
I FOUGHT BESIDE JOHN BROWN IN THE KANSAS BORDER WARS. HE TOLD ME OF YOUR DARING RAIDS. I'M COLONEL JAMES MONTGOMERY.
WHAT CAN I DO FOR YOU, COLONEL?
JOHN SAID YOU HAD A KNACK FOR AVOIDING PATROLS AND OUTFOXING PURSUERS--AND THAT YOU WERE AN EXPERT WITH SECRET NETWORKS.
SHE IS! SHE'S ALREADY BUILT A REGULAR SPY RING HERE IN SOUTH CAROLINA!
WHEN DID SHE FIND TIME TO BUILD A SPY RING?
MY THEORY IS THAT SHE NEVER SLEEPS.
THOSE SLEEPING FITS GIVE HER ALL THE REST SHE NEEDS.
HARRIET FOUND INFORMATION. SHE HAD CONTACTS IN THE SWAMPS,
IN BOATS ON THE WATERWAYS AND ON THE COAST,
AND IN SLAVE CAMPS DEEP BEHIND ENEMY LINES.
SHE RELAYED THAT INTELLIGENCE BACK TO THE UNION GENERALS.
GENERAL RUFUS SAXTON
HARRIET, DO YOU HAVE ANY NEWS FOR US?
THE SLAVES IN JACKSONVILLE, FLORIDA, ARE READY TO RISE UP. THERE IS LITTLE RESISTANCE.
I'LL GO. THIS WILL GIVE OUR BLACK REGIMENTS THEIR FIRST TASTE OF BATTLE.
COLONEL THOMAS WENTWORTH HIGGINSON
IT MIGHT GET US SOME NEW RECRUITS TOO. WE LEAVE IMMEDIATELY!
I HOPE YOU'RE RIGHT ABOUT THIS, HARRIET.
COLONEL JAMES MONTGOMERY

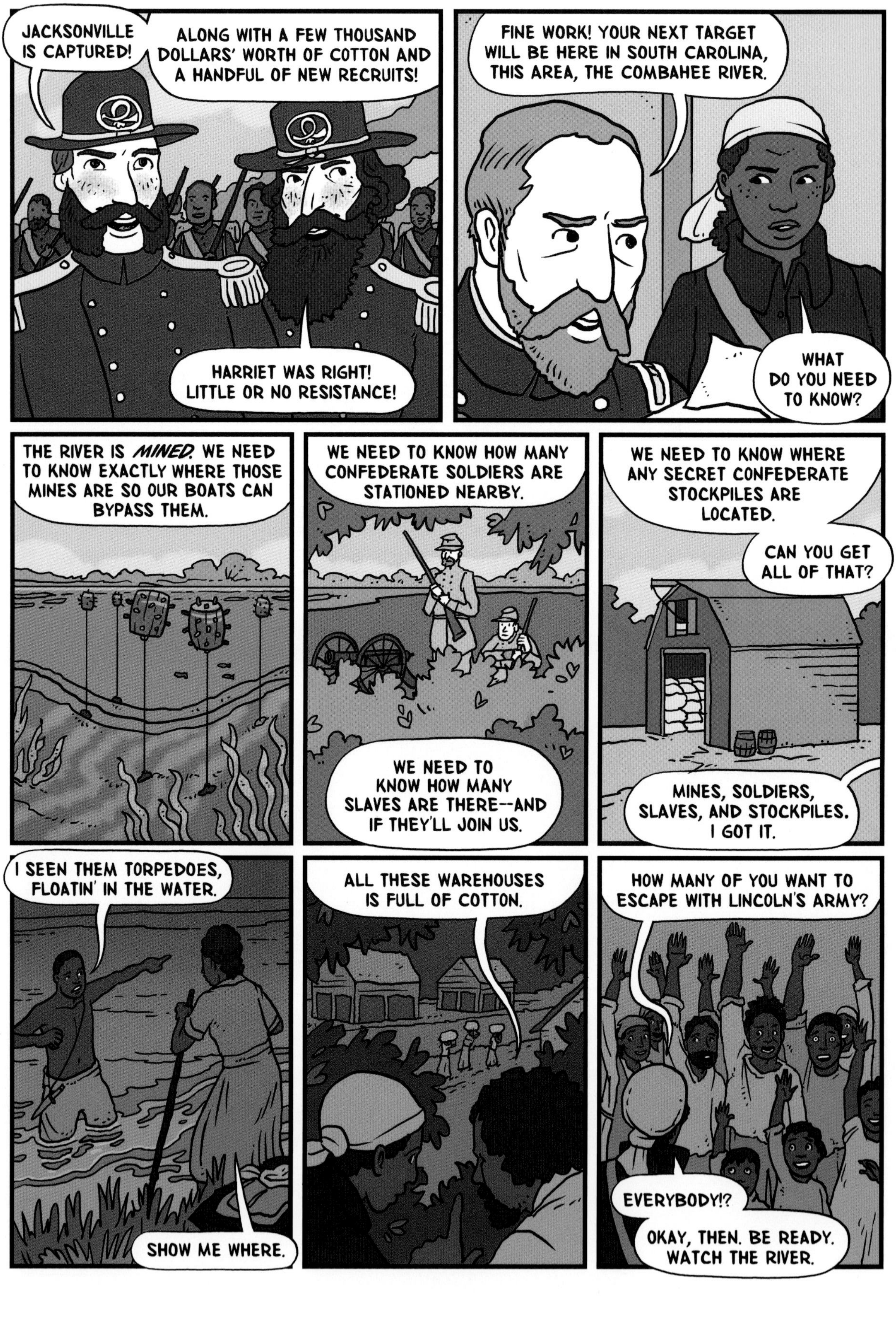
JACKSONVILLE IS CAPTURED!
ALONG WITH A FEW THOUSAND DOLLARS' WORTH OF COTTON AND A HANDFUL OF NEW RECRUITS!
HARRIET WAS RIGHT! LITTLE OR NO RESISTANCE!
FINE WORK! YOUR NEXT TARGET WILL BE HERE IN SOUTH CAROLINA, THIS AREA, THE COMBAHEE RIVER.
WHAT DO YOU NEED TO KNOW?
THE RIVER IS *MINED.* WE NEED TO KNOW EXACTLY WHERE THOSE MINES ARE SO OUR BOATS CAN BYPASS THEM.
WE NEED TO KNOW HOW MANY CONFEDERATE SOLDIERS ARE STATIONED NEARBY.
WE NEED TO KNOW HOW MANY SLAVES ARE THERE--AND IF THEY'LL JOIN US.
WE NEED TO KNOW WHERE ANY SECRET CONFEDERATE STOCKPILES ARE LOCATED.
CAN YOU GET ALL OF THAT?
MINES, SOLDIERS, SLAVES, AND STOCKPILES. I GOT IT.
I SEEN THEM TORPEDOES, FLOATIN' IN THE WATER.
SHOW ME WHERE.
ALL THESE WAREHOUSES IS FULL OF COTTON.
HOW MANY OF YOU WANT TO ESCAPE WITH LINCOLN'S ARMY?
EVERYBODY!?
OKAY, THEN. BE READY. WATCH THE RIVER.

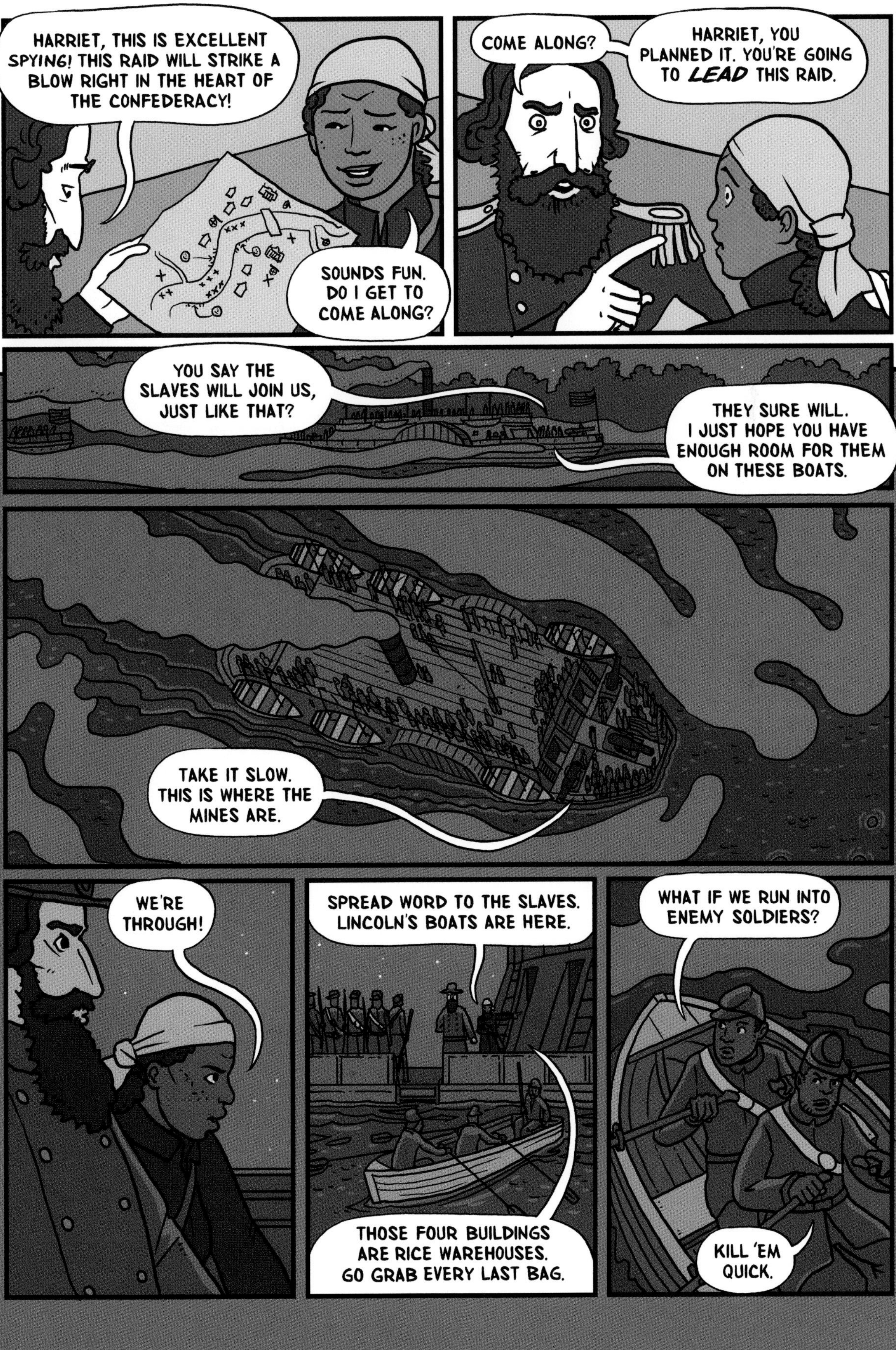
HARRIET, THIS IS EXCELLENT SPYING! THIS RAID WILL STRIKE A BLOW RIGHT IN THE HEART OF THE CONFEDERACY!
SOUNDS FUN. DO I GET TO COME ALONG?
COME ALONG?
HARRIET, YOU PLANNED IT. YOU'RE GOING TO *LEAD* THIS RAID.
YOU SAY THE SLAVES WILL JOIN US, JUST LIKE THAT?
THEY SURE WILL. I JUST HOPE YOU HAVE ENOUGH ROOM FOR THEM ON THESE BOATS.
TAKE IT SLOW. THIS IS WHERE THE MINES ARE.
WE'RE THROUGH!
SPREAD WORD TO THE SLAVES. LINCOLN'S BOATS ARE HERE.
THOSE FOUR BUILDINGS ARE RICE WAREHOUSES. GO GRAB EVERY LAST BAG.
WHAT IF WE RUN INTO ENEMY SOLDIERS?
KILL 'EM QUICK.

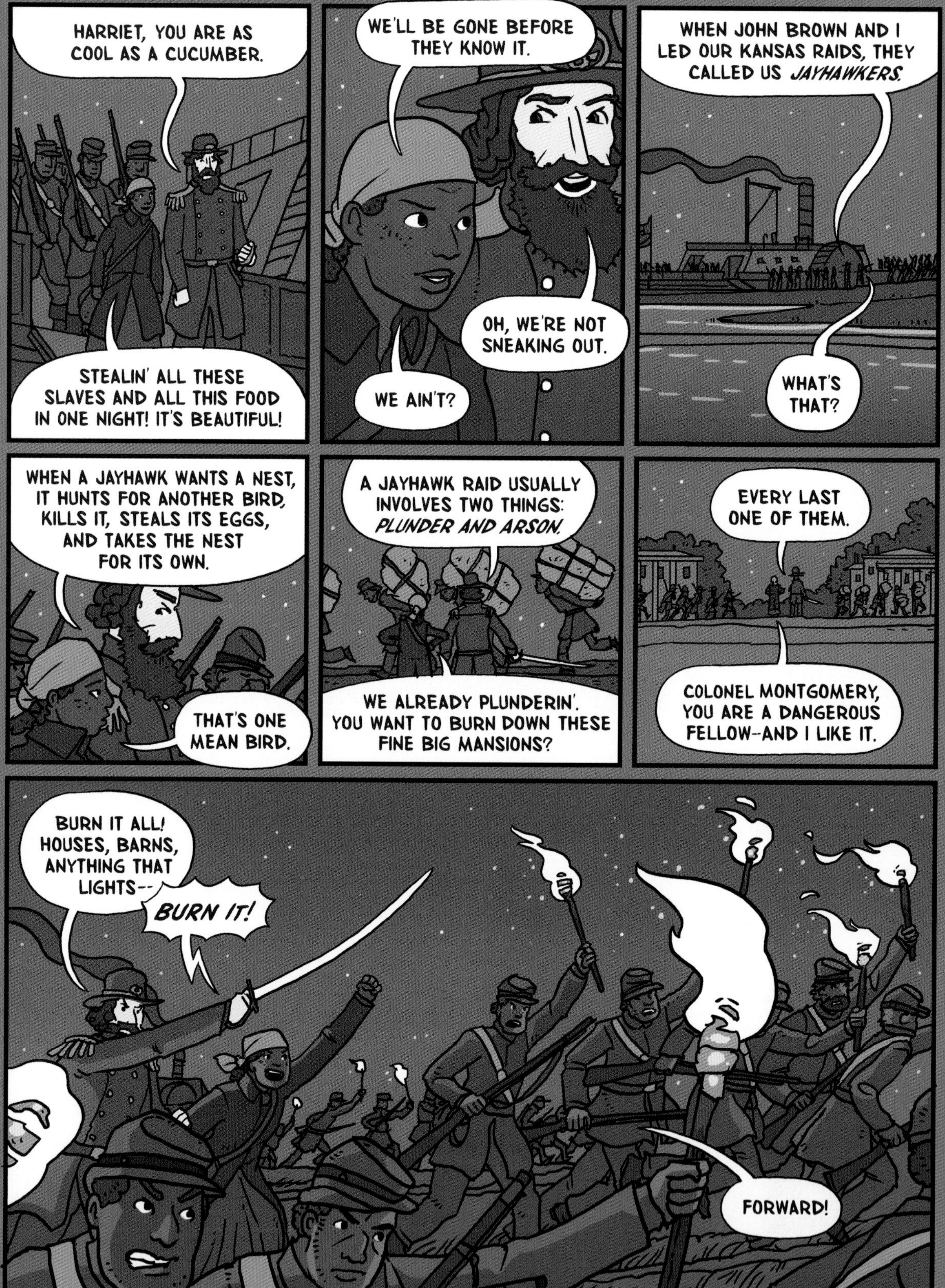
HARRIET, YOU ARE AS COOL AS A CUCUMBER.
STEALIN' ALL THESE SLAVES AND ALL THIS FOOD IN ONE NIGHT! IT'S BEAUTIFUL!
WE'LL BE GONE BEFORE THEY KNOW IT.
WE AIN'T?
OH, WE'RE NOT SNEAKING OUT.
WHEN JOHN BROWN AND I LED OUR KANSAS RAIDS, THEY CALLED US *JAYHAWKERS.*
WHAT'S THAT?
WHEN A JAYHAWK WANTS A NEST, IT HUNTS FOR ANOTHER BIRD, KILLS IT, STEALS ITS EGGS, AND TAKES THE NEST FOR ITS OWN.
THAT'S ONE MEAN BIRD.
A JAYHAWK RAID USUALLY INVOLVES TWO THINGS: *PLUNDER AND ARSON.*
WE ALREADY PLUNDERIN'. YOU WANT TO BURN DOWN THESE FINE BIG MANSIONS?
EVERY LAST ONE OF THEM.
COLONEL MONTGOMERY, YOU ARE A DANGEROUS FELLOW--AND I LIKE IT.
BURN IT ALL! HOUSES, BARNS, ANYTHING THAT LIGHTS--
BURN IT!
FORWARD!

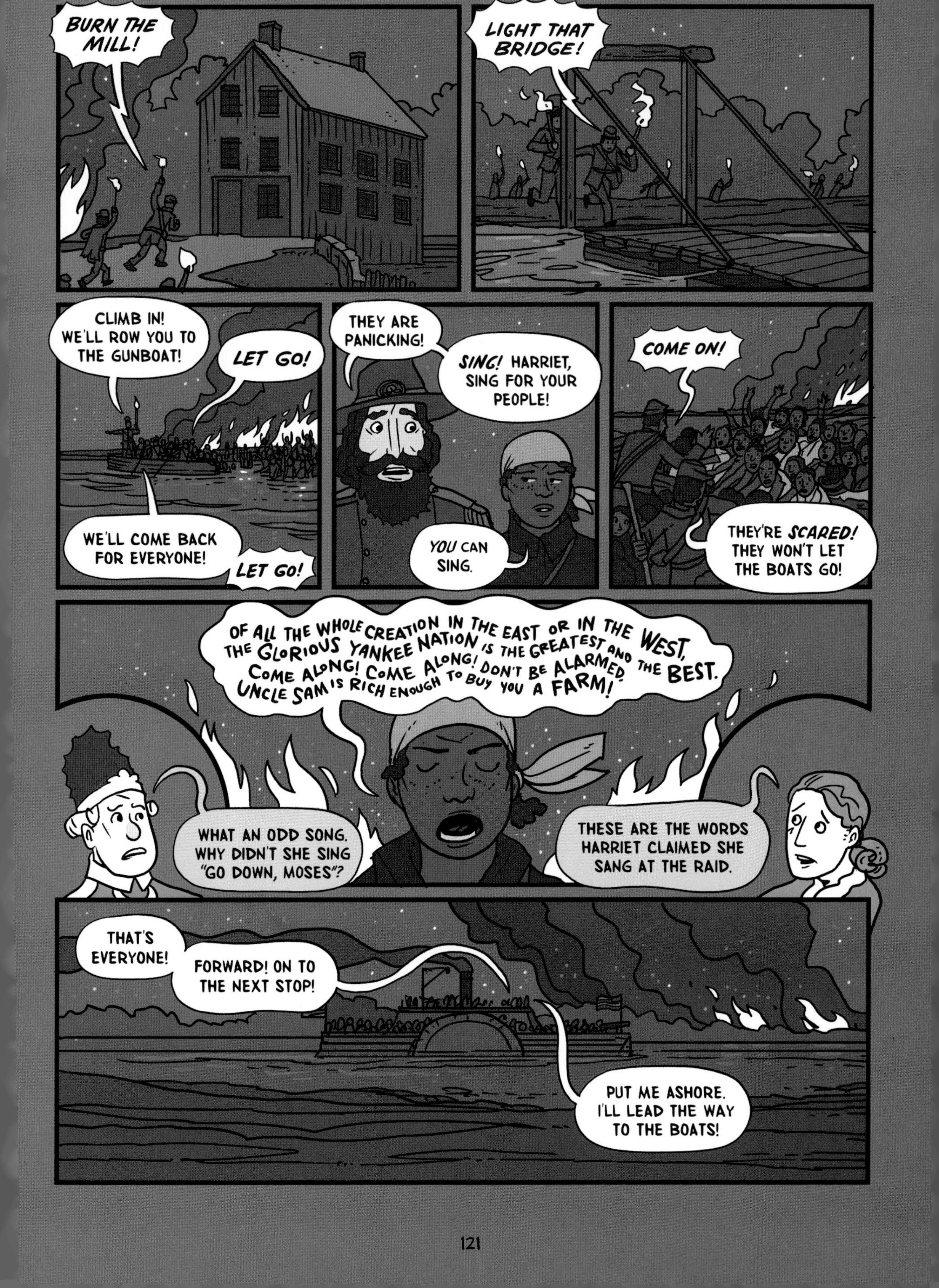
BURN THE MILL!
LIGHT THAT BRIDGE!
CLIMB IN! WE'LL ROW YOU TO THE GUNBOAT!
LET GO!
WE'LL COME BACK FOR EVERYONE!
LET GO!
THEY ARE PANICKING!
SING! HARRIET, SING FOR YOUR PEOPLE!
YOU CAN SING.
COME ON!
THEY'RE SCARED! THEY WON'T LET THE BOATS GO!
OF ALL THE WHOLE CREATION IN THE EAST OR IN THE WEST, THE GLORIOUS YANKEE NATION IS THE GREATEST AND THE BEST. COME ALONG! COME ALONG! DON'T BE ALARMED. UNCLE SAM IS RICH ENOUGH TO BUY YOU A FARM!
WHAT AN ODD SONG. WHY DIDN'T SHE SING "GO DOWN, MOSES"?
THESE ARE THE WORDS HARRIET CLAIMED SHE SANG AT THE RAID.
THAT'S EVERYONE!
FORWARD! ON TO THE NEXT STOP!
PUT ME ASHORE. I'LL LEAD THE WAY TO THE BOATS!

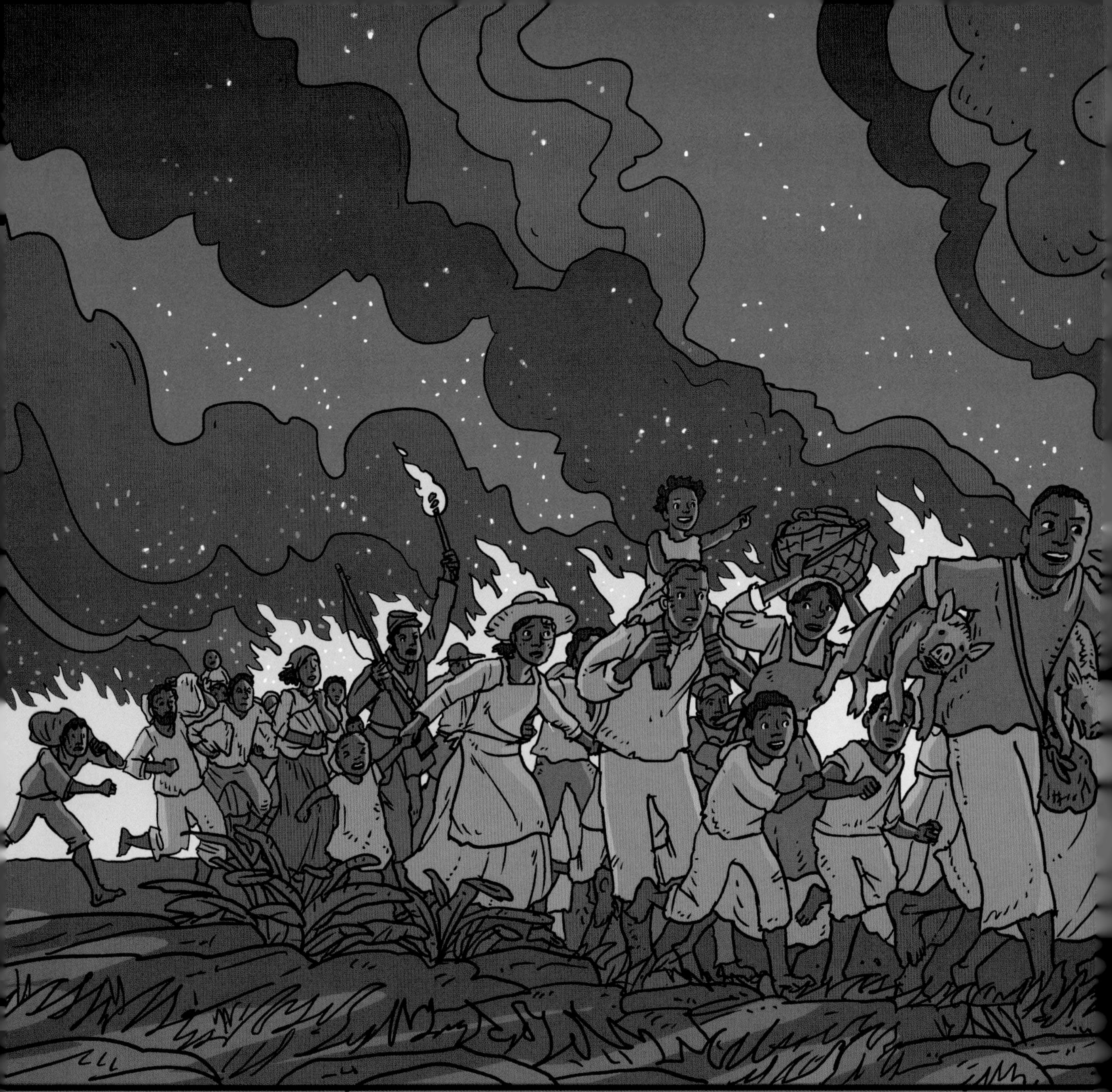

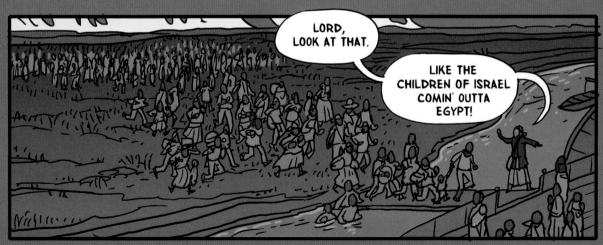

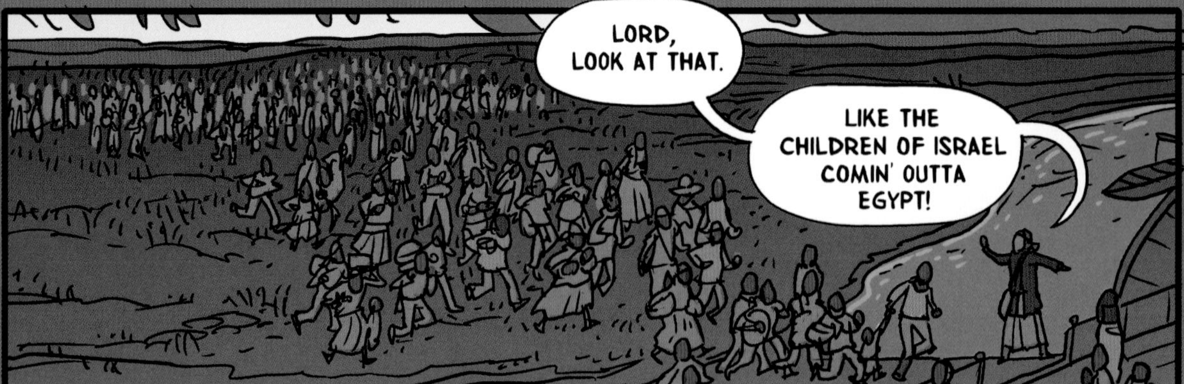
LORD, LOOK AT THAT.
LIKE THE CHILDREN OF ISRAEL COMIN' OUTTA EGYPT!

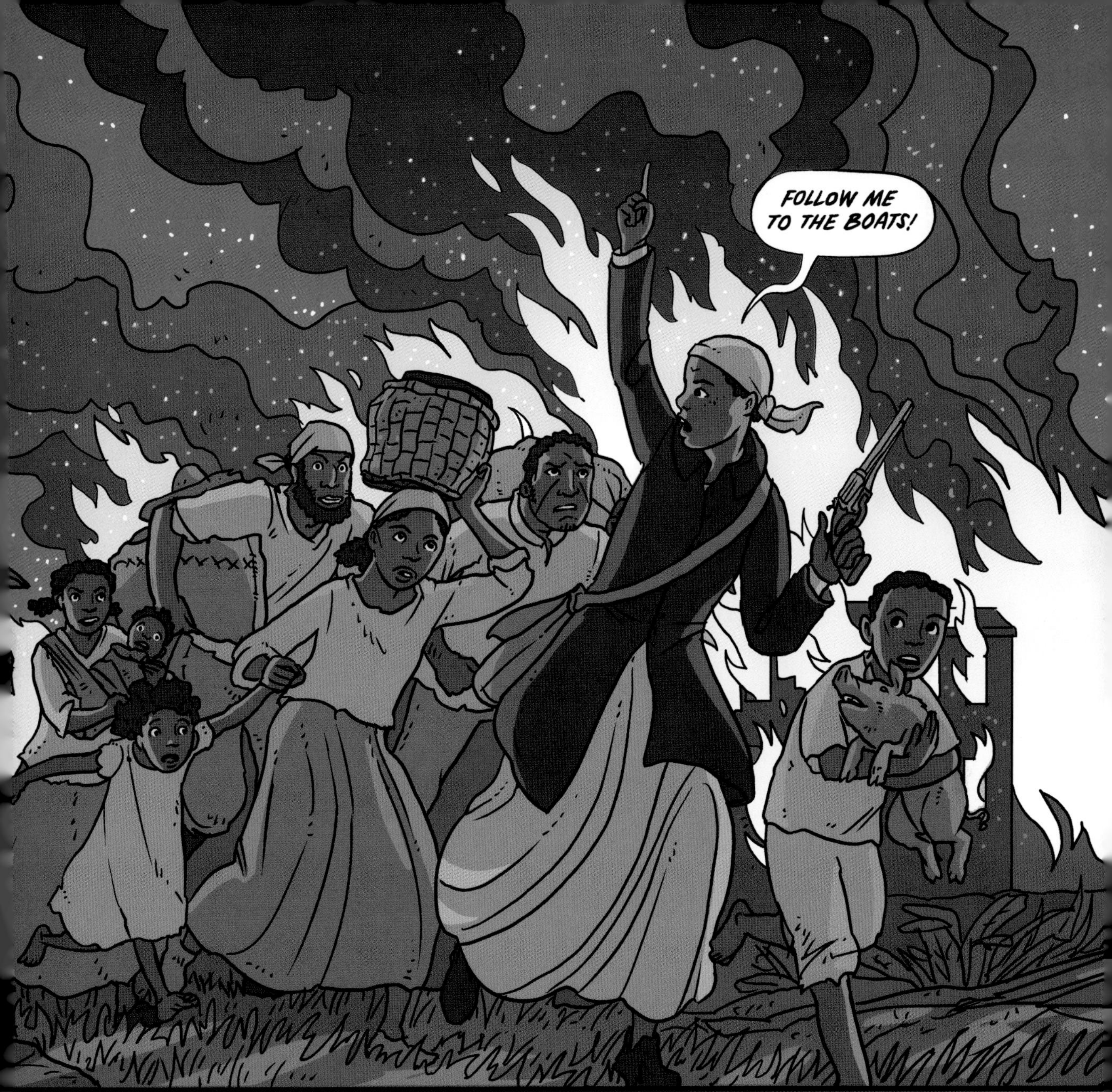
FOLLOW ME TO THE BOATS!

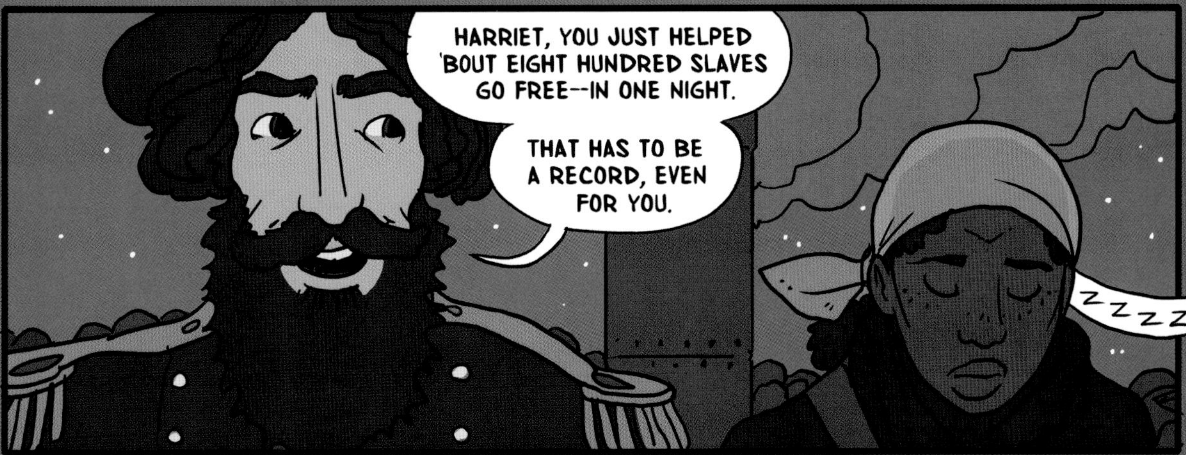
HARRIET, YOU JUST HELPED 'BOUT EIGHT HUNDRED SLAVES GO FREE--IN ONE NIGHT.
THAT HAS TO BE A RECORD, EVEN FOR YOU.
ZZZZZZ

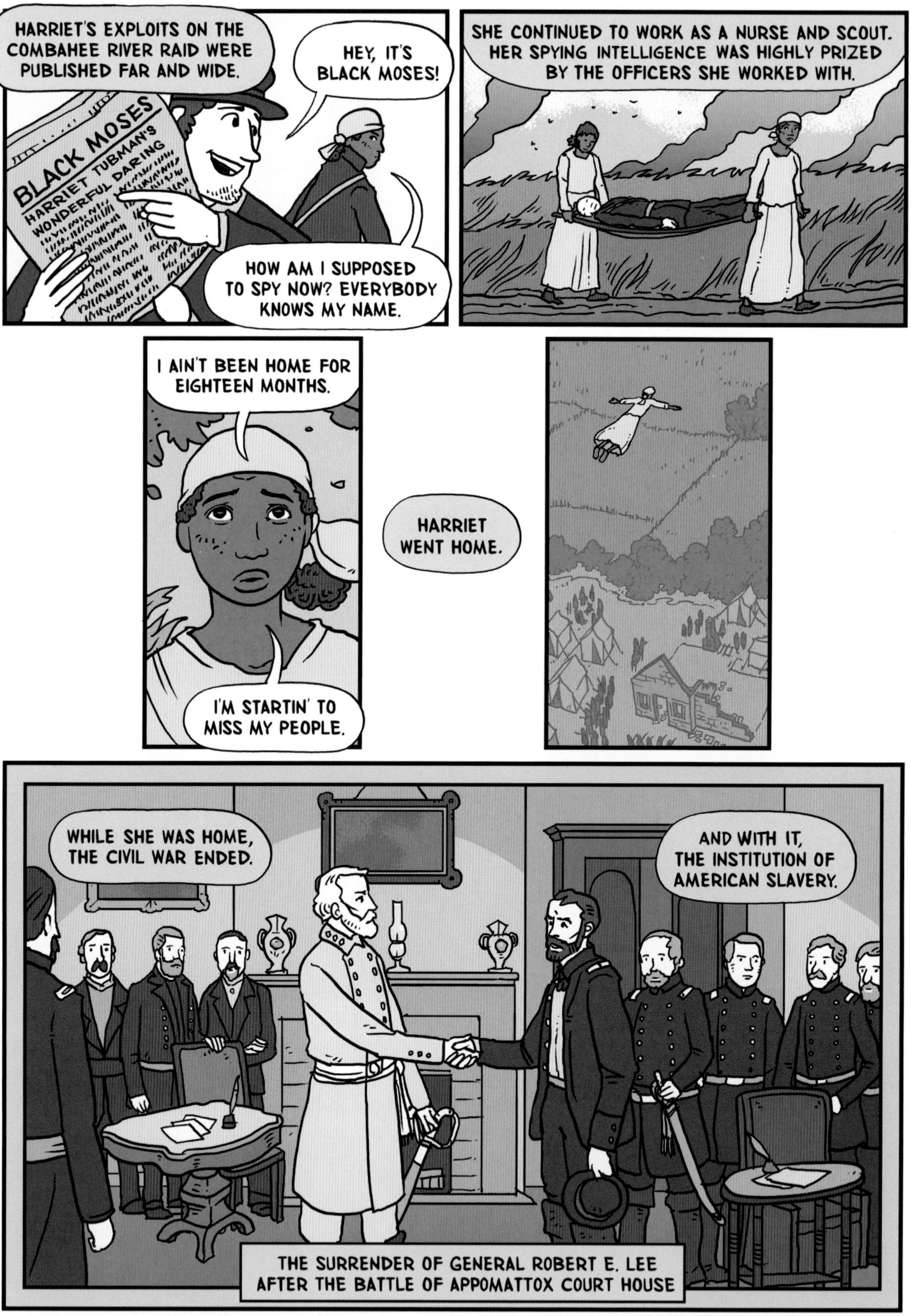
HARRIET'S EXPLOITS ON THE COMBAHEE RIVER RAID WERE PUBLISHED FAR AND WIDE.
BLACK MOSES
HARRIET TUBMAN'S WONDERFUL DARING
HEY, IT'S BLACK MOSES!
HOW AM I SUPPOSED TO SPY NOW? EVERYBODY KNOWS MY NAME.
SHE CONTINUED TO WORK AS A NURSE AND SCOUT. HER SPYING INTELLIGENCE WAS HIGHLY PRIZED BY THE OFFICERS SHE WORKED WITH.
I AIN'T BEEN HOME FOR EIGHTEEN MONTHS.
I'M STARTIN' TO MISS MY PEOPLE.
HARRIET WENT HOME.
WHILE SHE WAS HOME, THE CIVIL WAR ENDED.
AND WITH IT, THE INSTITUTION OF AMERICAN SLAVERY.
THE SURRENDER OF GENERAL ROBERT E. LEE AFTER THE BATTLE OF APPOMATTOX COURT HOUSE

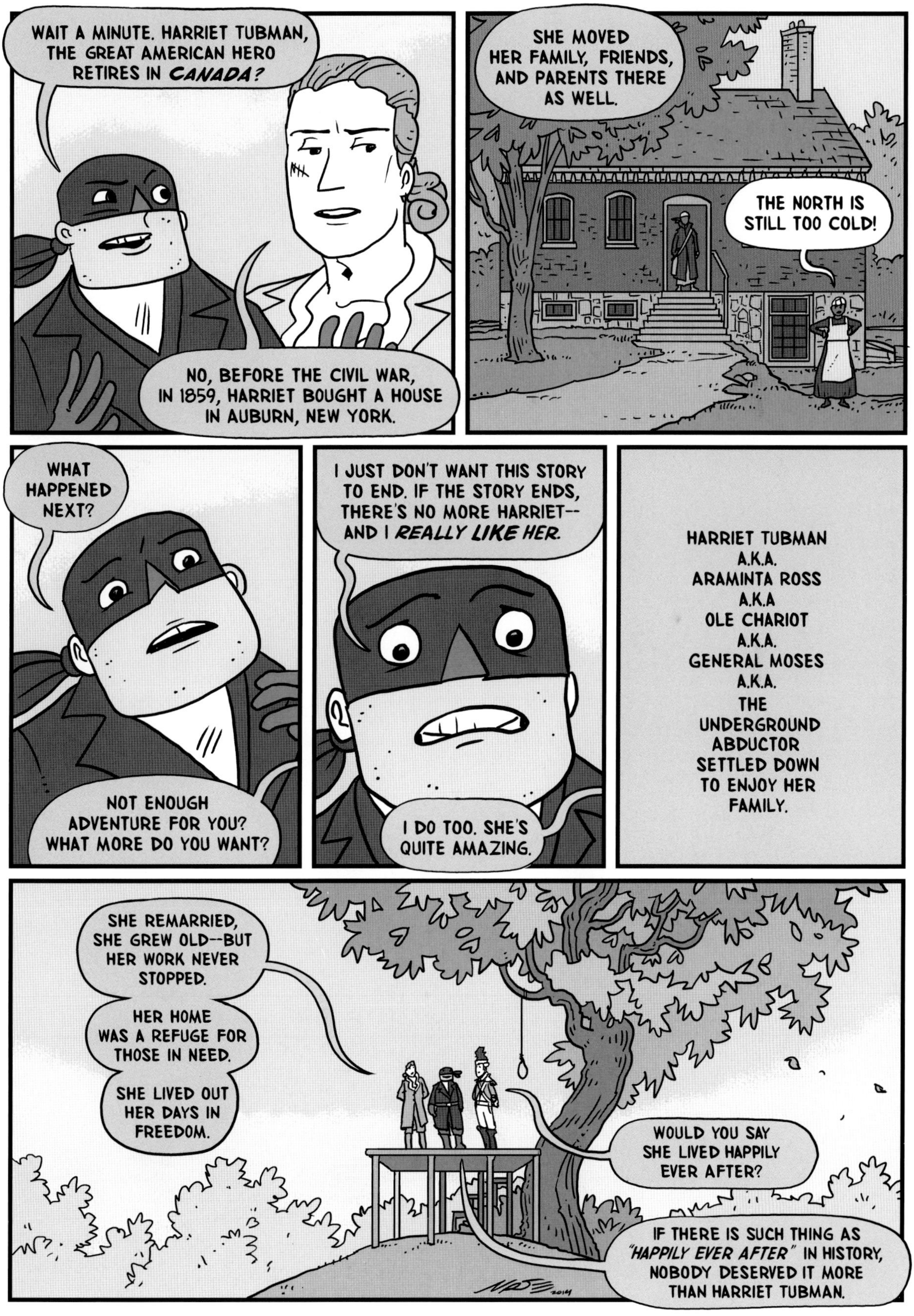
WAIT A MINUTE. HARRIET TUBMAN, THE GREAT AMERICAN HERO RETIRES IN *CANADA?*
NO, BEFORE THE CIVIL WAR, IN 1859, HARRIET BOUGHT A HOUSE IN AUBURN, NEW YORK.
SHE MOVED HER FAMILY, FRIENDS, AND PARENTS THERE AS WELL.
THE NORTH IS STILL TOO COLD!
WHAT HAPPENED NEXT?
NOT ENOUGH ADVENTURE FOR YOU? WHAT MORE DO YOU WANT?
I JUST DON'T WANT THIS STORY TO END. IF THE STORY ENDS, THERE'S NO MORE HARRIET-- AND I *REALLY LIKE HER.*
I DO TOO. SHE'S QUITE AMAZING.
HARRIET TUBMAN A.K.A. ARAMINTA ROSS A.K.A OLE CHARIOT A.K.A. GENERAL MOSES A.K.A. THE UNDERGROUND ABDUCTOR SETTLED DOWN TO ENJOY HER FAMILY.
SHE REMARRIED, SHE GREW OLD--BUT HER WORK NEVER STOPPED.
HER HOME WAS A REFUGE FOR THOSE IN NEED.
SHE LIVED OUT HER DAYS IN FREEDOM.
WOULD YOU SAY SHE LIVED HAPPILY EVER AFTER?
IF THERE IS SUCH THING AS *"HAPPILY EVER AFTER"* IN HISTORY, NOBODY DESERVED IT MORE THAN HARRIET TUBMAN.

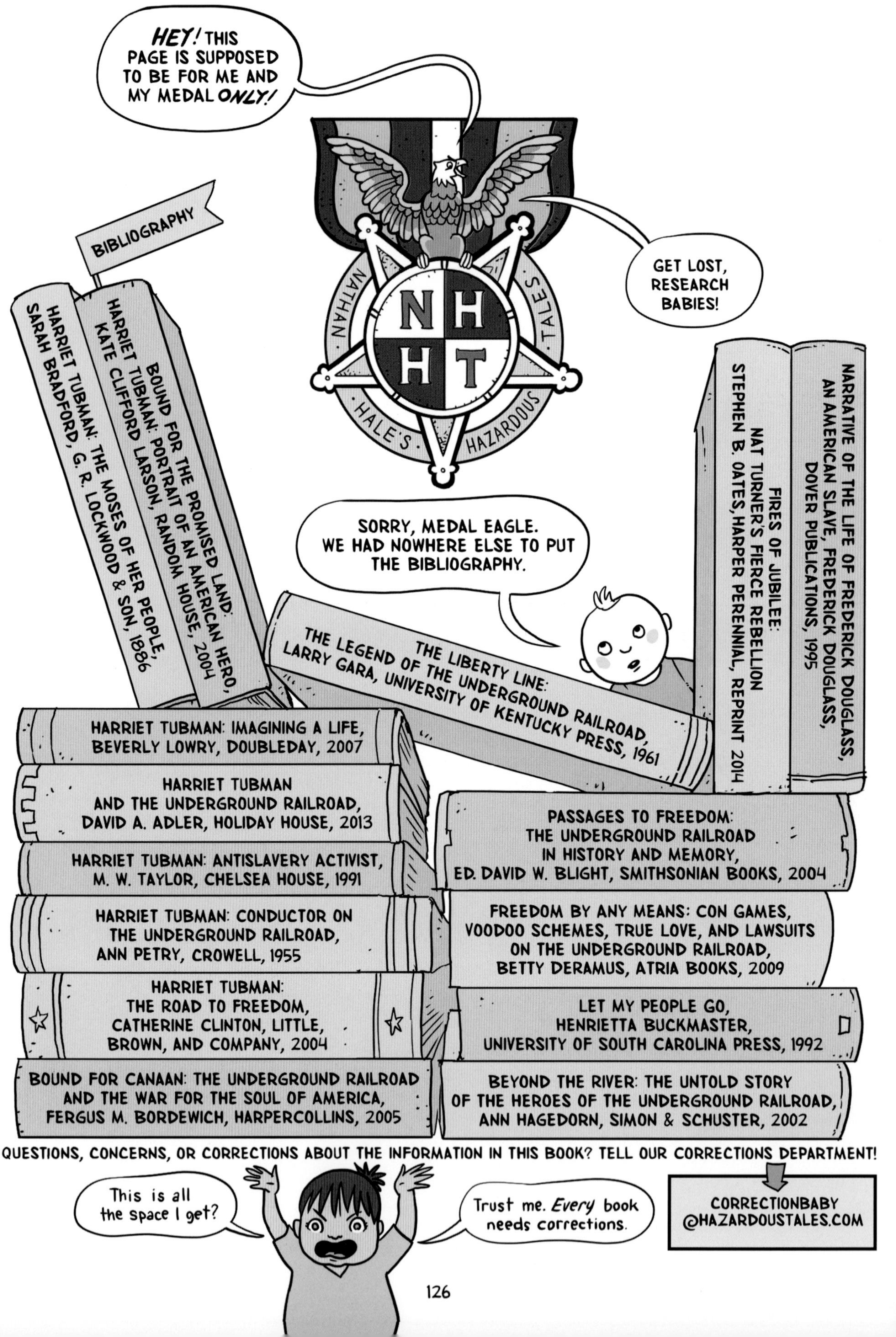

HEY! THIS PAGE IS SUPPOSED TO BE FOR ME AND MY MEDAL ONLY!
NATHAN HALE'S HAZARDOUS TALES
NH HT
GET LOST, RESEARCH BABIES!
SORRY, MEDAL EAGLE. WE HAD NOWHERE ELSE TO PUT THE BIBLIOGRAPHY.
BIBLIOGRAPHY
HARRIET TUBMAN: THE MOSES OF HER PEOPLE, SARAH BRADFORD, G. R. LOCKWOOD & SON, 1886
BOUND FOR THE PROMISED LAND: HARRIET TUBMAN: PORTRAIT OF AN AMERICAN HERO, KATE CLIFFORD LARSON, RANDOM HOUSE, 2004
THE LIBERTY LINE: THE LEGEND OF THE UNDERGROUND RAILROAD, LARRY GARA, UNIVERSITY OF KENTUCKY PRESS, 1961
FIRES OF JUBILEE: NAT TURNER'S FIERCE REBELLION STEPHEN B. OATES, HARPER PERENNIAL, REPRINT 2014
NARRATIVE OF THE LIFE OF FREDERICK DOUGLASS, AN AMERICAN SLAVE, FREDERICK DOUGLASS, DOVER PUBLICATIONS, 1995
HARRIET TUBMAN: IMAGINING A LIFE, BEVERLY LOWRY, DOUBLEDAY, 2007
HARRIET TUBMAN AND THE UNDERGROUND RAILROAD, DAVID A. ADLER, HOLIDAY HOUSE, 2013
HARRIET TUBMAN: ANTISLAVERY ACTIVIST, M. W. TAYLOR, CHELSEA HOUSE, 1991
HARRIET TUBMAN: CONDUCTOR ON THE UNDERGROUND RAILROAD, ANN PETRY, CROWELL, 1955
HARRIET TUBMAN: THE ROAD TO FREEDOM, CATHERINE CLINTON, LITTLE, BROWN, AND COMPANY, 2004
BOUND FOR CANAAN: THE UNDERGROUND RAILROAD AND THE WAR FOR THE SOUL OF AMERICA, FERGUS M. BORDEWICH, HARPERCOLLINS, 2005
PASSAGES TO FREEDOM: THE UNDERGROUND RAILROAD IN HISTORY AND MEMORY, ED. DAVID W. BLIGHT, SMITHSONIAN BOOKS, 2004
FREEDOM BY ANY MEANS: CON GAMES, VOODOO SCHEMES, TRUE LOVE, AND LAWSUITS ON THE UNDERGROUND RAILROAD, BETTY DERAMUS, ATRIA BOOKS, 2009
LET MY PEOPLE GO, HENRIETTA BUCKMASTER, UNIVERSITY OF SOUTH CAROLINA PRESS, 1992
BEYOND THE RIVER: THE UNTOLD STORY OF THE HEROES OF THE UNDERGROUND RAILROAD, ANN HAGEDORN, SIMON & SCHUSTER, 2002
QUESTIONS, CONCERNS, OR CORRECTIONS ABOUT THE INFORMATION IN THIS BOOK? TELL OUR CORRECTIONS DEPARTMENT!
This is all the space I get?
Trust me. Every book needs corrections.
CORRECTIONBABY @HAZARDOUSTALES.COM

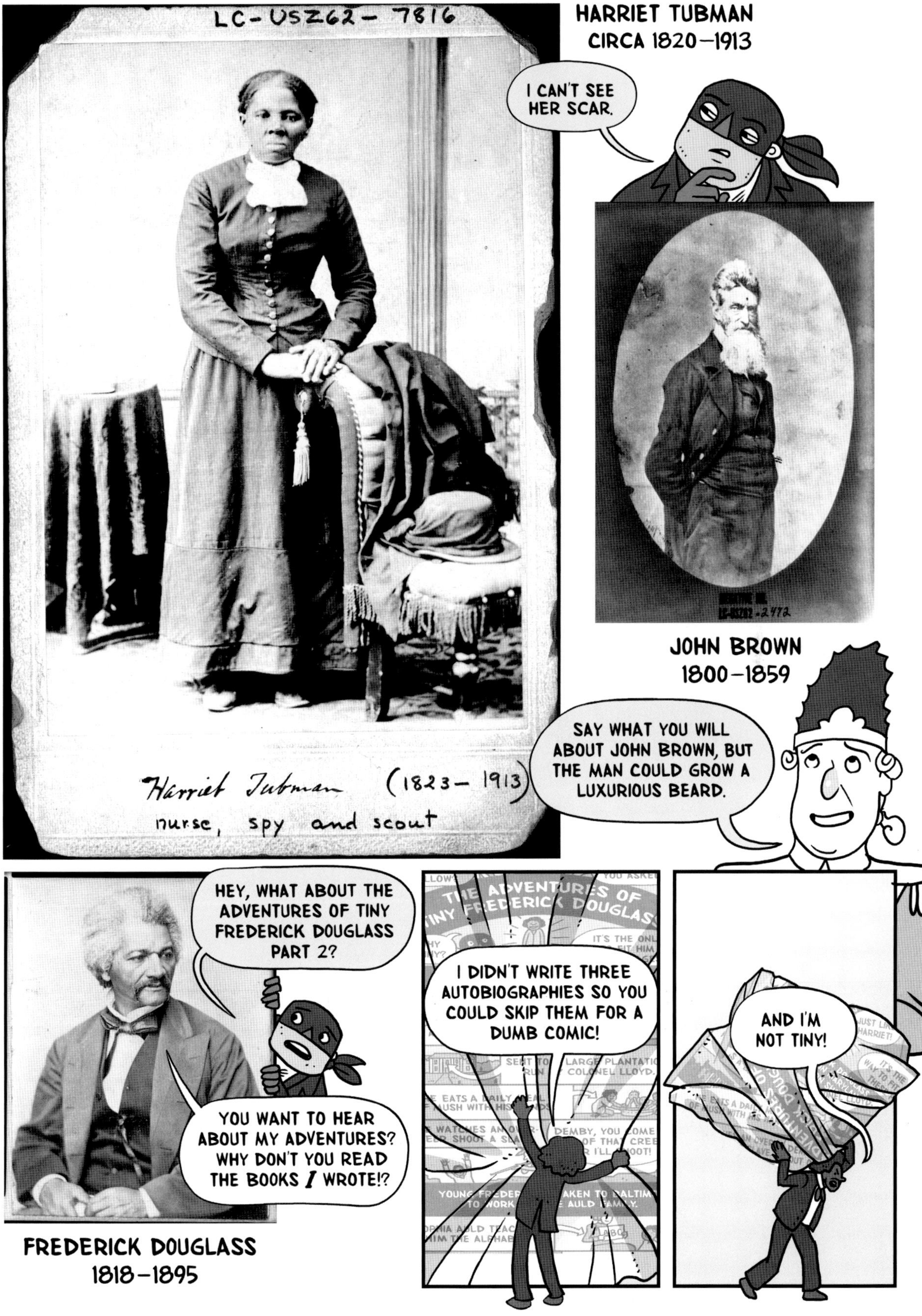

LC-USZ62- 7816
Harriet Tubman (1823- 1913)
nurse, spy and scout
HARRIET TUBMAN
CIRCA 1820–1913
I CAN'T SEE HER SCAR.
JOHN BROWN
1800–1859
SAY WHAT YOU WILL ABOUT JOHN BROWN, BUT THE MAN COULD GROW A LUXURIOUS BEARD.
HEY, WHAT ABOUT THE ADVENTURES OF TINY FREDERICK DOUGLASS PART 2?
YOU WANT TO HEAR ABOUT MY ADVENTURES? WHY DON'T YOU READ THE BOOKS *I* WROTE!?
FREDERICK DOUGLASS
1818–1895
I DIDN'T WRITE THREE AUTOBIOGRAPHIES SO YOU COULD SKIP THEM FOR A DUMB COMIC!
AND I'M NOT TINY!

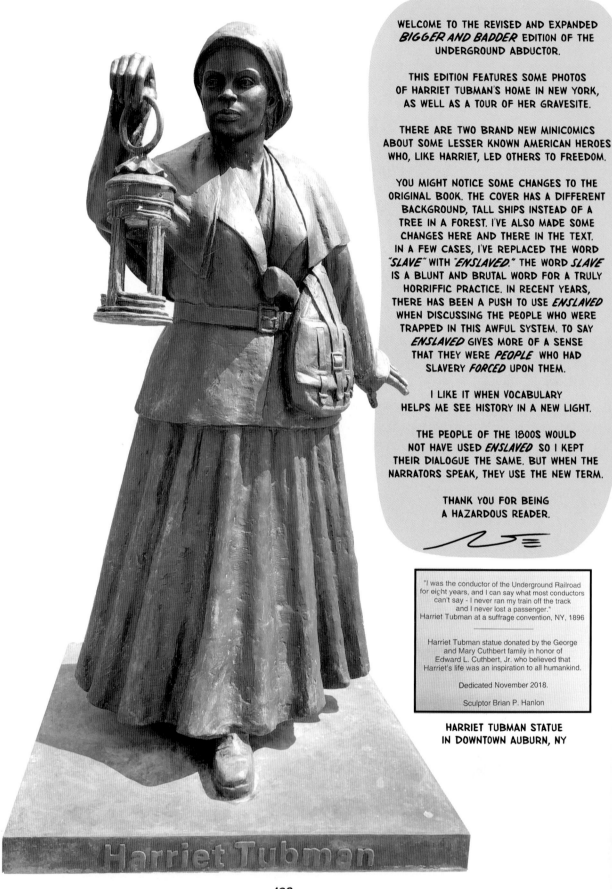

WELCOME TO THE REVISED AND EXPANDED *BIGGER AND BADDER* EDITION OF THE UNDERGROUND ABDUCTOR.

THIS EDITION FEATURES SOME PHOTOS OF HARRIET TUBMAN'S HOME IN NEW YORK, AS WELL AS A TOUR OF HER GRAVESITE.

THERE ARE TWO BRAND NEW MINICOMICS ABOUT SOME LESSER KNOWN AMERICAN HEROES WHO, LIKE HARRIET, LED OTHERS TO FREEDOM.

YOU MIGHT NOTICE SOME CHANGES TO THE ORIGINAL BOOK. THE COVER HAS A DIFFERENT BACKGROUND, TALL SHIPS INSTEAD OF A TREE IN A FOREST. I'VE ALSO MADE SOME CHANGES HERE AND THERE IN THE TEXT. IN A FEW CASES, I'VE REPLACED THE WORD *"SLAVE"* WITH *"ENSLAVED."* THE WORD *SLAVE* IS A BLUNT AND BRUTAL WORD FOR A TRULY HORRIFFIC PRACTICE. IN RECENT YEARS, THERE HAS BEEN A PUSH TO USE *ENSLAVED* WHEN DISCUSSING THE PEOPLE WHO WERE TRAPPED IN THIS AWFUL SYSTEM. TO SAY *ENSLAVED* GIVES MORE OF A SENSE THAT THEY WERE *PEOPLE* WHO HAD SLAVERY *FORCED* UPON THEM.

I LIKE IT WHEN VOCABULARY HELPS ME SEE HISTORY IN A NEW LIGHT.

THE PEOPLE OF THE 1800S WOULD NOT HAVE USED *ENSLAVED* SO I KEPT THEIR DIALOGUE THE SAME. BUT WHEN THE NARRATORS SPEAK, THEY USE THE NEW TERM.

THANK YOU FOR BEING A HAZARDOUS READER.

"I was the conductor of the Underground Railroad for eight years, and I can say what most conductors can't say - I never ran my train off the track and I never lost a passenger."
Harriet Tubman at a suffrage convention, NY, 1896

Harriet Tubman statue donated by the George and Mary Cuthbert family in honor of Edward L. Cuthbert, Jr. who believed that Harriet's life was an inspiration to all humankind.

Dedicated November 2018.

Sculptor Brian P. Hanlon

HARRIET TUBMAN STATUE IN DOWNTOWN AUBURN, NY

Harriet Tubman

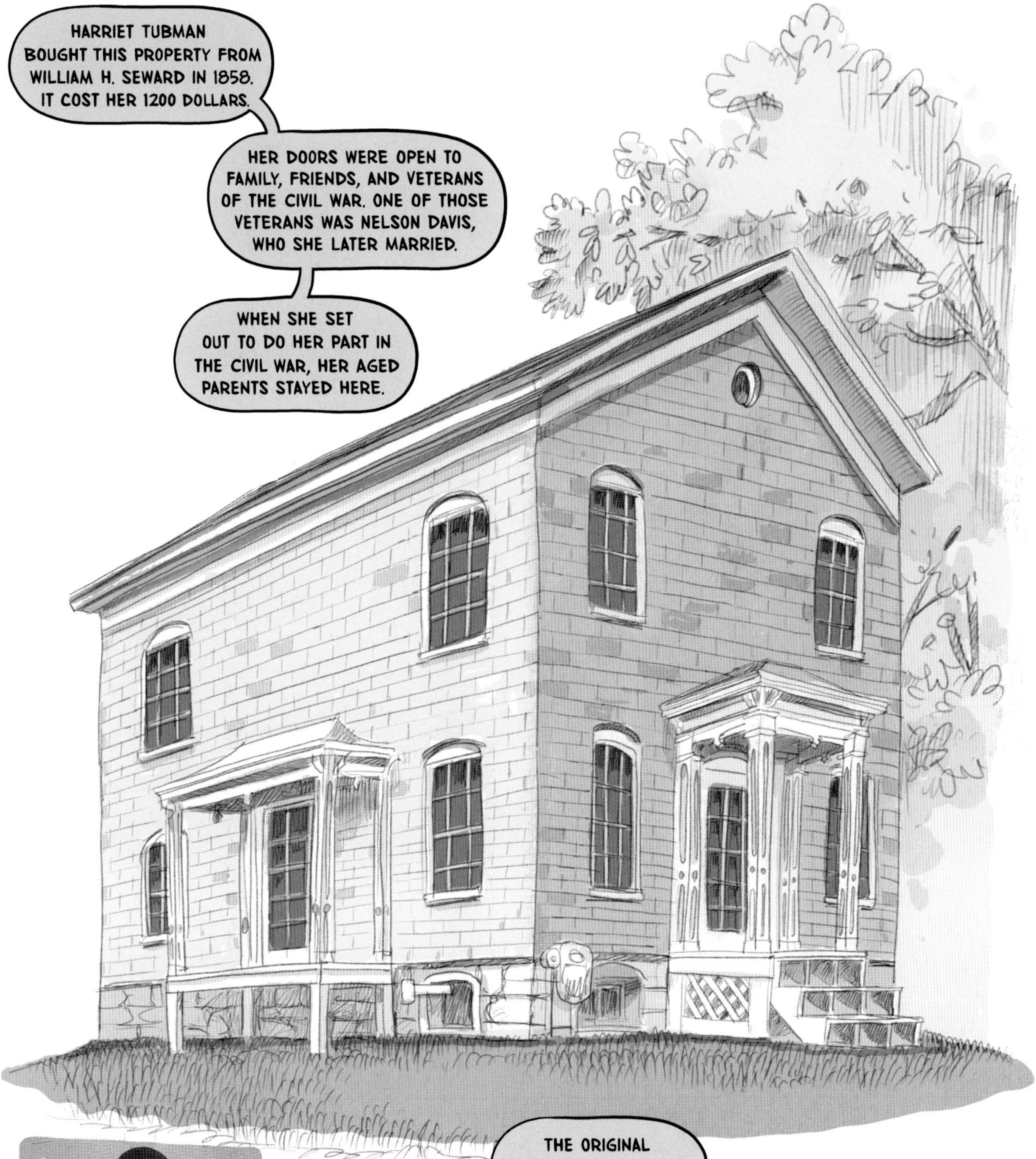
HARRIET TUBMAN BOUGHT THIS PROPERTY FROM WILLIAM H. SEWARD IN 1858. IT COST HER 1200 DOLLARS.
HER DOORS WERE OPEN TO FAMILY, FRIENDS, AND VETERANS OF THE CIVIL WAR. ONE OF THOSE VETERANS WAS NELSON DAVIS, WHO SHE LATER MARRIED.
WHEN SHE SET OUT TO DO HER PART IN THE CIVIL WAR, HER AGED PARENTS STAYED HERE.
THE ORIGINAL WOODEN HOUSE BURNED DOWN IN 1886.
IT WAS REBUILT WITH HELP FROM HARRIET'S HUSBAND, NELSON DAVIS, WHO WAS A BRICK MAKER.

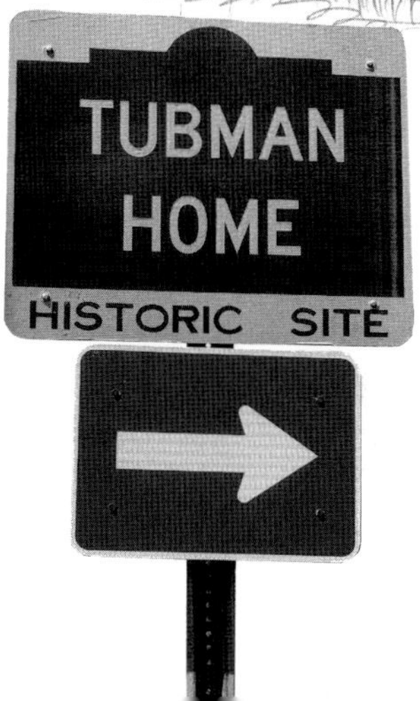
TUBMAN
HOME
HISTORIC SITE

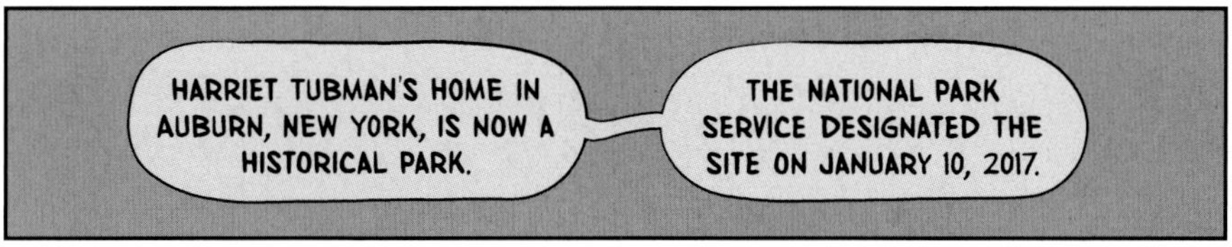
HARRIET TUBMAN'S HOME IN AUBURN, NEW YORK, IS NOW A HISTORICAL PARK.
THE NATIONAL PARK SERVICE DESIGNATED THE SITE ON JANUARY 10, 2017.

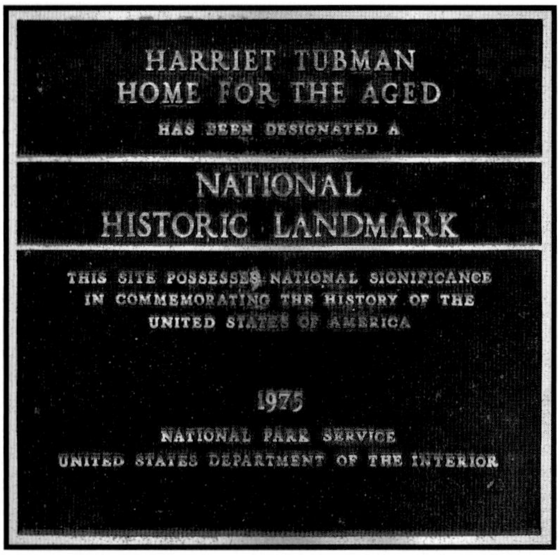
HARRIET TUBMAN
HOME FOR THE AGED
HAS BEEN DESIGNATED A
NATIONAL
HISTORIC LANDMARK
THIS SITE POSSESSES NATIONAL SIGNIFICANCE
IN COMMEMORATING THE HISTORY OF THE
UNITED STATES OF AMERICA
1975
NATIONAL PARK SERVICE
UNITED STATES DEPARTMENT OF THE INTERIOR

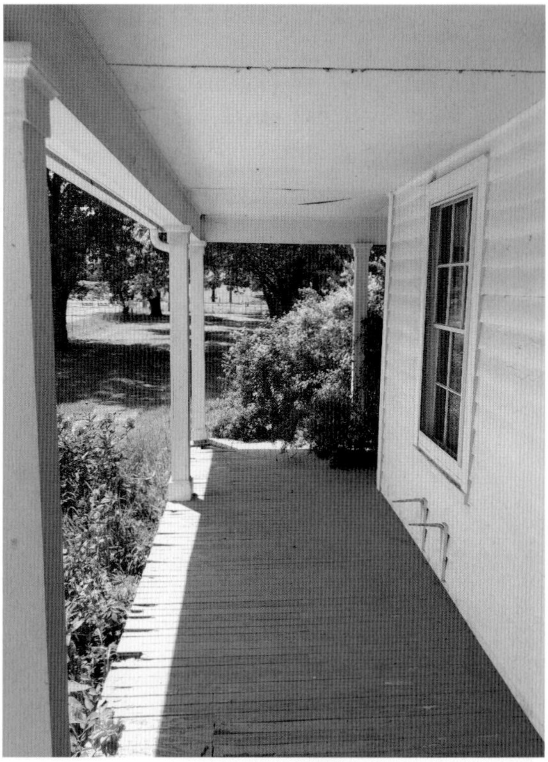

IN 1896, HARRIET TUBMAN ADDED TWENTY-FIVE MORE ACRES TO HER PROPERTY.

ON THIS LAND SHE BUILT HOMES AND HEALTH CARE SERVICES FOR FORMER ENSLAVED PEOPLE. THE MAIN BUILDING, NOW DESTROYED, SHE CALLED "JOHN BROWN HALL."

THE BUILDING BELOW IS HER HOME FOR THE ELDERLY.

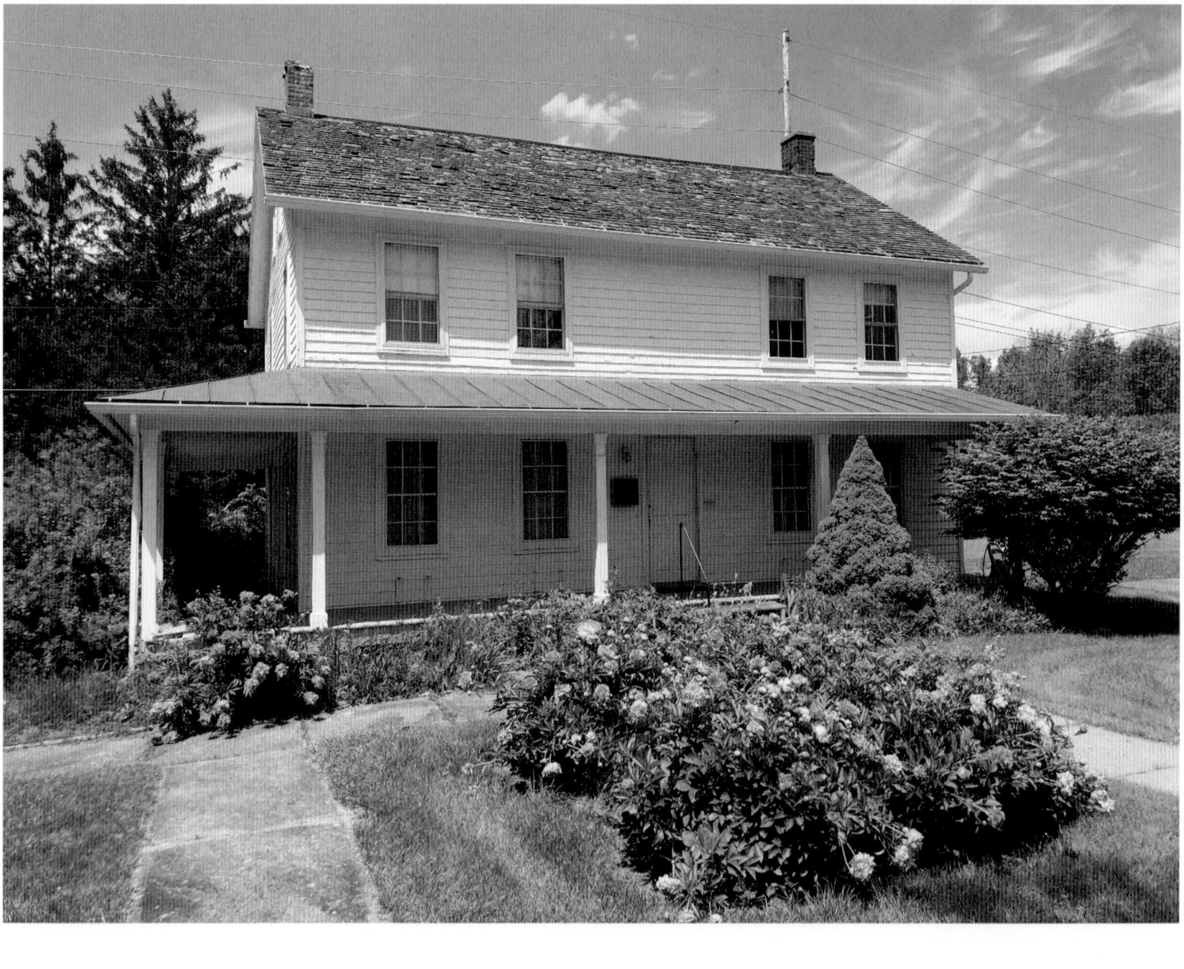

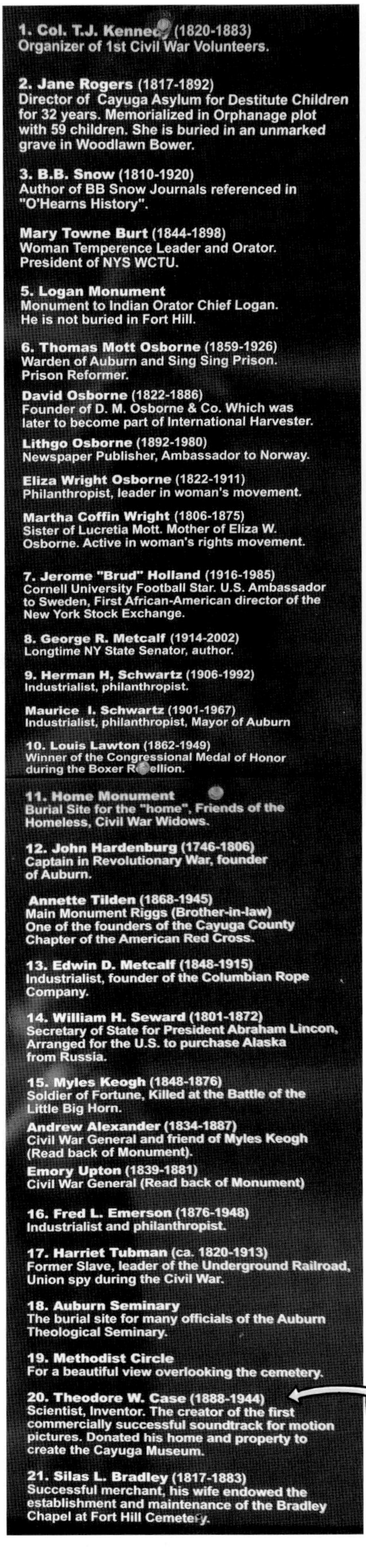
1. Col. T.J. Kenne (1820-1883)
Organizer of 1st Civil War Volunteers.
2. Jane Rogers (1817-1892)
Director of Cayuga Asylum for Destitute Children for 32 years. Memorialized in Orphanage plot with 59 children. She is buried in an unmarked grave in Woodlawn Bower.
3. B.B. Snow (1810-1920)
Author of BB Snow Journals referenced in "O'Hearns History".
Mary Towne Burt (1844-1898)
Woman Temperence Leader and Orator. President of NYS WCTU.
5. Logan Monument
Monument to Indian Orator Chief Logan. He is not buried in Fort Hill.
6. Thomas Mott Osborne (1859-1926)
Warden of Auburn and Sing Sing Prison. Prison Reformer.
David Osborne (1822-1886)
Founder of D. M. Osborne & Co. Which was later to become part of International Harvester.
Lithgo Osborne (1892-1980)
Newspaper Publisher, Ambassador to Norway.
Eliza Wright Osborne (1822-1911)
Philanthropist, leader in woman's movement.
Martha Coffin Wright (1806-1875)
Sister of Lucretia Mott. Mother of Eliza W. Osborne. Active in woman's rights movement.
7. Jerome "Brud" Holland (1916-1985)
Cornell University Football Star. U.S. Ambassador to Sweden, First African-American director of the New York Stock Exchange.
8. George R. Metcalf (1914-2002)
Longtime NY State Senator, author.
9. Herman H, Schwartz (1906-1992)
Industrialist, philanthropist.
Maurice I. Schwartz (1901-1967)
Industrialist, philanthropist, Mayor of Auburn
10. Louis Lawton (1862-1949)
Winner of the Congressional Medal of Honor during the Boxer R ellion.
11. Home Monument
Burial Site for the "home", Friends of the Homeless, Civil War Widows.
12. John Hardenburg (1746-1806)
Captain in Revolutionary War, founder of Auburn.
Annette Tilden (1868-1945)
Main Monument Riggs (Brother-in-law)
One of the founders of the Cayuga County Chapter of the American Red Cross.
13. Edwin D. Metcalf (1848-1915)
Industrialist, founder of the Columbian Rope Company.
14. William H. Seward (1801-1872)
Secretary of State for President Abraham Lincon, Arranged for the U.S. to purchase Alaska from Russia.
15. Myles Keogh (1848-1876)
Soldier of Fortune, Killed at the Battle of the Little Big Horn.
Andrew Alexander (1834-1887)
Civil War General and friend of Myles Keogh (Read back of Monument).
Emory Upton (1839-1881)
Civil War General (Read back of Monument)
16. Fred L. Emerson (1876-1948)
Industrialist and philanthropist.
17. Harriet Tubman (ca. 1820-1913)
Former Slave, leader of the Underground Railroad, Union spy during the Civil War.
18. Auburn Seminary
The burial site for many officials of the Auburn Theological Seminary.
19. Methodist Circle
For a beautiful view overlooking the cemetery.
20. Theodore W. Case (1888-1944)
Scientist, Inventor. The creator of the first commercially successful soundtrack for motion pictures. Donated his home and property to create the Cayuga Museum.
21. Silas L. Bradley (1817-1883)
Successful merchant, his wife endowed the establishment and maintenance of the Bradley Chapel at Fort Hill Ceme y.

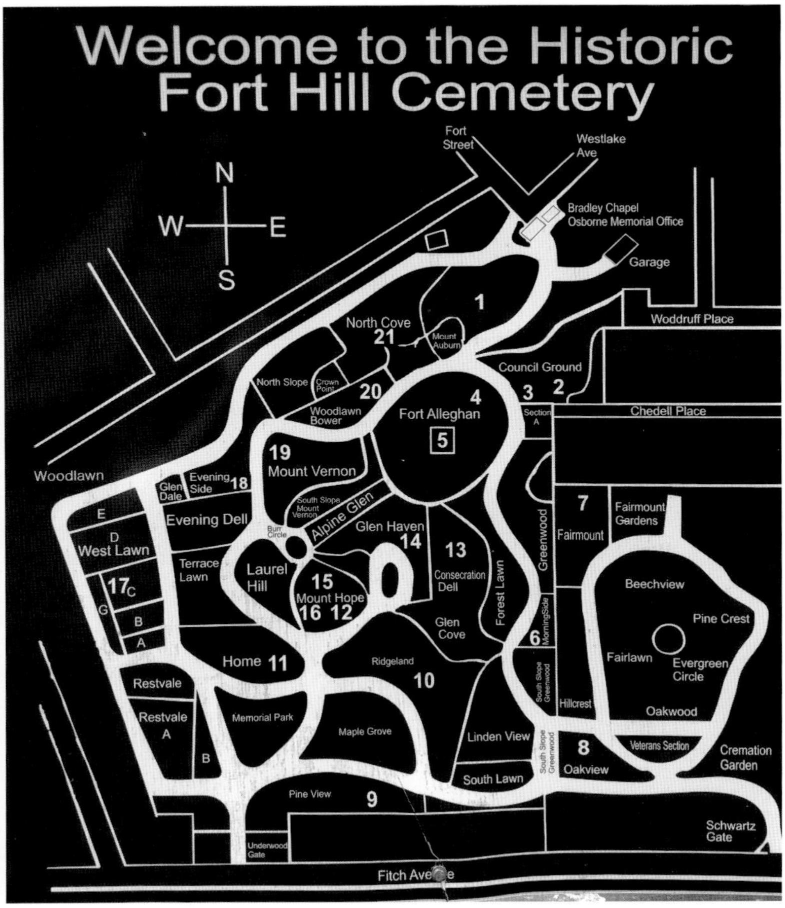
Welcome to the Historic
Fort Hill Cemetery
N
W
E
S
Fort Street
Westlake Ave
Bradley Chapel
Osborne Memorial Office
Garage
Woddruff Place
Chedell Place
Council Ground
North Cove
Mount Auburn
North Slope
Crown Point
Woodlawn Bower
Fort Alleghan
Section A
Woodlawn
Glen Dale
Evening Side
Mount Vernon
South Slope Mount Vernon
Alpine Glen
Evening Dell
Burr Circle
Glen Haven
West Lawn
Terrace Lawn
Laurel Hill
Mount Hope
Consecration Dell
Forest Lawn
Greenwood
MorningSide
Fairmount
Fairmount Gardens
Beechview
Pine Crest
Glen Cove
Ridgeland
Home
Restvale
Restvale A
Memorial Park
Maple Grove
Linden View
South Slope Greenwood
Hillcrest
Fairlawn
Evergreen Circle
Oakwood
Veterans Section
Cremation Garden
Oakview
South Lawn
Pine View
Underwood Gate
Schwartz Gate
Fitch Ave e

FORT HILL CEMETERY IN AUBURN, NEW YORK, IS HARRIET TUBMAN'S FINAL RESTING PLACE.

ABRAHAM LINCOLN'S SECRETARY OF STATE, WILLIAM H. SEWARD, IS ALSO BURIED HERE.

SEWARD'S HOME WAS A STOP ON THE UNDERGROUND RAILROAD. HE WORKED WITH HARRIET TUBMAN IN THE FIGHT AGAINST SLAVERY.

AFTER THE CIVIL WAR, SEWARD FOUGHT TO GET HARRIET A PENSION FOR HER WORK AS A SPY AND A NURSE FOR THE U.S. ARMY.

HARRIET TUBMAN BOUGHT HER SEVEN-ACRE HOMESTEAD FROM WILLIAM H. SEWARD.

ALSO IN THIS CEMETERY, THE INVENTOR OF THE *MOVIE SOUNDTRACK*.

HOW ABOUT *THAT!?*

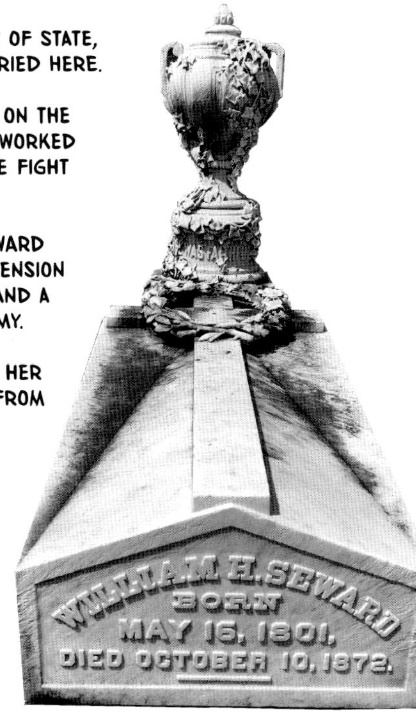
WILLIAM H. SEWARD
BORN
MAY 16, 1801.
DIED OCTOBER 10, 1872.

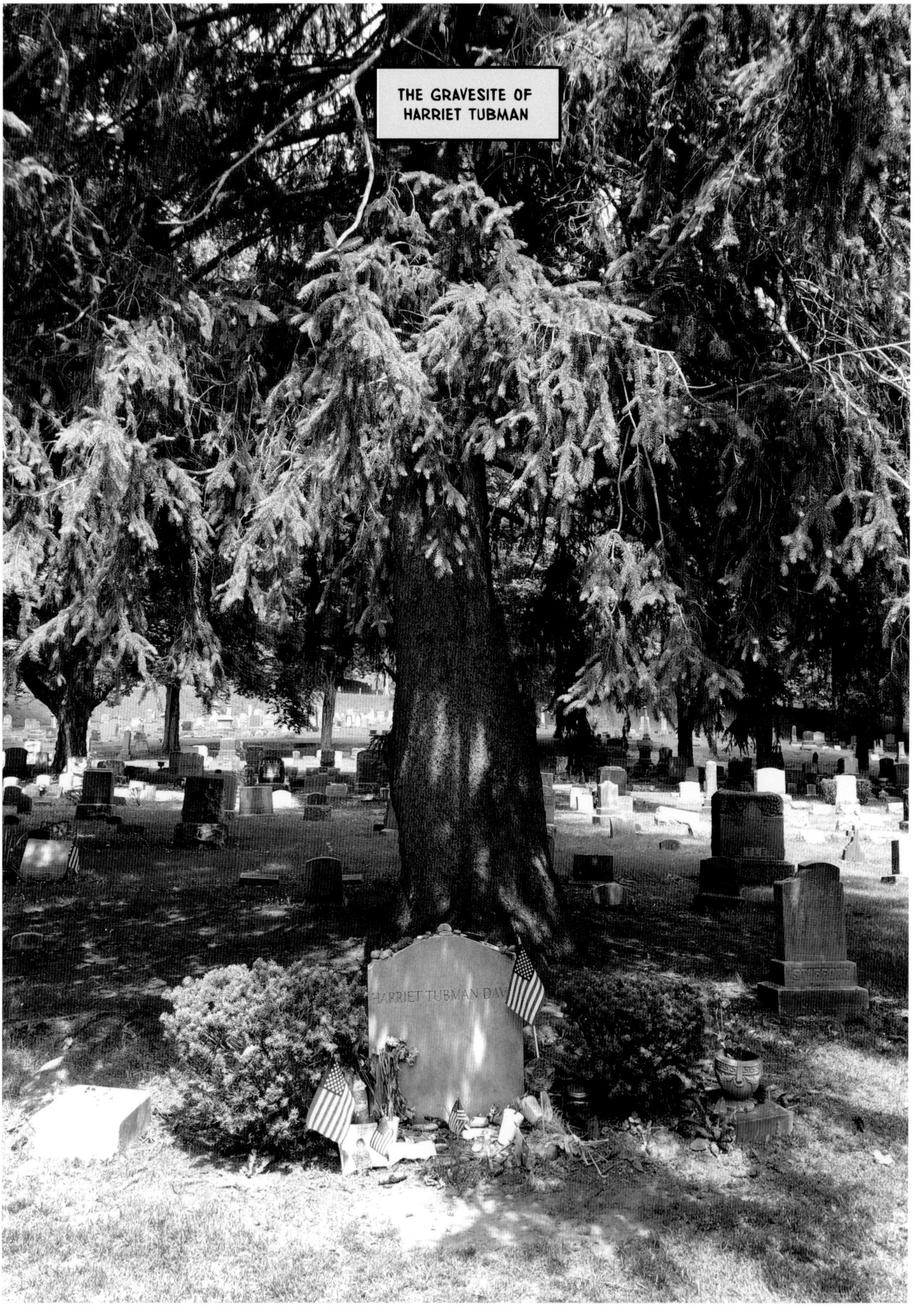
THE GRAVESITE OF HARRIET TUBMAN
HARRIET TUBMAN DAV

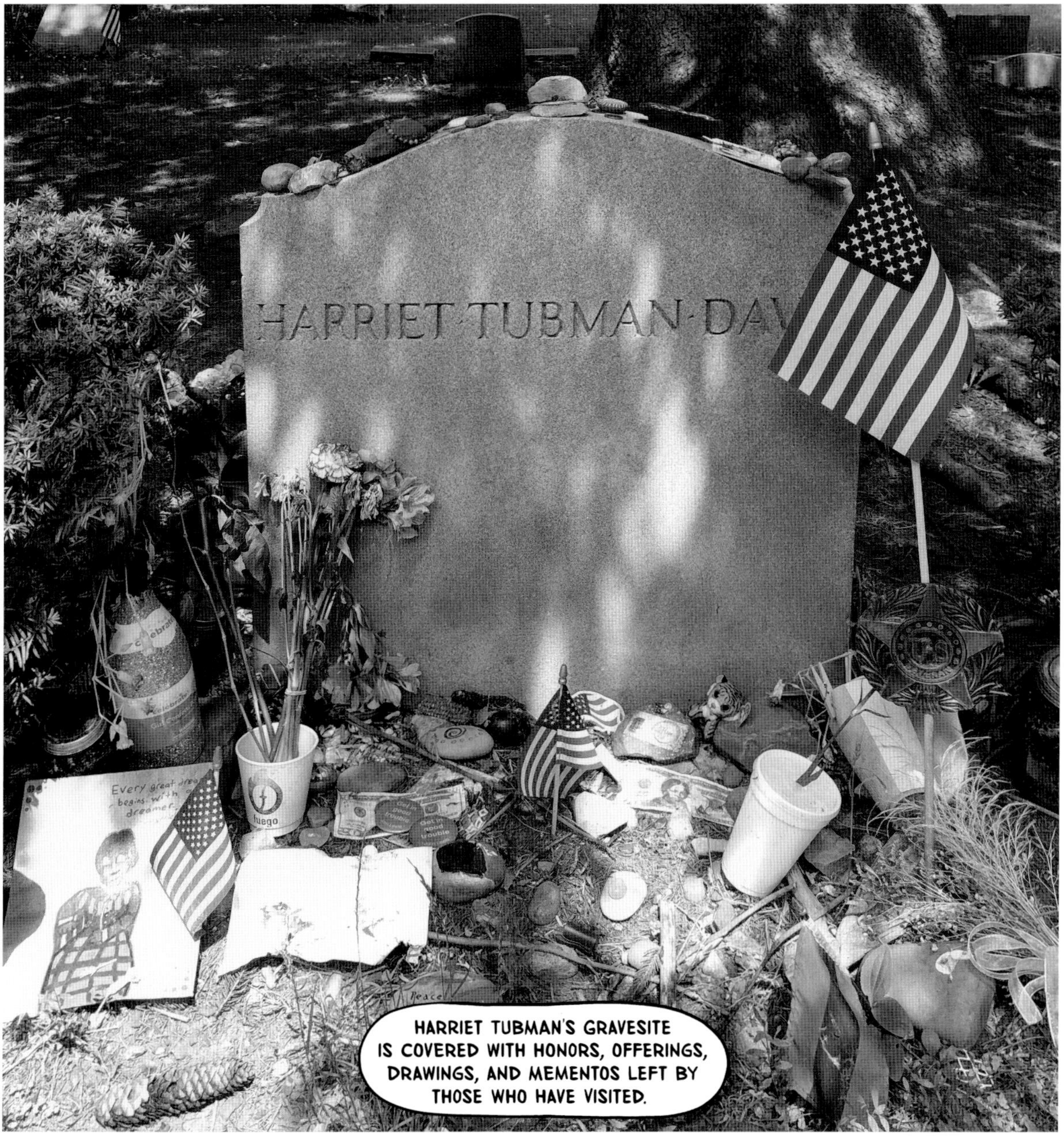
HARRIET TUBMAN'S GRAVESITE IS COVERED WITH HONORS, OFFERINGS, DRAWINGS, AND MEMENTOS LEFT BY THOSE WHO HAVE VISITED.

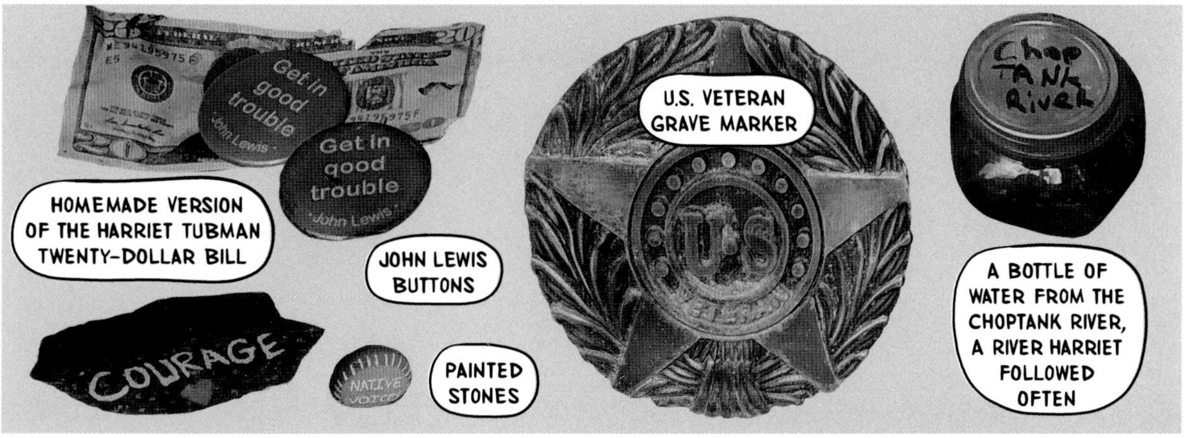
Get in good trouble
·John Lewis·
Get in good trouble
·John Lewis·
HOMEMADE VERSION OF THE HARRIET TUBMAN TWENTY-DOLLAR BILL
JOHN LEWIS BUTTONS
COURAGE
NATIVE VOICE
PAINTED STONES
U.S. VETERAN GRAVE MARKER
Chop TANK River
A BOTTLE OF WATER FROM THE CHOPTANK RIVER, A RIVER HARRIET FOLLOWED OFTEN

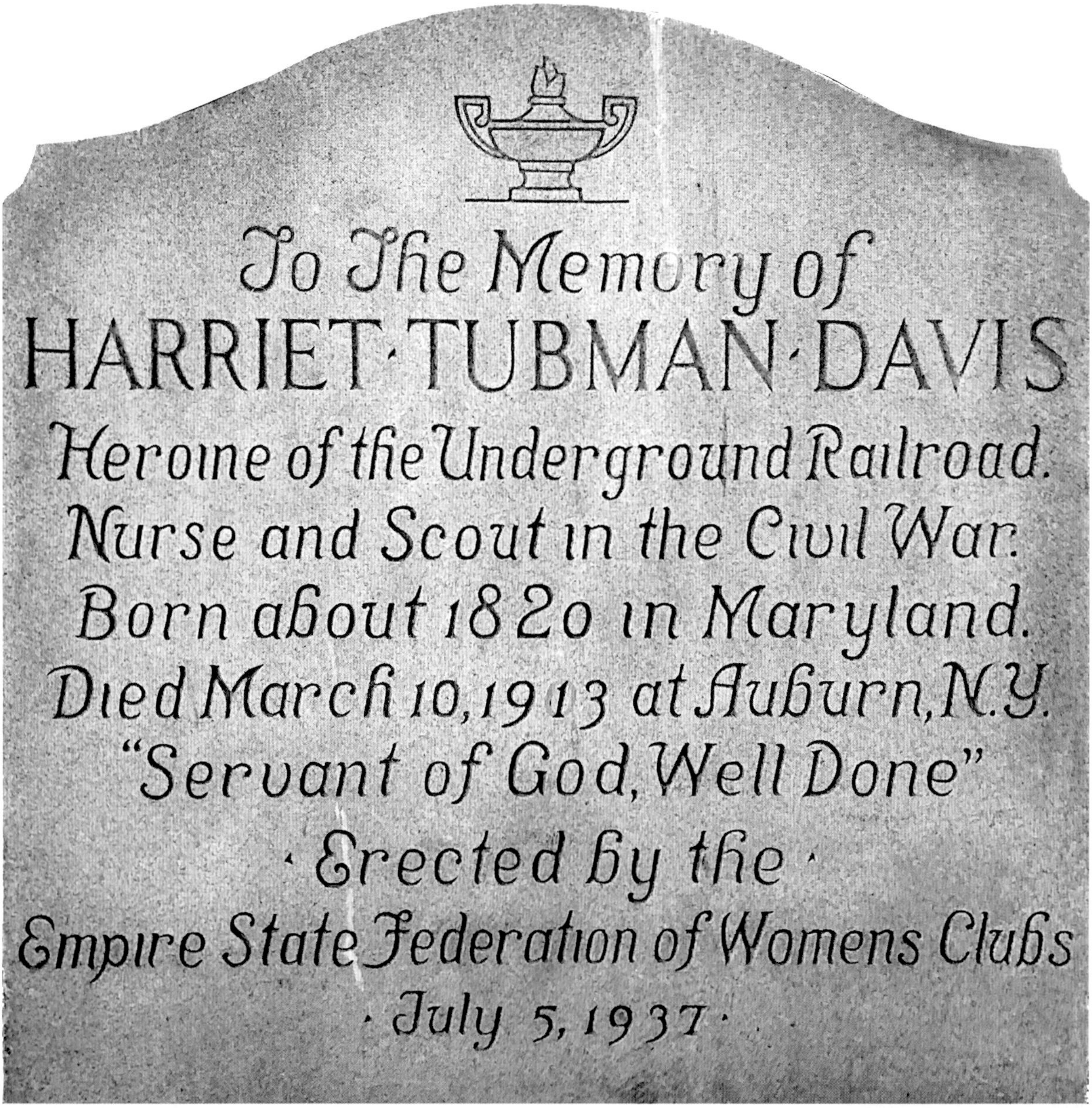
To The Memory of
HARRIET·TUBMAN·DAVIS
Heroine of the Underground Railroad.
Nurse and Scout in the Civil War.
Born about 1820 in Maryland.
Died March 10, 1913 at Auburn, N.Y.
"Servant of God, Well Done"
·Erected by the·
Empire State Federation of Womens Clubs
·July 5, 1937·

THE REVERSE SIDE OF THE HEADSTONE

HARRIET TUBMAN'S BROTHER AND NEPHEW ARE BURIED NEARBY.

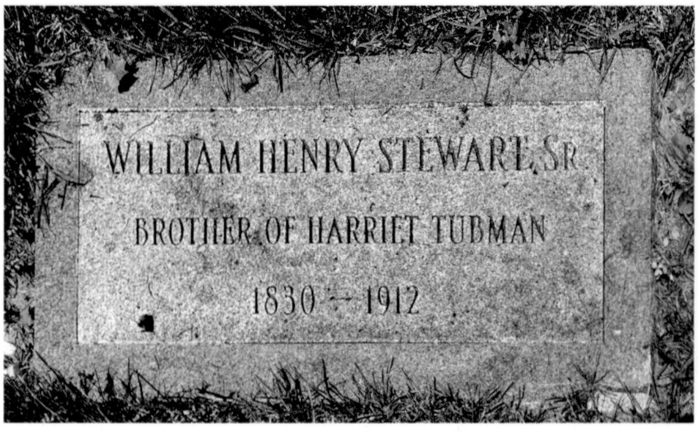
WILLIAM HENRY STEWART SR
BROTHER OF HARRIET TUBMAN
1830 — 1912

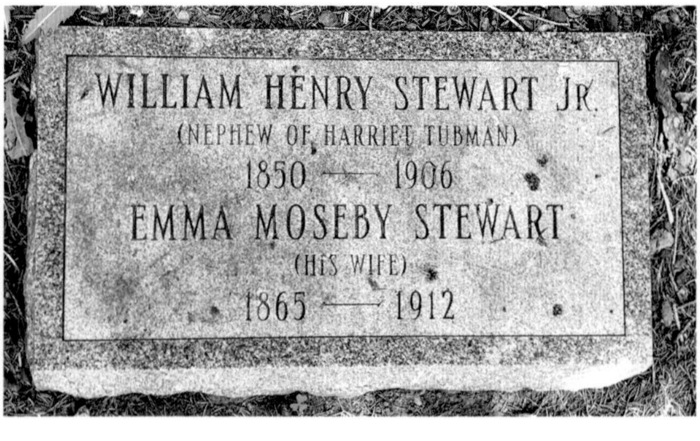
WILLIAM HENRY STEWART JR.
(NEPHEW OF HARRIET TUBMAN)
1850 — 1906
EMMA MOSEBY STEWART
(HIS WIFE)
1865 — 1912

The Court Case of MUM BETT

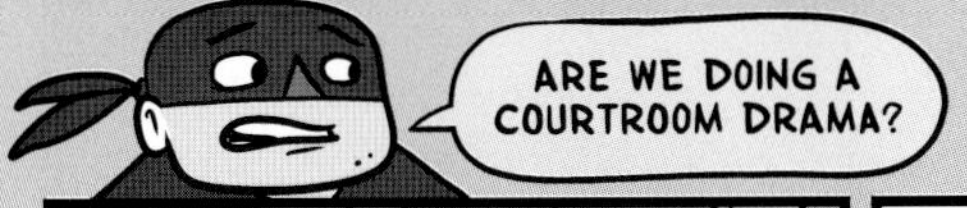
ARE WE DOING A COURTROOM DRAMA?

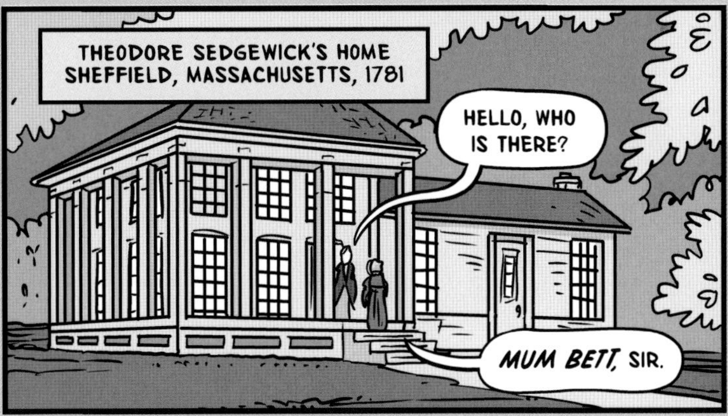
THEODORE SEDGEWICK'S HOME
SHEFFIELD, MASSACHUSETTS, 1781
HELLO, WHO IS THERE?
MUM BETT, SIR.

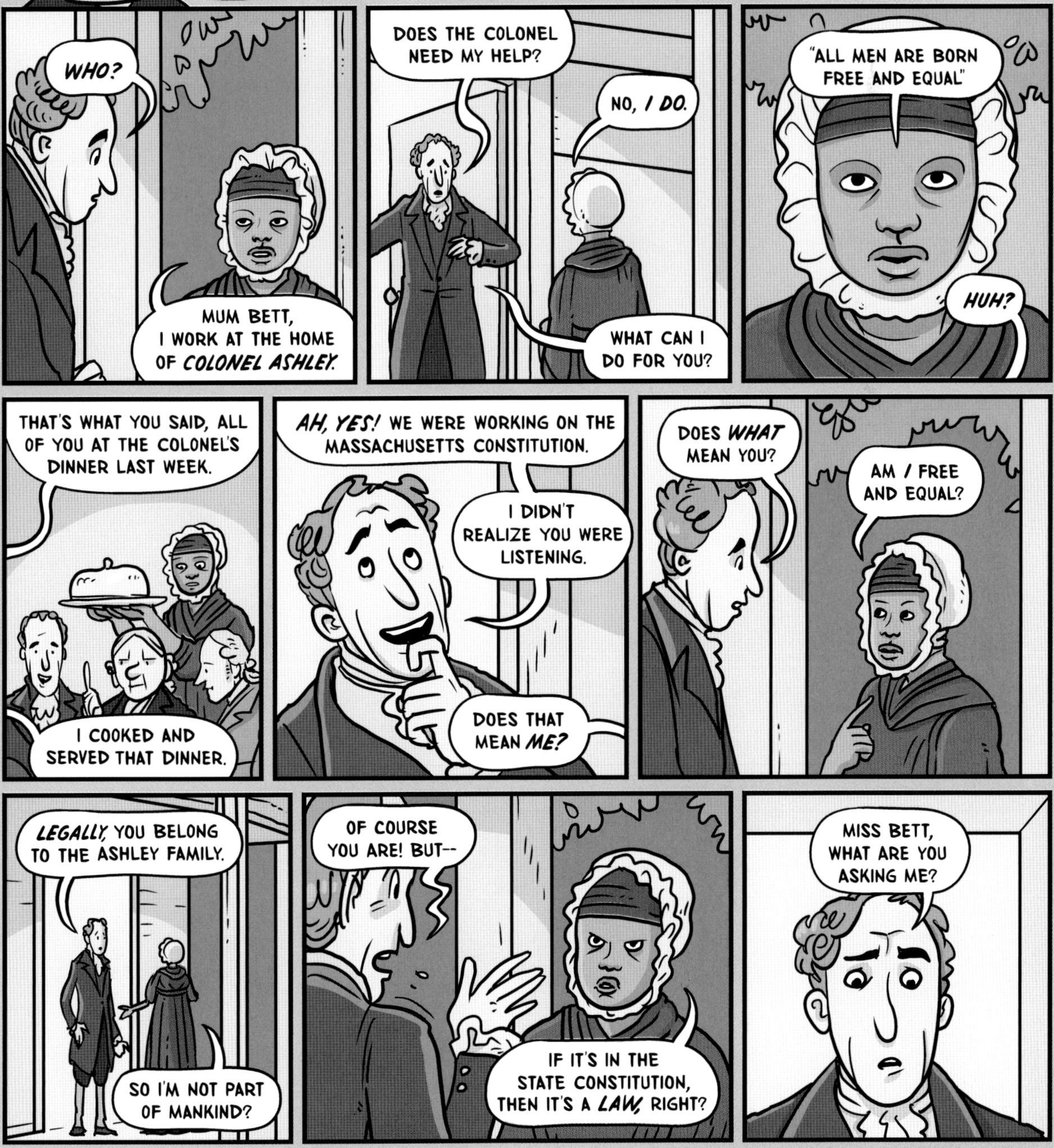
WHO?
MUM BETT, I WORK AT THE HOME OF COLONEL ASHLEY.
DOES THE COLONEL NEED MY HELP?
NO, I DO.
WHAT CAN I DO FOR YOU?
"ALL MEN ARE BORN FREE AND EQUAL"
HUH?
THAT'S WHAT YOU SAID, ALL OF YOU AT THE COLONEL'S DINNER LAST WEEK.
I COOKED AND SERVED THAT DINNER.
AH, YES! WE WERE WORKING ON THE MASSACHUSETTS CONSTITUTION.
I DIDN'T REALIZE YOU WERE LISTENING.
DOES THAT MEAN ME?
DOES WHAT MEAN YOU?
AM I FREE AND EQUAL?
LEGALLY, YOU BELONG TO THE ASHLEY FAMILY.
SO I'M NOT PART OF MANKIND?
OF COURSE YOU ARE! BUT--
IF IT'S IN THE STATE CONSTITUTION, THEN IT'S A LAW, RIGHT?
MISS BETT, WHAT ARE YOU ASKING ME?

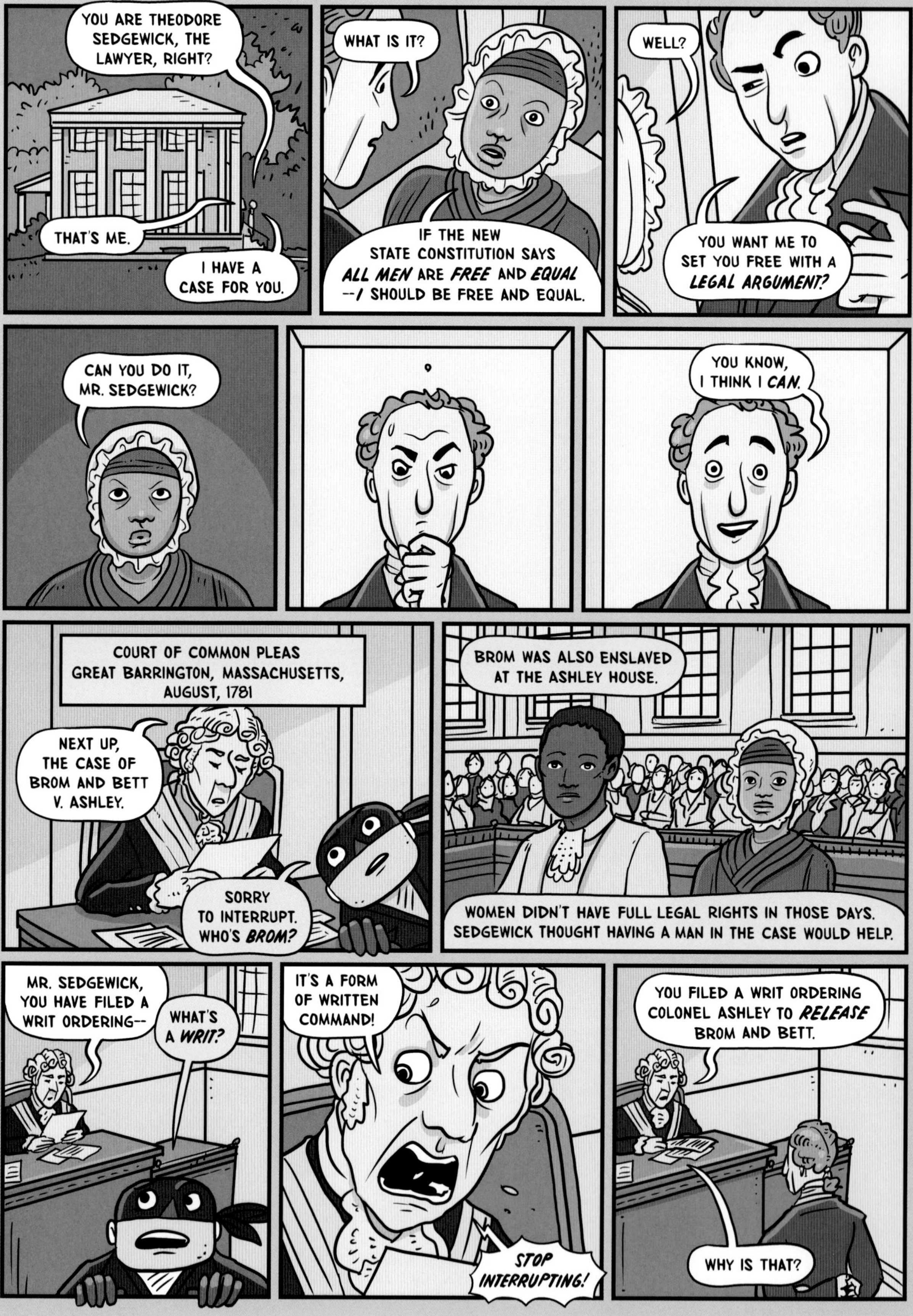
YOU ARE THEODORE SEDGEWICK, THE LAWYER, RIGHT?
THAT'S ME.
I HAVE A CASE FOR YOU.
WHAT IS IT?
IF THE NEW STATE CONSTITUTION SAYS ALL MEN ARE FREE AND EQUAL --I SHOULD BE FREE AND EQUAL.
WELL?
YOU WANT ME TO SET YOU FREE WITH A LEGAL ARGUMENT?
CAN YOU DO IT, MR. SEDGEWICK?
YOU KNOW, I THINK I CAN.
COURT OF COMMON PLEAS GREAT BARRINGTON, MASSACHUSETTS, AUGUST, 1781
NEXT UP, THE CASE OF BROM AND BETT V. ASHLEY.
SORRY TO INTERRUPT. WHO'S BROM?
BROM WAS ALSO ENSLAVED AT THE ASHLEY HOUSE.
WOMEN DIDN'T HAVE FULL LEGAL RIGHTS IN THOSE DAYS. SEDGEWICK THOUGHT HAVING A MAN IN THE CASE WOULD HELP.
MR. SEDGEWICK, YOU HAVE FILED A WRIT ORDERING--
WHAT'S A WRIT?
IT'S A FORM OF WRITTEN COMMAND!
STOP INTERRUPTING!
YOU FILED A WRIT ORDERING COLONEL ASHLEY TO RELEASE BROM AND BETT.
WHY IS THAT?

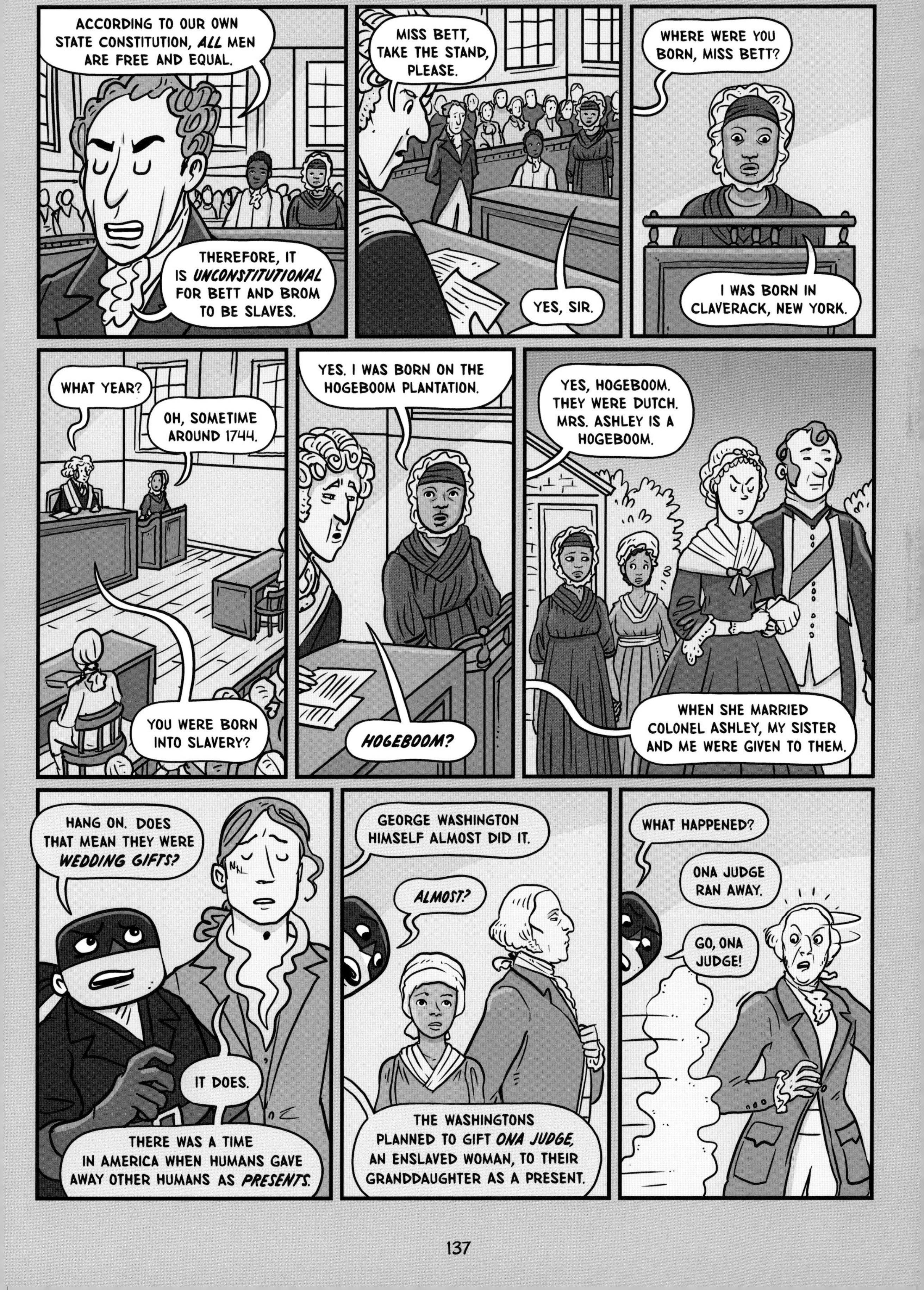
ACCORDING TO OUR OWN STATE CONSTITUTION, ALL MEN ARE FREE AND EQUAL.
THEREFORE, IT IS UNCONSTITUTIONAL FOR BETT AND BROM TO BE SLAVES.
MISS BETT, TAKE THE STAND, PLEASE.
YES, SIR.
WHERE WERE YOU BORN, MISS BETT?
I WAS BORN IN CLAVERACK, NEW YORK.
WHAT YEAR?
OH, SOMETIME AROUND 1744.
YOU WERE BORN INTO SLAVERY?
YES. I WAS BORN ON THE HOGEBOOM PLANTATION.
HOGEBOOM?
YES, HOGEBOOM. THEY WERE DUTCH. MRS. ASHLEY IS A HOGEBOOM.
WHEN SHE MARRIED COLONEL ASHLEY, MY SISTER AND ME WERE GIVEN TO THEM.
HANG ON. DOES THAT MEAN THEY WERE WEDDING GIFTS?
IT DOES.
THERE WAS A TIME IN AMERICA WHEN HUMANS GAVE AWAY OTHER HUMANS AS PRESENTS.
GEORGE WASHINGTON HIMSELF ALMOST DID IT.
ALMOST?
THE WASHINGTONS PLANNED TO GIFT ONA JUDGE, AN ENSLAVED WOMAN, TO THEIR GRANDDAUGHTER AS A PRESENT.
WHAT HAPPENED?
ONA JUDGE RAN AWAY.
GO, ONA JUDGE!

WHAT HAPPENED TO YOUR ARM, MISS BETT?
OH THIS? THAT'S BEEN THERE A LONG TIME.
I DIDN'T ASK WHEN, I ASKED HOW IT HAPPENED.
JUST A KITCHEN ACCIDENT.
MISS BETT IS WISELY KEEPING THIS TO HERSELF.
BUT I KNOW HOW SHE GOT THAT SCAR. AND I BELIEVE IT WOULD HELP OUR CASE TO TELL YOU.
THAT SCAR CAME FROM MRS. ASHLEY HERSELF!
THE HOGEBOOM!
ONE DAY, BETT AND HER YOUNGER SISTER, LIZZIE, WERE WORKING IN THE KITCHEN.
SOMETHING MUST HAVE INFURIATED MRS. ASHLEY, FOR SHE GRABBED A RED HOT SHOVEL OUT OF THE EMBERS
AND SWUNG IT RIGHT AT LIZZIE.
WHOK
SSSSS
YOU STOPPED THE SHOVEL FROM HITTING YOUR SISTER?
YES, SIR.
COLONEL JOHN ASHLEY, DID YOU WRITE THE WORDS, "MANKIND IN A STATE OF NATURE ARE EQUAL, FREE, AND INDEPENDENT OF EACH OTHER, AND HAVE A RIGHT TO THE UNDISTURBED ENJOYMENT OF THEIR LIVES, THEIR LIBERTY AND PROPERTY"?
YES, THAT WAS PART OF THE SHEFFIELD DECLARATION.
AND DID THOSE WORDS MAKE IT INTO THE STATE CONSTITUTION?
YES, THEY DID.
DO YOU BELIEVE THEM?
OF COURSE I DO!
BUT YOU OWN SLAVES.

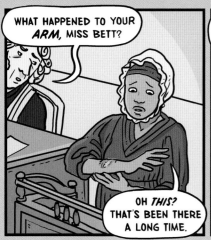

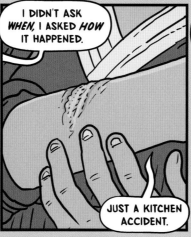

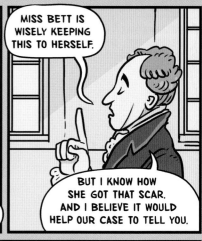

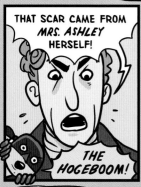

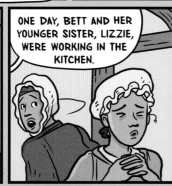

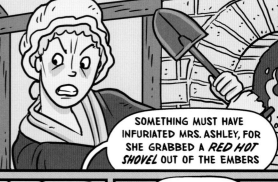

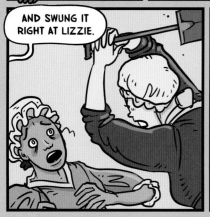

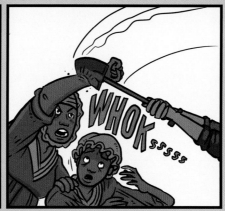

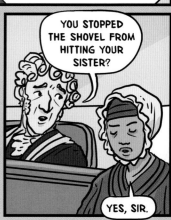

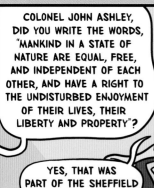

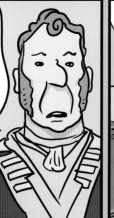

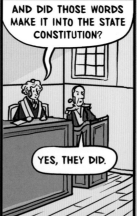

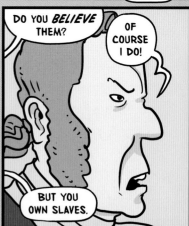

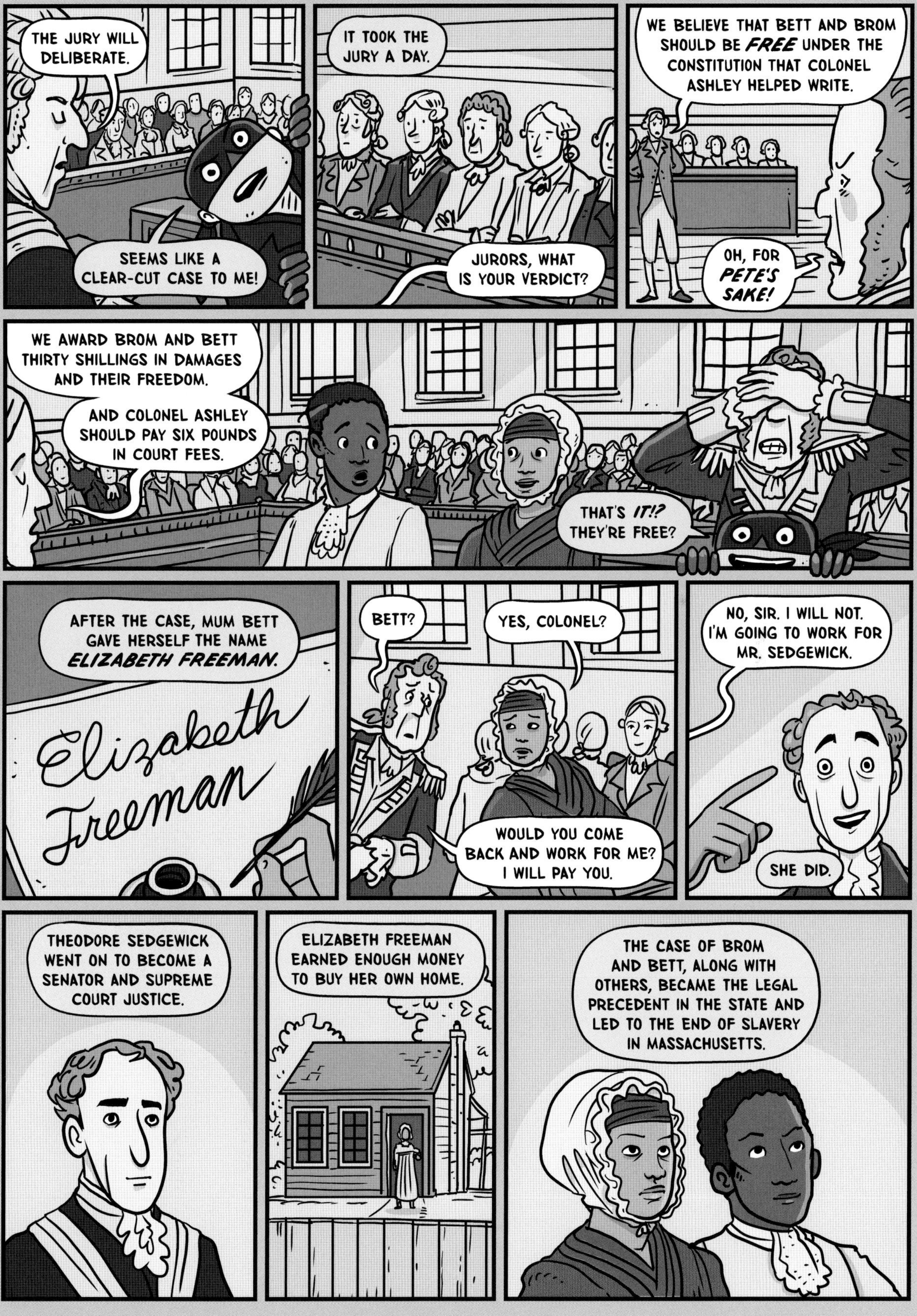
THE JURY WILL DELIBERATE.
SEEMS LIKE A CLEAR-CUT CASE TO ME!
IT TOOK THE JURY A DAY.
JURORS, WHAT IS YOUR VERDICT?
WE BELIEVE THAT BETT AND BROM SHOULD BE *FREE* UNDER THE CONSTITUTION THAT COLONEL ASHLEY HELPED WRITE.
OH, FOR *PETE'S SAKE!*
WE AWARD BROM AND BETT THIRTY SHILLINGS IN DAMAGES AND THEIR FREEDOM.
AND COLONEL ASHLEY SHOULD PAY SIX POUNDS IN COURT FEES.
THAT'S *IT!?* THEY'RE FREE?
AFTER THE CASE, MUM BETT GAVE HERSELF THE NAME *ELIZABETH FREEMAN.*
Elizabeth Freeman
BETT?
YES, COLONEL?
WOULD YOU COME BACK AND WORK FOR ME? I WILL PAY YOU.
NO, SIR. I WILL NOT. I'M GOING TO WORK FOR MR. SEDGEWICK.
SHE DID.
THEODORE SEDGEWICK WENT ON TO BECOME A SENATOR AND SUPREME COURT JUSTICE.
ELIZABETH FREEMAN EARNED ENOUGH MONEY TO BUY HER OWN HOME.
THE CASE OF BROM AND BETT, ALONG WITH OTHERS, BECAME THE LEGAL PRECEDENT IN THE STATE AND LED TO THE END OF SLAVERY IN MASSACHUSETTS.

BRISBY'S FISH WAGON

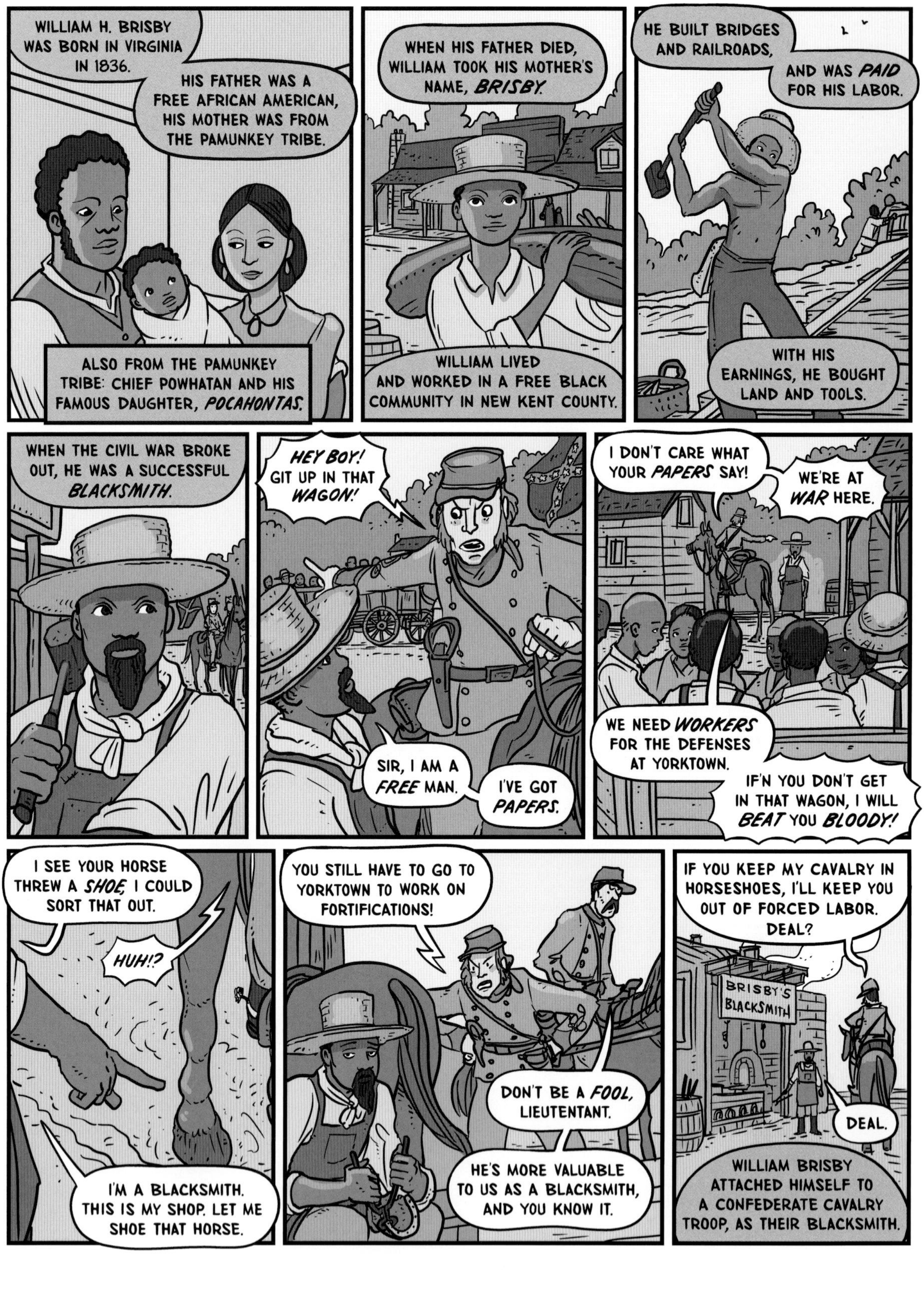

WILLIAM H. BRISBY WAS BORN IN VIRGINIA IN 1836.
HIS FATHER WAS A FREE AFRICAN AMERICAN, HIS MOTHER WAS FROM THE PAMUNKEY TRIBE.
ALSO FROM THE PAMUNKEY TRIBE: CHIEF POWHATAN AND HIS FAMOUS DAUGHTER, *POCAHONTAS.*
WHEN HIS FATHER DIED, WILLIAM TOOK HIS MOTHER'S NAME, *BRISBY.*
WILLIAM LIVED AND WORKED IN A FREE BLACK COMMUNITY IN NEW KENT COUNTY.
HE BUILT BRIDGES AND RAILROADS,
AND WAS *PAID* FOR HIS LABOR.
WITH HIS EARNINGS, HE BOUGHT LAND AND TOOLS.
WHEN THE CIVIL WAR BROKE OUT, HE WAS A SUCCESSFUL *BLACKSMITH.*
HEY BOY! GIT UP IN THAT *WAGON!*
SIR, I AM A *FREE* MAN.
I'VE GOT *PAPERS.*
I DON'T CARE WHAT YOUR *PAPERS* SAY!
WE'RE AT *WAR* HERE.
WE NEED *WORKERS* FOR THE DEFENSES AT YORKTOWN.
IF'N YOU DON'T GET IN THAT WAGON, I WILL *BEAT* YOU *BLOODY!*
I SEE YOUR HORSE THREW A *SHOE.* I COULD SORT THAT OUT.
HUH!?
I'M A BLACKSMITH. THIS IS MY SHOP. LET ME SHOE THAT HORSE.
YOU STILL HAVE TO GO TO YORKTOWN TO WORK ON FORTIFICATIONS!
DON'T BE A *FOOL,* LIEUTENTANT.
HE'S MORE VALUABLE TO US AS A BLACKSMITH, AND YOU KNOW IT.
IF YOU KEEP MY CAVALRY IN HORSESHOES, I'LL KEEP YOU OUT OF FORCED LABOR. DEAL?
BRISBY'S BLACKSMITH
DEAL.
WILLIAM BRISBY ATTACHED HIMSELF TO A CONFEDERATE CAVALRY TROOP, AS THEIR BLACKSMITH.

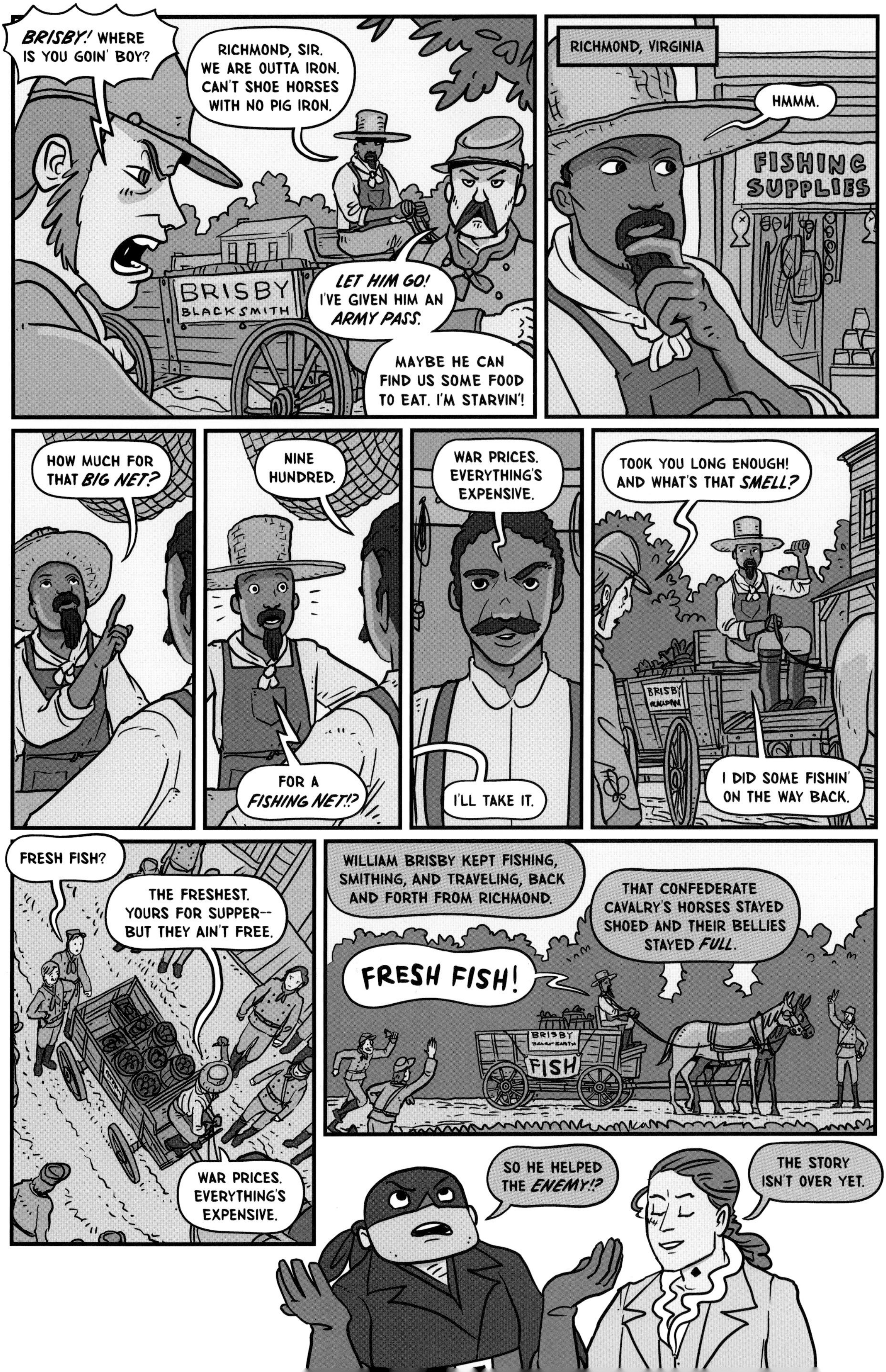
BRISBY! WHERE IS YOU GOIN' BOY?
RICHMOND, SIR. WE ARE OUTTA IRON. CAN'T SHOE HORSES WITH NO PIG IRON.
BRISBY BLACKSMITH
LET HIM GO! I'VE GIVEN HIM AN ARMY PASS.
MAYBE HE CAN FIND US SOME FOOD TO EAT. I'M STARVIN'!
RICHMOND, VIRGINIA
HMMM.
FISHING SUPPLIES
HOW MUCH FOR THAT BIG NET?
NINE HUNDRED.
FOR A FISHING NET!?
WAR PRICES. EVERYTHING'S EXPENSIVE.
I'LL TAKE IT.
TOOK YOU LONG ENOUGH! AND WHAT'S THAT SMELL?
BRISBY
I DID SOME FISHIN' ON THE WAY BACK.
FRESH FISH?
THE FRESHEST. YOURS FOR SUPPER-- BUT THEY AIN'T FREE.
WAR PRICES. EVERYTHING'S EXPENSIVE.
WILLIAM BRISBY KEPT FISHING, SMITHING, AND TRAVELING, BACK AND FORTH FROM RICHMOND.
THAT CONFEDERATE CAVALRY'S HORSES STAYED SHOED AND THEIR BELLIES STAYED FULL.
FRESH FISH!
BRISBY
FISH
SO HE HELPED THE ENEMY!?
THE STORY ISN'T OVER YET.

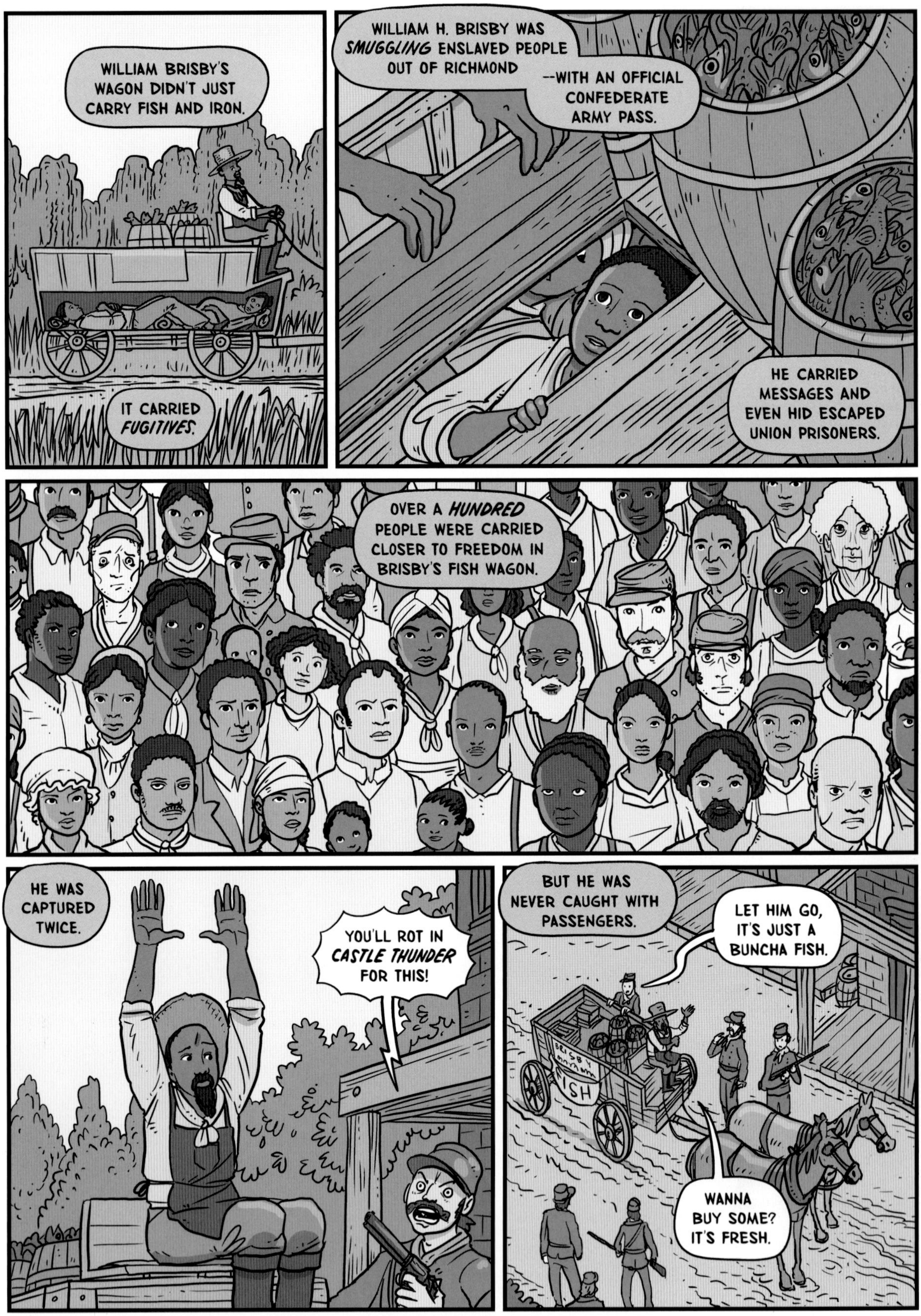
WILLIAM BRISBY'S WAGON DIDN'T JUST CARRY FISH AND IRON.
IT CARRIED *FUGITIVES.*
WILLIAM H. BRISBY WAS *SMUGGLING* ENSLAVED PEOPLE OUT OF RICHMOND
--WITH AN OFFICIAL CONFEDERATE ARMY PASS.
HE CARRIED MESSAGES AND EVEN HID ESCAPED UNION PRISONERS.
OVER A *HUNDRED* PEOPLE WERE CARRIED CLOSER TO FREEDOM IN BRISBY'S FISH WAGON.
HE WAS CAPTURED TWICE.
YOU'LL ROT IN *CASTLE THUNDER* FOR THIS!
BUT HE WAS NEVER CAUGHT WITH PASSENGERS.
LET HIM GO, IT'S JUST A BUNCHA FISH.
BRISBY
FISH
WANNA BUY SOME? IT'S FRESH.

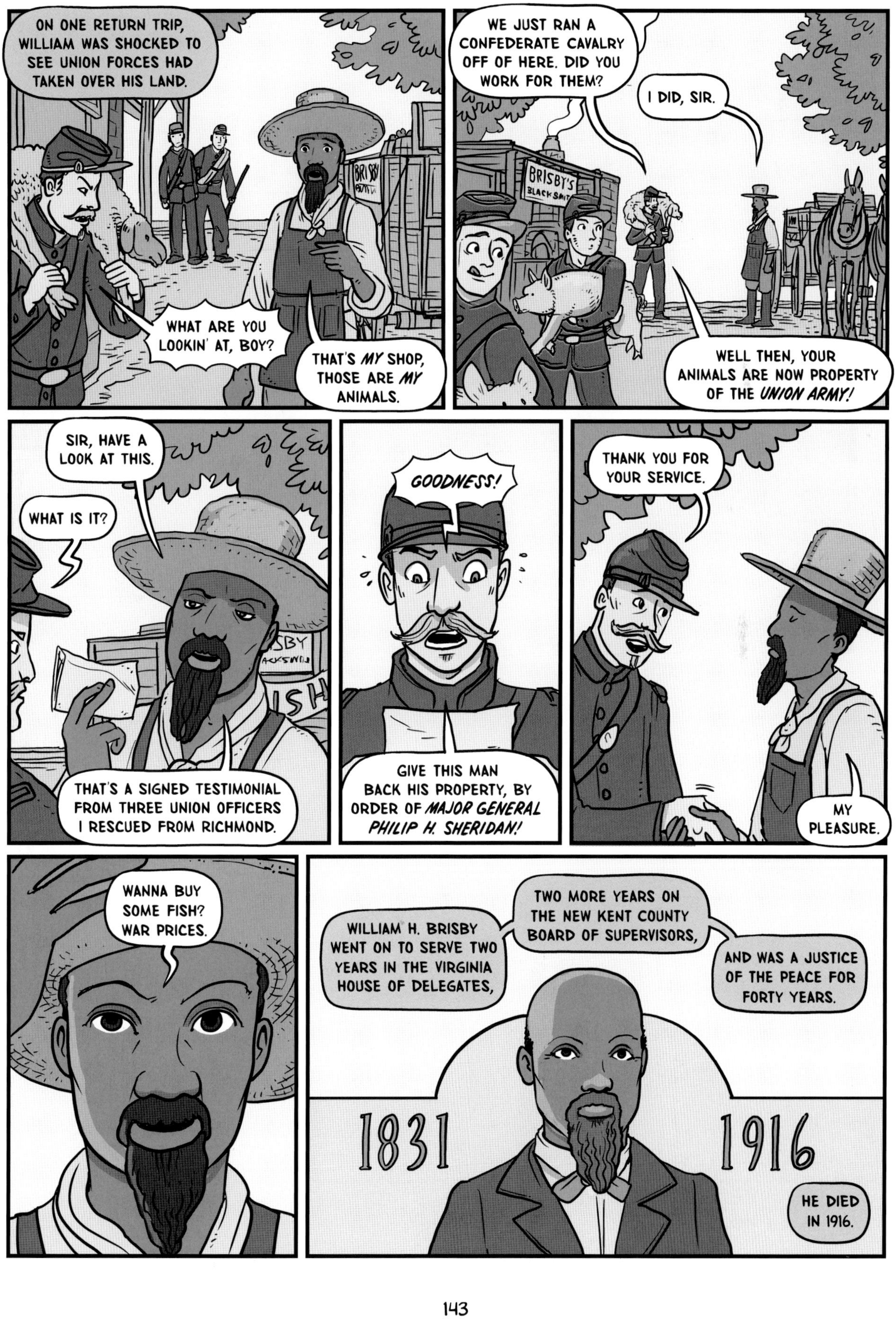
ON ONE RETURN TRIP, WILLIAM WAS SHOCKED TO SEE UNION FORCES HAD TAKEN OVER HIS LAND.
BRISBY
WHAT ARE YOU LOOKIN' AT, BOY?
THAT'S MY SHOP, THOSE ARE MY ANIMALS.
WE JUST RAN A CONFEDERATE CAVALRY OFF OF HERE. DID YOU WORK FOR THEM?
I DID, SIR.
BRISBY'S BLACKSMITH
WELL THEN, YOUR ANIMALS ARE NOW PROPERTY OF THE UNION ARMY!
SIR, HAVE A LOOK AT THIS.
WHAT IS IT?
THAT'S A SIGNED TESTIMONIAL FROM THREE UNION OFFICERS I RESCUED FROM RICHMOND.
GOODNESS!
GIVE THIS MAN BACK HIS PROPERTY, BY ORDER OF MAJOR GENERAL PHILIP H. SHERIDAN!
THANK YOU FOR YOUR SERVICE.
MY PLEASURE.
WANNA BUY SOME FISH? WAR PRICES.
WILLIAM H. BRISBY WENT ON TO SERVE TWO YEARS IN THE VIRGINIA HOUSE OF DELEGATES,
TWO MORE YEARS ON THE NEW KENT COUNTY BOARD OF SUPERVISORS,
AND WAS A JUSTICE OF THE PEACE FOR FORTY YEARS.
1831
1916
HE DIED IN 1916.

WHO WOULD WIN IN A FIGHT BETWEEN

HENRY KNOX, THE SPECTER OF DEATH, GUSTAVUS FOX, AND THE THE 1916 GOD OF WAR?

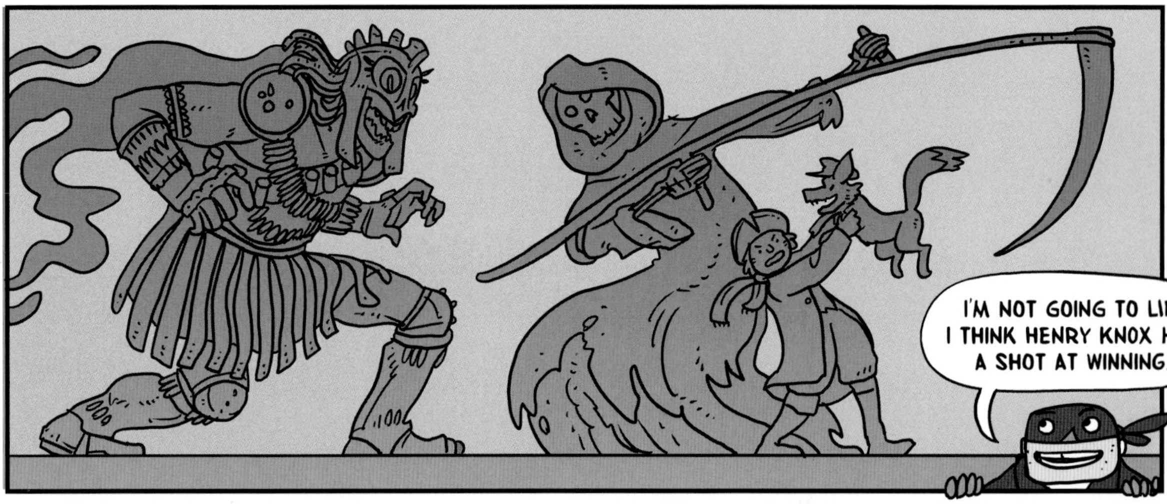
I'M NOT GOING TO LIE, I THINK HENRY KNOX HAS A SHOT AT WINNING.

THERE IS ONLY ONE WAY TO DECIDE: READ THE HAZARDOUS TALES SERIES!

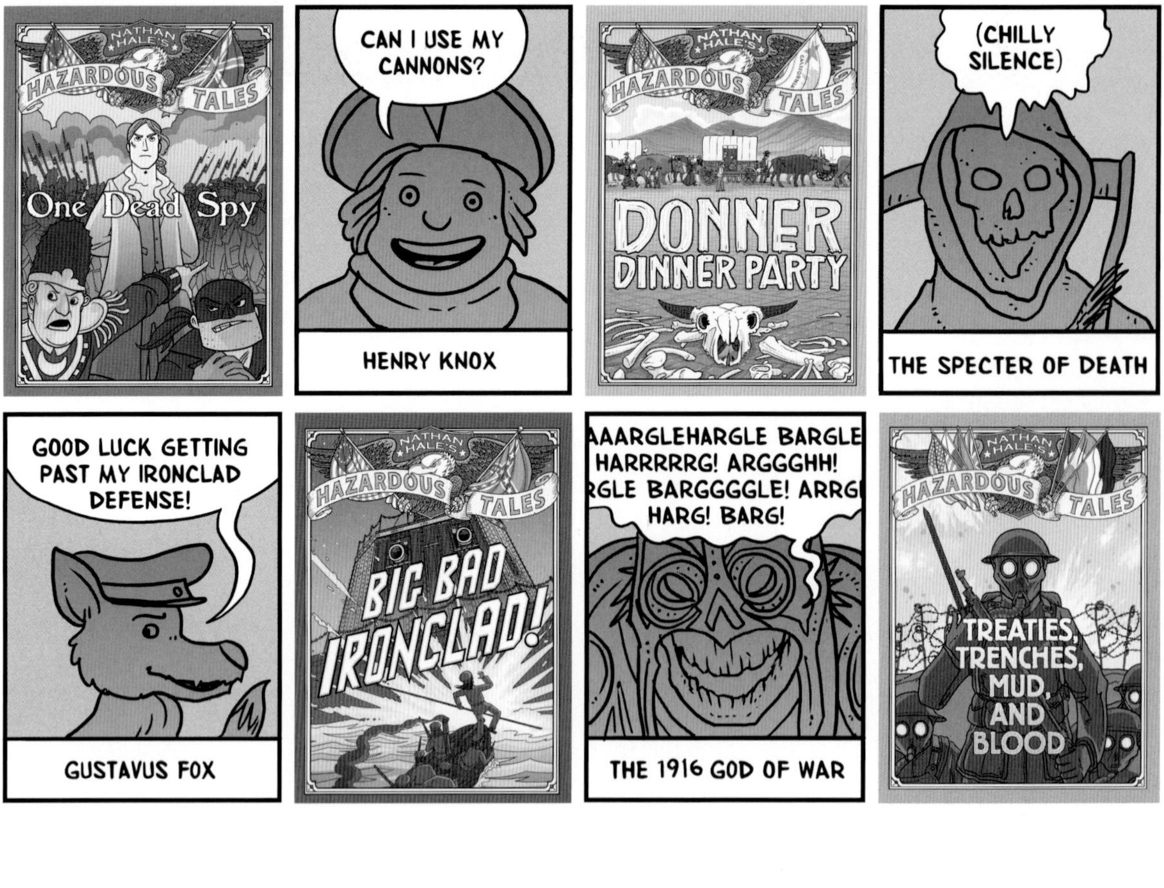
NATHAN HALE'S HAZARDOUS TALES
One Dead Spy
CAN I USE MY CANNONS?
HENRY KNOX
NATHAN HALE'S HAZARDOUS TALES
DONNER DINNER PARTY
(CHILLY SILENCE)
THE SPECTER OF DEATH
GOOD LUCK GETTING PAST MY IRONCLAD DEFENSE!
GUSTAVUS FOX
NATHAN HALE'S HAZARDOUS TALES
BIG BAD IRONCLAD!
AARGLEHARGLE BARGLE HARRRRRG! ARGGGHH! RGLE BARGGGGLE! ARRG HARG! BARG!
THE 1916 GOD OF WAR
NATHAN HALE'S HAZARDOUS TALES
TREATIES, TRENCHES, MUD, AND BLOOD

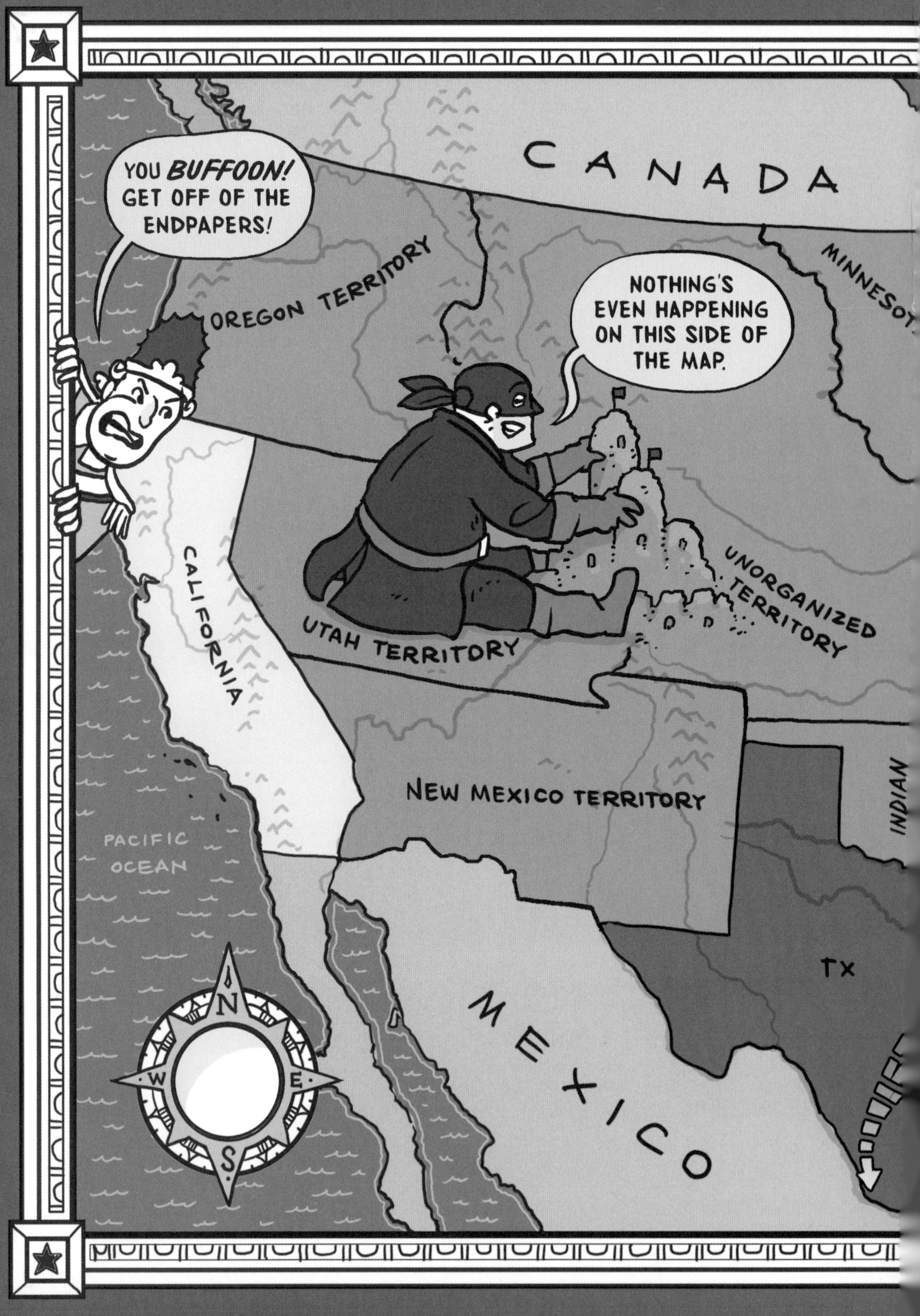
YOU *BUFFOON!* GET OFF OF THE ENDPAPERS!
NOTHING'S EVEN HAPPENING ON THIS SIDE OF THE MAP.
CANADA
MINNESOT
OREGON TERRITORY
CALIFORNIA
UTAH TERRITORY
UNORGANIZED TERRITORY
NEW MEXICO TERRITORY
INDIAN
PACIFIC OCEAN
TX
MEXICO
N
W
E
S